How to Misunderstand Kierkegaard

How to Misunderstand Kierkegaard

An Instruction Manual for Assistant Professors
and Other Immoral and Disreputable Persons

STUART DALTON

CASCADE *Books* • Eugene, Oregon

HOW TO MISUNDERSTAND KIERKEGAARD
An Instruction Manual for Assistant Professors and Other Immoral and Disreputable Persons

Copyright © 2022 Stuart Dalton. All rights reserved. Except for brief quotations in critical publications or reviews, no part of this book may be reproduced in any manner without prior written permission from the publisher. Write: Permissions, Wipf and Stock Publishers, 199 W. 8th Ave., Suite 3, Eugene, OR 97401.

Cascade Books
An Imprint of Wipf and Stock Publishers
199 W. 8th Ave., Suite 3
Eugene, OR 97401

www.wipfandstock.com

PAPERBACK ISBN: 978-1-6667-3225-2
HARDCOVER ISBN: 978-1-6667-2571-1
EBOOK ISBN: 978-1-6667-2572-8

Cataloguing-in-Publication data:

Names: Dalton, Stuart [author].

Title: How to misunderstand Kierkegaard : an instruction manual for assistant professors and other immoral and disreputable persons / Stuart Dalton.

Description: Eugene, OR: Cascade Books, 2022 | Includes bibliographical references.

Identifiers: ISBN 978-1-6667-3225-2 (paperback) | ISBN 978-1-6667-2571-1 (hardcover) | ISBN 978-1-6667-2572-8 (ebook)

Subjects: LCSH: Kierkegaard, Søren | Kierkegaard, Søren,—1813–1855—Criticism and interpretation | Kierkegaard, Søren,—1813–1855—Anonyms and pseudonyms | Philosophy, Modern | Philosophers | Literary criticism | Literature—Philosophy

Classification: B4377 D35 2022 (paperback) | B4377 (ebook)

VERSION NUMBER 092022

For Sara,
my favorite comedian.

"There are many vociferous and easily perspiring people who are stupid enough to assume that their stupidity is seriousness and seriously stupid enough to want to make other people believe it. So what is called seriousness is the easiest of all postures instead of having seriousness be the finest fruit of the uttermost reflection. . . . This is the source of that hypocritical outcry against everyone who is not stupid enough but who is witty and jesting and then, at the right point, serious: "He is not serious." On the contrary, the reverse is the case: Whoever does not dare at every moment to submit his seriousness to the test of jest, he is stupid, is comical." (*KJN* 2:213)

"Humor stands in opposition to irony, and therefore they could well be united in an individual, both parts conditioned by a refusal to be reconciled with the world. But with the one, this refusal takes the form of not caring a whit about it, while with the other, by contrast, one makes an attempt to influence the world, but is ridiculed by it for doing so. These represent the two ends of a see-saw (wave motion); for the humorist experiences moments when the world teases him, just as the other, in his battle with life, must often succumb and in turn often rise above it and laugh at it." (*KJN* 11.1:138)

"But humor is also the joy that has triumphed over the world." (*KJN* 2:88)

Contents

Preface: A note on the style of this book | ix
Acknowledgements | xi
List of Abbreviations | xiii

INTRODUCTION (actually more like a personal confession) | 1
How I, an assistant professor, found a way to justify writing a book about Kierkegaard's philosophy in spite of Kierkegaard's many excellent jokes about assistant professors who write books about his philosophy, and why this is a fragmentary, sketchy, scrappy, and crumby book
    or
Clearly what the world needs now more than anything else is another book on Kierkegaard's philosophy written by another assistant professor

CHAPTER 1 | 31
How to misunderstand Kierkegaard's journals and notebooks as nothing more than supplements and appendices to his other books rather than works of philosophy themselves
    or
Three forms of philosophical theatre in Kierkegaard's journals and notebooks

CHAPTER 2 | 71
How to misunderstand the many concluding summaries that Kierkegaard wrote to explain his strange indirect authorship by imagining that they are somehow outside his strange indirect authorship and therefore should be trusted completely
    or
Prefaces to nothing, points of view that are pointless, and non-concluding conclusions

CHAPTER 3 | 90
How to misunderstand religion in Kierkegaard's writing and thus succeed in completely overlooking some of the most interesting ideas in his philosophy
or
X reasons to understand religion as a metaphor in Kierkegaard's writing

CHAPTER 4 | 109
How to misunderstand what *Philosophical Fragments* can teach us about human (all-too-human) education
or
How to be a highly ineffective and highly confused teacher

CHAPTER 5 | 128
How to misunderstand *Either/Or* by assuming there's only one nihilist in the book, and that only Part I is comical
or
The Queen of Denmark was right! This book really should have been called *Either and Or*

CHAPTER 6 | 169
How to misunderstand *Repetition* by ignoring the fact that the book's author, Constantin Constantius, loves a good farce
or
Repetition repeats itself in *Repetition*: first as tragedy and then as farce

CHAPTER 7 | 196
How to misunderstand *Johannes Climacus* by missing the methodological manifesto that it contains
or
Lessons on how to end (and also begin) a philosophy book, from a philosophy book that did not end

CONCLUSION (actually more like a personal apology) | 221
And now this crumby book is finally over
or
Concluding ecstatic discourse in praise of scrappy philosophy

Endnotes | 223
Bibliography | 267

Preface

A note on the style of this book

KIERKEGAARD CHOSE TO WRITE his own philosophy books in a style that was so unorthodox and downright bizarre that most readers—in the nineteenth century and still today—have been shocked and even somewhat scandalized. This is one of his greatest accomplishments. I have no doubt that Kierkegaard was perfectly capable of writing in the style that has long been the rule for philosophy books: solemn, systematic, sterile prose, utterly oblivious to humor in any form as it trundles slowly and with grim determination toward its conclusion with all the charm and grace of a steamroller, smothering any objection that appears in its path with dispassionate, dull, dreary, desiccated arguments. But Kierkegaard decided that a philosophy book should be written differently; a philosophy book should be energetic, playful, humorous, free-spirited, surprising and joyous—even though this goes completely against the established tradition and therefore will leave everyone who reads it feeling somewhat stunned.

I wanted to write this book about Kierkegaard's philosophy in the style of Kierkegaard's philosophy. This is not to say that I claim to be able to write as well as Kierkegaard (I definitely do not make that claim), or that I wanted to imitate Kierkegaard's own unique voice, like a ventriloquist (there's not much point in that novelty act); however I did want to take seriously Kierkegaard's conviction that a philosophy book should be written in a style that is surprising and playful and free-spirited, and not oblivious to or hostile to humor (as if philosophy and comedy were total strangers or arch enemies). Obviously it's up to each reader to decide if this book succeeds in saying anything at all that is innovative, interesting, intelligent, or insightful, but I can at least say this much about the book myself very confidently: it's definitely a little bit weird. However, all of Kierkegaard's philosophy books were also quite weird, so at least this book is in good company.

Acknowledgements

THANK YOU TO CASCADE Books for allowing this strange and scrappy little book to sally forth into the cold, bleak, unwelcoming world of academic scholarship, where I hope it will find a few readers who discover some scrap of value in its pages.

Thank you to my fellow philosophy professors at Western Connecticut State University, Anna Malavisi and John Clark, for your constant friendship and support and for your unflagging efforts to keep philosophy alive and kicking in this corner of The Land of Steady Habits, in spite of all the obstacles.

Thank you to every student I have ever had the privilege to teach. I have learned something valuable from all of you. Thank you in particular to Daniel Koveleski and Amanda Jones, who read and commented on parts of this book and who also demonstrated to me in every day of every class that philosophy is supposed to be joyous.

Thank you to my sister Stephenie, who read much of this manuscript and discovered therein many grammatical and logical infelicities, thereby sparing me much embarrassment, and thank you to my brother Shane, who hosted me on two ski vacations (which were thoroughly renewing) while I worked on this book.

Thank you, finally, to my children—Sage, Jackson, and Marcus—for tolerating your often baffled and bewildered father, and thank you especially to Sara for sticking with me through everything.

Earlier versions of the following chapters appeared in these journals, and I thank the editors for permission to include this material.

Chapter 1: "Three Forms of Philosophical Theatre in Kierkegaard's Journals and Notebooks" *Philosophy and Social Criticism* 48.1 (2022) 86–127.

Chapter 2: "How to Avoid Writing: Prefaces and Points of View in Kierkegaard." *Philosophy Today* 44.2 (2000) 123–36.

Chapter 4: "How to Be a Terrible Teacher: Kierkegaard's *Philosophical Fragments* on What Education Is Not." *Philosophy and Social Criticism* 45.3 (2019) 241–64.

Chapter 6: "Kierkegaard's *Repetition* as a Comedy in Two Acts." *Janus Head* 4.2 (2001) 287–326.

Chapter 7: "*Johannes Climacus* as Kierkegaard's Discourse on Method." *Philosophy Today* 47.4 (2003) 360–77.

Abbreviations

THE FOLLOWING ABBREVIATIONS WILL be used for the works by Søren Kierkegaard that I will cite. (For pseudonymous works, the pseudonymous author is indicated after the title.)

AW "My Activity as a Writer" (including the appendix, "My Position as a Religious Author in Christendom' and my Strategy"). In *The Point of View for My Work as an Author and Related Writings*, Translated by Walter Lowrie, 141–58. New York: Harper, 1962. (I will quote from the Lowrie translation, but I will also include the page number from the Hong translation, following the abbreviation H: *The Point of View: Kierkegaard's Writings XXII*. Translated by Howard Hong and Edna Hong. Princeton: Princeton University Press, 1998.)

CI *The Concept of Irony*. Edited and Translated by Howard Hong and Edna Hong. Princeton: Princeton University Press, 1989.

COR *The Corsair Affair and Articles Related to the Writings*. Edited and Translated by Howard Hong and Edna Hong. Princeton: Princeton University Press, 1982.

CUP *Concluding Unscientific Postscript to Philosophical Fragments* (Johannes Climacus). Translated by Howard Hong and Edna Hong. Princeton: Princeton University Press, 1992. (All citations are from volume 1.)

EOI *Either/Or Part I* (Victor Eremita, editor). Edited and Translated by Howard Hong and Edna Hong. Princeton: Princeton University Press, 1987.

EOII *Either/Or Part II* (Victor Eremita, editor). Edited and Translated by Howard Hong and Edna Hong. Princeton: Princeton University Press, 1987.

JC *Johannes Climacus, or De Omnibus Dubitandum Est.* In *Philosophical Fragments* and *Johannes Climacus*, translated by Howard Hong and Edna Hong, 113–73. Princeton: Princeton University Press, 1985.

KJN *Kierkegaard's Journals and Notebooks.* General editor: Bruce H. Kirmmse. Princeton: Princeton University Press, 2007–20. (I will cite the volume number followed by the page number. There are eleven volumes in all and volume 11 has two parts, which will be designated as 11.1 and 11.2. The editors and translators for each volume vary; all the particulars for each volume are listed in the bibliography.)

P *Prefaces: Light Reading for Certain Classes as the Occasion May Require* (Nicolaus Notabene). Translated by William McDonald. Tallahassee: Florida State University Press, 1989. (I will quote from the McDonald translation, but I will also include the page number from the Nichol translation, following the abbreviation *N*: *Prefaces, Writing Sampler: Kierkegaard's Writings IX.* Translated by Todd W. Nichol. Princeton: Princeton University Press, 1997.)

PA "The Present Age." In *Two Ages: The Age of Revolution and the Present Age*, translated by Howard Hong and Edna Hong, 68–112. Princeton: Princeton University Press, 1978.

PF *Philosophical Fragments* (Johannes Climacus). In *Philosophical Fragments* and *Johannes Climacus*, translated by Howard Hong and Edna Hong, 1–111. Princeton: Princeton University Press, 1985.

PV "The Point of View for My Work as an Author" (including the supplement, "The Single Individual"). In *The Point of View for My Work as an Author and Related Writings*, Translated by Walter Lowrie, 5–138. New York: Harper, 1962. (I will quote from the Lowrie translation, but I will also include the page number from the Hong translation preceded by the abbreviation *H*: *The Point of View: Kierkegaard's Writings XXII.* Translated by Howard Hong and Edna Hong. Princeton: Princeton University Press, 1998.)

R *Repetition* (Constantin Constantius). In *Fear and Trembling* and *Repetition*, translated by Howard Hong and Edna Hong, 125–231. Princeton: Princeton University Press, 1983.

SLW *Stages on Life's Way* (Hilarius Bookbinder, editor). Edited and Translated by Howard Hong and Edna Hong. Princeton: Princeton University Press, 1988.

WS   *Writing Sampler*. In *Prefaces, Writing Sampler: Kierkegaard's Writings IX*, Translated by Todd W. Nichol, 69–90. Princeton: Princeton University Press, 1997.

Introduction

(actually more like a personal confession)

How I, an assistant professor, found a way to justify writing a book about Kierkegaard's philosophy in spite of Kierkegaard's many excellent jokes about assistant professors who write books about his philosophy, and why this is a fragmentary, sketchy, scrappy, and crumby book

or

Clearly what the world needs now more than anything else is another book on Kierkegaard's philosophy written by another assistant professor[1]

LIKE ALMOST EVERY ASSISTANT professor of philosophy on Planet Earth, one morning I woke up in a panic, sat bolt upright in bed, and shouted out loud: "I must write a book about Kierkegaard's philosophy! There are not nearly enough of them yet!" Most assistant professors, when this happens to them, quickly realize that it's way too early to get out of bed and start writing a book on an enigmatic nineteenth-century Danish philosopher, so they go back to sleep and what seemed like an epiphany quietly fades away, melting like hoarfrost as the sun comes up and good sense returns. If they recall the thought a few weeks later they shake their heads and laugh—"What a crazy idea!"

Because I lack the intelligence and good sense that most assistant professors possess I did not go back to sleep when this thought occurred to me; instead I leapt out of bed and immediately began writing with great zeal and enthusiasm, determined to add one more book to the rapidly rising pile of books about Kierkegaard that the human race had already produced. But as I wrote a haunting question took up residence in the back of my mind, taunting me and making me feel ashamed of myself. The question was this: "How can you, an assistant professor, write a book about Kierkegaard's philosophy when Kierkegaard wrote so many excellent jokes and cutting criticisms about assistant professors who write books about his philosophy? How is this even possible? Hasn't Kierkegaard preempted and rendered ridiculous such a book before you could even begin writing it?"

The cause of my anxiety and shame were Kierkegaard's many remarks about assistant professors and their many crimes—remarks that are so abundant that they constitute something like a mini-genre within his writing. Here are seventeen examples just from Kierkegaard's journals. (While seventeen examples of anything may seem like far too many examples—a quantity that amounts to clubbing the reader over the head with examples instead of trusting her to get the point after just one or two—in this case I believe that seventeen examples are the bare minimum necessary to impart the weight of Kierkegaard's disdain for the assistant professorial class; so please read them all, even though it will be a time-consuming and painful experience for you.)

> The essential thinker always states an issue in its most extreme form; this is precisely what is brilliant—and only a few can follow him. Then the professor comes; he takes away the "paradox"—a great many people, almost the entire multitude, can understand him, and then people think that now the truth has become truer!
>
> Even if a brilliant thinker came up with the idea of "a system," he would never get it completed—so honest would he be. But just a little hint to a professor about what he wanted to do—and the professor would straightaway have the system completed.
>
> The professor always seems to be a quite different sort of thinking fellow—this is how it must appear when the problem is reflected in the medium of the public, or when any and every Tom, Dick, or Harry is a thinker.
>
> Every essential thinker can only view the professor comically. The professor is what Leporello is in relation to a Don

Giovanni, only with the addition that he cheats his way into gaining great respect in the eyes of the half-learned. (*KJN* 6:161)

In early antiquity philosophy was a power, an ethical power, character. The empire protected itself by—paying them, by making them "professors." So also with Christianity.

The professor is a castrato, but he has not gelded himself for the sake of the kingdom of heaven, but the reverse, in order properly to fit into this characterless world. (*KJN* 8:460)

Hegel was a professor of philosophy, not a thinker, and he must also have been a rather insignificant personality without an impression of life—but a quite extraordinary professor, I do not deny that.

But surely someday the time will come when this concept—professor—gains acceptance as a comical character. (*KJN* 7:67)

But nowadays human beings are born without subjectivity, like knives without edges, like arrows without points. Millions live occupying themselves solely with the finite goals of this life. And those who ought to be a superior sort—yes, these are precisely the ones I have in mind when I say that nowadays human beings are just as unusable for spirit as sewing needles without eyes are unusable for sewing.

The superior ones are namely—assistant professors, i.e., they are lacking in subjectivity, blunted, sluggish objectivities, copies.... [T]here they remain, inhumanly—Yes, isn't it as I say: they are not human beings!—they remain objective, they lecture on it. And that is also how it is in relation to everything else that is glorious, that has had to suffer, and that has cried out for imitation: They remain objective and lecture on it. Yes, and what is still worse, this tranquility is not attained after a long struggle with something better within themselves, a struggle with conscience—no, this tranquility is original, there is nothing better in them that must be vanquished; on the contrary, they believe themselves to be glorious human beings who as such are capable of lecturing like this. (*KJN* 10:82–83)

There have been many hours when I have, as it were, felt the need for someone I could talk to, an ascetic. But everywhere I look, this nauseating figure, the professor who lectures and otherwise knows existentially only about bread-and-butter and career. And it would never occur to me to talk to someone like that; indeed, maybe I would not even be able to justify doing so, for naturally he would have tried to rid me of all modesty, so that in quite brazen security and with no further ado I would turn a livelihood into life's earnest. (*KJN* 9:55)

"The Professor" of course flatters himself and the respective graduate students and undergraduates together with prospective students with the idea that "the Professor" is the best and most excellent flower of the development.

No, this is a misunderstanding. The professor is really the greatest human folly. For he is the conceited human attempt that wants to exhaust in reflection something that is above reflection. . . .

An analogy to this may in fact be shown in the world of individual human beings. Take someone who is actually in love. While actually in love it never occurs to him to be able to comprehend it; rather it seems to him—oh, lovable humility!—inconceivable that the girl could love him. Then let him get the girl. And let the years pass—and then perhaps there will come a time when the impress of his love no longer tingles in him; no, the passion has quite subsided and he has become inordinately clever—that is to say, quite stupid. His having come to this point will be discernible in the degree to which he thinks he is able to understand perfectly his infatuation for this or that reason. This is something that happens often in people's lives. A husband or a wife who was once in love is 10 years later a professor or doyenne in his or her infatuation. As professors or docents are always recognizable by their fancying themselves to be the finest flowers of the highest evolution, so too these professors and doyennes think that the stage they are now in is the highest. (*KJN* 9:65)

It is this peaceful, steady life in the utmost heterogeneity that makes the assistant professor so abominable.

But, alas, in vain do you hope to influence the assistant professors. When I am dead, my work will be pressed into service—by the assistant professors.

And these assistant professors will find continuing approval in the eyes of the world. Because, just as, in a grammar school, where those most looked up to are those whom their classmates regard as the cleverest at fooling the teacher, so does the world always admire this one thing: a more clever form of dishonesty. (*KJN* 10:30)

The Two Ways

One is to suffer; another is to become a professor of someone else having suffered.

The former is "the way"; the latter is to go round-about (thus the preposition that serves as the motto for all lecturing and lecture-prating: about), and perhaps it ends with going downabout. (*KJN* 10:171)

"The assistant professor" is in reality a non-human; I could almost be tempted to call him a non-animal. No passion whatsoever is capable of making an impression on "the assistant professor." . . .

No, suffering makes no impression on "the assistant professor." He is, however, very busily engaged in studying the sufferings of others, in familiarizing himself with them—for this, of course, is the basis on which he makes a living, fattening himself up with wife and child and family, all tastefully enjoying life with the help of—the sufferings of others, which he knows how to prepare in such a way that the state and a highly esteemed public willingly pay a very high price for it. (*KJN* 10:400)

Right now, it would probably be easy to find someone to give lectures about my ideas. It would also be easy enough for me to help someone in this respect. And it would be something of a relief to me that I didn't have to stand entirely alone. . . .

The thing is, it ought not be presented as a lecture; what I have to say must not be lectured. As a lecture, it would become something completely different. What I need is a person who doesn't gesticulate with his arms from the pulpit, nor with his finger from the professorial chair, but someone who gesticulates with his entire personal existence, who is ready and willing, amid every danger, to express in deeds exactly what he professes. A docent is someone who has 17 objectives: he wants to make a living, he wants to get married, he wants to be well regarded, he wants to satisfy the times, etc. What I've said, when presented in a lecture by a docent, would *eo ipso* become something completely different. This is indeed the profound untruth about all modern lectures: there is absolutely no notion of how the idea is affected when the person who presents it doesn't dare express it in actions; precisely for this reason the heart and soul of the idea disappear; the power of the idea is eliminated. (*KJN* 4:322)

The fundamental misfortune of the world is this confounded lecturing and that one great discovery after another makes people able to lecture impersonally on an ever greater scale. There no longer live any human beings, any thinkers, any lovers, etc.—rather, with the help of the press, the human race has been enveloped in a sort of atmosphere of thoughts, feelings, moods, even decisions and intentions, that are no one's, that belong to no one and everyone.

It is painful to see the toughness or callousness with which a person can sneak to the place he supposes the truth to be, in order that he might learn how to speak it, so that he could include this piece in the repertoire of his barrel organ—but doing anything simply does not occur to him. (*KJN* 5:214–15)

This, too, can be the subject of lectures. And if a docent could steal my thoughts from me he would be a brilliant success.... No, if, as I would like, I were capable of reaching down into posterity, it would be in order to frustrate, if possible, this mendacious lecturing that also wants to live off me. But it cannot be done. (*KJN* 9:134)

When I die someday, there will be something here for the assistant professors. Those villainous scoundrels! And nonetheless, it does no good, it does no good even if these words get printed and read again and again—the assistant professors will lecture all the same, perhaps with the added remark: The peculiar characteristic of his writing is that it cannot be lectured on. (*KJN* 9:350)

Somewhere in a hymn about the rich man it says that he painstakingly amasses a fortune and "knows not who will inherit from him."

Likewise I will leave behind me, intellectually speaking, a by no means insignificant bit of capital. And alas, I know who is going to inherit from me, that figure to whom I am so deeply opposed, he who up to now has inherited all that is best and will continue to do so—namely the docent, the professor.

And even if "the professor" chanced to read this, it would not give him pause, would not cause his conscience to smite him; no, this, too, will be something on which to hold forth. Nor, again, would this latter observation, should the professor chance to read it, give him pause; no, this, too, would be something on which to hold forth. For longer even than the tapeworm (of which according to *Andresseavisen*, a woman was recently delivered, for which her husband expresses gratitude in *Andresseavisen*, informing us of its length: 200 feet), longer still is the professor; and no human being can purge another in whom this tapeworm "the professor," is lodged.... (*KJN* 9:76)

Even my bitterest enemy would scarcely deny that I shall acquire a certain fame. But now I am beginning to wonder whether I might not gain fame in an entirely different genre from the one in which I had imagined until now: whether I might actually become famous as a naturalist, inasmuch as I have discovered—or at least have made a very significant contribution to—the natural history of parasites; the parasites I have in mind are priests and professors, those greedy and prolific parasites who even have the brazenness (which, indeed, other parasites do not possess) to want to be counted as the true friends and adherents of those whose sufferings they live off. (*KJN* 10:444)

And some day, when I am dead, how busy all the assistant professors will be to get me and mine butchered and salted down, how much competition there will be to say the same things, if possible, in more elegant language—as if that were what mattered.

Ah, but how ridiculous an assistant professor is! We all laugh when some mad Meier carries around a mass of fieldstone that he thinks is money—but the assistant professor goes about proudly, proud of his cleverness, and no one laughs. (*KJN* 10:55–56)

I love the common man—I find the assistant professors loathsome.

It is precisely the assistant professors who have demoralized the race. If things were allowed to be as they truly are: the few who are truly in service of the idea, or, even better, in God's service—and then the people: everything would be better.

But the infamous situation is that under the appearance of also serving the idea, this group of scoundrels, this band of robbers, forces its way between those few and the people, all for the sake of some miserable earthly advantage.

Were there no hell, one would have to come into being in order to punish the assistant professors, whose crime is indeed precisely of the sort that cannot very well be punished in this world. (*KJN* 10:98–99)

Confronted with so much evidence that Kierkegaard did not want his philosophy to be tarnished by their analysis and their grubby little books, most sensible assistant professors would get the message and move on to another project. They would find some other author to analyze and write books about—someone who didn't tell a single joke about assistant professors and who actually welcomes their attention. However, because I am not a sensible person, and because I was determined to get my own grubby little book published come hell or high water, I persisted. Putting to work my impressive powers of sophistry I came up with five rationalizations, excuses, and exculpations that would allow me to write a book about Kierkegaard's philosophy in spite of his many excellent jokes and criticisms directed against assistant professors (which seem designed to prevent any such books from ever being written):

Rationalization/Excuse/Exculpation #1: Generate an endless parade of red herrings.

This diversionary tactic could be accomplished by constantly trumpeting about other things that Kierkegaard said or did, especially the very bizarre or slightly scandalous features of his life and his writing, for example: "Did you know that many of the books Kierkegaard wrote were intended as coded messages to his former fiancé Regine Olson, even after he had broken up with her? Did you know that even though he was the youngest of seven children and was born when his father was fifty-six years old, he fully expected his father to outlive him in order to fulfill a divine curse, and he was amazed when this didn't happen? Did you know that he invited a satirical magazine to write about him, and then was deeply offended when the magazine did just that—publishing cartoons of him with one trouser leg shorter than the other, which led to Copenhagen school boys taunting and laughing at him when he went out for his daily walks? All of these events and anecdotes are so interesting that you should definitely focus completely on them and pay no attention to those very boring remarks about assistant professors!" Such a strategy would require a vigorous, truly athletic effort to manufacture a continual stream of distractions that would prevent anyone from noticing that Kierkegaard called into question the very idea of any assistant professor writing a book about his philosophy.

Rationalization/Excuse/Exculpation #2: Transform myself into a martyr for the noble cause of correcting this mistake.

To accomplish this I would argue that all of Kierkegaard's criticisms of assistant professors are simply wrong. They are all based on an error, I would insist; an error that—heroically—I will now correct. Donning the mantel of a martyr I would proclaim with great solemnity: "While Kierkegaard's philosophy is certainly quite brilliant, his criticism of assistant professors is, sadly, the one area of his thought where he made a serious mistake, a truly grave and embarrassing error, and I have humbly accepted the weighty responsibility of correcting this mistake. For this act of noble self-sacrifice, honored reading public, you are welcome."

Rationalization/Excuse/Exculpation #3: Argue that there is no comedy in philosophy, therefore everything funny in Kierkegaard's writing—especially all of his hilarious remarks about assistant professors—can be safely ignored.

For this approach I would offer the following argument to prove that philosophy renounced comedy long ago: "The first and also the last philosopher who attempted to make a joke was Socrates and look what happened to him! After Socrates was executed for telling jokes all philosophers quickly learned from his mistake and immediately renounced their sense of humor, resolving never to tell a single joke for the rest of their lives and giving thanks to Socrates for having taught them this most important of all philosophical lessons. Philosophy has henceforth been a completely humorless affair; this is, in fact, the one definition that accurately describes all of philosophy, encompassing every tradition and school of thought from medieval scholasticism to twentieth-century logical positivism: philosophy is the discipline that is allergic to comedy and completely lacks a sense of humor. Any undergraduate student who has taken even one philosophy class can confirm the accuracy of this definition." I would then argue that since there are, by definition, no jokes in philosophy it is perfectly logical to ignore any jokes that Kierkegaard made, including all his jokes about assistant professors, and proceed to write one more completely humorless book about Kierkegaard's philosophy.

Rationalization/Excuse/Exculpation #4: Engage in semantic hair-splitting.

This clever maneuver would involve taking refuge in the fact that Kierkegaard was only talking about assistant professors, not associate or full professors, and fortunately the elaborate system of rank that organizes the university professoriate, like a strange army composed only of officers who never leave their offices, allows every assistant professor to escape from the ignominious caste to which they are currently consigned—that rankest of all academic ranks. Therefore, I would be within my rights to proclaim: "While I must confess that I am at the moment a lowly assistant professor, this book about Kierkegaard will get me promoted to associate professor, and then all of Kierkegaard's jokes about assistant professors will no longer apply to me. Consequently, though this book is written now by an assistant professor, in the future it will have been written by an associate professor. Therefore, thank The Gods for the future perfect tense since this grammatical loophole makes me immune to ridicule in the present tense while I compose this very serious and not at all ridiculous book."

Rationalization/Excuse/Exculpation #5: Embrace the contradiction.

This final strategy may safely be regarded as the Hail Mary in my own philosophical playbook—my final act of desperation as the game clock ticks down to zero. The play takes the form of the following argument: "Yes it is undeniably true that I, an assistant professor, have written a book about Kierkegaard's philosophy even though Kierkegaard said—at great length and with great hilarity—that this is the worst thing that could happen to his philosophy. This is an undeniable contradiction, but I embrace this contradiction! My work is contradictory, and I too am a living contradiction! But what's wrong with contradictions? Contradictions are not so bad; the prejudice against contradictions is really quite deplorable. I say let a thousand flowers bloom and let true statements and false statements and tautologies and contradictions flourish side by side and arm in arm like brothers! Also please consider that it's entirely possible that there really are no contradictions, only apparent contradictions, and that every apparent contradiction contains a higher synthesis in which the contradiction is canceled, but at the same time, I don't know, maybe sort of preserved, and then I guess somehow lifted up to a higher level. Ergo there is no shame at all in contradictions and I wear all my contradictions proudly, like a badge of honor." This solution to the problem of how to write about Kierkegaard's philosophy while also getting paid for assistant professing would result in a book praising Kierkegaard that would appear to have been written by Hegel, which Kierkegaard himself would surely find amazing as well as proof that anything is possible.[2]

I was ready to deploy any and all of these rationalizations/excuses/exculpations in order to defuse, deny and dodge Kierkegaard's many hilarious criticisms of assistant professors when it occurred to me that there is another alternative. Rather than trying so hard to run and hide from these criticisms I could instead try to learn from them. When I did this it became clear that these texts actually provide extremely useful directions to anyone who wants to write about Kierkegaard's philosophy: they offer a kind of instruction manual in the form of jokes. All I have to do, I realized, is figure out what exactly Kierkegaard means by "assistant professor"—the character flaws and crimes that Kierkegaard attributes to this class of immoral and disreputable persons—and then find a way to avoid these personality defects. So I set aside my sophistical project of defusing, denying, and dodging Kierkegaard's jokes about assistant professors and instead tried to learn from these jokes, and here is what I learned.

It seems to me that the criminal acts and the character defects of assistant professors, which are presented in Kierkegaard's many excellent jokes about them, are essentially four:

(1) An assistant professor for Kierkegaard is someone who has done everything in his power to cease to be human—someone who has transformed himself into something like an assistant-professor-machine. He has surrendered his human subjectivity and become a mere approximation or objective copy of a human being.

(2) An assistant professor is a parasite. He feeds off of other people's creations and never creates anything new himself. What seems to offend Kierkegaard the most about the parasitism of assistant professors—a theme he returns to again and again with truly delightful imagery and detailed descriptions that do seem to qualify him as something of a naturalist—is that it has the audacity to present itself as creative work. Consequently the readers, auditors, and other customers of assistant professors are tricked into thinking that this is what real philosophy looks like, and are thus defrauded. They are sold a recycled copy of a copy and told that it's the real thing.

(3) An assistant professor is someone who reduces and simplifies and systematizes Kierkegaard's ideas, chopping up his philosophy into small, easily packaged and easily marketed morsels for the consuming public, thereby making life easier for everyone. But Kierkegaard never wanted to make anyone's life easier, so again this is a fraudulent and greatly distorted facsimile of his philosophy.

(4) An assistant professor kills Kierkegaard's philosophy by lecturing on it, thereby turning it into a collection of dead ideas for non-humans such as himself rather than subjective truths that need to be lived. Kierkegaard argues that lecturing is not essentially different from taxidermy or mummification. It's a way of reducing living ideas into preserved relics, suitable for display in a natural history museum but now very much dead. Lecturing is the practice by which professors who have ceased to be human (character defect/criminal act #1) dry out and dehumanize the ideas that they have parasitically extracted

(character defect/criminal act #2), and reduced and simplified and systematized (character defect/criminal act #3), from what was once a living collection of ideas.

This is how I found a way to justify writing a book about Kierkegaard's philosophy in spite of Kierkegaard's many excellent jokes about assistant professors who write books about his philosophy: by using those jokes as guidelines for how not to write about Kierkegaard's philosophy. The cure for my anxious and guilty conscience became clear: If I wanted to write a book about Kierkegaard's philosophy I simply needed to write like an anti-assistant-professor. Since I am by nature a lazy person I was happy to adopt the method that Kierkegaard has already provided—through his many outstanding jokes about assistant professors—as my own. Consequently, the method that I have followed in all the chapters of this book is the anti-assistant-professor-method, which I will now make perfectly clear in a solemn public declaration written in boldface type:

The method I've followed in this book is the anti-assistant-professor method, by which I mean writing in a way that is human, that creates something new rather than just repeating and rearranging Kierkegaard's ideas like a parasite, that expands and amplifies Kierkegaard's ideas rather than reducing or simplifying or systematizing them, and that does not kill Kierkegaard's philosophy by lecturing on it.

I feel the need to elaborate somewhat on all four aspects of the anti-assistant-professor method that guided the writing of this book.

(1) What does it mean not to lose one's humanity when writing a book about Kierkegaard?

One thing that it definitely means is: don't misplace or renounce your sense of humor. There are many good reasons not to do so; here are just two of them.

First of all, please consider the extreme incongruity of writing a humorless book about an author for whom comedy was so important. Kierkegaard is one of the few authors in the history of philosophy who have taken laughter seriously and put it to work as a philosophical tool. This is someone who chose to write his master's thesis on "The Concept of Irony with Constant Reference to Socrates" when he was twenty-eight years old. The conventions of master's theses prevented that book from being even remotely funny, required as it was to maintain a grim seriousness even when discussing irony in order to satisfy the humorless examining faculty; still, just the fact that he chose this topic for his thesis is very revealing.[3] In all of his writing Kierkegaard argues that comedy has always been an important part of philosophy, and he also puts comedy to work as a way to explore philosophical ideas and arguments.[4] Those are both rare and wonderful characteristics of Kierkegaard's philosophy that make it marvelously insightful and also enjoyable—proof that the two are not mutually exclusive. Most philosophy is written with horrible pomposity and piety in a dreadful spirit of seriousness and gravity, as if the author were a very short person standing on his tip-toes and straining to stretch himself in order to convince everyone that he's actually a giant. Kierkegaard never hesitates to laugh at this hilarious spectacle.

Secondly, on a purely personal level, I must confess that if I wrote anything about Kierkegaard that was allergic to comedy I would be deeply ashamed. I hope that these essays are insightful and instructive, but also entertaining, playful, and fun. This is not a legal or moral or logical requirement: the world always has room for one more dreary, dull, gloomy, grave and humorless book on Kierkegaard, and writing such a book would break no laws, nor would it even surprise anyone. However, I personally would be so disgusted with myself if I were to write a dreary and deadly serious book about Kierkegaard's philosophy that I would quit my job, say farewell to my family, my friends, and all of human civilization, and go off into the desert to live out the rest of my days in shame and regret. If I wrote anything about Kierkegaard that didn't honor his ability to unite philosophy and comedy I would regard that as a complete failure of imagination on my part, and I would be terribly embarrassed.[5]

(2) What does it mean to write about Kierkegaard's philosophy in a non-parasitical way?

I think it means that your goal is always to create something new and never simply to repeat or rearrange the ideas that Kierkegaard already created. It means writing in a way that expands rather than reduces and that liberates Kierkegaard's writing from the many forces that seek to constrain it.

What philosophy looks like when it does not attempt to create anything new was described best by Nietzsche:

> Scholars who spend basically all their time "poring over" books . . . ultimately become completely unable to think for themselves. When they are not poring over books, they are not thinking. When they think, they are *responding* to some stimulus (—a thought they have read about). In the end, all they do is react. Scholars spend all their energy saying yes and no, criticizing what other people have already thought,—they do not think for themselves any more. . . . Their instinct for self-defence has worn out, otherwise they would be defending themselves from books.[6]

This is most of what passes for philosophy today: trundling piles of other people's books and other people's ideas from one location to another, rearranging these piles and occasionally commenting on them. Though this may be intellectually demanding work, and though clearly it is about philosophy, it isn't really philosophy—I would argue—because philosophy requires creating something new. Such an approach to philosophy is best summarized by Deleuze and Guattari, who argue that criticism and the history of philosophy (as they are generally practiced) are actually insidious dangers because they make people forget that real philosophy requires creating something new.

> [T]hose who criticize without creating, those who are content to defend the vanished concept without being able to give it the forces it needs to return to life, are the plague of philosophy. All these debaters and communicators are inspired by *ressentiment*. They speak only of themselves when they set empty generalizations against one another. Philosophy has a horror of discussions. It always has something else to do.[7]

> Nothing positive is done, nothing at all, in the domains of either criticism or history, when we are content to brandish ready-made old concepts like skeletons intended to intimidate any creation, without seeing that the ancient philosophers from whom we borrow them were already doing what we would like to prevent modern philosophers from doing: they were creating new concepts, and they were not happy just to clean and scrape bones like the critic and historian of our time. Even the history of philosophy is completely without interest if it does not undertake to awaken a dormant concept and to play it again on a new stage, even if this comes at the price of turning it against itself.[8]

Contemplation, reflection, dialogue, criticism, and scholarship in all of its many forms—all of these are just so much sound and fury, signifying nothing, if they fail to do the one and only thing that philosophy must always do: create new concepts.

> Concepts are not waiting for us ready-made, like heavenly bodies. There is no heaven for concepts. They must be invented, fabricated, or rather created and would be nothing without their creator's signature. Nietzsche laid down the task of philosophy when he wrote, "[Philosophers] must no longer accept concepts as a gift, nor merely purify and polish them, but first *make* and *create* them, present them and make them convincing. Hitherto one has generally trusted one's concepts as if they were a wonderful dowry from some sort of wonderland," but trust must be replaced by distrust, and philosophers must distrust most those concepts they did not create themselves.... Plato said that Ideas must be contemplated, but first of all he had to create the concept of Idea. What would be the value of a philosopher of whom one could say, "He has created no concepts; he has not created his own concepts."[9]

I think this is a model of philosophy that Kierkegaard would approve of and one that follows the anti-assistant-professor method for writing about Kierkegaard's philosophy. In these essays my aim is to create new concepts that expand and enlarge on Kierkegaard's philosophy and thus avoid philosophical parasitism.[10]

(3) What does it mean to write about Kierkegaard's philosophy in a way that doesn't reduce or simplify or systematize it?

One of the most common ways of reducing or simplifying or systematizing Kierkegaard's thought is to argue that it's really all about religion, specifically the Christian religion. None of the essays in this book will contribute to that reductive project. Instead, in these essays I will argue that everything Kierkegaard wrote about religion has an additional meaning that is not limited to religion, and it is this other-than-religion meaning that I want to explore. Disentangling philosophy from religion at every stage in the history of philosophy—from the pre-Socratics, all the way through medieval, modern, and contemporary philosophy—is a project that fascinates me because it goes right to the heart of why philosophy is a uniquely human achievement and why it is valuable.

Anyone reading the paragraph above may very well ask: "If that's what interests you why on earth would you choose to write about Kierkegaard, of all people, since his life and his thought were so completely and inextricably tied up with Christianity?" My answer is that I think Kierkegaard is perhaps the best and most interesting philosopher to use as a case study for disentangling philosophy and religion. In these essays I will argue that Kierkegaard wasn't just an apologist for Christianity; in his philosophy he created and defended something new—his own creation—which he called "Xnty." That Kierkegaard wrung Xnty from his own experience, having fallen into a family led by a father who imposed on his children a very austere and quite brutal form of Christianity, just makes that whole story more interesting biographically, but I'm not smart enough to write that biography so I won't even try. Instead, what I will focus on is how the conceptual creation that Kierkegaard called Xnty is a philosophical creation, not a religion, and the fact that the religion Christianity serves as camouflage for the conceptual machinery of the philosophy Xnty just makes Xnty as a theoretical construction even more fascinating.[11]

Kierkegaard may very well have derived much or even all of his philosophy from thinking about religion and especially from a reading of the New Testament, but he also recognized that his reading and interpretation was itself a creative act—that there was no necessity to the conclusions he came to. In these essays I'll argue that in the many arguments that Kierkegaard phrased using the language and categories of religion he was at the same time also creating philosophical concepts that exceed the limits of religion. These philosophical concepts took on a life of their own that no doubt would surprise Kierkegaard, in the same way that children always surprise their parents with the choices they make and the lives that they create for themselves—lives very different from what their parents had imagined for them. But Kierkegaard did recognize the essentially subjective and creative nature of his project; he recognized that he was creating new subjective truths—new philosophical concepts—with his interpretation of religion, as these journal entries make clear:

> God's Sublimity
> He gives human beings a holy book containing his will but no middle terms with regard to the ideal—and then he leaves it to each one how to understand it. He does not let us hear from him, keeps perfectly quiet, testing the single individual, for indeed, it really seems to be left completely up to us how we will understand scripture. (*KJN* 8:62)

> How the N.T. is read.

> We are now so used to the fact that there is a N.T.—and in having a mutual understanding that we are not to do what is written there. (*KJN* 8:86)

Kierkegaard recognized that an infinite interpretation of any text is always possible, and that humans take advantage of this fact mainly as a way to avoid making any decisions or taking any action (*KJN* 9:128–29). He posited his own interpretation of the New Testament and of religion generally and then acted upon it, but he certainly recognized that his interpretation was a subjective and creative act and not some objective thing that fell from the sky.

Similarly, it may very well be the case that some of Kierkegaard's greatest works were, in his mind, written for the purpose of breaking up with his one and only girlfriend, Regine Olsen—an extremely strange literary act that probably no one understood, especially not Regine. This breakup-by-means-of-philosophy-books was so complicated that Kierkegaard had to spend the last fourteen years of his life explaining it to himself so that at least one person could understand it. But the fact that Kierkegaard's intentions may have been so narrowly focused when he wrote books like *Either/Or* and *Fear and Trembling* has not limited the impact and effect of these books. The fact that almost no one could understand the very idea of a prolonged, textual break up, let alone the specific instantiation of that textual form that is performed in those books by a bizarre cast of characters such as Victor Eremita, Judge Wilhelm, and Johannes the Seducer—this fact has not at all prevented these texts from creating an explosion of new philosophical concepts that readers have been exploring and applying ever since. The concepts that were created by these books were, from the start, much more than Kierkegaard could ever have imagined.

Kierkegaard wrestled with some of the toughest questions and issues that humans can wrestle with, but he did it all using the cultural and conceptual paradigms that he happened to fall into—most importantly, a very austere and even oppressive understanding of Christianity which was taught to him by a father deeply committed to a tragic sense of life.[12] Within this context Kierkegaard worked through most of the big questions that came to define existentialism and created many new philosophical concepts along the way, but he probably didn't understand it that way; he may very well have thought that what he was doing was all about religion from beginning to end. Like any truly great thinker, he didn't really understand what he was doing. But even though his ideas and arguments were presented and framed in the language of a certain deadly serious version of Christianity, they were not limited to that version of Christianity—or to Christianity in general, or to religion in general. This is not to say that Kierkegaard's insights, ideas and arguments cannot be understood to be about religion; just that it would be a mistake to understand them to be only about religion. One of the primary projects of this book is to argue that whenever Kierkegaard refers to religion what he says applies to much more than that.

To write about Kierkegaard's philosophy in a way that doesn't reduce or simplify or systematize it also requires that you make a choice about which Kierkegaard to study, because there are lots of different Kierkegaards from which to choose: one is deeply melancholic and seems intent on defining himself as such, as if that were a badge of honor; one craves recognition and fame and resents those who are more respected than he is; one is full of guilt for some crime that he refuses even to name, perhaps because it was someone else's crime; one is so fixated on his broken engagement that he analyzes it almost every day for fourteen years and when he dies proclaims that being engaged is no different than being married (much to the surprise of his former fiancée, who is now married to someone else); one is something like a full-time professional protestor intent on tearing down institutional Christianity; one is someone who never stops dreaming and making plans to become a country pastor—a full-time employee of institutional Christianity—and seems to be constantly auditioning for that job by publishing sample sermons; one is such a nihilist that he thinks the entire human race is a crime that should be extinguished immediately, that the best thing for a human would be never to have been born, and the second best is to die as quickly as possible;[13] one is a philosopher who idolizes Socrates and follows in the Socratic tradition, creating philosophy that is not allergic to comedy but is very much allergic to thoughtless piety or orthodoxy in any form, and that is fundamentally affirmative and constructive, intent on celebrating the joy of creating new concepts; and there are many, many more.

I am only interested in the last Kierkegaard in this list, and I have deliberately chosen to focus on this aspect of Kierkegaard's thought and to ignore the others. However, this is not a reductive project because I'm not arguing that Kierkegaard is just this—that somehow all the other dimensions of Kierkegaard's thought can be ultimately squeezed and compacted and beaten down to this one dimension. Kierkegaard was an extremely compound and complex person, and his thinking was similarly compound and complex. I see no reason to deny that, or to insist that his thought be simplified or reduced in any way; but I also see no reason to hide the fact that I'm really only interested in one aspect or dimension of Kierkegaard's thinking and writing—one of the many Kierkegaards that are available and that have served as the focus of many other books. For anyone who (for some strange reason) may decide to read this book: please don't waste your time looking for any of these other Kierkegaards in these essays; they are not here.

(4) What does it mean to write about Kierkegaard's philosophy in a way that doesn't kill it by lecturing on it?

The point of Kierkegaard's writing was to create a new personality, not a lecture or a doctrine. Even a book can have a personality of its own, and any book about Kierkegaard's writing should also have a personality, as these journal entries suggest:

> The lecturing approach cannot be stopped by a new doctrine, but only by a personality. (*KJN* 9:16)
>
> On My Writings
> The heterogeneity must by all means be maintained: here we have an author, not a cause in the objective sense, but a cause for which an individual has stood on his own, for which he has suffered, etc. But, just as people have not understood why *Concluding Postscript* is structured comically—that precisely this is earnestness—and just as people therefore think they are improving the cause by taking individual theses and transposing them into a didactic mode, so here, too, it will probably also end with a new confusion, in which people treat me as a cause and transpose everything into objectivity, making it into something new, that here we have a new doctrine—rather than that what is new is that here we have a personality. . . . All of my work as an author and the whole of my existence as an author are like a challenge: I have surrounded the terrain, everywhere inciting people and watching to see whether the single individual might not arise . . . . (*KJN* 6 312–13)[14]

The anti-assistant-professor method that I have adopted enjoins writing about Kierkegaard's ideas in a way that doesn't lecture about those ideas, but instead performs those ideas and thereby catalyzes new ideas, new concepts, new philosophy. The only way to stop all the lecturing to which philosophy has become addicted is to replace the lecture with a personality.[15]

For this book I've chosen a personality that is fragmentary, sketchy, scrappy, and crumby. Writing crumby philosophy books is something that Kierkegaard himself pioneered in all of his writing, but most obviously in the strange and wonderful book *Philosophical Fragments*, so I will turn to that book for an explanation of the crumby personality that I want this book to have.

How should a reader understand *Philosophical Fragments*? The text itself suggests two distinct options:

On the one hand, the book invites us to treat it as an unruly, anarchic, unsystematic mess; a random assortment of scraps—mere philosophical crumbs.[16] The title, of course, suggests this approach, and so does the book's author, Johannes Climacus, who insists that what he has written is not really even a book: it's merely a pamphlet "without any claim to being a part of the scientific-scholarly endeavor in which one acquires legitimacy," not even "as an absolute trumpeter" (*PF* 5). The author further confesses that he is a lazy, thoroughly indolent fellow (*PF* 5) who has written his pamphlet just to appear busy, since everyone else around him seemed to have so many serious and important things to do, and he didn't want to be seen as "the only loafer among so many busy people" (*PF* 6). He also considers it too much of a burden to have any opinion of his own and he is indignant that anyone would even want to know what his opinions are (*PF* 7). Why then should we bother to read his pamphlet? The only reason he gives us is that he is not a bad dancer—"for I have trained myself and am training myself always to be able to dance lightly in the service of thought" (*PF* 7).[17] As a dialectical dancer, with no fixed convictions of his own, he plans simply to follow the arguments wherever they lead, and we're welcome to follow along. The net result of this unscripted dialectical dancing is (Climacus is proud to say) a large collection of philosophical fragments or crumbs, and the worst fate he can imagine for his work is that some well-meaning systematizer might try to impose order on these crumbs by sweeping them up into a neat and tidy pile, which would "prevent a kind and well-disposed reader from unabashedly looking to see if there is anything in the pamphlet he can use" (*PF* 7). "Please don't clean up my crumby book," Climacus begs; "please allow this pamphlet to remain an unruly, anarchic, unsystematic mess, a happy assortment of philosophical scraps and crumbs, and then perhaps among the crumbs you will find something useful." I will call this approach to the book the crumby approach, since it embraces and celebrates the book's crumbiness and vows to resist any attempt to impose a system on the fragments of philosophy that fill its pages.[18]

On the other hand, Johannes Climacus also seems to suggest another approach to *Philosophical Fragments* that directly contradicts the crumby approach. I'll call this the authoritative approach because it places *Philosophical Fragments*, along with its much longer, weightier, and more famous sequel (*The Concluding Unscientific Postscript to the Philosophical Fragments*) under the authority of a single thesis statement or question, which is announced with some fanfare on the title page:

> Can a historical point of departure be given for an eternal consciousness; how can such a point of departure be of more than historical interest; can an eternal happiness be built on historical knowledge?

The reader, confronted by this very somber and serious three-part question before she has even had a chance to turn the page and read the first word of the book, is immediately tempted to think of the book as a systematic response to a very stern and systematic set of questions, in spite of any apparent protestations to the contrary from the author. This approach leads to regarding *Philosophical Fragments* as fragmentary only in the sense that it is just part-one of a larger systematic discourse responding to a single set of questions (which just happen to be of interest primarily to Christian theology, thereby making it very easy to think of both the *Fragments* and the *Postscript* as *aufgehoben* into the larger system of Christian theology). The authoritative approach to the book makes it very easy to dismiss all the noise from this very noisy author about "fragments" and "crumbs" and "please spare my book from the system" as nothing more than sound and fury, signifying nothing. The authoritative approach does a neat job of simplifying and streamlining *Philosophical Fragments*; it sweeps up all the crumbs and organizes them into a larger systematic whole, and for most readers this approach to the book has proven to be irresistible.

Because Climacus offers us two possible interpretative approaches to *Philosophical Fragments* that seem to be polar opposites it's natural to assume that only one approach can be correct; but that would be a bad assumption. When *Philosophical Fragments* confronts us with two interpretative paradigms that appear to be mutually exclusive this gives us the opportunity to resist the seduction of an exclusive, either/or, style of thinking, and here again we should be grateful to Climacus for making good on his promise to create difficulties for us everywhere (*CUP* 186–87). *Philosophical Fragments*, along with all the rest of Kierkegaard's texts, supports *both* of these readings—the authoritative approach and the crumby approach (and of course many, many more). However, the authoritative approach to this book—and to all of Kierkegaard's books—has attracted the most attention by far, while the crumby approach has gotten almost none.

This unfortunate situation deserves to be corrected. One of my humble projects in this book is to make some space for the crumby approach to all of Kierkegaard's philosophical texts so that the rich dialectical and multifaceted character of these texts can be more fully appreciated. In these essays I will argue for the crumby approach to Kierkegaard's writing, which resists all temptations to sweep up or clean up the fragments, sketches, scraps, and crumbs into something resembling a system, and which also suggests that we should pay special attention to the crumbs that are left behind after the main course has been eaten, the serving trays cleared away, and the dinner guests thinking about retiring for a nap. These crumby ideas are the leftovers which are easy to ignore. These leftovers may turn out to be far more interesting, and far more useful, than the main course, even though the main course was spectacular and delicious and therefore attracted everyone's attention.[19]

This is the non-lecturing personality I would like these essays to have. Clearly this calls for another solemn declaration written in boldface type:

This book is a deliberately fragmentary, sketchy, scrappy, and crumby book. This is certainly not the only way to interpret Kierkegaard's philosophy, but it's a legitimate and useful approach that has been mostly ignored in favor of a more authoritative approach (and no doubt I also chose to adopt this personality for the book simply because it reflects my own personality, since I am a fragmentary, sketchy, scrappy, and generally crumby person).

At this point an attentive reader will certainly have noted that although I have now issued, with great fanfare, two boldface public declarations regarding the anti-assistant-professor methodology and the deliberately crumby personality of this book, I have not yet answered the question that I promised to answer right at the beginning of this introduction/confession: Why does the world need another book about Kierkegaard by another assistant professor, and how will this book be a tremendous boon to the whole world? Here, finally, is my humble explanation of this not-very-humble assertion: While this book is, I confess, just another book about Kierkegaard by another shameless assistant professor, it is also a book about the dangers of nihilism for the entire human race and a contribution to the ongoing project of recognizing and unmasking nihilism when it masquerades as something more respectable.

There is actually an astounding amount of nihilism in Kierkegaard's writing, and it's also astounding how little this has been recognized. Before I plunge ahead with a book celebrating the humor, playfulness, and affirmative spirit of Kierkegaard's philosophy it would be disingenuous in the extreme if I failed to acknowledge that there is another side to Kierkegaard's thought that is not at all joyous, or humorous, or playful, or affirmative, but is actually more like the polar opposite of all of those qualities. Kierkegaard is rightly credited with being one of the founding fathers of existentialism and therefore an enemy of nihilism in all its forms, but it's also true that Kierkegaard himself succumbed to nihilism at the end of his very short life in a truly spectacular way. The version of nihilism that Kierkegaard adopted at the end of his life was concealed behind a strange and twisted mask of religion—as if it were all God's idea and he had no choice in the matter.

The evidence for Kierkegaard's descent into nihilism at the end of his life is particularly clear in his final journals. Throughout all of Kierkegaard's journals there are brief moments of self-pity, bitterness, anger, and resentment that are somewhat nihilistic, but these occasional moments of pessimism seem like aberrations because the overall character of his thought remains affirmative, creative, and optimistic. But something different happens in his final journals, especially in the last three of them (NB 34, 35, and 36). Suddenly nihilism becomes the general rule rather than the exception. To be more specific, there are two sustained nihilistic arguments in Kierkegaard's final three journals that completely displace everything affirmative in his thought:

(1)

Beginning in NB 34, and continuing in NB 35 and 36, Kierkegaard argues at length for anti-natalism. In a total of thirty-five different journal entries he insists that birth is always a calamity and the entire human race should be extinguished. Here are a few examples:

> What constantly occupies "the human being" is to get this world made into a fine world, to get away from God's criminalist view that it lieth in wickedness, that for him it is a felonious existence.... To this end Xnty—which therefore immediately bars the way to propagation.... So even if someone became Xn and died unmarried, he is still a criminal, for his existence through propagation was a crime. (*KJN* 10:341)

> This world, the selfishness of this entire existence, is concentrated and culminates in the propagation of the race, a selfishness that (as I have shown elsewhere), if it cannot create (which is the right reserved to God's majesty), then at least wants to: give life. God does not want this selfishness; he wants it stopped—therefore Xnty immediately bars the way. God's kingdom is not of this world; the Xn is a stranger and foreigner. (*KJN* 10:343)

> The New Testament clearly rests on the view: to love God is to hate oneself, and love of God is hostility toward humanity. Thus, indeed, the entirely accurate view of Xnty held by the paganism of the times, that it is hostility toward humanity. (*KJN* 10:438)

> [T]he appearance of Xt was directed specifically at putting a stop to the race. (*KJN* 10:444)

The anti-natalism that Kierkegaard defends here is more often associated with Schopenhauer; but Kierkegaard's version is actually much more extreme than Schopenhauer's—a point that Kierkegaard himself makes in an extended discussion of Schopenhauer in his NB 32 journal. Schopenhauer, he argues, "*is not a thoroughgoing pessimist*" (*KJN* 10:140, the emphasis is Kierkegaard's own). Kierkegaard took his own arguments for pessimism much further: while Schopenhauer argues that human existence is merely an error, Kierkegaard argues that it is a crime.

> A lie is concentrated at precisely this point concerning the propagation of the race; if sin came into the world in this way, a lie was also set vigorously into motion on the same occasion. ... It is because of this lie that the child is filled full of all this: that it's a wonderful world, that the purpose of life is to be happy, to enjoy, etc., etc., which of course the child is indeed naturally disposed to believe (Schopenhauer is thus correct in saying that each person is born with the illusion that the aim of this life is to be happy), but which is also connected to the fact that the parents—were they to explain that the world is evil, that the purpose of life is to suffer, item that a child's life has its origin in the satisfaction of lust, etc.—would of course face embarrassment if it occurred to the child to ask, "Why then, do I exist?" (*KJN* 10:384–85)

> [I]t is completely impossible for a child to grasp the *punctum saliens* in Xnty: original sin, and were the child capable of understanding it, the parents would appear in an extremely strange light. (*KJN* 10:421)

> Xnty is pessimism. (*KJN* 10:156)

> Xnty is utter pessimism. (*KJN* 10:173)

(2)

In Kierkegaard's final journal (NB 36), there are several entries in which he makes plans for his own martyrdom. There's no way of knowing what connection there is between the ideas and arguments expressed in these journal entries and Kierkegaard's own death, which occurred less than a year later, so this is not an argument about what caused Kierkegaard's death (which can never be known with certainty, and it's not relevant to Kierkegaard's philosophy anyway). However, it is undeniable that Kierkegaard argued in NB 36 for the superiority of a martyr's death and an "early exit" from human life, which—according to the anti-natalism argument that dominates NB 34 and 35—is fundamentally a crime anyway. Here are some examples:

> Xnty rests on the notion that martyrdom has value in and of itself, absolute value. (*KJN* 10:93)

> I want to engage with my contemporaries. . . . I do not want to engage with them in a straightforward fashion—I want to be sacrificed. (*KJN* 10:76)

> The True Extraordinaries, Those of the First Class
> They do not feel happy enough in this world to want to settle down in it. No, they are travelers, on a mission, hurry away again, home, as soon as possible. Then, when they notice that the end approaches, when—having brought about the greatest possible effect in the shortest possible time—they have just about completed their mission: then they push a little button that only they know about—then their lives have a catastrophic effect, and in that way they are thrust out of the world. Here, from beginning to end, everything is heterogeneity: to exit this world catastrophically is the greatest heterogeneity in comparison with a steady, calm life and a quiet death. (*KJN* 10:426)

> To Bring About a Catastrophe
> However afraid people would be of me if they found out, however strange it would seem to them: it is certain that what has occupied me in recent times has been whether God in fact wants me to stake everything on bringing about a catastrophe, on getting arrested, convicted—if possible, executed. (*KJN* 10:435)[20]

I think the extremely nihilistic character of these two arguments has been generally overlooked because they are presented as religious arguments, which leads readers to treat them as articles of faith that should be respected and passed over in silence rather than philosophical theories that should be argued and interrogated. Thus, they are dismissed as nothing more than additional examples of Kierkegaard's very idiosyncratic and very extreme version of Christianity.[21] But the fact that Kierkegaard presents these nihilistic declarations as if they were natural requirements of Christianity is just another example of him using "Christianity" as a synonym for "subjective truth."

As I mentioned earlier, and as you've observed in many quotations already cited in this introduction/confession, in all of his journals Kierkegaard used the letter "X" to signify Christianity, Christ, or any variation thereof (for example "Xt" for Christ; "Xn" for Christian; "Xnty" for Christianity, "Xndom" for Christendom, etc.). One of the great values of Kierkegaard's journals is that they make it clear that this X really was a variable in Kierkegaard's thought: a placeholder that could stand for anything. When "Xnty" is understood in this way everything that Kierkegaard writes about "Christianity" no longer has any necessary connection to religion. In his journals, and in all of his other writings, the X of "Xnty" is instantiated in two very different ways:

(1) As a collection of ideals for a truly authentic human existence—standards for how to live which are so demanding and idealized that perhaps they can never be fully realized. (Xnty in this sense was one of Kierkegaard's greatest philosophical creations, and I'll have much more to say about it throughout this book.)

(2) As a particular kind of nihilism, which argues against all human relationships and all other attempts to create meaning in life, and even against life itself.

The first instantiation of X is dominant throughout the earlier journals and throughout most of Kierkegaard's other writing; but in Kierkegaard's final journals the first instantiation quickly fades from view and the second instantiation takes over.

One of the most persistent and troubling criticisms of existentialism has always been the claim that it is actually just an extraordinarily confused and verbose form of nihilism. Every author in the existentialist tradition has faced this criticism, and every one of them has been extremely annoyed by it because they all claim to be doing just the opposite: providing a cure for nihilism. One of the great philosophical contributions that Kierkegaard made at the end of his life was to demonstrate how easy it is for existentialism to become precisely the disease that it claims to cure.

Perhaps more than any other author in the existentialist tradition Kierkegaard argued for the legitimacy and even the primacy of "subjective truth" in human existence—a concept that he most famously defined in 1835, when he was twenty-two years old:

> [T]he thing is to find a truth which is truth *for me*, to find *the idea for which I am willing to live and die*. And what use would it be in this respect if I were to discover a so-called objective truth. ... What use would it be if truth were to stand there before me, cold and naked, not caring whether I acknowledged it or not, inducing an anxious shiver rather than trusting devotion? ... That's what I lacked for leading a *completely human life* and not just a life of *knowledge,* to avoid basing my mind's development on—yes, on something that people call objective—something which at any rate isn't my own, and to base it instead on something which is bound up with the deepest roots of my existence. (*KJN* 1:19–21, all the emphasis is Kierkegaard's own)

Subjective truth is a powerful idea that can create meaning and value in human existence regardless of one's external circumstances, and it is an absolutely central principle of existentialism that all values have no independent, objective existence and therefore must be created by individual subjects. But subjective truth is also completely amenable to nihilism, since nihilism too is nothing but a collection of values. At the end of his life Kierkegaard demonstrated very effectively what critics of existentialism have long maintained: that creating your own values can indeed be very dangerous because there is nothing to prevent you from creating values that are completely nihilistic.

This argument about Kierkegaard succumbing to nihilism at the end of his life may sound like an indictment of him as a person, but that is not at all my intention. That would be a biographical project which doesn't interest me, and it also wouldn't be appropriate for a philosophy book, which is what I'm trying to write here. It is certainly worth noting, however, that this is one of the great ironies of the history of philosophy: that someone who is often credited with creating existentialism, or at least being one of its primary founders,[22] was capable of embracing at the end of his life a system of nihilism that was so thorough it probably would have shocked even Arthur Schopenhauer—who is generally recognized as the world champion of nihilism. This illustrates the insidious danger of nihilism, especially for any philosophy that maintains that values are subjective.

"Go big or go home" seems like a very apt description of Kierkegaard's thought over the course of his lifetime. Very early in his life, at age twenty-two, he formulated an idea of subjective truth that was a radical rebuttal to philosophy's unquestioning worship of objectivity, and that idea became a founding principle of nineteenth- and twentieth-century existentialism; then at the end of his life, at age forty-two, he used that same concept of subjective truth to justify embracing a truly epic version of nihilism that glorified anti-natalism and martyrdom, and called for the extinction of the entire human race. Kierkegaard did not think small thoughts, and for this we should be grateful, because there is much to be learned from both his insights and his mistakes. As Kierkegaard himself recognized, his life was a "battle of ideas" and the many conflicts and even contradictions in his thinking were the result of "the border skirmishes of [his] nature" (*KJN* 8:191–92). That Kierkegaard could first create a philosophy that so fully and effectively opposed nihilism, using both humor and insight in his arguments, and then could also so completely succumb to nihilism himself—this is something that I regard as a major accomplishment in its own unique way. It demonstrates the power of Kierkegaard's ideas, and the serious consequences that are entailed by their application. But it's also a very sad story and an undeniable tragedy that Kierkegaard himself could not find a way to apply his own philosophy to his own life in a way that would allow him to create meaning and value for himself.

If someone put a gun to my head and demanded that I speculate on the reasons why one of the creators of existentialism became a nihilist, here's the explanation that seems most likely to me: I think Kierkegaard believed personally in the power and the value of affirmation and comedy, and through most of his life he lived accordingly; but gradually he became convinced that it was his religious duty to be miserable—that God didn't want him to enjoy life because he was to be sacrificed, like a "little dash of cinnamon" that is added to a soup to make it taste just right (*KJN* 9:48–49). He became convinced that "it was not in fact God's will that [he] should enjoy life" (*KJN* 9:42), and that his natural inclination to see the world as "lovely and wonderful" was in fact a mistake that he had to overcome, part of an examination that all humans have to take (*KJN* 10:21). The worldview that he inherited from his father he described as "the tragedy of my childhood: the terrifying, secret explanation of the religious that was granted me in a fearful presentiment which my imagination hammered into shape—my offense at the religious" (*KJN* 2:174). This offensive thought that was planted in his youth eventually overtook him. The conviction that God did not want him to be happy seems to seep slowly into Kierkegaard's thought until eventually it takes over and extinguishes his naturally affirmative spirit; and thus he was transformed into a nihilist by the belief that God wanted him to be a nihilist. The person who wrote "humor is also the joy that has triumphed over the world" (*KJN* 2:88) when he was young, gave up on humor when he was old.

I think this is a very sad story, and if anyone ever asked for my theory concerning why Kierkegaard seems to lose his sense of humor and also his will to live at the end of his life, this is the explanation I would offer.

However, no one has ever asked me for my opinion on this matter, and I am confident that no one ever will, so I will keep it to myself and not say another word about it. This book is not a biography of Kierkegaard and I'm not going to have any more to say about his biography because clearly no one wants to hear my thoughts on that and there are already plenty of good Kierkegaard biographies available if anyone wants to study Kierkegaard's life. But this fact of his life—that he allowed himself to become a nihilist in spite of his own powerful arguments for affirmation, humor, and joy—is relevant to this book, because I want this book to be joyous and affirmative (pretty much the polar opposite of the worldview that dominated Kierkegaard's final years) and I want it to contribute to the project of unmasking and overcoming nihilism in all of its many forms. Nihilism is so easy to succumb to in some form or another, and the fact that even someone like Kierkegaard, who had so many brilliant insights into the insidious nature of nihilism and the many masks that it can wear, still allowed himself to become a nihilist—this is an extremely instructive story and an important part of Kierkegaard's contribution to philosophy. For all of these reasons, the nihilism in Kierkegaard's thought is important to consider before anyone dives into this book. I am interested in liberating Kierkegaard's philosophy from many things, including any arguments that limit and reduce his ideas to religion, the spirit of gravity and occasional humorlessness, and also some forms of nihilism that were so subtle and sneaky that even someone as insightful and practiced in recognizing nihilism as Kierkegaard failed to notice them.

As I write this introduction/confession in January 2022 the world continues to struggle with the COVID-19 virus. After nearly two years in which almost every human gathering has been canceled or closed or transferred to a "virtual environment" (meaning one in which there are no other people present, since every person is potentially a threat to my own survival) everyone is quite tired of this virus and it has become a commonplace to say that this pandemic has certainly been one of the greatest calamities that has ever befallen the human species. But the greatest enemy of humanity is not and never will be a virus, or earthquakes, or bears, or alligators, or any other objective thing; it is and always will be a subjective system of ideas, which can easily become subjective truths for which people will live and die. Nihilism in its many forms is far more viral than even the angriest, nastiest rhinovirus, and even social isolation will not prevent its spread. These essays on Kierkegaard, in addition to following the anti-assistant-professor method and adopting a deliberately crumby personality, will also be an attempt to provide the human race with one more inoculation against the spread of nihilism, which is the worst disease that anyone can catch. That's why I humbly suggest that what the world needs now more than anything else is another book on Kierkegaard's philosophy written by another assistant professor.

Since the last few pages of this introduction/confession have been so horribly sober and serious I feel the need to insert one last hilarious quote from Kierkegaard about assistant professors in order to lighten the mood and wrap up this introduction on the right note:

> How easy with finite goals. One is a professor, has a permanent position, a salary, honor, and respect—and furthermore, his efforts are understood immediately. It is of course assumed that it is serious business. This is how everything worldly joins together here.
>
> Assume the relation to an idea, assume a more pure, ideal existence—then you are superfluous, a sort of madness. (*KJN* 6:209)

(That was actually more chilling than funny—a good candidate for a warning sign that should be nailed over every assistant professor's office door.)

Now please read the rest of the book. I hope you enjoy it.

CHAPTER 1

How to misunderstand Kierkegaard's journals and notebooks as nothing more than supplements and appendices to his other books rather than works of philosophy themselves

or

Three forms of philosophical theatre in Kierkegaard's journals and notebooks

IMAGINE THAT YOU COULD bring together all the people currently residing on Planet Earth and ask them this one question: "Was Søren Kierkegaard a philosopher, or was he something else entirely? Of all the eclectic, strange, and truly bizarre texts that Kierkegaard created in his life, are there any that deserve to be called works of philosophy? In other words: If you want to find philosophy in Kierkegaard's writing, where should you look?" At this point someone in the crowd would probably raise her hand and point out: "You said you were only going to ask one question, but already you have asked three, so please be more organized and more succinct." That is a good point, and I am sorry. I will correct that now. All the questions above really boil down to just one question: "Did Kierkegaard write any philosophy, and if so, where did he put it?" (I guess that was really two questions; sorry again.) By now almost all the people of Earth would have gone home, since they find all of these questions to be either meaningless or extremely boring or possibly both; but if you could now round up the people who stuck around because they do have an opinion on this question and gather them in one room (you would probably not need a very large room), here's the debate that would likely follow.

One group in the room, or perhaps just one extremely confident individual, would stand up and say: "You won't find philosophy anywhere in Kierkegaard's writing, so don't waste your time looking. Kierkegaard didn't write any philosophy because he didn't follow the rules of the philosophy game. There are really just three simple and very reasonable rules to this game, so it's hardly asking too much to expect a writer to follow them. Here they are:

(1) Give us clear and concise arguments that fit neatly within the traditional areas of philosophy.

(2) Don't waste our time with any nonsense, because we are serious people and we have no tolerance for nonsense.

(3) Take full responsibility for what you have written, and be prepared to spend the rest of your life defending your arguments at conferences and in articles that will attract smaller and smaller audiences.

Obviously Kierkegaard never wrote anything that follows these rules. Even his books that are most often claimed to be philosophy books—the books attributed to pseudonyms with ludicrous names such as Hilarius Bookbinder and Nicolaus Notabene, and which also have ludicrous titles such as *Philosophical Crumbs* and *Concluding Unscientific Postscript to the Philosophical Crumbs*—these books are actually the worst offenders, the most egregious examples of breaking all the rules of philosophical writing. They are neither clear nor concise (many are nearly five hundred pages or longer and there's no agreement on what they mean), they are filled with an abundance of nonsense, and in the end Kierkegaard refuses to take any responsibility for them, abandoning them like broken down, unwanted cars left by the side of the road. Instead, he claims that the books were written by non-existent pseudonyms and insists that he himself is not to blame for the mess that these non-existent authors made. It's really all very annoying, immature, childish nonsense, and, as we warned you earlier, we are serious people who don't have any tolerance for nonsense, because philosophy is a deadly serious business."

Everyone else in the room would believe that at least some of what Kierkegaard wrote deserves to be called philosophy. In response to the very confident and categorical speech that they just heard, some people in this group would argue that at the very least Kierkegaard's pseudonymous books are philosophy books, albeit highly unorthodox philosophy books that require the reader to do a lot of hard work and also possess (ahem) a sense of humor. A few others would argue that in addition to the pseudonymous books Kierkegaard's many "Upbuilding Discourses" and "Ethical-Religious

Essays" are also works of philosophy that use a veneer of religion to hide carefully coded philosophical arguments, and a few others would argue that the same could be said for all of the articles that made up Kierkegaard's "attack upon Christendom" in the final years of his life—that these too were fundamentally philosophical arguments, even though on the surface they appear to be nothing more than critiques of the Church of Denmark as it existed in the middle of the nineteenth century. There may even be a handful of people who would argue that the various other scraps of writing that Kierkegaard produced in his lifetime, such as book reviews and letters to newspapers, were also works of philosophy. In short, the people in this second group would disagree on exactly where you should look if you want to find philosophy in Kierkegaard's writing, but they would all agree that it's there.[23] So what sort of argument could they present to make the case that Kierkegaard was a philosopher in spite of the criticisms leveled by the first group (or extremely confident individual)? How could they respond to the claim that you can't find any philosophy in Kierkegaard's writing?

One argument that you would likely hear from the people in the second group is something like the following: "Yes, you're right about all the rules for writing philosophy that you spelled out. Philosophers are required to give clear and concise arguments with no nonsense, and then take full responsibility for what they have written, defending their clear and concise arguments with even more clear and concise arguments for the rest of time. You're right about all of this, and you're also right that Kierkegaard doesn't do this in any of his published writing—but he does do it in his journals. In his journals Kierkegaard drops the indirect communication and writes with the clarity, precision, and responsibility that philosophy requires, and he cleans up all the nonsense and confusion that are in the other texts. So if you allow Kierkegaard's journals to supplement and complete the rest of his writing he does become a philosopher who follows all the traditional rules of the philosophy game." Though probably no one has ever stated it quite so explicitly and bluntly, this is actually a pretty common argument. Among those who want to defend Kierkegaard as a philosopher his journals have been used primarily in this way: as a warehouse that is thought to contain nothing but directly communicated, clear and concise arguments endorsed by the author himself that can be called upon as needed to make Kierkegaard into a respectable philosopher.[24]

In this chapter I'm going to argue for a different approach to Kierkegaard's journals. I'll argue that the journals deserve to be read as works of philosophy themselves, and not just used as supplements to bring order and respectability to Kierkegaard's other writings. There are at least three specific philosophical values in Kierkegaard's journals and notebooks—three ways in which the journals create philosophy within their own pages and therefore deserve to be read as independent works of philosophy and not just as supplements to Kierkegaard's other writing. All three of these are best understood as philosophical performances or a kind of philosophical theatre,[25] so the argument that follows is something like a three-act play:

> Act 1: The journals and notebooks perform existential philosophy.
>
> Act 2: They contribute to Kierkegaard's theory of indirect communication.
>
> Act 3: They create new philosophical concepts.

As a preface to the three acts of this play I'll briefly summarize how Kierkegaard's journals and notebooks have been used since his death in 1855, and I'll speculate on why they have not been read as works of philosophy themselves. This is intended as an entertaining prelude to set the stage before the show begins.

Prelude: The long, strange trip that Kierkegaard's journals and notebooks have taken since 1855

After Søren Kierkegaard's death in November of 1855 the Copenhagen Probate Commission entered his apartment to make an inventory of his property. They reported that the apartment contained "a mass of paper, mostly manuscripts, that were found in various places" (*KJN* 11: xxix). Most of this "mass of paper" consisted of bound journals or notebooks in three different groups: (1) a set of ten journals labeled by Kierkegaard AA through KK (there is no II); (2) a set of fifteen notebooks that were not labeled or numbered by Kierkegaard but that were later numbered 1–15 by the editors of Kierkegaard's papers according to the order in which he wrote in them; (3) a final set of thirty-six journals labeled by Kierkegaard NB1–NB36. The "mass of paper" also included many loose papers that were found mostly in small piles in a writing desk and in a chest of drawers. This was the moment when it was discovered that—in addition to the truly prodigious quantity of books and articles that Kierkegaard published in his life—he was also a rather maniacal journal writer who by the time of his death at age forty-two had filled up sixty-one distinct volumes in a very anarchic collection of journals and notebooks.

Kierkegaard willed all of his belongings, including all of these unpublished journals and papers, to his former fiancée, Regine Olsen. This proved rather awkward, however, since Regine Olsen was now Regine Schlegel—married to Fritz Schlegel, the governor of the Danish West Indies (which later became the U.S. Virgin Islands). A letter was dispatched to Regine at her island home by steamship informing her that her former fiancée had left her all his worldy possessions—which mostly amounted to an enormous stack of paper covered with his scribblings. Regine's husband replied with a tersely worded letter indicating that his wife did not wish to have her former boyfriend's junk shipped to her, thank you very much. Regine did request just a few items pertaining to their brief engagement (mostly letters that she and Søren had exchanged) but otherwise she renounced any claim on Søren's estate.[26] Consequently at this point all of Søren's property, including his journals and papers, reverted to his brother Peter Christian Kierkegaard, who was his only living family, since both of their parents and all of their five siblings had died earlier.

Peter became the reluctant custodian of his brother's journals and notebooks but he had no interest in trying to organize them, so when his nephew Henrik Lund volunteered for that job Peter was happy to oblige.[27] Henrik Lund was a zealous enthusiast for his uncle Søren's ideas. He is perhaps best known for the impromptu rant he delivered graveside at Søren's burial: an angry diatribe against the Church of Denmark. (For this unruly outburst he was later compelled by the authorities to pay a fine of one hundred rixdollars.) However, Lund didn't make much progress in organizing his uncle's papers and when he left Denmark a few years later to take a job as a physician on the island of St. John in the Danish West Indies (where Søren's former fiancée Regine now lived as the wife of the islands's governor) Kierkegaard's papers were initially stored for a few years at Lund's parents's house until they decided they didn't want this pile of paper cluttering up their home any longer and they shipped everything back to Peter, who once again found himself unable to escape from the mountain of papers that his brother left behind. Since Peter was a bishop in the same Church of Denmark that Søren and his nephew Henrik had ridiculed so mercilessly, and was also the subject of many critical remarks in his brother's journals and papers, it's not surprising that he did not share Henrik Lund's enthusiasm for organizing and publishing these documents. However, he did—begrudgingly and very slowly—allow for the journals and papers to be cataloged (he hired H. P. Barford to do this work, since he was loath to do it himself), and eventually for a very few of them to be published.

Peter was initially of the opinion that at most a selection of twenty or thirty pages should be published, in part because he thought the collection as a whole was so wildly unsystematic and disorganized that no one could make sense of it if it were published in its entirety, but mainly because much of the material he regarded as spiritually dangerous and he worried that it would "ensnare many individuals in perdition."[28] When H. P. Barford released a small selection of the journals and papers in 1869 the reviews were almost universally negative. Barford expressed his frustration with the situation thus: "Some people urge me in the strongest possible terms to publish absolutely the whole of Kierkegaard's literary remains, every single line, every jot and tittle. Others wish to have only to have a particular aspect of his inner life or activity illuminated, and still others wish to have precisely that aspect excluded from discussion."[29] Now that Kierkegaard's journals, notebooks and other posthumous papers have been published in a completely unabridged form, both in the original Danish and in English translation, the trajectory of Kierkegaard's journals and papers has finally reached its terminus and the longstanding argument about what to do with these strange texts has effectively been settled. Finally every single line, every jot and tittle, has been published, and readers have the chance to experience these texts exactly as they were found by the Copenhagen Probate Commission in Kierkegaard's apartment after his death in November 1855.[30]

Ever since they were discovered after his death Kierkegaard's journals have been mined voyeuristically for details of his life, and they have also been wrung dry by people looking for some clue to make sense of the many other bizarre and mysterious texts that he produced. In both of these ways they have been used as a means to an end, but they haven't been respected as works of philosophy themselves. It's not hard to understand why this happened; there are at least four reasons:

(1) It does seem rather indecent to go digging in someone's private journals looking for philosophy. Isn't this an invasion of the author's privacy? Isn't the whole point of a journal to write things that you don't want others to read? There is a feeling of impropriety whenever we poke around in someone's journals for any reason, but doing so armed with an agenda, looking for philosophy, feels particularly wrong.

(2) A journal seems like a highly unlikely place to find philosophical arguments. Why would an author put such arguments in a personal journal, where no one would think to look for them? There is a presumption that there simply can't be any philosophy within someone's journal by definition—because you wouldn't call it a journal if it was actually full of philosophy.

(3) Kierkegaard's life was so full of melodrama that the temptation to peer voyeuristically into his journals has proven irresistible to many. This also helps to explain why there have been so many biographies of Kierkegaard written; lately almost one every year. The sadness and drama of Kierkegaard's strange and wonderful life continues to be very

hard to resist, and there is certainly plenty of material in Kierkegaard's journals for biographers to exploit for many years to come.[31] Anyone who reads Kierkegaard's journals with a focus on his biography would probably not notice any philosophy along the way even if they happened to trip over it.

(4) The demand for an answer book to make sense of Kierkegaard's philosophy has always been very high. This has been true ever since Kierkegaard published *Either/Or* in 1843, and with each new book that he released after that the demand only increased. Kierkegaard's methods of indirect communication can induce a feeling of panic in readers. These methods succeed admirably in doing exactly what Kierkegaard said he wanted to do: create difficulties everywhere—but most readers would still prefer that life be simplified rather than made more difficult, so when we encounter a text that doesn't have a clear meaning we look around madly for a reader's guide or an answer book. More than anything else Kierkegaard's journals have been used in this way: as a tool to reduce and simplify the complexity of his indirectly communicated writings. This approach to Kierkegaard's journals and papers uses them to advance an argument about other texts that Kierkegaard wrote and doesn't make any attempt to find intrinsic value in the journals themselves.[32]

For all of these reasons it isn't surprising that the possibility of reading Kierkegaard's journals as works of philosophy has mostly been overlooked. In the following three acts I'll try to change that by presenting three ways that the journals are themselves works of philosophy.

Act 1: The journals and notebooks perform existential philosophy

The complete unabridged collection of Kierkegaard's journals and notebooks in English translation was begun by Princeton University Press in 2007 and completed in 2020. It is a profoundly different experience to read Kierkegaard's journals and notebooks in this unabridged format rather than reading an abridged version containing selections that were edited and organized by someone else. Edited selections from the journals (most famously the Hong edition published by Indiana University Press, which is still in print) transform Kierkegaard's journals into highly systematic, thematically organized quote books, but that is a great distortion. Kierkegaard is rightly famous for his fragmentary, unscientific style of writing and his journals are actually the most fragmentary and unscientific texts that he produced by far, so it is very misleading that previous editions have made these messy texts look like they are carefully and systematically organized. The truth is that they are nothing like that; the journals are random, repetitive, raw, very unpolished, and sometimes almost embarrassingly personal.

Much of what you find in the journals is grumbling and complaining about the injustice of the universe. Kierkegaard is often quite bitter and resentful about how the world has treated him and many of his journal entries manifest great sadness and resignation, especially as he nears the end of his life.[33] He complains about the injustices he has suffered and he struggles to make sense of the bizarre twists and turns of his very strange existence. If you read an edited, greatest hits version of the journals you will easily get the impression that Kierkegaard was brilliant all the time, but reading the unabridged edition will quickly disabuse you of that idea. Kierkegaard does not always present himself as heroic or noble or even particularly intelligent in the pages of his journals. Though there are still moments of great brilliance, to get to them you have to wade through pages of resentment, self-pity, vanity, and some very obvious delusional thinking (as when Kierkegaard imagines that his old girlfriend Regine definitely wants to get back together with him because she just walked past him in the street [KJN 8:177–82]). There are, for example, many journal entries in which Kierkegaard complains that people he regards as intellectually inferior to him are treated with respect and admiration while he is not (such as Mynster, Martensen, Goldschmidt and Nielsen, just to cite a few names that appear over and over again, e.g., just in KJN 8: pages 196–98, 212, 240, 284, 308, 334, 349, 389).

The relevance of journal entries such as these for Kierkegaard's own biography or for the history of Denmark in the middle of the nineteenth century is obvious;[34] but how are these sections of Kierkegaard's journals relevant to philosophy? Here's one possibility: in these sections Kierkegaard's journals demonstrate what a true work of existential philosophy looks like because they present an authentic picture of human existence, including all of its confusion and disorder. All the features of human existence that Kierkegaard explored and analyzed in his philosophy come to life in his journals; in this way there is philosophical value even in those parts of the journals that don't seem to have anything to do with philosophy: the angry rants and complaints, the worried and frequently revised plans for his future; the confused and restless attempts to make sense of his past; the eager and anxious efforts to understand the implications of his choices; the occasional celebrations of good fortune or epiphanies of understanding and clarity.

Any story that embodies the principles of existential philosophy has philosophical value in that it demonstrates what those principles look like and feel like in actual lived experience—which Kierkegaard famously said can only be understood backwards but must be lived forwards (*KJN* 2:179). Even if a story built around principles of existential philosophy isn't a particularly good story in terms of its literary qualities it can still be highly educational, and it's one of the great accomplishments of existentialism that so many authors in this tradition have been willing to create not just abstract philosophical theories but also concrete imaginative stories that bring those abstract principles to life. Kierkegaard's journals can be seen as existential philosophy in this literary and phenomenological sense.[35]

There's at least one other way in which Kierkegaard's journals are valuable as a performance of existential philosophy: they provide a wonderful opportunity to get to know Kierkegaard better as a writer, and since Kierkegaard regarded philosophy and writing as inextricably bound together any insights we can gain concerning Kierkegaard as a writer should also illuminate his philosophy. His journals were, among other things, a writing workshop—an opportunity for an author who was obsessed with getting the presentation just right to try out first or second or third drafts. Everyone who has been impressed by Kierkegaard's writing should take the time to read at least one volume from his journals and notebooks if only to become better acquainted with Kierkegaard as a writer and to better appreciate his concern for style. For example, in a journal entry labeled simply "style" Kierkegaard writes this about his experience of writing:

> Sometimes I have sat for hours in this fashion, in love with the sound of language when it echoes with the fecundity of thought; thus I have sat for hours at a time, like a flautist who entertains himself with his flute. Most of what I have written has been spoken aloud many, many times, perhaps scores of times; it has been heard before being written down. My sentence constructions could be called a world of recollections, so much have I lived and enjoyed and experienced these thoughts as they came into being, as they searched for and found their form or, even if in a certain sense they possessed this more or less at the outset, then until every detail, even the least significant (because that work—the stylistic tinkering—was naturally done afterward: everyone who really has ideas also immediately has the form immediately)—was fully unfurled and arranged in such a way that the thought could find itself well situated in the form. (*KJN* 9:419–20)

For Kierkegaard, philosophy can never be divorced from how it is presented, so questions concerning writing and style are always already philosophical questions. Reading his journals in their complete, unabridged form provides a much more complete picture of Kierkegaard as both a writer and a philosopher.

Act 2: The journals and notebooks clarify and contribute to Kierkegaard's theory of indirect communication

There has always been a tension concerning what sort of authority should be assigned to Kierkegaard's journals and papers, especially since Kierkegaard was so meticulous about undermining his own author-ity as an author through the project he called "indirect communication." Confronted by a labyrinthine, indirectly communicated work such as the *Concluding Unscientific Postscript*, written (we are told) not by Søren Kierkegaard but rather by a certain "Johannes Climacus," who doesn't exist but who nevertheless informs us that what he has written "contains the notice that everything is to be understood in such a way that it is revoked, that the book has not only an end but has a revocation to boot" (*CUP* 619), a reader can feel disoriented almost to the point of panic. In such a disoriented condition we desperately want to find someone who is in charge—some voice of authority that can tell us what this unruly text means. There is a long tradition of turning to Kierkegaard's journals and papers for this authoritative voice because it's assumed that they contain no indirect communication, so here we can finally lift the veil and observe the author's true intentions. This approach to the journals makes them the ultimate authority and definitive last word in the cacophony of voices that constitute Kierkegaard's authorship.

Perhaps the best example of this approach is the fact that Kierkegaard's brother Peter initially chose to publish exactly one essay from the journals and papers when they were in his custody: "The Point of View for My Work as an Author," which is helpfully subtitled, "A Direct Communication, Report to History." There were two reasons why Peter chose to publish only that essay: first, because he thought it was obvious that the journals would have to be edited and organized in some way rather than published in an unabridged format, and he couldn't imagine any way to organize the material that would not seem completely arbitrary or biased; and second, because he was afraid that much of the contents of his brother's journals was "spiritually dangerous" and would lead people into perdition.[36] (Peter was employed at the time as a bishop in the Church of Denmark.) But "The Point of View for My Work as an Author" is different because it seems to present itself as a guide for the perplexed, a straightforward answer book for everyone who is puzzled by the bizarre menagerie of books that were attributed to pseudonymous authors and that speak in such a cacophony of conflicting voices; and the direct communication that this essay provides also has the virtue of returning Kierkegaard's work to a comforting place within the status quo, since it announces that everything he wrote was part of a single, univocal project: the purpose was religious from beginning to end. It's easy to see why Peter thought that this essay was all that needed to be published from the enormous collection of journals and papers that his brother left behind and why so many other readers since that time have turned to the journals and papers in the same spirit, looking for a final authority and a simplifying reduction for all of Kierkegaard's philosophy.[37]

Peter's choice to publish just "The Point of View" exemplifies three strategies that have been applied to Kierkegaard's journals and papers ever since in order to justify reading them as direct communications that can be used as the answer key for all of Kierkegaard's indirect communications:

(A) Use very selectively only a few parts of Kierkegaard's unpublished journals and papers, only the texts that suit your agenda. Ignore the much larger totality and the overall context of the journals and papers within which your preferred texts are situated. Use the texts that you have selected to reduce and simplify the complexity of Kierkegaard's philosophy, never to amplify or expand its meaning or its application.

(B) Assume that in his journals and papers Kierkegaard is a reliable narrator who has a master plan for his whole authorship, never changes his mind or his plans, and can always be trusted to tell you exactly what he is doing and why.

(C) Insist, or simply assume without argument (as if it were perfectly obvious) that there is no indirect communication in Kierkegaard's journals—that in his journals Kierkegaard neither adds to the theory of indirect communication nor practices that theory in any way.

All three of these strategies are attempts to circumvent or undermine indirect communication in Kierkegaard's writing. (This is especially obvious in the case of C, but it's true of A and B also.) They all use Kierkegaard's journals and papers as a tool to negate the carefully crafted indirect communication of Kierkegaard's other writing. However, all three of these strategies either ignore or distort what's actually in Kierkegaard's journals and papers. The (A) strategy is so obviously wrong that nothing more needs to be said about it, but (B) and (C) are a little more subtle so in the rest of this act I'll respond to those strategies and argue that rather than negating or neutralizing indirect communication in Kierkegaard's philosophy the journals and papers actually do the opposite: they clarify and contribute to the project of indirect communication in both theory and in practice.

Concerning Strategy (B): Assume that in his journals and papers Kierkegaard is a reliable narrator who has a master plan for his whole authorship, never changes his mind or his plans, and can always be trusted to tell you exactly what he is doing and why.

The (B) strategy assumes that in his journals and papers Kierkegaard is a reliable narrator who has a master plan for his whole authorship, never changes his mind or his plans, and can always be trusted to tell you exactly what he is doing and why, but none of this is true. In at least three different ways Kierkegaard presents himself as an unreliable narrator in his journals and papers.

As I noted in act 1, the author of *Kierkegaard's Journals and Notebooks* does not always present himself as someone who is a wise and trustworthy narrator. Those parts of Kierkegaard's journals where he presents himself as very confused or angry or overwhelmed by his existence (and these parts are legion) are good reminders that Kierkegaard too was human, all too human. He was often unsure of what he was doing, often doubted himself, and was often far from noble as he allowed himself to sink into self-absorption and self-pity. Like Nietzsche's Zarathustra, Kierkegaard is not wise or heroic all the time. In *Thus Spoke Zarathustra* from time-to-time Zarathustra gets discouraged, depressed, or just overwhelmed (cf. "The Soothsayer" in Part Two),[38] but these parts of the book are just as important as the more famous and more readily quoted parts of the book since they remind us that poets can't be trusted (and Zarathustra too is a poet—cf. "On Poets" in Part Two)[39] and that the true disciples of any teacher should run away from that teacher, lest they be crushed by a statue (cf. "On the Bestowing Virtue" at the end of Part One).[40] The less than wise or heroic moments in Kierkegaard's journals contribute to the philosophical value of these texts in the same way.

In addition to the many moments in the journals when Kierkegaard seemed overwhelmed by the circumstances and the challenges of his life, we should also notice how often he changed his mind, and how often he acknowledged that he didn't really know what he was doing. Here's one delightfully honest example:

> Furthermore, all that about the possibility of offense is more or less something that occurred to me at one point, which I had never thought of until then, something quite foreign to my

nature. . . . So from now on the decisive presentation of Christianity begins in a stricter sense than hitherto. . . . But what is and what has been the worst thing about this is that I have managed to get the matter so muddled in reflection that I scarcely know what I am doing. (*KJN* 5:23–24)

Perhaps the most obvious and most instructive examples of Kierkegaard changing his mind are the many, many journal entries in which he first makes plans to publish some piece of writing that explains his authorship as a whole in a direct way, and then later decides that this would be a mistake. *The Point of View* is the most well-known of these essays, but there were several others that Kierkegaard either wrote or thought about writing. Here is the moment of epiphany when Kierkegaard figured out that publishing *The Point of View* would be a mistake, and also speculates about what led him almost to make that mistake.

> NB. NB. NB.
> *The Point of View for My Work as an Author* must not be published. No, No!
>
> 1) And this is what is decisive . . . I cannot present myself entirely truthfully. . . .
>
> 2) I cannot quite say that my work as an author is a sacrifice. . . . I have surely been sacrificed, but my work as an author is not a sacrifice—it is indeed what I would absolutely most like to continue doing. . . .
>
> 3) Once I have spoken about what is extraordinary in myself, even with all the reservations I have employed, then I will be stuck with it; it will be a torment and a frightful responsibility for me to go on living when I am solemnly regarded as something extraordinary.
>
> 4) The fact that I cannot present myself fully means that I am, after all, essentially a poet—and here I will remain.
>   . . .
>
> I was in danger of a complete turnabout.
>
> This must not happen, and I thank God that it has been prevented, that I did not go ahead and publish *The Point of View for My Work as an Author*, (which something within me had indeed always resisted). . . .
>
> I would rather remain in my incognito and let everyone view me however he pleases than solemnly become a somebody, the extraordinary. (*KJN* 5:258–60)

Even after this epiphany Kierkegaard continued to write explanations of his writing that were similar to "The Point of View," and he contemplated similar essays that he never actually wrote; but in every case he decided that these direct, authoritative, simplifying, reductive summaries should not be published. It would be difficult to count all the non-concluding conclusions that Kierkegaard wrote or contemplated; he himself seems to have lost track,[41] but here are a few more entries from his journals that show how often he thought about this possibility and how often he reinterpreted his experience, revised his plans, and changed his mind.

> I have made yet another final attempt to say a word about myself and my entire authorship. I have written "A Supplementary Note" that should be called The Accounting and should accompany *The Discourses*. In my opinion it is a masterpiece; but that doesn't matter it can't be done. . . . Personally, I can't take ownership in that way. (*KJN* 5:362–63)

> The "Three Notes" shouldn't be published either. I must not speak directly about myself. . . .
> Nothing ought to be said directly about me personally:
> 1) because essentially, I am only a poet; but a poet's personality always contains something mysterious, which is why he should not be portrayed as, and, at all costs, not be confused with, an absolutely ethical character in the strictest sense. (*KJN* 5:351).

> On the Publication of Writings about Myself. "The Accounting" cannot be published now either. As I have always understood, there is a poetic element in me which precludes me from including myself in the account. . . . One single word concerning myself then a *metabasis eis allo genos* has been made and I will be unable to stop. (*KJN* 7:124)

> Thank God I did not come to publish the material about my work as an author or in any way want to force myself to be more than I am. . . . And so not one word about myself in relation to the entire authorship, such a word changes everything and misrepresents me. (*KJN* 6:147)

Kierkegaard was clearly tempted by the idea of explaining himself in very direct and clear language, but every time he considered doing this he realized that a direct explanation of his writing would undermine the whole purpose and project of his writing.

> Were I to dare accompany my actions with commentary explaining the cunning purposefulness behind the entire project, I would enjoy great success—but fail completely in my task. Then people would utterly fail to get the impression, the sting, of decision in the action, but would be enchanted by the interesting aspect of the reflection that underlies the action. (*KJN* 10:431)
>
> If the age were to ask me, of its own initiative: who are you, really? I would answer that it has the right to consider me to be whatever it wants me to be; I think I've done various things to prevent it from overestimating me, but I cannot do more. There is something that prevents me from speaking completely openly about myself and therefore I won't speak of what might possibly have been entrusted me in an extraordinary sense; for then it would be untrue. (*KJN* 5:270)

These journal entries make it clear that Kierkegaard himself recognized that he didn't always understand what he was doing, and that he often changed his plans and revised his interpretation of his experience. We can also observe in these texts that Kierkegaard understood that all of this was part of the overall indirect communication of his authorship.

> *On Indirect Communication and Myself*
> Here it must be noted, above all, that I am indeed not a teacher who originally envisioned everything and who then made use of indirect communication, conscious of every move, but that I am someone who has developed during the process of productivity. It follows that my indirect communication is on a lower level than direct communication because the indirectness was of course connected to the circumstance that I myself was not clear about it from the beginning and therefore did not dare speak directly at the beginning. Thus I myself am the one who has been released and has developed through indirect communication. (*KJN* 8:110)

In his less-than-noble, human-all-too-human moments, in his constantly changing plans and his recognition that he didn't always understand what he was doing, and in his oft-repeated decision not to publish any direct, simplifying or reducing summaries of his indirectly communicated philosophy, the author of *Kierkegaard's Journals and Notebooks* demonstrated that he was not a reliable narrator.[42]

Concerning Strategy (C): Insist, or simply assume without argument (as if it were perfectly obvious) that there is no indirect communication in Kierkegaard's journals—that in his journals Kierkegaard neither adds to the theory of indirect communication nor practices that theory in any way.

This assumption, or this insistence, is false because in at least two ways Kierkegaard's journals add to both the theory and the practice of indirect communication.

To see this we should first ask a question that most people never think to ask about this text, because it seems so obvious: Who exactly was the author of *Kierkegaard's Journals and Notebooks*? In one of the many moments when he considered and then rejected an essay that would explain all of his writing in a direct, authoritative voice, Kierkegaard offered a fascinating answer to this question:

> On the Completed Work Concerning Myself
> The difficulty with publishing the pieces about my writings is and continues to be that I have really been used without really knowing it myself, or without knowing it fully; and now, for the first time, I understand and can see the whole of it—but then of course I cannot say "I." . . . But this is my limit: I am a pseudonym. (*KJN* 6:287)[43]

This is a rather startling conclusion, but it makes perfect sense in terms of Kierkegaard's overall project of indirect communication. That "Søren Kierkegaard" could also be a pseudonym, even in *Søren Kierkegaard's Journals and Notebooks*, should not really surprise us. Actually, Kierkegaard effectively announced this very early in his journals:

> After my death no one will find in my papers (this is my consolation) the least information about what has *really* filled my life, find *that* script in my innermost being that explains everything, and which often, for me, makes what the world would call trifles into events of immense importance, and which I too consider of no significance once I take away the secret note that explains it. (*KJN* 2:157)

That entry from one of the earliest notebooks is probably the most famous example of Kierkegaard effectively disappearing from his own journals, but it's not alone. Throughout the journals there are numerous entries labeled "On Myself" (in *KJN* 9 alone there are thirty-one entries with that label, or some very close variation thereof), and these entries often contribute to Kierkegaard's disappearance from his own journals Here are two examples:

> No doubt in what has been written concerning myself in the journals from '48 and '49 a literary touch has nonetheless often crept in. It is not so easy to exclude things of this sort when someone is as poetically productive as I am. It happens as soon as I take pen in hand. For, strangely enough, privately I have a remarkably clear and succinct sense of myself. But as soon as I want to write it down, it immediately becomes literary invention. (*KJN* 9:259)

> But I end my notes here. They are too wordy for me, and yet they do not exhaust everything I carry in my inner self.... (*KJN* 5:25)

In journal entries such as these Kierkegaard makes it clear that he was fully aware of the distance between the pseudonym "Søren Kierkegaard" and the real Søren Kierkegaard, and that he wanted to preserve that distance. If we take these texts seriously we can't accept at face value the picture that Kierkegaard paints of himself in his journals, and we also can't assume that he's telling the truth about his deepest thoughts on any subject. The "Søren Kierkegaard" who speaks in these texts is just as much of a pseudonym as Victor Eremita, Johannes Climacus, or any of the other pseudonyms that Kierkegaard deployed in his authorship.[44] These journal entries are reminiscent of Plato's "Seventh Letter," where Plato declared that he never wrote down his most cherished ideas—what he truly believed—on any subject:

> There is no writing of mine about these matters, nor will there ever be one. For this knowledge is not something that can be put into words like other sciences.... [N]o sensible man will venture to express his deepest thoughts in words, especially in a form which is unchangeable, as is true of written outlines. ... [A]nyone who is seriously studying high matters will be the last to write about them and thus expose his thought to the envy and criticism of men. What I have said comes, in short, to this: whenever we see a book, whether the laws of a legislator or a composition on any other subject, we can be sure that if the author is really serious, the book does not contain his best thoughts; they are stored away with the fairest of his possessions. And if he has committed these serious thoughts to writing it is because men, not the gods, "have taken his wits away."[45]

The "Seventh Letter" makes "Plato" indistinguishable from the many other characters who appear in his dialogues, and in the same way the

"Søren Kierkegaard" of the journals must also be regarded as just one more pseudonym—one more mask or point of view, with no decisive authority to tell us who is in charge of all the strange characters who wander through his writings.[46]

The idea that even one's own journal can be written by a pseudonym is certainly an innovation, and consequently "Søren Kierkegaard" may be the best concealed and most effective pseudonym that Søren Kierkegaard ever created; but as with all of Kierkegaard's pseudonymous texts we should be grateful that Kierkegaard managed to make himself disappear from the text of his journals and papers. This was a gift to the reader, as the pseudonym A.F. . . . explained so well in his wonderful essay "Who is the Author of *Either/Or*?" published seven days after *Either/Or* in 1843:

> Most people, including the author of this article, think it is not worth the trouble to be concerned about who the author is. They are happy not to know his identity, for then they have only the book to deal with, without being bothered or distracted by his personality. (*COR* 16)

In addition to the transformation of "Søren Kierkegaard" into a pseudonym, Kierkegaard's journals also add to the theory and practice of indirect communication by demonstrating how committed Kierkegaard was to using indirect communication all the time, with no exceptions, and by indicating the great variety of forms that indirect communication could take. Contrary to the assumption—or tradition, or wishful thinking—that has led so many readers to follow Peter's lead and treat Kierkegaard's journals as if they contained no indirect communication whatsoever, the journals do just the opposite: they explain and they demonstrate that Kierkegaard never wanted indirect communication to end, and he wanted to find new ways of deploying indirect communication beyond pseudonymous texts.[47]

There is a fascinating journal entry that illustrates the difficulty—even the impossibility—of separating Kierkegaard's presentation of himself in the journals from his practice of indirect communication. The journal entry is labeled, "On Myself—On Indirect and Direct Communication." (Note that in the very title of this journal entry Kierkegaard suggests that the presentation of himself was inextricable from indirect communication.) In this text Kierkegaard argues that even though indirect communication will always make the author's life more difficult, and the communication won't be understood until later, (probably not until after the author's death, if it is understood at all), still it's a necessity whenever you're trying to explain something to the world that the world is convinced it already knows (*KJN* 9:174). Kierkegaard then explains that he regards every moment in his life when he reverted to direct communication as something of a failure, because the ideal situation would be to communicate indirectly from beginning to end.

> [I]t is very far from being the case that less is accomplished through indirect communication. No, but the effect comes only afterward, and then all the more powerfully....
>
> The matter comes to this. From a purely ideal point of view, what I have accomplished ought to have been done as follows. There ought to be a person who, when he began, was fully and firmly in accord with himself, before God, that he was a Xn, also fulfilling a Christian ethic existentially—and who then began with indirect communication. Then he would also stick with indirect communication, unwavering to the end. He would quite genuinely be God's spy.... (*KJN* 9:175)

This was Kierkegaard's highest aspiration: to be God's spy, and he regarded anything short of constant indirect communication as falling short of this ideal. This aspiration shaped even the writing in his own journals.

> An understanding of the totality of my literary activity, its maieutic purpose, etc., requires also an understanding of my personal existence as an author, what I qua author have done with my personal existence to support it, illuminate it, conceal it, give it direction, etc., something that is more complicated than, and just as interesting as, all the literary work. And in this way, it all leads back in a more ideal sense to "the single individual," who isn't me in an empirical sense, but is the author.... All this is needed to illuminate my position during the development of the authorship. Objectivity is believed to be superior to subjectivity; it's just the opposite. That is, objectivity within a corresponding subject is the endpoint. The system was an inhuman something than no human being as auctor and executor could answer. (*KJN* 5:304)

From journal entries such as these it's clear that indirect communication should apply to all of Kierkegaard's writing, without exception. Once indirect communication has been turned loose in Kierkegaard's texts there is no way to turn it off—no way to put the genie back into the bottle.[48] All of Kierkegaard's authorship should be understood as indirectly communicated because indirect communication has no finish line.

> As long as I live, I act, indirectly, so as to incite [people] against me, and then I am silent .(*KJN* 4:152)

> As an author I am a genius of a rather unusual sort—neither more nor less than that—absolutely devoid of authority, and therefore continually assigned to annihilate himself so that he does not become an authority for anyone. (*KJN* 5:30)

> The very instant I communicate directly, the truth loses in intensity. . . . But for every serious person who wants to understand, isn't there enough in what I have accomplished to permit him to understand? (*KJN* 5:43)

Really all it should take to prove this conclusion is a quick reminder of why Kierkegaard used indirect communication in his writing—the purpose it was meant to serve.[49] These two journal entries succeed admirably in reminding us of what Kierkegaard was trying to accomplish with indirect communication:

> There are many people who arrive at answers in life just like schoolboys; they cheat their teacher by copying the answer out of the arithmetic book without having worked the problem out themselves. (*KJN* 2:75)

> My destiny seems to be to discourse upon truth, to the extent that I discover it, in such a way that I simultaneously annihilate all possible authority. By becoming a minor, in the highest degree becoming untrustworthy in people's eyes, I speak the truth and thus place them in the contradiction from which they can be rescued only by appropriating the truth themselves. Only *that* personality who can appropriate truth and make it his own is matured, no matter whether it is Balaam's ass talking, or a guffawing grouch, or an apostle and an angel. (*KJN* 2:158)

Indirect communication forces every reader to speak only with themselves, because the writer has hidden himself behind mirrors.

> If you wish to be and to remain enthusiastic, then, quickly, draw the silk curtain of a scoundrel's (irony's) guise, and be enthusiastic in secret. Or replace your window glass with mirrors, so that your enthusiasm is hidden, because curiosity and envy and partisan sympathy see only their own mug. There is absolutely no hiding place for inwardness more secure than behind a mirror. And this is possible when you train yourself to alter your phenomenal behavior in a light, deft, accurately reflecting fashion, just like a mirror, to suit better that of the other person, so that no person speaks with you but converses always and only with himself—in spite of the fact that he believes himself to be speaking with you. (*KJN* 4:164)[50]

Since Kierkegaard wanted to teach the value of individuality, that message had to be communicated in a way that made followers or disciples or any kind of organized group or club impossible.

> Had someone else come up with the idea of individuality, he would have immediately acquired so many adherents that the whole thing would miscarry, because the swarm of followers would obscure the idea of individuality. Qua dialectician, I am somewhat better versed in the matter. . . . To live alone in a remote place with the idea of individuality is not a consistent nor the most precise expression of the idea. (*KJN* 4:144)

In all of these respects the journals add to Kierkegaard's theory of indirect communication by making it clear that there's no off switch for indirect communication. None of Kierkegaard's writing should be considered free of indirect communication, including his journals and posthumous papers.[51]

Act 3: The journals and notebooks create new philosophical concepts

I noted at the beginning of this chapter that the overall idea of philosophy as a kind of performance or theatre is informed by Deleuze and Guattari's book *What Is Philosophy?* In this third act I'll begin by detailing some of the arguments in this book that are particularly important to the third philosophical value I see in Kierkegaard's journals: the fact that they create new concepts. *What Is Philosophy?* opens new possibilities for understanding both the history and the value of philosophy and the arguments in this book are extremely useful for making sense of Kierkegaard's philosophy, particularly the philosophy in his journals. For purposes of clarifying how Kierkegaard's journals create new philosophical concepts there are four arguments in *What Is Philosophy?* that are particularly relevant, so I'll summarize those arguments briefly.[52]

(a) The essential activity of philosophy has always been creating new concepts, and everything else that philosophy does is peripheral.

I discussed and endorsed this part of Deleuze and Guattari's argument in the Introduction/Confession as a way to satisfy the requirement of the anti-assistant-professor method to write about Kierkegaard's philosophy in a non-parasitical way. Here I will add just a few more comments to fill out this ideal of philosophy as creating new concepts.

Deleuze and Guattari wrote *What Is Philosophy?* after writing several other philosophy books that were so unorthodox that most people didn't know what to make of them. Predictably many of these books were rejected as not-philosophy by confused readers. Only at the end of their work together (*What Is Philosophy?* is the last book in their joint authorship) did they pause to explain how the strange and unorthodox texts they created together were in fact philosophy books, and this explanation had the effect of enlarging the philosophical canon significantly to include many other works that had also been rejected as not-philosophy.[53]

Philosophy is "the discipline that involves *creating* concepts,"[54] they argue, and everything else that philosophy does, or has done, or has thought of as essential to its nature, is actually peripheral and secondary to this central creative activity. To appreciate the force of this idea perhaps it's easiest to consider what it rejects as essential to philosophy. Deleuze and Guattari argue that many of the traditions and practices that philosophy has clung to as its most cherished possessions are actually completely irrelevant to philosophy, and perhaps even get in its way.

> We can at least see what philosophy is not: it is not contemplation, reflection, or communication. This is the case even though it may sometimes believe it is one or other of these, as a result of the capacity of every discipline to produce its own illusions and hide behind its own peculiar smokescreen. It is not contemplation, for contemplations are things themselves as seen in the creation of their specific concepts. It is not reflection, because no one needs philosophy to reflect on anything. It is thought that philosophy is being given a great deal by being turned into the art of reflection, but actually it loses everything. Mathematicians, as mathematicians, have never waited for philosophers before reflecting on mathematics, nor artists before reflecting on painting or music. So long as their reflection belongs to their respective creation, it is a bad joke to say that this makes them philosophers. Nor does philosophy find any final refuge in communication, which only works under the sway of opinions in order to create consensus and not concepts. . . . Philosophy does not contemplate, reflect, or communicate, although it must create concepts for these actions, or passions. Contemplation, reflection and communication are not disciplines but machines for constituting Universals in every discipline.[55]

The last activity on this list is perhaps the most surprising. Philosophy has regarded dialogue and discussion as almost holy activities that have something like mystical or magical powers. This tradition extends back to

Socrates, who prized philosophical dialogue so much that he never wrote a single word since any time spent writing was time not spent discussing, and therefore time wasted. Deleuze and Guattari argue that this is actually a misunderstanding of Socrates, because "[i]n fact, Socrates constantly made all discussion impossible" since he deployed a "pitiless monologue that eliminates the rivals one by one."[56] Whatever you think of this highly unorthodox reading of Socrates, the essential point of their argument is clear: philosophy is the activity of creating new concepts, and that doesn't happen by magic whenever people simply start talking about a philosophical issue. There are so many ways to avoid creating a new concept, and discussion can easily be one of them.

> For this reason philosophers have very little time for discussion. Every philosopher runs away when he or she hears someone say, "Let's discuss this." . . . The best one can say about discussions is that they take things no farther, since the participants never talk about the same thing. . . . Communication always comes too early or too late, and when it comes to creating, conversation is always superfluous.[57]

(b) There is a productive alliance between philosophical concepts and chaos, but opinions and beliefs have no such alliance and instead just try to negate chaos or to ignore it.

Here's the essential fact of the human condition that we want philosophy to address, according to Deleuze and Guattari: we don't want to be completely at the mercy of chaos and disorder, but we also don't want to lose the energy and innovation that can only be found in chaos. Philosophy, along with art and science, are disciplines that form a productive alliance with chaos. They venture into chaos in order to bring back concepts (philosophy), functions (science), and sensations (art) that create order from complete disorder. But the order that philosophy, art and science create is different from the order created by mere opinions or beliefs, which are what most people fall back on to defend themselves against chaos. "[T]he struggle with chaos is only the instrument of a more profound struggle against opinion, for the misfortune of people comes from opinion."[58] Opinion attempts to smother or deny chaos completely rather than derive meaning and value from it, whereas philosophy, art, and science approach chaos with respect because they know that while too much chaos is overwhelming, no chaos at all is death.

> We require just a little order to protect us from chaos. Nothing is more distressing than a thought that escapes itself, than ideas that fly off, that disappear hardly formed, already eroded by forgetfulness or precipitated into others that we no longer master.... We constantly lose our ideas. That is why we want to hang on to fixed opinions so much. We ask only that our ideas are linked together according to a minimum of constant rules. ... That is all we ask for in order to *make an opinion* for ourselves, like a sort of "umbrella," which protects us from chaos. Our opinions are made up from all this. But art, science, and philosophy require more: they cast planes over the chaos. These three disciplines are not like religions that invoke dynasties of gods, or the epiphany of a single god, in order to paint a firmament on the umbrella, like the figures of an *Urdoxa* from which opinions stem. Philosophy, science, and art want us to tear open the firmament and plunge into the chaos. We defeat it only at this price.... The philosopher, the scientist, and the artist seem to return from the land of the dead.[59]

Philosophy, art, and science venture into chaos ("the land of the dead") so that they can bring back the kind of order that we truly want: order that continues to be energized and animated by chaos.[60] This means that genuine philosophy, art, and science will always be somewhat risky, messy, and chaotic. These are signs of the authenticity and value of these disciplines. On the other hand, opinion seems perfectly safe, stable, and still, which makes it both attractive and dangerous.

> It is as if one were casting a net, but the fisherman always risks being swept away and finding himself in the open sea when he thought he had reached port. The three disciplines advance by crises or shocks in different ways, and in each case it is their succession that makes it possible to speak of "progress." It is as if the *struggle against chaos* does not take place without an affinity with the enemy, because another struggle develops and takes on more importance—the *struggle against opinion,* which claims to protect us from chaos itself.[61]

(c) Philosophy deploys the new concepts it creates on a plane of immanence.

Every aspect of the definition of philosophy in *What Is Philosophy?* is prescriptive, but that is especially obvious in this case. The argument is that philosophy should create concepts that remain here on Earth and should never succumb to the temptation of transcendence.

> Philosophy began with this insistence, and this is what differentiates it from religion. In short, the first philosophers are those who institute a plane of immanence like a sieve stretched over the chaos. In this sense they contrast with sages, who are religious personae, priests, because they conceive of the institution of an always transcendent order imposed from outside by a great despot or by one god higher than the others, inspired by Eris. . . . Whenever there is transcendence, vertical Being, imperial State in the sky or on earth, there is religion; and there is Philosophy whenever there is immanence . . . .[62]

"Can the entire history of philosophy be presented from the viewpoint of the instituting of a plane of immanence?"[63] This is quite an audacious proposal, but Deleuze and Guattari don't hesitate to answer "yes." They proceed in the six pages that follow to argue that throughout its history philosophy has always created new concepts on a plane of immanence, even when it didn't realize it or perhaps intended to do otherwise. You might think, for example, that the entire medieval period (well over a thousand years), dominated as it was by philosophers who saw themselves as servants of religion, might have given up on the plane of immanence, but Deleuze and Guattari are undaunted. Here's what happened to philosophy in the Middle Ages, they argue:

> [t]he positing of immanence remains pure philosophical instituting, but at the same time it is tolerated only in very small doses; it is strictly controlled and enframed by the demands of an emanative and, above all, creative transcendence. Putting their work and sometimes their lives at risk, all philosophers must prove that the dose of immanence they inject into world and mind does not compromise the transcendence of a God to which immanence must be attributed only secondarily.[64]

In other words, medieval philosophy consists of those moments when very creative medieval philosophers managed—when no one was looking—to create new concepts that remained on a plane of immanence, in spite of the fact that their employer (the church) demanded otherwise. The same rule applies to every moment of the history of philosophy: individual philosophers may have sometimes strayed from the plane of immanence, but whenever they did they were no longer creating philosophy because philosophy is by definition creating new concepts on a plane of immanence. Transcendence is just one of the many dreams and delusions that offer themselves as alternatives to the plane of immanence, and philosophy must resist all of these temptations.

> The plane is surrounded by illusions. These are not abstract misinterpretations or just external pressures but rather thought's mirages.... We must draw up a list of these illusions and take their measure, just as Nietzsche, following Spinoza, listed the "four great errors." But the list is infinite. First of all there is the *illusion of transcendence*.... Then there is the *illusion of the eternal* when it is forgotten that concepts must be created....[65]

On the plane of immanence philosophical concepts create events. Concepts are not things or objects; they are event-generators, they exist only through the events that they bring about.[66]

> The concept is an incorporeal, even though it is incarnated or effectuated in bodies. But, in fact, it is not mixed up with the state of affairs in which it is effectuated. It does not have spatiotemporal coordinates, only intensive ordinates. It has no energy, only intensities.... The concept speaks the event, not the essence or the thing—pure Event....[67]

> Every concept shapes and reshapes the event in its own way. The greatness of a philosophy is measured by the nature of the events to which its concepts summon us or that it enables us to release in concepts.[68]

In other words, what we should look for in concepts, and what we should expect from concepts, is results. The standard for a concept's value is purely pragmatic: a powerful concept creates powerful events on a plane of immanence, and it also creates more concepts.[69]

(d) There's an art to naming new philosophical concepts.

Like every new child that comes into the world, the new concepts that philosophy creates must be given a name. Philosophy must create new concepts, but it can only use an old language to name those concepts. This immediately presents all sorts of interesting challenges and possibilities. Artistry, style, and taste all play a part in naming a new concept, and as with all art forms this creates numerous opportunities for both deeper insights and also misunderstandings.

> [S]ome concepts must be indicated by an extraordinary and sometimes even barbarous or shocking word, whereas others

make do with an ordinary, everyday word that is filled with harmonics so distant that it risks being imperceptible to a nonphilosophical ear. Some concepts call for archaisms, and others for neologisms, shot through with almost crazy etymological exercises: etymology is like a specifically philosophical athleticism. In each case there must be a strange necessity for these words and for their choice, like an element of style. The concept's baptism calls for a specifically philosophical *taste* that proceeds with violence or by insinuation and constitutes a philosophical language within language—not just a vocabulary but a syntax that attains the sublime or a great beauty.[70]

The names assigned to concepts are important to consider especially because they have so much to do with newly created concepts not being recognized as concepts. One must be attuned to all the art and athleticism that went into the name that was given to a concept in order to discern that a new philosophical concept has just been added to the world, even though the name is something we may have heard before. The problem or challenge of paleonyms is especially acute when philosophy uses the language of something very different from philosophy (such as religion) to name a philosophical concept. When that happens the possibilities for misunderstanding are legion, but the opportunities for deeper insight are also abundant.[71]

These four arguments from *What Is Philosophy?* about how and why philosophy creates new concepts help to clarify how Kierkegaard creates new philosophical concepts in his journals. I'm going to focus on one concept in particular: the concept to which Kierkegaard gave the name "Xnty." This concept is not limited to the journals—arguably it is one of the main projects of Kierkegaard's authorship as a whole—but the journals make a major contribution to this project that should not be overlooked. This concept emerges from a productive alliance with chaos, especially the chaos of Kierkegaard's own experience trying to make sense of Christianity as he confronted it in his own demanding upbringing and in his reading of the New Testament. Like all philosophical concepts this concept aims to create order and meaning on a plane of immanence, and its true enemy is the contentment and false sense of order created by opinion. Finally, this concept is given a name that seems both commonplace and bizarre and is certainly "filled with harmonics so distant that it risks being imperceptible to a nonphilosophical ear." Something like "a specifically philosophical athleticism" is required to recognize the "strange necessity" of this name, just as it is required to recognize the events that are created by this new concept and how innovative and important they are for all of us struggling to bring order from the chaos of our own existence. The discussions of Xnty in Kierkegaard's journals are generally regarded as theological and apologetic—not philosophical or creative—but that, I will argue, is simply a lack of imagination and a failure to recognize how and why philosophy creates and names new concepts.[72]

The chaos out of which the concept Xnty was born is the first thing that needs to be clarified in order to recognize it as a philosophical concept. Kierkegaard wrestled the concept Xnty out of the chaos of his own experience, especially the chaos of his religious upbringing and his struggle to make sense of Christianity.[73] Though Kierkegaard's thinking about Xnty was initiated and catalyzed by his attempts to make sense of Christianity and by his reading of the New Testament, Xnty becomes something much more than this starting point. In Kierkegaard's thinking Xnty develops into a philosophical concept on a plane of immanence that is quite different from Christianity or any other form of religion.

Kierkegaard begins using "Xnty" almost immediately in his journals, and continues to the very end. It appears for the first time in the AA journal shortly after the following journal entry which makes it clear that he is unafraid to criticize Christianity and has already begun using religion as an occasion to think about philosophical issues.

> On looking at a fair number of particular phenomena in the Christian life, it occurs to me that Christianity, instead of bestowing strength on them—yes, that in contrast to the pagan, such individuals are deprived by Christianity of their manhood and are now like the gelding in relation to the stallion.
> —Christianity made an impressive figure when it strode vigorously upon the world and said what it meant. But from that moment on, when either it tried to stake out boundaries with a Pope or wanted to beat people over the head with the Bible, or now most recently with the Apostles's Creed, it is like an old man who thinks he has lived long enough and wants to make an end to himself. (KJN 1:28)

Just a few pages later Kierkegaard writes the following mysterious and metaphysical journal entry:

> The first creation produces the immed. consciousness (that's the impression, but just like the wind, one knows neither whence it comes nor wither it blows); beyond this we cannot go. Xnty is the second creation (that's why Xt is born of a pure virgin, which is again a creation out of nothing . . .). (KJN 1:36)

"Xnty" has generally been understood as nothing more than a quirky and idiosyncratic abbreviation, so most readers just translate "Xnty" into

"Christianity" and don't give it any further thought. But we should give Kierkegaard the chance to define "Xnty" himself before we rush to impose our own meaning on it. What exactly does the X of Xnty stand for? It's well known that Kierkegaard attacked Christendom because it strays from the biblical text of Christianity—because it ignores the text that is supposed to define it. In the same way, we should figure out what Xnty means by reading what's actually in Kierkegaard's texts, in all of their complexity, and not rely on some pre-conceived or traditional idea of Christianity. In one of his final journals Kierkegaard notes that if we actually read the New Testament, instead of regarding it as a consoling and comforting book that makes a suitable gift for children we would realize what terrifying demands the book makes of us and we would ask God to take it back (*KJN* 10:13). Something similar may happen if we read what Kierkegaard has to say about Xnty in his journals; we may find something shocking there that we didn't expect at all if we assumed that Xnty was nothing more than shorthand for Christianity or religion.

Xnty as Kierkegaard presents it in his journals is actually almost the exact opposite of religion as religion is generally understood. Xnty bears no resemblance to any form of religion that has ever existed, or perhaps ever could exist. Xnty is so de-institutionalized, individualized, and anarchic that it no longer has any meaningful connection to religion. (It should be noted that based on his understanding of Xnty Kierkegaard spent his final days protesting and trying to eradicate religion as everyone else in Denmark understood it.) Religion is about binding people together (*re-ligo*), but Xnty does the opposite: it separates and isolates every individual and requires her to confront the extreme, even impossible demands of her existence alone. Xnty is a purely individual, theoretical, and philosophical construction. Xnty "does not exist," as Kierkegaard often reminds us in his journals, and in a sense it never could exist, because it's an impossible existential ideal—a collection of standards for how to live that could never be fully realized. The variable X of Xnty stands for what Kierkegaard understood to be the overwhelming, offensive, obscene, X-rated, and even impossible demands of individual existence.[74]

The new concept Xnty was catalyzed by Kierkegaard's reading of the New Testament, among other things, but just as Kierkegaard insisted that his own writing could be understood in many different ways, and that the responsibility for that interpretation lies with the reader, he also recognized that his own reading and interpretation of the New Testament was his responsibility and couldn't be blamed on God or anyone else. Just because Kierkegaard may have been writing about Christianity doesn't change the fact that fundamentally this was just another act of textual interpretation.

As Kierkegaard often reminded us, he had "no authority"; he just had a reading, an interpretation, and a few arguments to support it.

> A philosopher with authority is nonsense. For a philosopher extends no farther than his teachings extend; if I can prove that his teachings are self-contradictory, erroneous, etc., then he has nothing to say to us.... And therefore it is indeed nonsense for a philosopher to require faith. (*KJN* 6:427)

The fact that the conceptual creation Kierkegaard called "Xnty" may have been based in part on his reading of the New Testament doesn't change the fact that what he created was an act of textual interpretation, and not the thing itself.

It seems likely that the chaos of Kierkegaard's fundamentalist Christian upbringing also led him to conceptualize Christianity as a collection of impossible existential ideals—standards for how to live that could never be fully realized. The requirements of Christianity as Kierkegaard understood them were so demanding and idealized that Christianity had to become a strictly individual matter, something that was fundamentally incompatible with collectives or groups of any kind. For all of these reasons it was natural for Kierkegaard to conclude that "Xnty simply does not exist" (e.g., *KJN* 8:122–24) and to be amazed that the entire "Christian" world could be so oblivious to this fact—so out of sync with the truth of its own nonexistence. Once Kierkegaard conceptualized Christianity as Xnty in these extreme and idealistic terms Xnty really did become the equivalent of the variable "X," a placeholder that could stand for any collection of ideals that emphasize being true to one's own existence and lived experience. As Kierkegaard writes quite often in his journals, everyone assumed that he was arguing for a new version of Christian fundamentalism, but he wasn't; instead, he just wanted honesty. For example, consider this entry in NB 21 which Kierkegaard titles, "What I have Wanted and Want":

> I have never in the remotest manner suggested or attempted to extend the cause in the pietistic direction, to pietistic strictness and the like.
>
> No, but what I want is truth in our talk and above all in our preaching, and not, as now, almost pure untruth respecting the existential so that not only is what is higher abolished but the lower even placed in its stead; the prototypes are misused, nothing is made present, and possibility and actuality and their existential relations, etc., etc., are dealt with quite wrongly. (*KJN* 8:47–48)

Since Kierkegaard understands Xnty in starkly existential terms he will eventually conclude that any sort of institutional Xnty is a contradiction.

> The interest of human beings is for there to be a religious establishment; the more complex and grandiose it is, the better, all the more so because of the security and the distance from decisions—which we hum. beings love so much.
>
> God's interest is that there be no religious establishment whatsoever...
>
> How, then, can these two ideas be united: an established order—there is no established order? In such a way that we hum. beings confess that the established order exists for the sake of our frailty....
>
> But then it ends with people deifying "an established order." People forget that beyond "the established order" there is, as the ideal, the thought: No established order
>
> The order is: No 1—there is no established order. (*KJN* 8:125)

That Kierkegaard was inspired by religion to create philosophy is nothing new in the history of philosophy. It's philosophy's nature to be present in all sorts of things that don't call themselves philosophy, such as literature, art, politics, and religion. Part of philosophy's job has always been to find and extract philosophy wherever it may be. We can find philosophy all over the place living under an assumed name, an alias, and this work of discovery and unmasking has always been an important part of philosophy. This has been especially true with regard to religion. In the longest period of philosophy—the medieval period—this is just about all that happened. At various other times philosophy has occasionally confused itself with religion (for example, pre-Socratic philosophers such as Pythagoras and Empedocles sometimes struggled to see clearly where religion ended and philosophy began); but it has also used religion very successfully as a vehicle for exploring philosophical questions and issues. Medieval philosophy is only philosophy if we are willing to look past all the discussions of religion (primarily Christianity) to discover the philosophy that is concealed behind them. To lose sight of the differences that distinguish philosophy and religion and to allow philosophy to get confused with religion or to get absorbed back into religion would be a disaster. It would negate all the progress that philosophy has made since the pre-Socratics. It would negate all the clever strategy, subterfuge, and misdirection that allowed philosophy to survive in the Middle Ages.

Did Kierkegaard create the philosophical concept Xnty unintentionally and inadvertently? That certainly seems possible, and Kierkegaard himself seemed to acknowledge this possibility. As I've already discussed, one of the main things you discover in the journals is Kierkegaard struggling to make sense of his own writings. He constantly classifies and reclassifies his creations, his concepts, and his pseudonyms, perpetually turning the kaleidoscope and rearranging his ideas to try to make sense of them. If you're looking for an authoritative voice or unity in Kierkegaard's authorship here it is: the author never stopped trying to comprehend his own writing as a unity—a unified production that spoke with a single authoritative voice—but he never succeeded. Kierkegaard tried as hard as he could to discover or to impose some sort of order or system on the concepts he created, but he couldn't do it. From time to time he writes something along the lines of, "at least God understands what it all means," but this is just another way of saying that the concepts he created escaped from him. "God" becomes another word for "thought" or "philosophy" when Kierkegaard uses it in this way, another way of acknowledging that the full meaning and impact of the concepts he created would have to be determined by someone else in the future. This is sort of like prophesying something that will happen in the future without realizing that's what you're doing.

> It is indeed rather analogous to the prophetic (and this is something every more or less intelligent nature has experienced) for a person to say something that he himself understands in his own way—end eventually he understands that something much more profound lay within it. . . . Thus the fulfillment is not merely a part of making the prophecy a prophecy, but actually the prophecy is only completed in the fulfillment—even though it is predicted in advance. (*KJN* 7:36)

In one of his most honest moments in the journals he acknowledged: "I am actually an author for authors; I do not relate directly to a public; no, qua author I make others productive" (*KJN* 6:390). The journals demonstrate that Kierkegaard produced concepts that exceeded his own understanding and took on a creative life of their own.

Metabasis eis allo genos is perhaps Kierkegaard's favorite phrase. He returns to it over and over again in his writing, including in his journals, to explain what he is doing. This phrase can be translated very succinctly as "paradigm shift." In his writing Kierkegaard is constantly trying to create paradigm shifts. Out of the chaos of his own experience with religion and his own attempts to make sense of Christianity and the New Testament, Kierkegaard created Xnty—a new philosophical concept on the plane of

How to misunderstand Kierkegaard's journals   63

immanence.⁷⁵ This concept was created through a productive alliance with chaos. Unlike opinion or belief, which attempt to shelter us from chaos by denying or negating chaos completely, this concept brings order out of chaos but maintains a respect for chaos, and thus it continues to be animated and energized by chaos. It casts a plane of immanence through chaos, but it does not think of chaos as the enemy. The real enemy is opinion, "for the misfortune of people comes from opinion."⁷⁶ "Xnty is not a doctrine . . . but an existence communication," Kierkegaard writes (*KJN* 5:39). This summarizes very concisely the paradigm shift from religion to philosophy that Xnty aims to bring about.

Deleuze and Guattari emphasize that philosophical concepts are event-generators, and that they should be judged by the events that they generate.

> Every concept shapes and reshapes the event in its own way. The greatness of a philosophy is measured by the nature of the events to which its concepts summon us or that it enables us to release in concepts.⁷⁷

As an existence communication, the new philosophical concept that Kierkegaard names Xnty creates order and meaning on the plane of immanence by generating at least three different events, which I will explore in the remainder of this chapter.

(a) The event of radical individuality

This event is a transformation of reality. Our natural inclination is to believe that crowds are more real than single individuals, but actually just the opposite is true. A crowd is any group at all, any collection of people beyond one, and its ontological status seems obvious: it seems self-evident that crowds have a reality of their own, and that this reality exceeds the lesser reality of a lone individual. But Xnty reveals this to be a false ontology. Crowds actually have no reality at all; they are illusions and abstractions with no underlying actuality or being.

> The numerical's law of existence is: they live comparatively. From this one sees that the numerical is the sophistical, an expansive element that, when examined more closely, dissolves into nothingness. (*KJN* 10:261)

Only single individuals are real and a crowd is just a collection of single individuals who may or may not be confused about their own ontological status. Xnty corrects the ontological confusion that causes many people to lose themselves in crowds, to be intimidated by crowds, or to doubt their own significance. Xnty clarifies that reality only belongs to single individuals, even when those single individuals happen to be in the presence of many other single individuals, and that the metaphysical superiority we assign to crowds is simply a mistake. Xnty dispels the intoxicating illusion that somehow we acquire greater reality and importance when we allow ourselves to be absorbed into a crowd.

> If there is a certain truth in that saying that human beings have been granted speech in order to conceal their thoughts, or, as I say, in order to conceal the fact that they have no thoughts—if there is a certain truth in this, namely the truth that this is not why they have been granted it, but is what they use it for—then one can truthfully say something similar about the numerical: the numerical is used in order to conceal how empty the whole of existence is, the numerical displaces a person into an exalted state just as opium does—and then he is tranquilized, tranquilized by this enormous reliability of millions. And yet, in truth millions are equally unreliable, absolutely equally unreliable as one person. But one person does not have a stupefying effect—that is something the millions have: and thus it is quite clear that he is absolutely unreliable. That means that "millions" displace a person into a stupefaction, he swoons under the power of numbers, he expires qua spirit, he goes along with it, but it is not expressed in this manner, no, he believes that he possesses the most complete certainty and reliability—so greatly is he deceived. (*KJN* 10:124)

> [I]n the world of spirit, there is no counting, or rather, what counts is: difference, i.e., there is no counting. . . . For number is a mystification, the mystification that there is more than one. This is a sort of mystification that one rarely thinks about: to mystify by disguising oneself as many. (*KJN* 10:264–65)

The event of radical individuality can save us from the tragedy of surrendering the reality of our own individual existence to an abstraction such as "the public." This is a kind of salvation on the plane of immanence, and it rescues us from an ontological error that seems almost hardwired in human thought: the instinct to defer to a crowd, or to long to be swept up in a crowd. Like Christianity, Xnty is, in its own way, trying to save people. The condition from which Xnty is trying to deliver individual humans is the animal condition that fears standing out from the herd.

> In the *Laws* Plato says ... that what binds people in obedience to the laws is a sense of shame. ...
>
> In this lies the human trait that being the single individual, the exception, is impudence.
>
> In immediacy, this power of shame that binds the particular individuals in conformity with the common is really an animal property; they lack the self-awareness to be able to endure being different from the others; to be different from the others would be the most awful anguish. (*KJN* 9:45)

Losing oneself in a crowd is certainly instinctive and "natural," but that only makes it all the more insidious.

> Instinctively (just as the octopus knows how to muddle things, and the skunk knows how to spread an odor, and the hedgehog knows how to raise its quills), the "human being" has a tactic against "spirit": Let us form a mass—that is the human being's tactic, his mode of protecting himself. Just as a person puts on many coats to keep out the cold, so does "mass" keep idea and spirit away. Just as the ostrich sticks its head in the ground and believes that I cannot be seen, so does the human being form a mass and then think that he cannot be seen. ... Like a person who says he is not home, thus does the human being deny that he is home: by becoming a third person—i.e., in the mass—instead of being I.
>
> As mass, then, a human being is a sensate power, behaves en masse as an animal creature, and is extremely happy and satisfied to be protected as a mass against God, the unconditioned, the idea, spirit, the ideals. Lamentable happiness, for whatever is mass is always what is wasted in every generation, and through its own fault. (*KJN* 10:127–28)

> [E]xistences, lives as actually lived, demonstrate that no one believes in "the single individual" and in intensive actions—existences everywhere demonstrate: Let us form a group.
>
> But Xnty is diametrically opposed to this.
>
> And the existential always expresses truly what a person believes. (*KJN* 8:217)[78]

The ontological transformation that follows from the event of radical individuality does not prevent relationships or communities from existing. Single individuals can still interact with each other and form relationships and communities as much as they want, but the fundamental ontology remains unchanged. In any relationship or community the only thing that is real is single individuals—who now happen to be interacting with other single individuals—but their interaction never creates a new reality, a new level of metaphysical being beyond the single individual. There is no ontological expansion when individuals form relationships and communities with other individuals. The ontological totality of the human world never changes: it always consists exclusively of single individuals, no matter how many relationships and communities those single individuals create. Xnty itself can be a kind of community, but that community can exist only when the individuals in the community realize that this community has no reality that exceeds their own reality, that single individuals remain the only reality.

> This is the enormous illusion that has actually abolished Xnty.
> ...
> In brief, the confusion is this, but it has continued from generation to generation of these millions and millions: one enters into Xnty in the wrong way. Instead of entering as an individual, one enters with the others; the others are Xns—ergo I am one, too, and in the same sense that the others are. (KJN 7:79)

This is why communities are possible, but "the public" remains an illusory abstraction. Kierkegaard explains this distinction, and also provides a very effective summary of the event of radical individuality, in a journal entry labeled, "The Difference between 'Crowd,' 'Public,'—and 'Community'":

> In "the public" and the like, the single individual is nothing; there is no individual; the numerical is what is constitutive and is the law for coming into being, a *generatio aeqvivoca*; apart from "the public" the single individual is nothing, and in a deeper sense, he is also nothing within the public.
> In the community, the single individual *is*; the single individual is dialectically decisive as the *Prius* for forming a community and in the community the single individual is qualitatively something essential and at any moment can also become higher than "the community," namely, as soon as "the others" fall away from the idea. What binds the community together is that each is an individual, and then the idea. What binds the public together, or its looseness, is that the numerical is everything. Every individual guarantees the community; the public is a chimera. In the community, the single individual is the microcosm who qualitatively repeats the macrocosm; here *unum noris omnes* holds true in a good sense. In the public there is no single individual; the whole is nothing; here it is impossible to say *unum noris omnes*, for here there is no One. "The Community" is certainly more than a sum, but it is nonetheless a sum of ones. The public is nonsense: a sum of negative ones, of

ones who are not ones, who become ones by means of the sum instead of the sum having to become the sum by means of the ones. (*KJN* 7:37–38)[79]

(b) The event of immanent idealism

This event is a transformation of time. It transforms both the present and the future. The present is deepened and intensified until it becomes inexhaustible. The future too becomes inexhaustible, and also unattainable: a future that will never be present. This transformation of time is accomplished through a form of idealism that remains on the plane of immanence. While idealism has often been associated with transcendence, there is no necessary connection between them—no reason why a limitless idealism can't be deployed on the plane of immanence. This is possible through intensification, and through a deliberate embracing of impossibility. Kierkegaard accomplishes this by making Xnty an impossible existential ideal and therefore always out of reach. "The task is not to comprehend Xnty," he writes, "but to comprehend that one cannot comprehend it" (*KJN* 5:70).[80] As he wrote in the last lines of NB 34, one of his last journals:

> What shamelessness and what a base lie, that religion is something for children and women, presumably because its task is too easy for the strong person: the man. Thanks, but no thanks—especially for such menfolk as those living nowadays. No, religion, Xnty, is an ideality, a task, under which the greatest ideality. (*KJN* 10: 365)

Setting aside the ridiculous part about only "menfolk" being strong, this much is clear from this journal entry: Kierkegaard understood Xnty to be so extreme and so demanding that it was effectively an impossible ideal.[81]

The event of immanent idealism of Xnty requires the event of radical individuality as a necessary condition, since the extreme demands of Xnty would be incoherent if they were presented through an abstract nonexistence such as a group. The transformation of reality accomplished by radical individuality must take place first, and then time can be transformed through immanent idealism. Most people would prefer to avoid both of these events since they are demanding and difficult.

> Either there has to be an individual who presents ideals—or these cannot be presented at all. When there are many—then there is relativity.

> The misfortune of the age, now, is exactly that sociality has completely strangled ideals. Finally, then, there is an individual who in the most modest way makes the attempt—but, as mentioned, an individual it has to be—and then it is called an arrogant usurpation by the individual.
>
> There is at bottom a natural cunning in this remark. For the very last thing one wants expressed is ideals; people want to stay with societal haggling. But in fact ideals can be presented only by an individual—ergo, they try to intimidate the individual into not daring, and then they escape the ideals. They may perhaps still find that there is something to the question—and appoint a committee, or drive around in a spacious four-seater Holstein carriage—to look for ideals. (*KJN* 8:93)

This event transforms time by embracing the impossible. Impossibility is chaotic, but rather than trying to stifle or suffocate this chaos the concept of Xnty preserves its energy and power on a plane of immanence. The order that is brought out of the chaos of impossibility is a directional order: a relentless focus on the future, which then becomes an infinitely deferred and inexhaustible future.[82] This creates just enough order to protect us from chaos while also preserving everything that's good about chaos. The impossible and unattainable ideals of Xnty deepen and intensify time; they create a productive temporal infinity that animates life and doesn't succumb to the deadening illusions of opinion.

(c) *The event of subjective truth*

This event is a transformation of thought and knowledge. Xnty creates this event when it maintains that all values must be created on the plane of immanence, just as philosophical concepts must be created, since there are no objective values waiting to be discovered like things in the world. Xnty calls for a purely subjective decision concerning values to be made right now, in this instant, but every decision that creates values has eternal implications. For human understanding this is paradoxical and even incomprehensible, but that only makes it more interesting. "Xnty is not a doctrine . . . but an existence communication" (*KJN* 5:39), and this is perhaps the most dramatic and unavoidable fact of human existence: that we must create our own values, right here and right now, and when we do that it has infinite, eternal consequences.

> [C]an something eternal be decided in time? This is how one could, philosophically, properly address the question to Xnty.
> ...
> [E]xistence, which surely knows what it wants, has of course arranged things such that no one can know whether he will be alive for the next hour—and Xnty believes that precisely this unrest is part of bringing about a decision regarding eternity.
> For an eternal decision in time is the most intensive intensity, the most intensive leap. (*KJN* 10:5)

Perhaps the most famous account of subjective truth is the one that Kierkegaard gave in 1835 when he was twenty-two years old:

> [T]he thing is to find a truth which is truth *for me*, to find *the idea for which I am willing to live and die*. And what use would it be in this respect if I were to discover a so-called objective truth. ... What use would it be if truth were to stand there before me, cold and naked, not caring whether I acknowledged it or not, inducing an anxious shiver rather than trusting devotion? ... That's what I lacked for leading a *completely human life* and not just a life of *knowledge*, to avoid basing my mind's development on—yes, on something that people call objective—something which at any rate isn't my own, and to base it instead on something which is bound up with the deepest roots of my existence. (*KJN* 1:19–21)

This early journal entry captures the drama and the value of subjective truth, but it's not a definition. Can subjective truth be defined? In one of the most unappreciated moments of comedy in the *Concluding Unscientific Postscript* Kierkegaard offers this "definition" of subjective truth: "*the objective uncertainty maintained through appropriation in the most passionate inwardness is truth*, the highest truth there is for someone *existing*" (*CUP* 171). The joke is that this "definition" actually makes it clear that subjective truth is undefinable by any conventional means, since a standard definition requires drawing boundaries around a concept, limiting it in space and time, and establishing a meaning that everyone can understand. This "definition" of subjective truth makes it clear that subjective truth is something that will have to be shown rather than said; the best we can do is define it ostensively, by pointing to it or performing it.[83]

That subjective truth must be performed rather than defined follows from the transformation of time that was effected by the event of immanent idealism. Subjective truth is situated in an intensified and inexhaustible present, and in an infinitely deferred and impossible future that can never become present. If subjective truth were ever realized in the past, present, or future it would cease to be an objective uncertainty. A performance of subjective truth must express unlimited possibility so that it can show what an inexhaustible present and a future that can never become present look like. All that Kierkegaard can do in his journals is point us in this direction—in the direction of an inexhaustible, idealized, and impossible future. Anything more than that would contradict the very idea of subjective truth. This gesturing or pointing is the final performance, the final form of philosophical theatre, in Kierkegaard's journals.

Chapter 2

How to misunderstand the many concluding summaries that Kierkegaard wrote to explain his strange indirect authorship by imagining that they are somehow outside his strange indirect authorship and therefore should be trusted completely

or

Prefaces to nothing, points of view that are pointless, and non-concluding conclusions

> It is, in the literary world, customary to take a holy vow. The ceremony is less definite. In olden times one swore, as is known, by Freyr's boar; Hamlet swears by the fire tongs; the Jews are even said to have done it in an indecent manner. However, the ceremony is unimportant; the vow is the main thing. Accordingly I swear: as soon as possible to realize a plan contemplated for thirty years to publish a logical System, as soon as possible to honor my vow taken ten years ago concerning an aesthetic System; furthermore I promise an ethical and dogmatic System, and finally *the* System. As soon as this has been published, future generations will not even need to learn to write, for there will be nothing further to write, but only to read—the System. (*P* 30–31/*N* 14)

WHAT WAS THE POINT of *The Point of View for My Work as an Author?* The pseudonymous works that started in 1843 with *Either/Or* were brought to a conclusion very effectively by the *Concluding Unscientific Postscript*, which was attributed to a writer whose very name signaled that this was to be the climax, the end of the road, the final rung on the ladder that Kierkegaard started climbing three years earlier. As if that wasn't enough, the conclusion of the *Concluding Unscientific Postscript* takes the form of a "First and Last Explanation" in which Kierkegaard himself finally steps out from behind the curtain and announces, as directly and explicitly as possible, that the show is over:

> For the sake of form and order, I hereby acknowledge, something that can scarcely be of interest to anyone to *know,* that I am, as is said, the author of *Either/Or* (Victor Eremita), Copenhagen, February 1843; *Fear and Trembling* (Johannes de Silentio), 1843; *Repetition* (Constantin Constantius), 1843; *The Concept of Anxiety* (Vigilius Haufniensis), 1844; *Prefaces* (Nicholaus Notabene), 1844; *Philosophical Fragments* (Johannes Climacus), 1844; *Stages on Life's Way* (Hilarius Bookbinder—William Afham, the Judge, Frater Taciturnus), 1845; *Concluding Postscript to Philosophical Fragments* (Johannes Climacus), 1846 . . . . (*CUP* 625)

> [I]n the pseudonymous books there is not a single word by me. I have no opinion about them except as a third party, no knowledge of their meaning except as a reader, not the remotest private relation to them, since it is impossible to have that to a doubly reflected communication. A single word by me personally in my own name would be an arrogating self-forgetfulness that, regarded dialectically, would be guilty of having essentially annihilated the pseudonymous authors by this one word. (*CUP* 626)

> The opportunity seems to invite an open and direct explanation, yes, almost to demand it even from one who is reluctant—so, then, I shall use it for that purpose, not as an author, because I am indeed not an author in the usual sense, but as one who has cooperated so that the pseudonyms could become authors. (*CUP* 628)

> With this I take leave of the pseudonymous authors with doubtful good wishes for their future fate, that this, if it is propitious for them, will be just as they might wish. Of course, I know them from intimate association; I know they could not expect or desire many readers—would that they might happily find the few desirable readers.
> Of my reader, if I dare to speak of such a one, I would in passing request for myself a forgetful remembrance, a sign that it is of me that he is reminded, because he remembers me as irrelevant to the books. (*CUP* 629)

> Oh, would that no ordinary seaman will lay a dialectical hand
> on this work but let it stand as it now stands. (*CUP* 630)

Given the unequivocal language here, it's quite a surprise that just two years later Kierkegaard thought it necessary to supplement this "First and Last Explanation" with another explanation. And not just one, in fact, because after writing *The Point of View for My Work as an Author* he decides not to publish the main text in his lifetime, and instead spins off a smaller pamphlet called *My Activity as a Writer* (also translated as *On My Work as an Author*), which he publishes in 1851. Both of these works also have supplements that accompany them: *The Point of View* is supplemented by a piece called "The Individual: Two Notes Concerning my Work as an Author," and *My Activity as a Writer* is supplemented by a short article called "My Position as a Religious Writer in 'Christendom' and My Tactics." So in the end we have not just one, climactic, definitive, first and last conclusion to the pseudonymous works, but two (or, depending on how you count, four): the first explanation, which was supposed to be the first and the last explanation, has been upstaged by the last explanation, (and its supplement), which the author asserts is now both the first word and the last word, even though some of its words are also repeated in the other explanation, (and its supplement), that came between the first and the last, and although the author suppressed his last report to history—which has now become the first—until he himself was history.

What exactly is the point of all this?

In this chapter I will argue that the point of *The Point of View*, and the other conclusions that Kierkegaard wrote for his work as an author, was to make sure that there could be no definitive conclusion to the indirect communication that he so carefully crafted. Or, to phrase this conclusion in a slightly different form: regardless of what Kierkegaard himself intended when he wrote his various concluding summaries of his work as an author, the effect of these multiple concluding summaries is to call into question the possibility of writing any kind of unitary and unifying point-of-view for Kierkegaard's textual production.[84]

To arrive at these conclusions about Kierkegaard's conclusions, I will begin by going back to the beginnings in Kierkegaard's writing—to his prefaces, of which he also wrote too many. My argument, in a nutshell, is that Kierkegaard's indirect communication resists being put in a nutshell, and that the extraordinary attention that Kierkegaard gave to writing beginnings and endings was one of the defenses that he used to protect his indirect communication—the composition of which necessarily had to have a beginning and an ending—from having a beginning and an ending imposed upon it in terms of its existential effects. By writing multiple beginnings and endings for his writing, and by writing these beginnings and endings in a very particular way, Kierkegaard anticipated the demand that the present age (both his and ours) would make for a systematic, totalized, conveniently packaged and easily digestible version of his unruly, ill-behaved, and indirectly communicated philosophy, and he derailed that helpful undertaking before it ever got started.

Of course, these efforts have not deterred numerous concerned and well-meaning assistant professors from offering up Kierkegaard's indirect communication in a systematic nutshell, but this is just one more irony in a story that has lots of irony. The best place to begin in this story is with a book that is nothing but beginnings, but which never manages to get anything started.

Foreplay: Prefaces

> The Dialectic of Beginning.
>
> Scene in the Underworld.
>
> Characters: Socrates
> Hegel.
>
> Socrates is sitting by running water, listening to it in the cool air. Hegel sits at a desk and is reading Trendelenburg's *Logische Untersuchungen:* Part 2 p. 198. and walks over to Socrates to complain.
>
> Socrates: Should we begin by disagreeing entirely or by agreeing about something that we will call a presupposition?
>
> Hegel: [says nothing—apparently stunned speechless by the stupidity of Socrates's question]
>
> Socrates: what presupposition are you starting from?
>
> Hegel: from none whatever.
>
> Socrates: now you're talking; so perhaps you do not begin at all.
>
> Hegel: I? Not begin—I, who have written 21 volumes?
>
> Socrates: Ye gods, you have sacrificed a hecatomb.
>
> Hegel: But I start with nothing.
>
> Socrates: isn't that with something?

> Hegel: No—the inverse movement. It becomes clear only at the conclusion of the whole, where I have treated all knowledge, world history, etc.
>
> Socrates: How can I overcome this difficulty.... You know that I did not even allow Polus to speak for more than 5 minutes at a time, and you want to speak XXI volumes (*KJN* 11.2:30).

In the preface to *Prefaces* Nicolaus Notabene explains that he can only write prefaces because his wife will not allow him to write a book. "[A] husband who is an author is not much better than a husband who goes to the club every evening," his wife argues; "indeed even worse. For he who goes to the club must himself still confess that it is a breach, but to be an author is a distinguished infidelity which cannot arouse resentment even though the consequences are worse" (*P* 25/*N* 9). "'To be an author when one is a husband,' she says, 'is open infidelity, just the contrary of what the pastor said. For this is the validity of marriage, that the man sticks firmly by his wife, and then nothing more'" (*P* 25/*N* 10). Nicolaus protests that this will make him nothing more than "an *encliticon* to her" (*P* 26/*N* 10), but his wife is unmoved. The logic of his arguments fails to impress her. "[E]ven though I can argue with the devil himself," he notes, "I cannot argue with my wife. She has, you see, only one syllogism, or more correctly not even one. What learned people call sophistry, she, who does not count herself among the learned, calls teasing" (*P* 22/*N* 7). She threatens to confiscate all of his manuscripts and use the paper as backing for her embroidery (*P* 21–22/*N* 7). When he brings out the one "introductory paragraph" that he has managed to write so far, she lights it on fire (*P* 23/*N* 8).

Nicolaus is about to give up. "An author's position can hardly be more hopeless than mine," he surmises (*P* 22/*N* 7). But then he discovers an ingenious way to get around his wife's objections:

> The result was that I promised not to be an author. But as at learned dissertation defenses, when the candidate has disarmed all one's objections, one at last produces some linguistic trifle in order to be proved right in something at least, and the candidate politely agrees in order to agree with one in something at least, in this way I reserved for myself license to write *Prefaces*. I appealed in this regard to analogies, that men who had promised their wives never to take snuff anymore had been allowed as compensation to have as many tobacco tins as they wanted. She accepted my proposal, perhaps in the opinion that one could not write a preface without writing a book—which indeed I do not dare. (*P* 28/*N* 12)

Prefaces, Nicolaus Notabene's book of prefaces, cannot be a book because Nicolaus is under an injunction not to write a book. If he is going to be an author his only alternative is to write a book that resists being a book; a book that in the end will not have been a book.[85]

For Hegel such a book could only be regarded as a first-rate scandal. Some thirty-seven years before Nicolaus Notabene published his book of prefaces, Hegel voiced his own concerns about prefaces in the *Phenomenology of Spirit*. But unlike Nicolaus Notabene's wife, who is convinced that you can't write a preface without also writing a book, Hegel is convinced that once you've written a book (if it's a book of philosophy), there's no point in writing a preface. A preface to a work of philosophy is "not only superfluous," but also "inappropriate and misleading" because it gives the reader the wrong impression about the true nature of philosophy.[86] For Hegel, philosophy is not philosophy unless it is comprehensive. "[P]hilosophy moves essentially in the element of universality, which includes within itself the particular."[87] True philosophy, which is scientific (*Wissenschaftliche*), systematic, comprehensive, and totalizing, must be written in a book with no preface because a preface to such a system is already a refutation of the system. The system must be complete within itself, with no need of any kind of introduction or supplementation.

Consequently, in Hegel's systematic philosophy the preface is disowned and abandoned. As Derrida explains in "Outwork," his preface to *Dissemination*, a preface is precisely the kind of fragment that can never find a place in Hegel's comprehensive system:

> [e]ither the preface already belongs to this exposition of the whole, engages it and is engaged in it, in which case the preface has no specificity and no textual place of its own, being merely a part of philosophical discourse; or else the preface escapes this in some way, in which case it is nothing at all: a textual form of vacuity, a set of empty, dead signs which have *fallen* . . . outside the living concept. Then it is nothing but a mechanical, hollow *repetition*, without any internal link with the content it claims to announce.[88]

Nicolaus Notabene accepts Hegel's separation of the preface and the book and adopts it as his starting point. From Hegel, Notabene writes, "the preface has received its mortal wound[,] . . . for if one begins the book with the subject matter and the System with nothing, then it is considered that there is nothing left to say in a preface" (*P* 18/*N* 4). Notabene agrees with Hegel that prefaces do not belong in systematic philosophy because they lack the essentialism that characterizes systematic philosophy. "Prefaces bear the stamp of the accidental just as dialects, idioms, provincialisms do. They are subjected to the rule of fashion in quite another sense than the works themselves; they change like clothing" (*P* 17/*N* 3).

But instead of concluding, along with Hegel, that the preface is now useless and superfluous, Notabene argues that the separation of the preface and the book confers new life on the preface. It is time for the preface to celebrate its newly won independence. And the new role that Notabene defines for the preface, now that Hegel has given it its independence, is one that has important consequences for Hegel's ideal of systematic philosophy. The scorned and rejected preface now returns to call into question the possibility of that System that disowned it. Notabene writes:

> The incommensurable, which in earlier times one set down in the preface to a book, can now find its place in a preface that is not the preface to any book. Thus I believe that the strife is settled to their mutual satisfaction and pleasure—if the preface and the book cannot get on well together, then let the one give the other a bill of divorce. (*P* 18/*N* 4)

For Hegel, the System is a book with no preface: it comprehends and circumscribes all of existence within the self-contained movement of its chapters. The very existence of a preface belies the completeness of the System because the preface is always already outside of the book. The preface is a counter-example to everything that follows in the book; it introduces the book by refuting it. All of this is due to the fact that a preface necessarily contains something incommensurable to the System, something that the book forgot. Hegel understood this, and he explained it all very clearly—in a preface, which means (by his own admission) that his explanation is either redundant or meaningless. So Hegel, who dealt the preface its "mortal wound," also provided the clearest example of how the preface is the repository of the incommensurable.[89]

Nicolaus Notabene proposes to accentuate this incommensurabilty even further by writing prefaces that are prefatory to nothing.

> [I]t must not deal with a subject, for otherwise the preface itself would become a book, and the question of preface and book would revert. The preface as such, the emancipated preface, must then have no subject to discuss but must deal with nothing, and as far as it is thought to deal with something, this must be an appearance and a feigned movement. (*P* 19/*N* 4–5)

The preface that has been emancipated from the book, and the author who writes such a preface, have no concern for the serious business of systematic philosophy.

> Writing a preface is like ringing at a man's door to bamboozle him; ... it is like lashing with one's stick in the air at the wind; ... like tipping one's hat though one greets no one; ... like bowing in invitation to dance, then not moving; like pressing the left leg in, tightening the reins to the right, and hearing the steed say "Prrf," and oneself not caring a fig for the whole world; it is like joining in without suffering the least inconvenience from joining in. (P 19–20/N 5)

> And what is the one who writes them like? He goes in and out among people like a jester in winter and a fool in summer; he is hello and goodbye in one person, always happy and carefree, pleased with himself, a really frivolous good-for-nothing, indeed an immoral person[;] ... he does not run errands for the System. (P 20/N 6)

Prefaces that don't even pretend to be part of a larger system, written by an author with no interest in completing the System, bring into relief even more clearly what Hegel himself unwittingly demonstrated when he wrote, and apologized for, his own prefaces: the fact that any system always leaves something out. The nine prefaces in *Prefaces* are fragments of philosophy that nevertheless yield an insight into the whole. They are like "something insignificant, a trifle, a heedless remark, an unguarded outburst, a chance facial expression, an involuntary gesture" through which "one has been given the opportunity to steal into a person and discover what has eluded more careful observation" (P 17/N 3). What they reveal about the whole is that systematic philosophy has not yet found a way to integrate all of the fragments that constitute human existence.

Kierkegaard's arguments against the possibility of an existential system in the *Concluding Unscientific Postscript* are well known.[90] One of these arguments concerns the impossibility of beginning a system with nothing.[91] In the *Postscript* Johannes Climacus argues that an immediate beginning to systematic philosophy is inconceivable simply because existence always precedes any possible system of existence. Since the systematic philosopher is also a person who exists, she can effect a beginning to her system of philosophy only through an act of will, only by making a leap that asserts a beginning in order to bring to a halt the otherwise infinite regression of reflection. In other words, the beginning of anything is always arbitrary—not absolute, as systematic philosophy maintains. "[T]his thought in all its simplicity," Climacus writes, "is capable of deciding that there can be no system of existence and that a logical system must not boast of an absolute beginning, because such a beginning is just like pure being, a pure chimera" (*CUP* 112).

Nicolaus Notabene's prefaces challenge the systematic character of a book—or any collection of books—by bringing into relief the arbitrary and open-ended nature of their beginnings. *Prefaces* is a book of beginnings that never gets anything started. "[T]his light reading will not possibly be able to begin strife and dispute ... for a word in advance begins no dispute" (*P* 99/*N* 68). Instead of offering a foothold for a systematic study, *Prefaces* disrupts at the outset all efforts to draw systematic boundary lines around texts.

The relevance of this disruption for the interpretation of Kierkegaard's own indirect communication is obvious. For anyone who would argue, for example, that Kierkegaard's writings can be brought together into a thematically unified totality—a textual system—*Prefaces* suggests a very telling question that we might ask of such an approach: Will this textual system have a preface? As soon as there is a preface the system is disrupted, disseminated, finished (in the sense of undermining the very possibility of being finished or completed). But without a preface it never gets started. Since textual interpretation is an activity practiced by existing beings, its beginnings are always arbitrary acts of will with no claim on the absolute. In Kierkegaard's case, the act of will required to postulate a unifying system for his various texts would have to be a formidable one, because of the extraordinary pains that Kierkegaard took in his writing to prevent that kind of reading. *Prefaces* serves to remind anyone who feels inspired to make such an attempt that his attempt could only have a beginning that is willful and arbitrary, thus calling into question the systematic character of the whole endeavor before it ever gets started.

For a misunderstanding with the reader: Point(s) of View

> [T]he desire to prevent all misunderstanding about an enterprise ... is a thing that could occur only to a youth. There is nothing that so easily gets beyond one's control and so easily becomes misunderstood, as a misunderstanding. Even if one were to undertake nothing more than merely to avoid misunderstanding—then in that case one would presumably become the most thoroughly misunderstood of all men. (*PV* 125/*H* 116)

After writing *The Point of View* in 1848 Kierkegaard quickly decided that he couldn't publish it. In an important journal entry from 1849 he explains his reasons, and also provides some interesting clues about his intentions for the future of the manuscript:

> NB. NB. NB.
>
> *The Point of View for My Work as an Author* must not be published. No, No!
>
> 1) And this is what is decisive . . . I cannot present myself entirely truthfully. . . .
>
> 2) I cannot quite say that my work as an author is a sacrifice. . . . I have surely been sacrificed, but my work as an author is not a sacrifice—it is indeed what I would absolutely most like to continue doing. . . . But I have also been something of a lofty dreamer, and therefore I could possibly have deceived myself concerning the degree to which I might prefer being put to death, if it came to that, over seeking some quieter activity.
>
> 3) Once I have spoken about what is extraordinary in myself, even with all the reservations I have employed, then I will be stuck with it; it will be a torment and a frightful responsibility for me to go on living when I am solemnly regarded as something extraordinary.
>
> 4) The fact that I cannot present myself fully means that I am, after all, essentially a poet—and here I will remain.
>
> But the fact is this. Last year (when I wrote that piece) was very wearing for me, I suffered a great deal. In addition to this, abuse at the hands of vulgarity has disturbed my incognito a bit, and this has tended to force me into an immediacy—instead of the dialectical, where I always am—forcing me beyond myself. My incognito was to be a sort of nothing, eccentric, peculiar to look at, with thin legs, a drifter, etc. All of this was of my own free will. Now the rabble has been taught to stare at me bestially and caricature me, day in and day out. At times this has caused me to tire of my incognito. So I was in danger of a complete turnabout.
>
> This must not happen, and I thank God that it has been prevented, that I did not go ahead and publish *The Point of View for My Work as an Author*, (which something within me had indeed always resisted).
>
> The book itself is true and, to my way of thinking, masterly. But this sort of thing can only be published after my death. . . . But I must be careful about the idea of dying, so that I don't

go and take some step in the thought that I am to die in half a
year—and then live to 82. No, this is the sort of thing one can
finish and put in one's desk, sealed and labeled: To Be Opened
after My Death.

...I would rather remain in my incognito and let everyone
view me however he pleases than solemnly become a somebody,
the extraordinary. (*KJN* 5:258–60)

Several other journal entries, all from 1849, show the strength of Kierkegaard's determination not to have *The Point of View* published:

> I must not speak directly about myself and if indeed much more
> ought to be said, *The Point of View* should be published. All
> of that material ought to be left ready, as it is, until after my
> death. Nothing ought to be said directly about me personally:
> 1) because essentially, I am only a poet; but a poet's personality
> always contains something mysterious.... (*KJN* 5:351)

> No, quite right, there shouldn't be a word said about me, above
> all not about assuming responsibility for all my literary activity as if it were my own idea and my own intention. No matter
> how many qualifications I might add while making the case, it
> wouldn't be enough. I ought to keep silent. Above all it would
> be untrue if, at the definitive moment I decided to continue qua
> religious author, I were to assure myself of the whole course of
> the foregoing. No, I am a poet. My writing is essentially my education.... (*KJN* 5:370–71)

> The texts called *The Point of View for My Work as an Author, A
> Note, Three Notes,* "Armed Neutrality" cannot be published. All
> this productivity will be properly pseudonymous.... What has
> happened here is a battle of ideas. In the real world, this entire
> matter about whether to publish them under my own name or
> not would be a bagatelle. But in the world of my ideas, it is a
> monstrously stressful problem that is like everything to me:
> neither untruthfully to hold myself back nor untruthfully to go
> too far, but truthfully to understand myself, to remain true to
> myself. (*KJN* 6:65)

> Nothing pertaining to my authorial persona can be used at all.
> (*KJN* 6:124)

> Thank God I did not come to publish the material about my
> work as an author or in any way want to force myself to be more
> than I am.... And so not one word about myself in relation

to the entire authorship, such a word changes everything and misrepresents me. (*KJN* 6:147)

> On the Completed Work Concerning Myself
> The difficulty with publishing the pieces about my writings is and continues to be that I have really been used without really knowing it myself, or without knowing it fully; and now, for the first time, I understand and can see the whole of it—but then of course I cannot say "I." . . . But this is my limit: I am a pseudonym. (*KJN* 6:287)

Two years after he wrote these journal entries and decided not to publish *The Point of View*, however, Kierkegaard did publish another text which includes everything that he claimed he could never say about himself in *The Point of View*. While *My Activity as a Writer* is quite a bit shorter than *The Point of View for My Work as an Author*, it is essentially the same work. In what appears to be an exceedingly direct communication, it provides a univocal reading of Kierkegaard as an author, summarizing his whole authorship as fundamentally a religious production. When *My Activity as a Writer* was at the press, two years after Kierkegaard gave thanks to the Almighty that he did not make the serious mistake of publishing *The Point of View*, he writes the following in his journal:

> Now they are being printed. Oh, I feel so inexplicably, unspeakably happy and relieved and confident and overwhelmed. . . .
> I have suffered much during these days, terribly much. Ah, but still it comes back, an understanding of my task once again confronts me, but in an intensified form. And even if I have got it wrong seventeen times, in its grace, an infinite love has nonetheless made everything turn out for the best. (*KJN* 8:388)

> *On My Work as an Author*
> The Significance of This Little Work.
> The state of affairs in "Christendom" is that people have utterly displaced the point of view for what Xnty is, transposing it into something objective, something scientific and scholarly, making differences such as genius and talent into what is decisive.
> This little work turns the whole thing around. It says (precisely because it is preceded by that enormous literary production): to hell with genius and talent and scholarship and so on—Xnty is the existential, it is a task for character. . . .
> That is why this little book is not a literary work, a new literary work, but an act. . . .

This little book is not authorship but action. It is an intensive action that will not be understood immediately. (*KJN* 8:411–12)

What was the act that *My Activity as a Writer* performed? And why is it that Kierkegaard was able to publish this text without any anxiety at all, when two years earlier he had insisted that no such unifying point of view could ever be published?

Obviously the psychological question concerning Kierkegaard's intentions remains forever undecidable, and in the end that is not my interest anyway. What I want to argue is that *My Activity as a Writer* (which Kierkegaard published himself), as well as *The Point of View* (which he did not publish in his lifetime but which he left behind in such a way that it seems likely he hoped that someone else would publish it after his death),[92] can be understood just as Kierkegaard suggested (in 1849) that any such works would have to be understood if they ever were to be published: as pseudonymous, indirectly communicated, poetic works that do not totalize his work as an author but instead destabilize it. It is possible that Kierkegaard figured this out in the interval between the anxious 1849 journal entries which I cited above, and the publication of *My Activity as a Writer* in 1851, which he greeted so calmly. On the other hand, maybe this isn't what Kierkegaard was thinking at all. Either way, regardless of Kierkegaard's intentions, the effect of the texts is the same: Kierkegaard's points of view on his work as an author function, like his prefaces, to resist any kind of completion or totalization of his indirect communication.[93]

The destabilizing effect of *My Activity as a Writer* is evident in at least two ways. First of all, if one is looking for a conclusion to Kierkegaard's authorship, it's no longer clear where to look. Which conclusion is the real conclusion? In his excellent article, "The Eyes of Argus: *The Point of View* and Points of View on Kierkegaard's Work as an Author," Joakim Graff notes that there are at least three different points of view that precede *The Point of View*. These include: (1) Johannes Climacus's comments on the writings of Magister Kierkegaard in the "Glance at a Contemporary Effort in Danish Literature" in the *Postscript*; (2) Kierkegaard's comments on the pseudonymous authors in "A First and Last Declaration," also in the postscript; (3) Kierkegaard's comments on all the authors and texts that fall within his authorship in *My Activity as a Writer*.[94] By the time *The Point of View* is delivered to the world in 1859 (not by Søren Kierkegaard, but by his brother Peter, who believed that it was the only thing in the journals and papers that should be published since it would clear up all confusion about Søren's writing for evermore), it is clear that there is no single point of view for

Kierkegaard's work as an author. Nothing makes that point more effectively than the multiple points of view authored by Kierkegaard himself. But if Kierkegaard's writings are to be regarded systematically, having more than one conclusion to the system is just as unacceptable as not having any conclusion at all. Either way the desired system is disrupted because the systematic point of view that it required has been displaced by a plurality of points of view which resist any kind of unification.

The multiple conclusions that Kierkegaard wrote for his authorship echo the multiple prefaces Nicolaus Notabene created. In both cases their multiplicity contributes to the dissemination of the systematic book, from which they have now become separated. As Johannes Climacus writes in the *Postscript*:

> [I]t is indeed ludicrous to treat everything as completed and then to say at the end that the conclusion is lacking. In other words, if the conclusion is lacking at the end, it is also lacking at the beginning. This should therefore have been said at the beginning. But if the conclusion is lacking at the beginning, this means that there is no system. A house can indeed be finished even though a bell pull is lacking, but in a scholarly construction the lack of a conclusion has retroactive power to make the beginning doubtful and hypothetical, that is, unsystematic. (*CUP* 13)

By hanging on to *The Point of View* instead of publishing it in 1848, as he originally planned, Kierkegaard ensured that he would "again have something in reserve" (*KJN* 5:305), but he did not give his authorship a conclusion. When *The Point of View* is published after his death it only reinforces the position that was already staked out by *My Activity as a Writer*. *The Point of View* doesn't say anything radically new or different from *My Activity as a Writer* about the meaning of Kierkegaard's authorship, it just says it with a lot more feeling (and a lot more words). The displacement of a systematic conclusion to Kierkegaard's authorship has already been effected by *My Activity as a Writer*.[95]

Secondly, *My Activity as a Writer* destabilizes any systematic approach to Kierkegaard's writings by ironically displacing precisely the kind of systematic conclusion that it seems to promise. To see this, it's helpful to go back to some of Nicolaus Notabene's arguments in *Prefaces*. Even though *Prefaces* is not a book, and the prefaces it contains are prefaces to nothing, there are a few consistent themes that run through the whole text. One of these themes can be summarized as follows: In the future people will no longer read books, they will only read book reviews.[96] According to Nicolaus Notabene, book reviews respond to the public's demand to be able to discuss a book without actually reading it—because reading the book takes too much time and is far too boring. In the future literature and journalism will work hand in hand to ensure that the public will be able to continue talking about books without actually reading any books (*P* 42/*N* 22). A book will be considered a success when it pays dividends to everyone involved—the author, the publisher, the printer, the binder, the reviewer, the reader—without costing any of them much effort (*P* 29/*N* 13). "[I]t is not unthinkable that a book could be published, cause a sensation, occasion a review that was read, while the book could just as well be unwritten. . . . If only chatter can get into motion, then all is well" (*P* 35/*N* 17).[97]

In such a rushed and superficial literary climate, Notabene argues, the greatest friend that an author can have is an ironic reviewer. An ironic reviewer makes no attempt to give the general reading public a complete summary of the book, or a definitive statement of the book's meaning that can immediately be put to use in conversation. Instead, he merely "pronounces with all possible indolence an unappealable judgment based on his personality and mood" (*P* 36/*N* 17-18). This kind of purely subjective and comical review shields the author from the public's demand that the author and his books be reducible to something that can be easily consumed, digested, and then regurgitated in literary conversation. The ironic reviewer throws the public off track, and preserves the book for the kind of individual appropriation that the author intended. "Whereas an author therefore has his worst enemies and traitors in those orthodox exclamation marks, he often has in such a humorist a secret friend who has read the book with all inwardness but only seeks in this way to save his soul and the book from all connection with prattle" (*P* 37/*N* 18).

An author who doesn't have the benefit of such an ironic reviewer is at the mercy of the reading public which only wants to systematize the author's works—to find out what they mean, in a nutshell, so that they can be discussed at parties. Given this demand by the reading public the author is no better off than the cat that gets beaten out of the barrel (*P* 37/*N* 18). "It must be the very devil to be an author if one does not know how to have one's private pleasure from such treatment and above all know how to fool the reading public, so it certainly has something in the barrel, but not one's self, one's deeper personality, but a personality one supplies oneself" (*P* 37-38/*N* 18).

My Activity as a Writer can be understood as precisely this kind of book review—as an ironic review of his own work that Kierkegaard published in order to protect his authorship from being reduced to a paragraph in a book review, or a paragraph in the System. But the irony in *My Activity as a Writer* will be apparent only to one who has taken the trouble to read Kierkegaard's pseudonymous books. Anyone who is looking for a way to avoid reading those texts will completely miss the irony, because (unlike Kierkegaard's previous ironic, indirect communications), there is nothing in the tone of this piece to tip off the reader that the text is not to be taken at face value. In *My Activity as a Writer* Kierkegaard presents himself with a completely straight face. This sobriety and sincerity of tone can only reinforce the opinion of one who is looking for the ultimate Kierkegaardian book review that she has come to the right place. In addition, the text is extraordinarily concise. It summarizes all of Kierkegaard's work in a grand total of ten paragraphs, none of which demand much effort from the reader. Kierkegaard emphasizes that he is trying to provide the most concise and straightforward summary of his work possible. "Prolixity of statement would nowhere be more out of place than here," he writes. "What is here required is to be able to fold together in simplicity that which is unfolded in the many books" (*AW* 150/*H* 12). Though those many books may seem complicated on the surface, Kierkegaard reassures the reader that this complexity is just an illusion. In reality everything that he wrote boils down to just one thing: "the authorship, *integrally* regarded, is religious from first to last" (*AW* 143/*H* 6).

Of course, all of what Kierkegaard writes in *My Activity as a Writer* may be true. What is comical about the argument is the idea that this is the only way to read Kierkegaard's writings, the only legitimate point of view on his authorship.[98] And it is also comical to imagine that Kierkegaard would ever think to make things so easy for his readers. The same author who had one of his pseudonyms explain how he discovered his life's purpose in the project of making life more difficult for other people (*CUP* 186–87)—the same author who cloaked himself in a multitude of different pseudonyms, of whose writing he claimed to have "no opinion . . . except as a third party" (*CUP* 626), who discoursed at length on the need for subjective truths to be communicated indirectly, and who concluded his most complicated book of all with the notice that everything in the book "is to be understood in such a way that it is revoked" (*CUP* 619)—can hardly be expected to offer ten helpful, straightforward paragraphs at the end of his career to summarize the twenty-eight books that he had written up to that point. Such kind consideration from an author who had previously gone out of his way to make life difficult for his readers, and to force them to think for themselves, is not impossible, it's just extremely unlikely and completely out of character.

And it's also very funny. For anyone who had taken the trouble of reading any of those previous twenty-eight books (and there were not many who had: by 1849, when Kierkegaard first started thinking about publishing *The*

Point of View, only *Either/Or* had sold more than 525 copies), *My Activity as a Writer* would immediately appear to be a work of comedy—a tremendous incongruity when placed in the context of everything that Kierkegaard had written about indirect communication up to that point. It announces itself as a work of comedy with its title: *My Activity as a Writer* promises to tell you all about the writer who was behind the creation of the books, and who therefore (presumably) is in complete control of their meaning. Shifting the focus to the master writer (Kierkegaard) is just what the superficial reader wants, because otherwise she is faced with the daunting task of trying to come to terms with more than twenty-eight different authors and their multiple personalities. These authors often criticize each other's books and otherwise disagree with each other, which only solidifies the impression that there is no one to turn to who can tell you—authoritatively—what the books mean. But *My Activity as a Writer* promises to eliminate all of these difficulties by tracing everything back to the intentions of the one-in-charge. Suddenly there is just one book and one author—the book of Kierkegaard's overarching plan as an author—instead of twenty-eight books and at least as many authors. And the text of his activity as an author is, Kierkegaard assures us, a simple one. Everything that he produced as an author was produced "*uno tenore,* in one breath" (*AW* 143/*H* 6). "[C]orresponding to this authorship there is an originator who, as author, 'has only willed one thing,'" and the road travelled by this author "has the aim of *approaching, of attaining* simplicity" (*AW* 143/*H* 7).

But anyone who has read and taken seriously the pseudonymous texts understands that the author is irrelevant to a work of indirect communication. Anyone who appeals to the authority of the author behind a work of indirect communication has *eo ipso* misunderstood the work (*CUP* 618).[99] Writing in the 1843 article, "Who Is the Author of Either/Or?" Kierkegaard's pseudonym (A. F. . . .) answers his own question this way: "Most people, including the author of this article, think it is not worth the trouble to be concerned about who the author is. They are happy not to know his identity, for then they have only the book to deal with, without being bothered or distracted by his personality" (*COR* 16). In "A First and Last Explanation," where Kierkegaard for the first time speaks directly about his role in the production of the pseudonymous texts, he states very clearly that he is "irrelevant to the books" (*CUP* 629).

> Thus I am the indifferent, that is, what and how I am are matters of indifference, precisely because in turn the question whether in my innermost being it is also a matter of indifference to me what and how I am, is absolutely irrelevant to this production.

> ... My facsimile, my picture, etc., like the question whether I wear a hat or a cap, could become an object of attention only for those to whom the indifferent has become important—perhaps in compensation because the important has become a matter of indifference to them. (*CUP* 626)

One constant throughout Kierkegaard's authorship was the insistence that he wrote "without authority."[100] The only time that Kierkegaard claims to have any authority is in *My Activity as a Writer*, (and later in *The Point of View*), where he claims to have an author's authority to reduce all of his texts to a single meaning. One can take this claim seriously only if one is willing to reject all of Kierkegaard's texts that preceded this claim, and in that case the claim becomes meaningless, because there is no more authorship over which the author can claim authority.[101]

If one reads the pseudonymous works first, and then turns to *My Activity as a Writer* as a conclusion to those works, it's immediately apparent that it doesn't bring anything to a conclusion. Anyone who knew Kierkegaard's work first hand, and who consequently was not looking for a book review that could put the authorship in a nutshell, would understand that what they had found in *My Activity as a Writer* is another pseudonymous text that only further complicates the indirect communication that it claims to explicate so straightforwardly. Kierkegaard gave the public what it wanted: an apparently serious and succinct book review of a very complicated authorship that reduces the whole thing to one very simple and socially acceptable idea: that the whole production was religious from first to last.

Perhaps this is also what Kierkegaard intended; perhaps it was his own personal interpretation of his texts, which he also wanted to share with his readers. At any rate, regardless of what Kierkegaard wanted to achieve with *My Activity as a Writer*, what he did achieve was the creation of one more pseudonym. By publishing *My Activity as a Writer* in his lifetime he tapped into all the traditional expectations that the public has concerning writers and their relationship to their work, and he used this massive body of stereotypes to create a new personage: a pseudonym named "Søren Kierkegaard." This was the last and best defense available to Kierkegaard both to protect his own independence, the independence of the text, and the independence of the reader—all of which were crucial to him.[102] By publishing *My Activity as a Writer* and using his own name and his own voice in a way that his careful readers would recognize as ironic—in spite of its serious tone and sober claim to be an honest and direct communication—Kierkegaard effectively foreclosed on the option of referring to him for authoritative guidance in understanding his writings.[103] By seeming to write a definitive conclusion to his authorship, Kierkegaard has actually contributed to the delimitation of his authorship. By making his own name into a pseudonym, Kierkegaard revokes any authority that he might seem to have over his texts, and also renders it more difficult to bring his fragmented texts together into a unified system.[104]

In conclusion: How to avoid finishing anything

The system that Kierkegaard wanted to avoid is a system of human existence that denies the truth of human existence: the fact that existence is always incomplete, in process, underway, surprising, unfinished, like this sentence . . . To avoid writing a system that would bring an end to the writing of existence Kierkegaard wrote philosophy books that were deliberately scrappy and crumby, and he deployed writing that also unwrote itself with irony—writing that won't stay in place, that slips through your fingers before you can use it to build walls around truths that can never be more than subjective truths; truths that refuse to be contained, in the same way that individual personalities and identities refuse to be contained.[105] Kierkegaard wrote both beginnings and endings to his philosophy that undermined the possibility of any beginning or ending to his philosophy, and in this way he undermined the possibility of bringing his texts together into some kind of systematic totality. A system that lacks both a beginning and an end is clearly not much of a system (*CUP* 13); it's really more like a joke.[106]

Not surprisingly, most people didn't get the joke; but this is also funny, and the laughter that this misunderstanding occasions is one more report to history that Kierkegaard's textual project has successfully resisted and undermined all attempts to turn it into a system.

Chapter 3

How to misunderstand religion in Kierkegaard's writing and thus succeed in completely overlooking some of the most interesting ideas in his philosophy

or

X reasons to understand religion as a metaphor in Kierkegaard's writing[107]

IN CHAPTER 2 I tried to clarify, and also heap praise upon, the elaborate scam that Kierkegaard perpetrated when he wrote multiple conclusions for his writing. These multiple conclusions make any simple or systematic conclusion about Kierkegaard's philosophy impossible and create a self-undermining and self-effacing machine that is truly a work of art. The beautiful and cunning "clandestine machinery" (*KJN* 6:414) of these multiple conclusions delimits the interpretation of Kierkegaard's philosophy and makes any effort to reduce its meaning to something straightforward or simple look quite ridiculous. Given the creativity and artistry manifest in Kierkegaard's non-concluding conclusions, we really ought to be embarrassed if we are so totally lacking in imagination that we can't think of any other way to read Kierkegaard except as a "religious writer." If that's the best that we can do we should be ashamed because that's an obvious failure of imagination.

What would a reading of Kierkegaard's texts look like if it aspired to the same level of artistry and imagination that Kierkegaard himself applied to those texts when he wrote multiple non-concluding conclusions for his work? I suggest that we start by considering the range of metaphorical meanings that religion can have. While it's true that much of Kierkegaard's writing appears on the surface to be interested only in religion, everything that Kierkegaard wrote about religion can be understood as a metaphor and therefore about something other than religion. This is not to suggest that there's anything wrong with taking Kierkegaard's writing about religion at face value and not reading it as metaphorical;[108] I'm only arguing that if we can't think of any other possible readings for these eccentric and eclectic texts there's definitely something wrong with us.

In this chapter I will argue that there are at least ten good reasons for understanding everything Kierkegaard writes about religion as metaphorical. Such a reading makes Kierkegaard's thought more relevant and more useful. It creates new meanings and new concepts that can be put to work in the larger project of understanding and giving meaning to human experience. I am going to argue for recognizing and liberating these new meanings and concepts in Kierkegaard's writing, but at the same time I will never argue for eliminating any previously recognized meanings and concepts. My project in this chapter is an affirmative, creative project that has no interest in arguing against anything, except the insistence that religion can have only one meaning in the texts of Kierkegaard—that's a mistake that I do want to correct.

Many of the ten reasons for understanding religion as a metaphor that I will discuss in this chapter have been mentioned already, especially in chapter 1 when I argued that Kierkegaard's journals contribute to his theory of indirect communication (Act two in that chapter) and also create new philosophical concepts (Act three in that chapter). Kierkegaard's journals are particularly relevant to the arguments I'm offering for understanding religion as metaphor because they, along with the multiple conclusions that Kierkegaard created for his writing, have been used as the primary justifications for doing the opposite—for reading everything that Kierkegaard writes about religion in a strictly literal fashion and never considering its metaphorical possibilities. My arguments for reading religion as a metaphor in Kierkegaard's writing won't be limited to the journals, but the journals will play an outsize role in this chapter because I'm trying to make the point that what we actually find in the journals are many good reasons to expand and diversify the meanings and concepts generated by Kierkegaard's discussion of religion in those pages, which is contrary to how the journals have predominantly been used in the past.

Throughout its history philosophy has had a tendency not to recognize or respect its own metaphors, and consequently something like a secret history has developed within the history of philosophy—an alternate universe where the metaphors that mostly go unrecognized in the official and orthodox version of the philosophical narrative go about their business without costume or mask. Philosophy has abandoned and orphaned its metaphors here and for the most part never bothered to conduct a census or otherwise check in on what's happening in this parallel universe. Uncovering and re-covering this secret history can make philosophy more relevant and useful as a tool to make sense of human existence in the twenty-first century, and also a lot more fun. This chapter will be an exploration of philosophy's secret history and the alternate universe it has created in which these many orphaned metaphors have been living quite joyous and productive lives, happily ignored by philosophy's orthodox official history.

X reasons for understanding religion as a metaphor in Kierkegaard's writing

(1) Because Kierkegaard made it almost impossible for us not to do so when he used the letter X in his journals to signify Christianity, Christ, or any variation thereof.

Reading the X of Xnty as a variable—as a placeholder that could be instantiated by anything—is such an obvious and excellent possibility; so really how could we resist? Kierkegaard practically begs us to do it. It may seem like a trivial typographical accident, a reflection of an author's understandable reluctance not to write a long, five-syllable word like "Christianity" over and over again (just as I have the word "Kierkegaard" assigned to its own command in Microsoft Word so that I don't have to type out all eleven of its painful letters over and over again); and if there were nothing more to my argument than this very low-hanging fruit I agree that I should be ashamed. There is, in fact, more to the argument (so I'm not ashamed), but we really should take a moment at the outset to be grateful that Kierkegaard has given us this very obvious invitation to regard religion as a metaphor in his thought. Kierkegaard's journals are thought to be dominated by discussions of religion, but the words that we actually see on the pages of those journals are not "religion" or "Christianity" or anything else like that; instead what we find for the most part on these pages over and over again is "Xnty," "Xn-dom," etc. The X of Xnty, which almost irresistibly invites us to regard it as a variable, should serve as a constant reminder that Kierkegaard's thinking about religion was utterly unique and idiosyncratic, and very likely applicable to much more than either religion in general or Christianity in particular.

(2) Because Xnty bears no resemblance to any form of religion that has ever existed, or perhaps ever could exist.

At this point someone will likely leap to his feet and object rather indignantly: "Yes we know all about Xnty since you discussed it already *ad nauseam* in chapter 1, and we are tired of hearing about it! So please, talk not to me any more about Xnty! Furthermore, I must point out that even if I do grant your highly suspect claim that Xnty isn't really about religion but in fact creates a collection of new philosophical concepts (which I certainly do not grant), it remains the case that Kierkegaard discussed and explored religion in many other ways and using many other words. He doesn't always use the word 'Xnty' or its many variations in these discussions and explorations; often he uses very plain and common words like 'religion' and 'Christianity' that cannot be so easily twisted and distorted by your sophistry into something other than what they plainly are: straightforward discussions of religion, understood very literally, and not even remotely metaphorical. So what are you going to do about that, you unredeemable quibbler and paralogist? Xnty will not save you now!"

These are excellent points and I welcome this intervention by my angry friend who is tired of hearing about Xnty. Xnty is certainly not the beginning and the end of everything Kierkegaard has to say about religion in his writing, so if I want to make the case that everything Kierkegaard said about religion can be understood metaphorically (which I most certainly do) it would be a massive mistake for me to stop with Xnty. (That would also result in a very short and disappointing list, consisting of exactly one item, whereas I promised you a list with a full ten items.) So yes, I will stop talking about Xnty and move on to other ways in which religion is a metaphor in Kierkegaard's philosophy—after I say one last thing about Xnty.

Before I leave Xnty behind forever I think it is important to recall how truly different this new conceptual creation is from everything that has been understood as religion so far, and also every form of religion that we could imagine. I discussed this a little bit already, in chapter 1 (as my angry friend noted), but never in a particularly well-organized or systematic way, so please tolerate some repetition here as I try to enumerate in a more precise fashion some of the ways that Xnty as Kierkegaard presents it is not like anything that anyone would be inclined to call religion, and is also just profoundly weird. It seems to me that there are at least five of Xnty's characteristics that are particularly worth highlighting in this respect. All of these are reasons for understanding Xnty as a metaphor—as something other than religion. I've included a few additional selections from the journals for each of these characteristics just because they are so fascinating and therefore irresistible.

(a)

Xnty is for single individuals only. All groups or collectives or institutions of any kind are barred at the door. In this respect Xnty is the polar opposite of "religio" because instead of binding people together it separates and isolates them.

> Xnity is certainly accessible to all—though, be it noted, insofar, and only insofar, as each separately becomes an individual, becomes the single individual. (*KJN* 4:87)

> That is how Xnty has been abolished, by everywhere forcing personality to withdraw. People seem to fear that an I could be a sort of tyranny, and therefore every I is to be leveled, pushed back behind an objectivity. I must not be allowed to say, I believe there is a God. I am to say, This is Xnty's doctrine: I believe. But then this I is something more universal, not my personal I. (*KJN* 6:322)

> The principle is this: as soon as there exists one single true Xn in the strictest sense, Xnty exists; and on the other hand, even there were 7 billion, 5 million, 696,734, or 35 Xns, sort of, to a certain degree, Xnty does not exist on that account.... Viewed from another perspective, we human beings are perhaps well served by the fact that no Xns in the strictest sense exist, for one such would explode existence, and would probably cause all of us others to fall away completely. (*KJN* 8:123)

(b)

Xnty is an impossible existential ideal. It is unattainable and even incomprehensible. This characteristic is worth pondering for a moment. Xnty was meant to be impossible: impossible to realize and impossible even to understand. It follows that it never has existed, and never could exist, except as an ideal.

> The task is not to comprehend Xnty, but to comprehend that one cannot comprehend it. (*KJN* 5:70)

> Xnty of course declares itself to be against the understanding, to be paradoxical. . . . In general, all objections to Xnty are made by virtue of the understanding—but without sufficient understanding to stop at this sign: that Xnty itself proclaims that it is contrary to the understanding. (*KJN* 10:5)

> The ideality of it has been completely lost. The result is that being Xn is regarded as something that can surely be done by everyone. Then, by contrast, it becomes a mark of distinction to go further, to become a philosopher, a poet, or God knows what. (*KJN* 8:342)

> Christianity is superhuman. (*KJN* 8:350)

Given that Xnty is an impossible and incomprehensible existential ideal it follows that "Xnty simply does not exist" (e.g., *KJN* 8:122–24). Hence, the incongruity of so many humans claiming to be Xns, as if that were the easiest thing in the world.

> And this teaching, which fills me with fear and trembling, has now been embraced by all these millions upon millions, among whom there are millions who perhaps have scarcely an extra half-hour a year in which to think about their inner lives—but they are all Xns. (*KJN* 8:348–49)

(c)

The ideal and incomprehensible nature of Xnty makes it genuinely offensive. If it doesn't offend you, Kierkegaard argues, you haven't understood it:

> When a person first comes to reflect on Xnty, it must at first—before he has immersed himself in it—undoubtedly have been his downfall, a cause of offense. Indeed, he must have wished that it had never come into the world, or at least that the question regarding it had never arisen in his consciousness. It is therefore revolting to hear all this talk by officious and chattering middlemen about how Xt is the greatest hero, etc., etc.—therefore the humorous view is far preferable. (*KJN* 2:76)

The X of Xnty suggests, among other things, something X-rated: obscene, indecent, and scandalous. These are qualities that we generally don't associate with religion. No one has ever succeeded in formulating a satisfactory definition of obscenity; perhaps the closest anyone has come is the famous "definition" given by Supreme Court Justice Potter Stewart in Jacobellis v. Ohio:

> I shall not today attempt further to define the kinds of material I understand to be embraced within that shorthand description; and perhaps I could never succeed in intelligibly doing so. But I know it when I see it, and the motion picture involved in this case is not that.[109]

All we can say about the obscene is that we would prefer not to see it or experience it in any way; we would prefer that it remain invisible and hidden from us.

(d)

Xnty emphasizes heterogeneity with the world. It makes you an alien and an outlaw in this world.

> For Xnty is heterogeneity with this world—at the very instant that it begins to be official Xnty, even in the least way, at that very instant Xnty begins to become homogeneity with this world.
>
> Official Xnty is the precise, diametrical opposite of true Xnty; in every way, every way, even in the least things, it reverses things . . . . (*KJN* 9:312)

> . . . let us assume—let me consider this possibility—that I succeeded in attaining something of this loftiness. It seems to me that I must then become alien to all human beings, that they must hate me (alas, and this is indeed what Xnty predicts), it must seem to them as if I wanted to annihilate everything they hold dear. (*KJN* 8:348)

(e)

"Xnty is not a doctrine . . . but an existence communication" (*KJN* 5:39). Which of course changes everything. Works of literature, works of art, and works of philosophy are all existence communications, so Xnty belongs with them—that's where you should be looking if you want to understand Xnty.

> And this entire distinction about poetic communication is in turn related to the fundamental Christian category, that Xnty is an existence-communication and is not—as people have

meaninglessly and unchristianly made Xnty into—a doctrine
.... (*KJN* 6:359)

And now I shall say no more about Xnty. My objective in this chapter is to argue that every time Kierkegaard seems to be writing about religion what he writes can be understood metaphorically—that religion can always be productively and usefully read as a metaphor for something else. The overall purpose of this argument is to blow up one of the most pervasive strategies that have been used to reduce and simplify Kierkegaard's philosophy: to insist that in the end it's obviously just about religion and nothing more. Everything Kierkegaard writes about Xnty is certainly relevant to the project of constructive demolition that I am undertaking here, but there are many other aspects and dimensions of Kierkegaard's philosophy that have been used to support the claim that he is nothing more than a religious writer and I will focus on those for the remainder of this chapter. So now I bid farewell to Xnty forever, with doubtful good wishes for its future fate, that this, if it is propitious for it, will be just as it might wish. I know that it could not expect or desire many readers—would that it might happily find the few desirable readers.

(3) Because indirect communication applies to all of Kierkegaard's writing, including the texts that seem to be direct communications, such as the journals, and it applies to all of the topics that Kierkegaard discusses in those texts, including religion.

This too was discussed somewhat in chapter 1, so here again I beg the reader's pardon for repeating myself just a little, and here again I promise to make it worth your time by adding something that was missing from the previous discussion. There are two distinct arguments that should be considered here: one about text, and one about topics.

Kierkegaard makes it clear in his journals that it was his goal to use indirect communication all the time, in all of his writing, with no exceptions. In order truly to be "God's spy," a writer would "stick with indirect communication, unwavering to the end" (*KJN* 9:175). This means that those texts that have been generally assumed to be direct communications, such as the journals, can no longer be taken at face value. In these texts too indirect communication is the rule. This reasoning extends the logic of indirect communication to *all* of Kierkegaard's writing, so every text must be read suspiciously.

Kierkegaard explained how what appeared to be a direct communication could be part of the larger machinery of indirect communication:

> A real ironist must always be inexhaustible in varying the deception. The moment that a person has not himself unconditionally understood something, one can rob him of it by means of the deception. For a few moments he says: Aha, that is a trick! He thus relies on the direct communication. But then the deception is placed between us, and my art then consists in remaining in character. As soon as I am consistently able to do so, he is again confused. Only he who himself understands what he understands is immune to deception. (*KJN* 4:145)

We should remind ourselves also that indirect communication was such a thorough production and performance art for Kierkegaard that it even included daily walks on the streets of Copenhagen (*KJN* 4:22, 248, 271).[110]

> But, that all this is in service to the idea, that it is my highest interest, my artistic effort in support of my literary production.... [T]hat this is my real identity, the source of my legitimacy; that I have acted against reason; that without this I would simply have been a productive literary braggart, as authors are nowadays, to whom it never occurs to transform into reality a tiny fraction of what they write: alas, who thinks of this, who would not say that it was madness or lies! Well, let it be, my art is all the greater for it.... My productions have been maieutic; my existence has been supportive by being a stumbling block. (*KJN* 4:22)

What follows from all of this is a conclusion about Kierkegaard's texts: that there is no reason to regard any of them as exempt from the overall project and performance of indirect communication that Kierkegaard worked on throughout his life and throughout his authorship.

The same reasoning applies to all of the topics that Kierkegaard wrote about in his texts. Given all of the effort that Kierkegaard invested to create difficulties by means of indirect communication it is truly remarkable that so many readers have approached Kierkegaard's writing as if they were entering a metaphor-free zone whenever the subject is religion. Whenever Kierkegaard begins to discuss religion in any of his books or in his journals a spirit of piety often takes control of the reader's imagination and results in a very literal-minded reading. On this one aspect of Kierkegaard's philosophy a strange consensus seems to have emerged, confident that indirect communication no longer applies and everything is exactly what it seems to be. This consensus seems to rest on the assumption that a discussion of religion could not possibly be a metaphor for anything else, because that's simply too obscene, too indecent to fathom.

But there are no good reasons for this strange tendency to assume that as soon as Kierkegaard starts talking about religion—or any other topic—indirect communication can no longer apply. Once indirect communication has been turned loose in Kierkegaard's texts there is no way to turn it off—no way to put the genie back into the bottle in terms of either texts or topics. For an author who puts such tremendous emphasis on indirect communication, it's amazing that we have generally regarded everything he wrote as having a doubly-reflected double-meaning—except (for some reason) religion. As soon as Kierkegaard starts talking about religion we all bow down in reverence, paralyzed with fear (apparently) that the Lord will smite us if we dare to think that perhaps even this is an indirect communication.

This is, first of all and most embarrassingly, an utter failure of imagination, but it also goes completely against what Kierkegaard himself told us about the importance of using indirect communication when discussing religion.

> What matters is to present Xnty once again in all its radicality, and—as we are situated in Xndom—indirectly. I must be kept outside it—the awakening will be all the greater. People love direct communication because it makes the matter easy, and those who communicate love it because it makes life less strenuous for them because they do, after all, always find a few people with whom they can band together and escape the strain of solitude. (*KJN* 5:44)

> The single most deplorable idea in the world is that "eloquence" has become the medium for proclaiming Xnty. Sarcasm, irony, humor are much more closely related to the existential aspect of Christianity. (*KJN* 6:130)

Actually, the very fact that Kierkegaard claimed that everything he wrote was about religion (e.g., in *The Point of View*) gives us an excellent reason to think that this is *not* the case. For an author who deliberately wrote with such complexity and tried to make life more difficult to suddenly offer us such a reduction and simplification of his meaning—it seems to me that any reader who takes that at face value has not been paying attention.

None of Kierkegaard's texts, and none of the topics he wrote about, are ever free of indirect communication, so the tradition of regarding religion as somehow exempt from indirect communication can't be justified. There's no reason to take anything that Kierkegaard writes in any text literally. This means that when Kierkegaard writes about religion in any text, even an apparently direct text, it is always potentially an indirect communication that should not be taken at face value, and therefore it's always possible that religion can have a metaphorical meaning in these texts.

(4) Because it creates new concepts on a plane of immanence, which is philosophy's job.

I made the case in chapter 1, relying on arguments from Deleuze and Guattari, that it is philosophy's job to do this, and I argued at length that Xnty in particular could be understood as a collection of new philosophical concepts that Kierkegaard created—and I did promise not to say another word about Xnty—so I won't try everyone's patience by repeating any of those arguments here. I will simply add four thoughts that build on those arguments:

(a) All of the arguments in chapter 1 about how Xnty is a new conceptual creation also constitute arguments for understanding religion as a metaphor in Kierkegaard's writing—in all of the ways that religion is discussed and analyzed. Xnty can only be recognized as a new conceptual creation if one is willing to first make the move we're discussing now: willing to allow religion (in all of the ways that religion can be named, discussed, and analyzed) to be a metaphor for something other than religion. That paradigm shift was a necessary condition; without it Xnty would never get recognized as anything other than a strange abbreviation for "Christianity."

(b) The fact that you can create new philosophical concepts when you understand religion as a metaphor is an argument for doing so. In the spirit of pragmatism I would argue that an idea that allows you to do something new—to create new meanings and values and to make sense of your experience in new ways—has already justified itself, and also already proven its value. So the fact that religion can be understood as a metaphor, combined with the fact that interpreting religion as a metaphor creates new philosophical concepts, these are already good reasons to understand religion as a metaphor. The fact that this approach is philosophically productive, that it creates an extremely useful set of new philosophical concepts that work very well to organize the chaos of human existence, is an argument for the approach.

(c) The whole paradigm of philosophy creating new concepts provides a new way to understand what metaphors can do, and why they are valuable in philosophy. In this case we can see how Kierkegaard is using the language of transcendent religion to create entirely new philosophical concepts in a framework that doesn't require transcendence. The use of metaphor in these texts can then be understood not as a transfer of meaning, but rather as creating new meaning by creating new concepts, which is philosophy's job.

(d) Assigning the name "religion" to the many new philosophical concepts that Kierkegaard created was probably the very best way to hide all these new concepts in plain sight. This has proven to be a very effective form of camouflage. Deleuze and Guattari discuss the "philosophical athleticism" and "strange necessity" involved in naming a new concept.[111]

> The concept's baptism calls for a specifically philosophical *taste* that proceeds with violence or by insinuation and constitutes a philosophical language within language—not just a vocabulary but a syntax that attains the sublime or a great beauty.[112]

"Religion" is definitely a very old name, a true paleonym, that calls forth all sorts of other associations that don't seem very philosophical at all, but it certainly does work well as a way to conceal these new creations from anyone who isn't looking for them.

(5) Because it's philosophy's nature to be present into all sorts of things that don't call themselves philosophy, such as literature, art, politics, etc.

Philosophy has always had the ability to take up residence almost anywhere. It is the most adaptable and malleable of all the creatures in the academic animal kingdom. It can make a home for itself in almost any medium or activity or circumstances or environment; it's natural habitat is nearly universal. This is one of the reasons why the earliest philosophers recognized very quickly that there can be no predetermined limits to philosophy—because you never know where you might find a philosophical theory or argument, casually and comfortably lurking someplace no one would have ever thought to go looking, and thus if you draw up a map with territorial boundaries and confidently declare: "this is where you will find philosophy, and no place else!" you are bound to be hoisted by your own petard and proven wrong in a most embarrassing fashion. The fact that philosophical theories and arguments can be expressed through every method and means that humans have of expressing themselves, the ability that philosophy has to lurk and hide in media other than a traditional philosophical argumentative essay and in activities and pursuits that don't seem to have anything to do with philosophy—this is one of philosophy's most remarkable and glorious attributes.

Everyone knows what a traditional philosophical essay looks like: it is usually quite boring and dry, over-written, over-argued, under-edited, and generally devoid of all humor or any other traces of human life. But even the most humorless and traditional philosopher who devotes himself exclusively to this sort of writing has never hesitated to point out philosophical assumptions that non-philosophers make without realizing what they are doing. This is usually done with a great deal of self-satisfaction and even something that approximates human joy. But blowing the whistle on philosophical assumptions when they are made in areas that don't claim to be philosophy has not always been followed by the recognition that it's not just philosophical assumptions that abound far and wide, in every conceivable discourse and discipline, but also philosophy itself abounds there as well.

Part of philosophy's job has always been to find and unmask and extract philosophy wherever it may be. We can find philosophy all over the place living under an assumed name, an alias. So philosophy can be hiding, for example, in what appears to be a straightforward discussion of religion—and that, I would argue, is very often the case with Kierkegaard's philosophy. Much of what Kierkegaard writes about religion doesn't just make philosophical assumptions or occasionally allude to philosophy; it *is* philosophy—philosophy that is working undercover and incognito, as philosophy has so often done in its long and strange and wonderful history.

(6) Because philosophy has always done this, particularly with religion.

In the very longest period by far in the history of philosophy (the medieval period) this is basically all that happened: philosophy was created and smuggled into the world by calling it religion. Medieval philosophy only gets recognized as philosophy if we are willing to read all the discussions of religion (primarily Christianity) as actually discussions of philosophy. It's true that philosophy has sometimes confused itself with religion, especially in its earliest infancy (e.g., Pythagoras and Empedocles), but it has also used religion very successfully as a means to camouflage and conceal its ideas, especially during times when these ideas were considered dangerous, disruptive, or diabolical.

This strategy for concealing philosophy within religion takes advantage of the fact that most of the world has always confused and conflated philosophy and religion. One of philosophy's greatest achievements throughout all of its history has been to see through this confusion and be clear about how it is different from religion, even if the rest of the world remains baffled about the difference. Clever philosophers, especially during the Middle Ages, have used the world's confusion to their advantage by creating innovative philosophy and allowing it to be labeled as religion.

Through this clever ruse their philosophy was able to get published and make its way into the world masquerading as religion, and they also got paid enough to go on living. This wily act of camouflage is perhaps the greatest single accomplishment of medieval philosophers, who found a way to keep philosophy alive and even flourishing in spite of an intellectual environment that was extremely inimical to independent thinking.

To lose sight of the differences that distinguish philosophy and religion, and to allow philosophy to get confused with religion or to get absorbed back into religion would be a disaster. It would negate all the progress that philosophy has made since the pre-Socratics. It would negate all the clever strategy, subterfuge, and misdirection that allowed philosophy to survive in the Middle Ages. This is what happens when all of Kierkegaard's philosophy is understood as religion instead of being recognized as philosophy masquerading as religion in the grand and noble medieval tradition.

(7) Because in all of human history nothing has had more meanings than "religion."

It seems unlikely that any word or concept in the history of the world has been assigned as many meanings as "religion"—and always deeply felt and deeply serious meanings. If you could assemble all of these meanings at once and present them together this would constitute the history of the literal meanings of "religion." The range of meanings here assembled would be so vast that almost nothing would be excluded; so even if you understand religion literally it can still mean nearly anything; certainly its range of meaning is broad enough to include all the philosophical meanings that Kierkegaard attaches to it. This pointed question ought to be posed to anyone who insists that "religion" must always be understood literally: "What exactly is the literal meaning of religion"? If you wanted to choose a name or concept that has had a unified and singular meaning throughout history, "religion" or "Christianity" would both be terrible choices—perhaps the worst possible choices.

(8) Because Kierkegaard found the study of theology and religion to be extremely boring.

This is, I confess, an argument about the author's intentions, which normally I regard as an indecent and disgraceful argument. Obviously the author's intentions do not control the meaning of any author's writing, and they are ultimately unknowable and undecidable; and perhaps more than any other author Kierkegaard took pains to prevent anyone from appealing to his intentions or blaming those intentions for their own interpretation of his philosophy. Consequently I won't blame anyone who decides to ignore this part of the argument and regard it as completely irrelevant to the effects that Kierkegaard's texts have actually had in the world.

Still, though I am somewhat embarrassed to present this argument, I do think it's worth noting two biographical details in connection with Kierkegaard's thinking about religion that are very clear in his journals. It deserves to be noted that Kierkegaard—who has been widely and confidently portrayed as a "religious writer"—made no secret of the fact that he found the study of theology and religion to be extremely boring, and that he gravitated to the study of philosophy instead. His official academic education culminated in his defense of a very philosophical doctoral dissertation on *The Concept of Irony with Constant Reference to Socrates*. Whenever he discussed or explored religion he always preferred to do so through the lens of philosophy.

In a letter to P. W. Lund on 1 June 1835, written when he was twenty-two years old, Kierkegaard explained that he found the study of theology to be very dry and dull and that he was a theology student only to please his father.

> —as far as little irritations are concerned, I will remark only that I am embarked on studies for the theological degree, an occupation that does not interest me in the least, and which therefore is not going particularly quickly. I have always preferred free, perhaps therefore also rather indefinite, studies to the offerings at private dining clubs where one knows beforehand who the guests will be and what food will be served each day of the week. Since it is, however, a requirement, and one is hardly permitted entry to the scholarly commons without first being branded, and regarding it in view of my present state of mind as beneficial to myself, in the knowledge that by doing this I can also make my father very happy (he thinks that the real Canaan lies on the other side of the theological degree, but also, like Moses of old, ascends Mount Tabor and declares that I will never get in—yet I hope that this time the prophecy will not be fulfilled), then I had better knuckle down. . . . To me the scholarly world of theology is like Strandveien on Sunday afternoon in the Deer Park season—they rush past one another, yell and shout, laugh and make fools of one another, drive their horses to death, tip over and are run over, and when they finally reach Bakken covered in

dust and out of breath—yes, then they look at one another—and go home. (*KJN* 1:17–18)

Kierkegaard's disinterest in theology and religious studies generally is also verified in a very graphic and hilarious fashion in his journals and notebooks. The scribbles and doodles in his notebooks, many of which have become quite well known, are found almost exclusively in the sections of his notebooks where he is taking notes on readings or lectures in theology or church history. These doodles make plain Kierkegaard's state of mind with regard to this material. In volume 11, part 1 of the current edition of *Kierkegaard's Journals and Notebooks* you will find an enormous collection of designs and absent-minded drawings that occur exclusively in the first two sections, and those sections deal with church history, biblical exegesis, Schleiermacher's dogmatics, Baader's dogmatics, etc. Kierkegaard obviously found these topics to be extremely dull and uninspiring since he resorted to filling the paper with sketches of mysterious faces and heads, strange geometrical designs, and repeated words or fragments of words over and over in an apparent attempt to keep himself from dying of boredom. In addition to all the sketches and doodles that fill these pages, there are also many incomplete sentences—thoughts that Kierkegaard didn't even bother to complete, indicating that he found it boring and burdensome just to write down these ideas.

Again, I am embarrassed to advance any argument that ties the meaning of a text to its author's biography or intentions, and I justify doing so now only as a kind of corrective (or emetic, as Johannes Climacus might say). Since there has been such zeal for turning to Kierkegaard's biography to support interpretations of his writing I think it is only fair to point out that all the evidence in Kierkegaard's biography suggests that the study of theology and religion did not interest him at all. For what it's worth, which is perhaps exactly nothing: there isn't any biographical support for the idea that Kierkegaard was nothing but a religious writer; actually all the biographical evidence suggests that this is the last thing he ever wanted to be.[113]

(9) Kierkegaard seems to have concluded that it would be the job of future generations to figure out what he had done—the meanings and concepts he created—especially with regard to "religion."

This is another argument that considers the intentions of the author, but I am less embarrassed about this one because this time it's a case of the author recognizing the irrelevance of his own intentions—the impossibility of determining or containing the meaning of his conceptual creations. Kierkegaard's acknowledgment of this fact deserves our attention because it emphasizes the responsibility that we have, since we are the readers of the future that Kierkegaard imagined.

I would argue that Kierkegaard is perhaps the greatest case study in the history of philosophy for Deleuze and Guattari's contention that philosophy is all about creating new concepts. (This would also make Kierkegaard one of the greatest philosophers in the history of philosophy.) Kierkegaard created so many concepts that he felt the need to create different authors and voices for them also—so many new concepts that he quickly gave up on even trying to contain them himself. He created a huge and diverse menagerie of new concepts, and then when he tried to herd them all together into some kind of unified corral, as if everything he had done fit together in a unified project, he was disappointed by every attempt and never felt he succeeded. In the end he acknowledged that he had in fact created and turned loose on the world a whole bunch of new concepts that he didn't really understand himself. Kierkegaard was the first reader of his own writings who came to this conclusion. After many attempts to make sense of his own conceptual creations Kierkegaard seemed to come to this conclusion: I can't do it; it's up to the future to decide what I accomplished.

> I have made yet another final attempt to say a word about myself and my entire authorship. I have written "A Supplementary Note" that should be called The Accounting and should accompany *The Discourses*. In my opinion it is a masterpiece; but that doesn't matter it can't be done.... Personally, I can't take ownership in that way. To take an example.... I wrote *Either/Or*, especially "The Seducer's Diary," for her sake, to help her get out of the relationship.... Governance takes what concerns me personally and forms it into something with wide application. I'm thinking here of what one pseudonym wrote about Socrates: his whole life was a personal preoccupation with himself, and then Governance comes along and intensifies it with world-historical significance. (*KJN* 5:362–63)

Every time Kierkegaard refers to God or Governance making something more from his writing or thinking than he realized himself, this can be understood as just another way of expressing the higher power of philosophy, the fact that concepts always take on a life of their own and then create even more concepts. "Governance" can be understood as Kierkegaard's word for the process of philosophical creation wherein concepts create new concepts of their own, all beyond the intentional control of the author. "God" becomes another word for "thought" or "philosophy" when Kierkegaard uses it in this way.

> I dare not, and cannot, take ownership [of] the whole authorship as if it were something I *intended*. For it is *also* the possibility that resided in my essence as poet (the possibility of the dialectical) that became a reality—that developed as something favorably endowed, that attained its balance in every way by the work of Governance, that was also supported by circumstances, though all this was beneath the threshold of my consciousness from the very beginning. (*KJN* 5:379)

Kierkegaard recognized that he created concepts that exceeded him and that therefore they would only be understood once he was out of the way—after his death.

> As long as I live I will not be understood. Death must mitigate things in order to help the times out of their difficulty. I really have much too much ideality to be alive. (*KJN* 7:128)

He also acknowledged that his indirect communication was in part due to the fact that he himself didn't understand what he was doing:

> *On Indirect Communication and Myself*
> Here it must be noted, above all, that I am indeed not a teacher who originally envisioned everything and who then made use of indirect communication, conscious of every move, but that I am someone who has developed during the process of productivity. It follows that my indirect communication is on a lower level than direct communication because the indirectness was of course connected to the circumstance that I myself was not clear about it from the beginning and therefore did not dare speak directly at the beginning. Thus I myself am the one who has been released and has developed through indirect communication. (*KJN* 8:11c)

Kierkegaard gradually came to the conclusion that authority comes only from textual interpretation. The unpublished *Book on Adler* (actual title: *The Religious Confusion of the Present Age Illustrated by Magister Adler as a Phenomenon, A Mimical Monograph*, by Petrus Minor), which Kierkegaard revised repeatedly but never published, is a textual defense of that textual principle. Kierkegaard certainly recognized that an infinite interpretation of any text is possible, and one reason we do this is in order to defer acting (*KJN* 9:128–29). He posited an interpretation of the New Testament and then acted upon it, but he also recognized that his interpretation was his own act, something he willed, and not something that fell from the sky. He may have derived many of his new concepts from his own idiosyncratic reading of the New Testament, but he also recognized that this reading and interpretation was itself a creative act—that there was no necessity to the conclusions that he came to.

> God's Sublimity
> He gives human beings a holy book containing his will but no middle terms with regard to the ideal—and then he leaves it to each one how to understand it. He does not let us hear from him, keeps perfectly quiet, testing the single individual, for indeed, it really seems to be left completely up to us how we will understand scripture. (*KJN* 8:62)

Like Nietzsche's Zarathustra, who at first is confident that he understands exactly what he wants to teach and therefore marches right into town and begins proclaiming his big idea ("I teach you the overman. Human being is something that must be overcome. What have you done to overcome him?")[114]—and yet never seems able to figure out exactly what his new creation means, exactly what all of its implications are, and in the end seems to give up trying to figure this out and instead celebrates the fact that this is the job for free spirits and philosophers of the future,[115] Kierkegaard also seems to have come to the same conclusion.

(10) Because now the list has ten (X!) items, which justifies the clever chapter title, (and a clever chapter title is no small accomplishment, so this is perhaps the best reason of all).

Chapter 4

How to misunderstand what *Philosophical Fragments* can teach us about human (all-too-human) education
or
How to be a highly ineffective and highly confused teacher

THIS CHAPTER MARKS THE midpoint of the book—three chapters before and three to follow—which is likely a cause for celebration for any reader who has persevered this far in spite of the rapidly and ominously accumulating evidence that almost any other activity would be a better use of his time. To refresh your memory, my dear long-suffering reader, the anti-assistant-professor method for writing about Kierkegaard that I'm striving to follow in this book has four requirements:

1. Write in a way that's human.
2. Write in a way that creates something new rather than just repeating and rearranging Kierkegaard's ideas like a parasite.
3. Write in a way that expands and amplifies Kierkegaard's ideas rather than reducing or simplifying or systematizing them.
4. Write in a way that does not kill Kierkegaard's philosophy by lecturing on it.

Philosophical Fragments was the primary inspiration for how to satisfy the fourth requirement: by giving this book a non-lecturing personality that is fragmentary, sketchy, scrappy and crumby in every way. Since Kierkegaard wrote nothing but fragmentary, sketchy, scrappy, and crumby philosophy books himself we could turn to any of those books for inspiration, but the most obvious and explicit demonstration of the crumby approach to philosophy that I want to imitate is *Philosophical Fragments*—the title of which could just as easily and appropriately be translated as *Philosophical Crumbs*. I explained all of this in the introduction, so I will not add to your oppression and your sorrow, dear reader, by repeating that argument here. The explication of the crumby approach that *Philosophical Fragments* provides is already a marvelous contribution to philosophy, but in addition to clarifying and elucidating this approach *Philosophical Fragments* also performs it, and that performance is what I want to consider in this chapter—particularly with regard to what we can learn from this book about the nature of merely human (all-too-human) education.

In *Philosophical Fragments* two different theories of teaching and learning are presented: one that focuses on education when all of the parties involved (both teachers and students) are merely human, and a separate theory of education that considers how everything changes when God gets involved.[116] The crumby approach to Kierkegaard's writing resists all temptations to sweep up or clean up the fragments, sketches, scraps, and crumbs into something resembling a system, and it also suggests that we should pay special attention to the crumbs that are left behind after the main course has been eaten, the serving trays cleared away, and the dinner guests thinking about retiring for a nap. These crumby ideas are the leftovers that are easy to ignore—leftovers that may turn out to be far more interesting, and far more useful, than the main course, even though the main course was spectacular and delicious and therefore attracted and absorbed everyone's attention. The first theory of merely human education is clearly the crumbier of the two, while the second theory of divine education is obviously the main course. Climacus had so much more to say about the second theory in *Philosophical Fragments*—and even this wasn't enough, so two-years later he published the much longer *Concluding Unscientific Postscript to the Philosophical Fragments* in which he continued to explore all of the consequences for education when God steps into the role of teacher. Also this second theory of education (focused on God as educator) ventures rather spectacularly into the territory of passion and paradox, which leads to many dazzling dialectical fireworks and some very memorable imagery concerning leaps of faith and the special kind of madness that belongs to objective truth, and these rhetorical explosions are hard to ignore. For these reasons it seems like the first theory of merely human education in *Philosophical Fragments* functions primarily to set up the second theory, and the first theory easily gets left behind (like so many crumbs) once the second theory takes the stage. It's easy to run right past the first theory of education—the human, all-too-human theory—without even noticing it; but that would be a great loss because it's an amazing and profound theory of education, and it certainly contains many useful ideas.[117]

My defense of this crumby approach to *Philosophical Fragments* will rest on a purely pragmatic foundation: I will argue that this approach yields some truly fascinating and useful results, just as Climacus suggested in the preface. I will focus on a few of the really excellent crumbs (and/or fragments) in this book (and/or pamphlet) which concern how merely human teaching (and/or learning) are possible—and also how they can utterly fail. This really ought to be a topic of interest to the entire human race since education is the key to our survival, but we're obviously not very good at it.[118]

The ideas in *Philosophical Fragments* about the possibility and impossibility of merely human education may also be useful to a much smaller and stranger sub-culture within the human race: that very odd congregation of lost souls who desperately desire to understand the bizarre menagerie of texts assembled under the name "Søren Kierkegaard." This menagerie includes writing attributed to at least twenty-eight different pseudonyms, many more texts published under Kierkegaard's own signature, and an enormous collection of journals, papers, and scraps that were published posthumously. Whatever else you may think of this eclectic and unruly body of work it is at least clear that it's an extraordinary attempt to pass along some ideas within the human, all-too-human sphere. If some of Kierkegaard's own ideas on teaching and learning in *Philosophical Fragments* could be applied to some of the central puzzles in his own very complicated authorship, that would certainly be a fortuitous fringe benefit.

To make a case for the value of the theory of merely human education offered in *Philosophical Fragments* I will proceed in three stages. Not surprisingly, this educational theory is presented in a very crumby fashion, with bits and pieces scattered throughout the book, so first I will bring these scraps together and clarify the five essential attributes of what Climacus calls "Socratic" teaching. Then I will do the same for Climacus's defense of his Socratic theory of education, which is presented as a series of *reductio ad absurdum* proofs. I will argue that these proofs are especially useful because they clarify how education often fails because we love paradox and mystery more than simple human truths and therefore tend to conceptualize the educational enterprise in religious terms, as if teaching and learning were utterly beyond our limited human abilities and consequently only possible by means of divine intervention. Finally I will apply the theory of merely human education in *Philosophical Fragments* to Kierkegaard's authorship as a whole and argue that it gives us a paradigm for understanding all of his writing that is more fundamental than the distinction between direct and indirect communication, which has been the primary focus of the perplexed and persistent mortals who have labored for so long to make sense of these strange texts.

The crumby theory of merely human education in *Philosophical Fragments*: Five essential attributes of "Socratic" teaching and/or learning

"Can the truth be learned and/or taught?" Chapter 1 of *Philosophical Fragments* begins with this question; however, it's worded much less awkwardly in Danish because the single Danish word *laere* means both "to teach" and "to learn." This is, I believe, a brilliant insight on the part of the Danish language, since teaching and learning really are inextricable. Because *laere* means both "teach" and "learn," to choose one or the other in English translation would be merely arbitrary;[119] so I'm going to embrace the limitations of the English language when it comes to expressing the inextricable nature of teaching and learning and always use the awkward phrase "learn and/or teach" or some variation thereof in this chapter in spite of how annoying this will be to you, dear reader.

"Can the truth be learned and/or taught?"[120] In the "thought-project" that initiates his answer to this audacious and awkwardly worded question Climacus immediately summons Socrates for assistance. "It was a Socratic question," he insists, "or became that by way of the Socratic question whether virtue can be taught—for virtue in turn was defined as insight" (*PF* 9). Since from this point on Climacus will refer to authentic human teaching as "Socratic teaching" we should address the historical accuracy of this reference, lest anyone object that Climacus is guilty of getting Socrates all wrong.

To avoid all such nagging questions concerning historical accuracy I think we should recognize right at the outset that the theory of teaching and learning that *Philosophical Fragments* calls "Socratic" really has no necessary connection to the historic Socrates. Socrates merely serves as the occasion for Climacus to conceptualize a system of education that he calls "Socratic," a system that certainly includes a few well-known elements of Socrates's maieutic method but also goes well beyond what Socrates himself actually said or did. This is a "thought-project," not a history or biography project, and in this respect Climacus is just continuing the somewhat ignoble tradition that began with Plato of putting your own ideas in the mouth of Socrates. For example, even though Socrates himself said that he wasn't a teacher, and actually thought of teaching as a shameful and disreputable profession (since he equated it with sophistry),[121] Climacus unabashedly names a full-blown pedagogical theory after him. This is roughly the equivalent of naming a theory of how to be a happy and successful capitalist after Karl Marx, or naming a theory about the psychic health benefits of religious faith after Sigmund Freud. Clearly it's not fair or accurate to attribute to Socrates all of the pedagogical principles that Climacus does assign to him, but that is really beside the point, so it would be a mistake to allow this to stand in the way of appreciating the theory itself. I will continue to refer to the theory of teaching and learning presented in *Philosophical Fragments* as "Socratic," following Climacus, but if the name "Socrates" offends please replace it with "Diogenes" or "Prodicus" or "Sara" or "Clarence" or "Henrietta": it really makes no difference.

Philosophical Fragments outlines five essential attributes of "Socratic teaching," and all of them are truly insightful and full of fascinating implications.

(1) First, a Socratic teacher is a midwife who helps the student give birth to his or her own ideas. A maieutic relationship is the highest and best possible relationship that can exist between two people, Climacus argues, and so a Socratic teacher must establish such a relationship not out of necessity but rather out of principle (*PF* 10). Socrates demonstrated this in his own life because "[h]e was and continued to be a midwife not because he 'did not have the positive,' but because he perceived that this relation is the highest relation a human being can have to another" (*PF* 10).

This is one aspect of "Socratic" teaching that, of course, can be ascribed directly to Socrates, who explained to anyone who would listen that all he ever tried to do was help people give birth to their own ideas. However, Socrates gave his version of the maieutic method a different spin when he insisted that it was precisely because he aspired to nothing more than midwifery that no one could ever accuse him of trying to be a teacher—which was fine with him because he thought of teaching as sophistry and therefore wanted no part in it. So Climacus borrows only some of Socrates's ideas about teaching and midwifery, not the whole story, and this is one more example of how what the *Philosophical Fragments* calls "Socratic teaching" bears no necessary connection or resemblance to the historical Socrates. For Climacus, maieutic teaching is indeed teaching, and in fact the highest possible form of teaching.

(2) The second essential attribute of Socratic teaching concerns temporality. Viewed Socratically, when does teaching and learning occur? Climacus's fascinating answer to this question is: never. Or, to say the same thing: always. Or, to say the same thing yet again, but this time with far more words: teaching and learning have no instant or moment, they have only an

occasion, which amounts to a vanishing point—a moment in time that is capable of performing a disappearing act, and transforming past, present, and future along with it. Contrary to what you are probably thinking right now, these answers are not pure nonsense.

"Viewed Socratically," Climacus writes, "any point of departure in time is *eo ipso* something accidental, a vanishing point, an occasion" (*PF* 11). Therefore, the time of Socratic teaching and learning is accidental and vanishing. A moment of instruction and enlightenment occurs in time, but then vanishes from time, because time itself is transformed. This argument about the unique temporality of teaching and learning has this innovative and intriguing implication: learning Socratically transforms the student's past, and present, and future simultaneously. But this doesn't happen in a moment; rather it has always already happened.

Several thousand years ago Plato expressed something similar about the temporality of teaching and learning by means of his theory of learning as recollection, which maintains that what we call "learning" is really just "remembering." According to Plato, the truth—now recollected—was within you all along, and now that you have remembered it, all the time of your entire life is transformed at once. Climacus gives Plato's theory of recollection a different spin, which emphasizes the temporal transformation that is inherent in human learning and leaves behind all the metaphysical baggage required for Plato's theory of Forms.

> The temporal point of departure is a nothing, because in the same moment that I discover that I have known the truth from eternity without knowing it, in the same instant that moment is hidden in the eternal, assimilated into it in such a way that I, so to speak, still cannot find it even if I were to look for it, because there is no Here and no There, but only an *ubique et nusquam* [everywhere and nowhere]. (*PF* 13)[122]

Though this may sound suspiciously like a magical incantation, or a description of a paradox that resists understanding, Climacus insists that neither is required to explain how human, all too human, education occurs. In the other theory of teaching and learning presented in *Philosophical Fragments*, which concerns how teaching and learning are transformed when God enters the picture and assumes the role of teacher, paradox and the supernatural are essential parts of the story; but Climacus insists that they have no part in teaching and learning between mere humans. In fact, as we'll see later on, Climacus uses the absurdity of relying upon paradox or the supernatural to explain merely human teaching and learning as the punch line in many of the *reductio ad absurdum* arguments that he deploys in defense of his Socratic model of teaching.

But in addition to the *reductio ad absurdum* or indirect proofs that Climacus will offer later on in *Philosophical Fragments*, there is also empirical—or more accurately, phenomenological—evidence for these surprising claims about the temporality of teaching and learning. All you have to do is reflect honestly and thoroughly on your own educational experience, in all of its dimensions, to recognize that these claims about teaching and learning are true. Time really is transformed whenever learning occurs, and past, present, and future are always already transformed all together. Gaining a new insight retroactively resets one's past and proactively reconfigures one's future; so past, present, and future are all transformed in the same (vanishing) instant. It's as if the truth was there all along, as in Plato's theory of recollection, just waiting to be recovered.

(3) Thirdly, just as the moment of Socratic teaching becomes a vanishing point, the teacher herself must also vanish. "Viewed Socratically, any point of departure in time is *eo ipso* something accidental, a vanishing point, an occasion. Nor is the teacher anything more, and if he gives of himself and his erudition in any other way, he does not give but takes away. Then he is not even the other's friend much less his teacher" (*FF* 11). Time provides a template for the teacher to imitate, but the teacher has to understand the need to follow this template—he has to have the insight to know that "if he gives of himself and his erudition in any other way, he does not give but takes away," which would make him "not even the other's friend, much less his teacher" (*PF* 11).

To imitate successfully the way the moment vanishes and time transforms itself when learning occurs, a Socratic teacher must practice and perfect a vanishing act. She must learn how to disappear and never be found, thus leaving a student transformed but not indebted to anyone. Climacus emphasizes how much self-understanding and will are required in order to perform this disappearing act. There is nothing natural, instinctive, or easy about it; self-discipline and self-sufficiency are required, as well as love. "Socrates had the courage and self-collectedness to be sufficient unto himself, but in his relations to others he also had the courage and self-collectedness to be merely an occasion even for the most stupid person" (*PF* 11). It's far more natural for a teacher not to disappear, to linger in a student's life and continue to cast a long shadow while collecting praise, honor, glory, money, and perhaps even the Teacher of the Year Award. To will her own disappearance a teacher must be truly wise and in tune with the temporality of teaching and learning, and also motivated by a desire to benefit the student—because anything less than a total vanishing act will harm the student. To practice this art of transforming oneself into a vanishing point or accidental occasion in the life of a student requires,

> rare magnanimity—rare in our day, when the pastor is little more than the deacon, when every second person is an authority, while all these distinctions and all this considerable authority are mediated in a common lunacy and in a *commune naufragium* [common shipwreck], because, since no human has ever truly been an authority or has benefited anyone else by being that or has ever really managed successfully to carry his dependent along, there is better success in another way, for it never fails that one fool going his way takes several others along with him. (*PF* 11–12)

(4) As is evident from the text above, a fourth essential attribute of Socratic teaching is closely connected to the self-understanding that leads a good teacher to make herself disappear: a true Socratic teacher does not think of herself as an authority. This is another striking claim, but it follows quite naturally from the paradigm of teaching as deliberately vanishing midwifery in an accidental-and-vanishing-transformative-moment-of-time that Climacus has outlined so far. There is definitely an art to teaching, but it's the art of catalyzing the student's own creative process and then erasing yourself—vanishing before anyone notices (which is no mean art); it's not the art of possessing or asserting authority. A Socratic teacher stands on the same plane and shares the same world as the student; there is no hierarchy of authority that makes the teacher transcendent.

> Understood in this way . . . the teacher stands in a reciprocal relation, inasmuch as life and its situations are the occasions for him to become a teacher and he in turn the occasion for others to learn something. His relation, therefore, is at all times marked by autopathy just as much as sympathy. (*PF* 23)

This is one more aspect of Socratic teaching that is counter-intuitive to the point of appearing paradoxical, but again Climacus insists that there is no unthinkable paradox here: this paradigm of teaching simply follows naturally and logically from everything else that he has argued concerning education so far.

(5) Finally, a true Socratic teacher recognizes that for the student who learns from a teacher who is a mere vanishing point and accidental occasion, learning amounts to creating her own truth. Here again Climacus is borrowing some ideas from Plato's argument that all learning is recollection but adding some key modifications of his own. Instead of learning

as remembering, the spin that Climacus gives to this theory turns it into something more like learning as creating or inventing. Again, all the metaphysical baggage of Plato's Forms is no longer necessary; all that's required to support the conclusion that a student who learns creates her own truths is taking seriously the other four essential attributes of Socratic teaching that Climacus has already outlined, especially the idea that a Socratic teacher has abundant skill and art but zero authority. "[T]he teacher is only an occasion, whoever he may be . . . because I can discover my own untruth only by myself, because only when *I* discover it is it discovered, not before, even though the whole world knew it" (*PF* 14).

> If this is the case with regard to learning the truth, then the fact that I have learned from Socrates or from Prodicus or from a maidservant can concern me only historically or—to the extent that I am a Plato in my enthusiasm—poetically. But this enthusiasm, even though it is beautiful, . . . Socrates would say is still but an illusion, indeed, a muddiness of mind in which earthly distinction ferments almost grossly. Neither can the fact that the teaching of Socrates or of Prodicus was this or that have anything but historical interest for me, because the truth in which I rest was in me and emerged from me. Not even Socrates would have been capable of giving it to me, no more than the coachman is capable of pulling the horse's load, even though he may help the horse do it by means of the whip. . . . If I were to imagine myself meeting Socrates, Prodicus, or the maidservant in another life, there again none of them would be more than an occasion, as Socrates intrepidly expresses it by saying that even in the underworld he would only ask questions, for the ultimate idea in all questioning is that the person asked must himself possess the truth and acquire it by himself. (*PF* 12–13)

The absurd defense of Socratic teaching and/or learning, Or, how education gets confused with religion

Kierkegaard summarizes these five essential attributes of Socratic teaching in only five pages, thereby demonstrating that he's capable of writing very succinctly when he wants to. This is something that will seem nearly miraculous to anyone who has weathered the seemingly endless prolixity of *Either/Or* Part II, or *Stages on Life's Way*. This admirably brief summary is followed by many more pages of "proofs" that follow a classic *reductio ad absurdum* model—and this is where the argument really gets interesting.

To prove that the truth can be taught and/or learned only when the principles of Socratic teaching and learning summarized above are followed, we are asked to assume the contrary: that somehow the truth is learned even though these principles are not applied—and then we are led to see that laughable consequences follow, thus demonstrating that the assumption that led to these consequences had to be false. Though this proof is much longer than five pages it is never boring because Climacus seizes on the comic possibilities inherent in *reductio ad absurdum* arguments and exploits them fully, turning them into a very entertaining comedy show.[123]

All of these *reductio* arguments follow the same pattern: if we imagine that the truth can be taught and/or learned in a non-Socratic way, it follows that merely human education becomes indistinguishable from religion. This is quite funny, and therefore obviously false, because—as anyone who has spent ten minutes inside any classroom knows with perfect certainty: there is nothing less like the sublime and transcendent mysteries of religion than the messy and inefficient realities of a school in which humans struggle to educate other humans. Nothing is less worthy of worship than the human, all-too-human comedy of one mere mortal trying to teach another mere mortal; nothing else on earth would make a more ridiculous religion. A religion of human, merely human, education is reminiscent of "The Ass Festival" in *Thus Spoke Zarathustra,* when Zarathustra's followers—wanting desperately to worship something—decide to worship an ass. In their zealous desperation they quickly construct an elaborate system of dogma and rituals so that they can worship, with appropriate solemnity, the ass they find lingering outside Zarathustra's cave; however, even the ass who is the object of their adoration immediately recognizes how ridiculous this is and finds the whole spectacle hilarious.[124]

There are scraps of *reductio ad absurdum* arguments concerning the necessity of Socratic teaching and/or learning scattered throughout the *Philosophical Fragments,* in keeping with the generally crumby nature of this book. In what follows I'll bring these crumbs together to form a series of classic *reductio ad absurdum* proofs. Since the five essential characteristics of Socratic teaching and/or learning naturally overlap to form a package deal, a proof of each of the five would be tedious and unnecessary. Instead, Climacus provides three indirect proofs: (1) If merely human education occurred in a non-Socratic way, what would the consequences be for temporality? (2) What would the consequences be for the teacher? (3) What would the consequences be for the student? The real value of all three of these indirect proofs is that they clarify how education so often fails: they explain how to be a terrible teacher; how to be an unhappy student; how to be utterly disappointed by the whole educational enterprise.[125]

(1) If merely human education occurred in a non-Socratic way what hilarious consequences would follow for temporality?

This is a question about the meaning of the "moment" when teaching and/or learning occurs. In the Socratic model of education this moment is accidental and vanishing; but if teaching and/or learning could be imagined to occur in a moment that were neither, that moment "must have such decisive significance that for no moment will I be able to forget it" (*PF* 13). Every moment when something is learned would become a great earthquake in the student's life, absolutely dividing the past from the future. "A moment such as this is unique. To be sure, it is short and temporal . . . and yet it is decisive, and yet it is filled with the eternal. A moment such as this must have a special name. Let us call it: *the fullness of time*" (*PF* 18). So if you imagine that merely human teaching and/or learning were possible in a non-Socratic way the moment when learning occurs would have to be understood as something like the second coming of the Lord.[126]

This is the first instance in the book of Climacus deploying religious imagery in a highly sarcastic way to clarify the absurdity of non-Socratic teaching and/or learning. In all of these *reductio* arguments religious imagery is called upon only to demonstrate the absurd consequences that follow were we to imagine that humans could teach and learn in a non-Socratic fashion. Religion appears in these proofs only to make the point that if education is not understood in the merely human terms that structure Socratic pedagogy, then education becomes something completely mystical and mysterious to humans and we have to confess that only a god can save us.

A non-Socratic paradigm requires the moment of learning to be a miracle, an interruption of the temporal continuum that will dominate and overshadow the student's life forever. According to this paradigm, every time anyone learns anything a moment so miraculous has occurred that no other moment could possibly match it; but then if one managed to learn more than just one thing in life one would soon have an accumulation of miraculous moments that would threaten to drown out the normal flow of temporality completely. Just one such miraculous moment deserves to be worshipped forever; so wouldn't just two moments of learning be completely overwhelming? For anyone who hopes to learn more than one thing in her life the situation becomes utterly untenable because any mere mortal would find herself disoriented and displaced from her daily mundane existence by the occurrence of these educational miracles.

This story is absurd, obviously, but that was the whole point: to demonstrate by means of an obvious absurdity that the assumption that led to this bizarre result must be false. (*Reductio ad absurdum* arguments are supposed to be funny. They are the stand-up comedians of logic.)

(2) If merely human education occurred in a non-Socratic way what hilarious consequences would follow for the teacher?

Since the moment in which teaching/learning occurs is a miracle, teachers must now be understood as miracle workers. But even this grandiose designation is too humble; more accurately teachers really must be recognized as gods. This is quite obviously hilarious, since no one could possibly be less god-like than a teacher—especially a college professor who teaches four classes every semester while also serving on five different committees and advising forty-eight students, and who is expected to spend any time that remains calling and writing the state legislature begging them not to cut the university's budget again: no one would ever mistake this frantic and frazzled soul for a deity. Consequently, it's not at all difficult for Climacus to bring out the absurdity of this particular conclusion. The sarcastic honor and glory that he piles upon this imagined, deified version of a merely human teacher is boundless. The strains of Handel's *Messiah* can almost be heard playing in the background as one reads the following description of a god-like teacher:

> What, then, should we call such a teacher? . . . Let us call him a *savior*, for he does indeed save the learner from un-freedom, saves him from himself. Let us call him a *deliverer*, for he does indeed deliver the person who had imprisoned himself, and no one is so dreadfully imprisoned, and no captivity is so impossible to break out of as that in which the individual holds himself captive! And yet, even this does not say enough, for by his un-freedom he had indeed become guilty of something, and if that teacher gives him the condition and the truth, then he is, of course, a *reconciler* who takes away the wrath that lay over the incurred guilt. A teacher such as that, the learner will never be able to forget . . . . (*PF* 17)

To further emphasize the absurdity of such a god-like teacher, Climacus points out that when the learned hear about this teacher they will "no doubt first submit sophistic questions to him, invite him to colloquia or put him through an examination, and after that guarantee him a tenured position and a living" (*PF* 57). To this I can only add: Q. E. D.

(3) If merely human education occurred in a non-Socratic way what hilarious consequences would follow for the student?

The student who needs to be saved by the divine intervention of a god-like teacher must be understood as horribly damaged, in a fallen condition—more like an animal than a person. This may seem less hilarious than the ecstatic description of teachers reimagined as gods, but it's really just as absurd. In every way that teachers are elevated to the heavens in the previous *reductio* proof, students are abased and desecrated in this one, and again there is no limit to the hyperbole employed to make this point. (Suitable background music for Climacus's account of a student's wretched condition would be "*Confutatis Maledictis*" from Mozart's *Requiem*, or some other accompaniment appropriate for the damned.)

> The teacher, then, is the god himself, who, acting as the occasion, prompts the learner to be reminded that he is untruth and is that through his own fault. But this state—to be untruth and to be that through one's own fault—what can we call it? Let us call it *sin*. (PF 15)

> When the learner is untruth . . . and he now receives the condition and the truth . . . he becomes a person of a different quality or, as we can also call it, a *new* person. . . . Let us call this change *conversion*. . . . Inasmuch as he was in untruth through his own fault, this conversion cannot take place without its being assimilated into his consciousness or without his becoming aware that it was through his own fault, and with this consciousness he takes leave of his former state. But how does one take leave without feeling sorrowful? Yet this sorrow is, of course, over his having been so long in the former state. Let us call such sorrow *repentance*. . . . Let us call this transition *rebirth*, by which he enters the world a second time just as at birth. . . . Just as the person who by Socratic midwifery gave birth to himself and in so doing forgot everything else in the world and in a more profound sense owed no human being anything, so also the one who is born again owes no human being anything, but owes the divine teacher everything. (PF 18–19)

How to be a terrible teacher and an unhappy student: *Philosophical Fragments* as a guide to educational failure

The picture that emerges from all three of these *reductio ad absurdum* proofs is one of a truly ridiculous religion: a religion of pedagogy that desperately believes in a supernatural solution to a purely human problem. But while these proofs are highly entertaining, they are also opportunities to learn valuable lessons about why teaching and learning so often fail. Here's what we can learn from these proofs—and from the principles of Socratic teaching and/or learning that these proofs defend—about why we humans are so often terrible teachers and miserable students.

First, we are far too pious about education. We want education to be a miraculous intervention involving supernatural powers instead of the mundane and human, all-too-human enterprise that it actually is. Trying to teach or learn in a non-Socratic way is like hiring God to teach a few sections of introduction to philosophy (preferably on an adjunct basis, since the budget is always tight and we're always looking for ways to save money): it may seem like an excellent solution to your staffing problems (best adjunct ever! And we don't even need to pay for benefits!), but it brings with it a whole host of impossible mysteries and unthinkable paradoxes that will make education impossible to understand (and therefore—most terrifyingly—impossible to assess!) since God exists on a different plane entirely from merely mortal students and thus completely beyond our understanding. As soon as we impose a transcendent, supernatural paradigm on merely human education we effectively make education impossible—we place it beyond our own reach. This conclusion seems so obvious that it's hard to imagine how we could ever make such a bizarre mistake, but the *reductio ad absurdum* proofs in *Philosophical Fragments* clarify how quickly, easily, and often we do make this mistake—and thus how we unknowingly transform education into a religion—as soon as we attempt to teach and/or learn in a non-Socratic fashion.

Our excessive piety concerning education can also be understood as a misplaced passion for paradoxes. Climacus has much to say in *Philosophical Fragments* about paradox, but only when he turns to his second theory of education: how education is transformed when God becomes the teacher. In the second theory of education paradox is unavoidable and must be embraced; but if we're looking for paradox in the context of merely human education we're looking for it in all the wrong places. This is most likely due to the fact that we love paradoxes more than we care to admit in polite society.

The story we like to tell about paradoxes is that we consider them to be embarrassing and somewhat indecent. We speak of paradoxes as if they were rare and unintended consequences that occasionally surprise us when we are in search of clear and distinct truths. Certainly we would never go actively looking for paradoxes, we insist; the very idea seems perverse. But in the second theory of education in *Philosophical Fragments* Climacus argues that we don't really believe this story. The truth about paradoxes is exactly the opposite: we love them more than anything else and we actively seek them out. Our passion for paradox is itself paradoxical, since it amounts to the (impossible) desire to think an unthinkable thought, but we love even that paradox. We are, in short, paradoxical creatures who love their paradoxes, and secretly we are not at all embarrassed about this; actually we are quite proud, and boast to ourselves about our passion for paradoxes along the following lines:

> One must not think ill of the paradox, for the paradox is the passion of thought, and the thinker without the paradox is like the lover without passion: a mediocre fellow. But the ultimate potentiation of every passion is always to will its own downfall, and so it is also the ultimate passion of the understanding to will the collision, although in one way or another the collision must become its downfall. This, then, is the ultimate paradox of thought: to want to discover something that thought itself cannot think. (PF 37)

This argument about our lust for paradox reverses a tradition that is at least as old as Aristotle, who claimed in the first line of the first book of the *Metaphysics* that all people by nature desire to know.[127] According to *Philosophical Fragments*, this is false: what we really desire is not to know—to find an unthinkable thought that signals the limits of the understanding and the impossibility of knowledge.

Climacus argues that everything about religion is paradoxical. These well-known arguments are presented at great length in *Philosophical Fragments*,[128] and then at even greater length in the *Concluding Unscientific Postscript to the Philosophical Fragments*. These arguments have attracted much of the attention in these books; but behind them there is a crumby theory of merely human education in which there are no paradoxes, only simple human truths. One of the things we should learn from this crumby theory is that in the realm of purely human education our passion for paradox is misplaced and leads to absurd consequences. We expect miracles in merely human education when none are required, and we long for paradoxes that simply are not there. Thus we conflate education with religion, and succeed—very admirably—in making ourselves terrible teachers and miserable students.

In addition to our misplaced passion for paradox, Climacus's arguments about Socratic teaching clarify how other misplaced passions render merely human teaching and/or learning nearly impossible for us. For example, we desperately love authority. We want the world to be fully stocked with authorities who can tell us what to do at all times, and we also want to be among the ranks of authorities ourselves. Thus we cling to the illusion of authority even when that is the exact opposite of what good teaching requires. We also have far too much love for spectacular, world-historical, momentous events, and not enough appreciation for accidental, vanishing, merely occasional instants. So we cling to an impossible ideal of spectacular presence and never practice the skills required to transform the present into a vanishing instant, and to make ourselves disappear as well. We have no passion at all for the arts and skills that are truly required for effective teaching: the art of midwifery; the art of vanishing; the art of allowing students to create their own truths. Effective teaching does not require world famous, authoritative, god-like teachers; it requires teachers who are wise enough to know that they have no authority, who have practiced and perfected the art of disappearing, and who have the insight to understand that the moment of teaching and learning is also accidental and vanishing and that the student learns only insofar as she creates her own truth. These are not shadowy paradoxes, they are just simple human truths; but instead of embracing these truths we retreat into the realm of paradox, we conflate education with religion, we confuse ourselves with exalted gods and fallen sinners, and we content ourselves to wait patiently for the series of miracles that our absurd conception of human education seems to require.

Therefore, it is clear that we are generally satisfied to remain uneducated about the true nature of education, and *Philosophical Fragments* suggests that this should be understood as willful ignorance because the true nature of merely human education is not a great mystery. To emphasize this fact there's a recurring dialogue in the book between the author and an unnamed antagonist who reappears from time to time to point out to the author that he is effectively just a plagiarist because he is only repeating ideas that everyone already knows. Here are just a few excerpts from their delightful conversation:

> But perhaps someone will say, "This is the most ludicrous of all projects, or, rather, you are the most ludicrous of all project-cranks, for even if someone comes up with a foolish scheme, there is always at least the truth that he is the one who came up with the scheme. But you, on the other hand, are behaving like a vagabond who charges a fee for showing an area that everyone can see. You are like the man who in the afternoon exhibited for a fee a ram that in the forenoon everyone could see free of charge, grazing in the open pasture." (*PF* 21)
>
> Now if someone were to say, "What you are composing is the shabbiest plagiarism ever to appear, since it is nothing more or

less than what any child knows" then I presumably must hear with shame that I am a liar. But why the shabbiest? After all, every poet who steals, steals from another poet, and thus we are all equally shabby; indeed, my stealing is perhaps less harmful since it is more easily discovered. . . . And was this perhaps why you called my plagiarism the shabbiest ever, because I did not steal from any one person, but robbed the human race and, although I am just a single human being—indeed, even a shabby thief—arrogantly pretended to be the whole human race? (*PF* 35)

But someone may be saying, "You really are boring, for now we have the same story all over again; all the phrases you put in the mouth of the paradox do not belong to you at all. (*PF* 53)

Stop a moment. If you go on talking this way, I cannot get a word in edgewise. You talk as if you were defending a doctoral dissertation—indeed, you talk like a book and, what is unfortunate for you, like a very specific book. Once again, wittingly or unwittingly, you have introduced words that do not belong to you and that you have not put in the mouth of the one speaking, but they are familiar to everyone, except that you use the singular instead of the plural. (*PF* 68)

But someone may be saying, "How very curious! I have read your discussion to the end, and really not without some interest, and I have been pleased to find no slogans, no invisible writing. But how you do twist and turn. Just as Saft always ends up in the pantry, you always mix in some little phrase that is not your own, and that disturbs because of the recollection it prompts." (*PF* 105)

In this dialogue Climacus never denies the accusation that he is a plagiarist, that he is not saying anything new; he agrees completely with that assessment, and he's glad that his unnamed antagonist has figured this out. This conversation reappears from time to time in *Philosophical Fragments* to remind us that the theory of Socratic teaching and/or learning outlined there is something that we already know, though for some reason we insist on making education far more complicated than it is—even to the point that we can only make sense of it using supernatural, paradoxical, miraculous concepts borrowed from religion. But rather than acknowledge what we already know about the nature of merely human education, we continue to worship thoughtlessly at the altar of mystery, paradox, and the spectacular, and we continue to make merely human education into a thoroughly unpleasant and unsuccessful enterprise for both teachers and students.[129]

Applying the theory of merely human education in *Philosophical Fragments* to Kierkegaard's authorship as a whole
Or,
Why "Søren Kierkegaard" is the most interesting pseudonym of them all!

In addition to explaining how to be a terrible teacher and an unhappy student, the crumby theory of merely human education in *Philosophical Fragments* also provides some excellent clues concerning how to understand Kierkegaard's bizarre and complicated authorship as a whole (for anyone who is interested). So many debates about Kierkegaard's authorship have focused on indirect communication in his writing without ever considering the theory of merely human education in *Philosophical Fragments*. This is a mistake simply because a theory of education is always more basic than a theory of communication; the question "Can the truth be learned and/or taught?" is more fundamental than the question "How should the truth be communicated?" Consequently we can use the theory of merely human education presented in *Philosophical Fragments* to disentangle some of the classic *conundra* of indirect communication.[130]

Indirect communication gets a lot of attention because some of its best-known elements resonate purely on the level of spectacle: the twenty-eight (at least) pseudonyms that Kierkegaard employed in various texts (many of them with silly and highly memorable names such as Hilarious Bookbinder or Nicolaus Notabene); the jokes directed at Hegel and other extremely serious speculative philosophers; the prefaces to books in which the author informs the reader that the book is a waste of time; the book reviews that Kierkegaard wrote for his own books; etc. These same spectacular elements are also the focus of attention whenever indirect communication is belittled or dismissed as childish or pointless, as often happens. Finally, it's very common for those texts in Kierkegaard's authorship that seem to be direct communications, such as his journals and papers, to be assigned greater authority precisely because they seem to promise an answer key for the indirectly communicated texts—so a hierarchy emerges wherein the texts signed "Søren Kierkegaard" are put in charge of the texts signed by pseudonyms.

All of these conflicts and misunderstandings are eliminated when we recognize that Kierkegaard's system of indirect communication should be understood as one of the consequences of his theory of education. Recognizing this, the debate about which texts should be read as indirect communications and which texts are direct communications simply vanishes, like the vanishing, accidental moment of Socratic teaching and/or learning. The theory of merely human education in *Philosophical Fragments* clarifies the application and the value of Kierkegaard's indirect communication, including the very interesting question of what to make of the texts that are signed "Søren Kierkegaard." Understanding Kierkegaard's theory of merely human education leads one to read all of his work as pseudonymous and indirectly communicated regardless of who signed the text, because that's the only way merely human teaching and/or learning is possible.[131] To attempt to reduce this marvelously messy authorship to a single, simple idea, or a single authoritative voice, is antithetical to these pedagogical principles. Once the theory of merely human education in *Philosophical Fragments* is understood "Søren Kierkegaard" becomes perhaps the most interesting pseudonym of them all, because this pseudonym was the most successful in making life more difficult.

Chapter 5

How to misunderstand *Either/Or* by assuming there's only one nihilist in the book, and that only Part I is comical

or

The Queen of Denmark was right! This book really should have been called *Either and Or*

> I had said to the King that I had already made some of these observations as early as the day he ascended the throne. To this he replied, "Yes, isn't that right—that was the time there was a general meeting where you were the president."—He did have a memory.—At that very moment the door to the adjoining room was opened but was quickly closed again. I took a step back. He went over to the door, saying that it must surely be the Queen, "She has so very much wanted to see you; now I will fetch her." Then he came back, leading the Queen by the hand—and I bowed. It was really a discourtesy to the Queen, who did not get to make a very grand impression; she indeed looked rather insignificant—but is anything else possible when a queen is to make an entry in this manner?
>
> The Queen said that she certainly recognized me, for she had once seen me on the ramparts (when I ran and left Tryde in the lurch) and that she had read a bit of "your *Either and Or*, but that she could not understand it." To this I replied: "Your majesty will appreciate that it is so much the worse for me." (*KJN* 5:233–34)

How to misunderstand *Either/Or*   129

The Queen of Denmark was probably both the first and the last person to feel that she didn't understand *Either/Or*. Almost every reader since that time has been confident that they understand the book perfectly. If one of these very confident and conventional interpreters of the book had been present at the Royal Palace in 1849 when the Queen confessed her confusion he might have stepped forward and responded (very confidently) as follows:

> With all due respect, your Majesty, I humbly disagree! This book is not at all difficult to understand. First of all, please note that the title of the book is not *Either and Or*, it's simply *Either/Or*, and this simple title already makes it clear how easy it is to understand this simple book. It's really two books—an *Either* book and an *Or* book—written by two different authors, and these two books and their two authors couldn't possibly be more different. The first book is written by a disreputable, dissolute, unemployed hedonist who argues for a purely aesthetic life of enjoyment even though living such a life makes him deeply unhappy. The second book is written by a decent and upright family man who is serious and stable and has a good job (he's a judge!), and in every way is thoroughly respectable. This fine citizen argues in favor of the ethical form of life that he lives, and his argument is further strengthened by the fact that he is very happy and fulfilled living this life. So the very simple title announces to the reader the very simple choice that we all must make: *Either* live a degenerate and shameful life dedicated to aesthetic pleasure, which will leave you feeling extremely unhappy, *Or* live an honorable, respectable and truly fulfilling life of ethics. That's the choice the book places before us, and it's obviously a very easy and simple choice to make![32]

With all due respect to this very confident interpreter of *Either/Or*—who probably speaks for almost everyone who has ever given the book any thought at all—I humbly disagree! In this chapter I will argue that the Queen of Denmark was right: *Either/Or* is not as simple and straightforward as it seems, and her reconstruction of the title was also very insightful because the choice that the book presents isn't a simple exclusive disjunction, it's more like a messier and murkier inclusive disjunction, and therefore *Either and Or* would actually be a better, more accurate title for the book. I will focus on two ways in which *Either/Or* reveals itself to be more of a conjunction than a disjunction. The disjunctive reading of *Either/Or* proclaimed by almost all interpreters of the book rests on the assumption that there are fundamental differences between Part I and Part II and therefore the two parts of the book are disconnected and disjoined and have nothing in common; but there are at least two forms of continuity between Part I and Part II, two ways in which the two parts of the book are connected and continuous, conjoined rather than disjoined:

> (1) All the characters in the book are nihilists who are deeply in love with their nihilism. Though these characters represent different forms of life (aesthetic, ethical, and religious), they all find great pleasure in living their lives nihilistically.
>
> (2) The whole book is a comedy from beginning to end, and therefore great fun to read when this comedy is recognized. The comedy in Part I has been widely recognized, but the comedy in Part II has been almost entirely overlooked—a very unfortunate oversight that I will try to correct by demonstrating that B is just as comical as A, and also just as much of a nihilist.

These two conjunctions establish continuity between Parts I and II and they reveal that the choice that *Either/Or* presents to readers is actually a choice between several different forms of nihilism embodied by several different nihilists, all of which are equally comical and equally pleased with themselves. These are surprising results in a book that claims to have no results (*EOI* 12), and they are valuable results because of the insights into nihilism and comedy that they provide. In this chapter I will explore both of these conjunctions and thereby hopefully persuade you that the Queen of Denmark was onto something when she called the book *Either and Or*.

But before exploring these two conjunctions, and the many forms of nihilism and comedy that are performed in *Either/Or*, we should first take a moment to consider the very strange and elaborate opening act that starts the whole show and sets the stage for everything that follows.

The opening act: Victor Eremita warms up the audience with a bizarre love story, and also gives us several important clues for understanding the book

The preface to *Either/Or* is many things, but first and foremost it's a love story about a man who falls in love with a desk. For weeks Victor Eremita has been gazing longingly at a writing desk in the window of a secondhand shop. To justify the purchase of a piece of furniture that he doesn't need and can't afford he deploys a rationalization that is itself quite a work of art. "This is the last time you are going to be so prodigal," he tells himself.

"In fact, it is really lucky that you did buy it, for every time you look at it you will be reminded how prodigal you were; with this desk commences a new period in your life" (*EOI* 5). After bringing his beloved desk home a honeymoon period ensues. "[J]ust as in the first phase of my infatuation I had my pleasure in gazing at it from the street, so now I walked by it here at home. Gradually I learned to know its numerous features, its many drawers and compartments, and in every respect I was happy with my desk" (*EOI* 5). But the romance doesn't last forever and as in most relationships the cause of the conflict is money. Victor needs cash for a trip to the country but the desk won't give him any—the money drawer will not open, and this makes him so furious that he delivers a terrible blow to the desk with a hatchet. This does nothing to open the money drawer, but it does open a secret compartment containing the papers that make up the text of *Either/Or*. Victor Eremita writes that the whole experience confirmed his long-standing suspicion that we should "doubt somewhat the accuracy of that familiar philosophical thesis that the outer is the inner and the inner is the outer" (*EOI* 3, see also *EOI* 6).

Victor's hard-won lesson is one we should keep in mind as we try to make sense of *Either/Or*. Just as the desk confirmed his suspicion that the outer and the inner are not always aligned, the papers within the desk may also support the same thesis. Victor tells us that he found "a marked external difference" (*EOI* 6–7) in the papers that allowed him to organize them into two groups, and there also seemed to be differences in the papers's internal content that corresponded to the external differences, with the first group of papers containing aesthetic essays while the second group contained nothing but "ethical content, it seemed" (*EOI* 7). However, he also makes it clear that he has learned nothing about the authors themselves and has been unable to track them down after many years of trying (*EOI* 11–12). He can't even rule out the possibility that both sets of papers were written by the same person, and he even finds himself quite persuaded by this thought. If this were the case, he notes, the papers would certainly "take on a new aspect" (*EOI* 13).[133] The possibility that two distinct persons, who believe that they are radically different—even polar opposites—could in fact be conceptual twins, is a truly intriguing possibility, so I am grateful to Victor Eremita for suggesting it, and I will enthusiastically explore this possibility later in this chapter

Victor Eremita also tells us that he had the single author theory in mind when he chose the title *Either/Or*, and this suggests that we should understand the title not as an exclusive disjunction with fundamentally different and irreconcilable alternatives, but rather as a very resigned inclusive disjunction which means to inform us that there is no essential difference between these two forms of life, and so effectively we have something very close to a conjunction: it's possible that both A and B are essentially the same, so if you choose one or the other there's no essential difference. (Again it seems like the Queen of Denmark actually understood the book quite well, in spite of her protestations to the contrary.) This is another intriguing possibility that I will explore further later in this chapter.

Before we leave behind Victor Eremita's warm-up act in the preface we should also note his editorial impact on *Either/Or* as a whole. He not only gave the book its title, he's also responsible for many of the titles assigned to particular sections of the text (including both of the letters of B in Part II) and for the order in which each section appears. He claims to have found a logical sequence for the letters and the Ultimatum in Part II, and he also thinks the titles he assigned to the letters make sense, but he freely admits that he may have gotten all of this completely wrong (*EOI* 10–11). Victor Eremita, the Victorious Hermit, was the first reader of these chaotic papers, and also the first person who tried to impose some order and discipline on them. We should not feel any obligation to regard the structure he chose for the book as (ahem) authoritative or definitive. His editorial interventions reflect the panic that almost everyone feels when encountering one of Kierkegaard's unruly pseudonymous books: we feel compelled to impose some organization on the text immediately, to clothe it with some vestige of dignity and respectability—as if we had just found this poor befuddled book wandering about outside completely naked, absentmindedly forgetting to get dressed before leaving the house.

In summary, Victor Eremita's preface calls our attention to three important facts about the strange collection of papers that he discovered in a secret drawer when he attacked his beloved desk with a hatchet—facts we should keep in mind as we consider the rest of the book:

- Because this book begins with a story about a man who falls in love with a piece of furniture, it seems appropriate to suspect that it might harbor some comic aspirations. Taking any of the assorted pseudonymous authors of such a text at their word, as if they were nothing but honest and sober journalists intent only on reporting the facts and the unvarnished truth, seems like a big mistake. Perhaps it makes more sense to understand all the authors in this book as comedians who are intent on concealing and also revealing their deeper meaning with humor.

- In this book "one author becomes enclosed within the other like the boxes in a Chinese puzzle" (*EOI* 9). "Thus, when the book is read, A and B are forgotten; only the points of view confront each other" (*EOI*

14). We don't really know who these authors are or even, in a sense, how many authors there are, since there remains the distinct possibility that what seem to be two points of view may actually be a single point of view embodied in a single conceptual persona.

- The book that Victor Eremita passed along to us has already had an order imposed upon it by the editor, which may only serve to further confuse and conceal its true meaning. We should be wary of the interpretations already inscribed on this text by its editor (and this should also remind us to be wary of our own impulse to look for an authority within any of Kierkegaard's pseudonymous texts, since the only authors we find there are all purely imaginary *conceptual personae*).

And now let the comedy commence! The first conjunction: All the characters in this book are nihilists, and they are very happy being nihilists—very much in love with their nihilism

There are four philosophical characters in *Either/Or* (1) A, the author of all the papers collected in Part I except for the final text of that volume (he is also sometimes called "The Young Man" or "The Aesthete" but I will generally just refer to him as A); (2) Johannes the Seducer, the author of the final text in Part I—"The Seducer's Diary"—which A hurriedly copies after finding it unguarded on Johannes's writing desk; (3) B, the author of all the papers collected in Part II except for the final text of that volume (he is also sometimes called "Judge Wilhelm" but again I will generally just refer to him as B); (4) B's friend, the Stocky Little Pastor, who is the author of the final text of Part II, an unpublished sermon called "The Upbuilding That Lies in the Thought That in Relation to God We Are Always in the Wrong." B decides that this sermon should be the "Ultimatum" in Part II. (I'm not including Victor Eremita in this list because he's not a philosophical character, though he is definitely a character. The story he tells in the preface is very entertaining, and he gives us some very useful information about the editorial decisions he made as he prepared the papers for publication, but he refrains from telling us any more about his own thinking; so he provides us with something of an editorial philosophy for the book but no account of the philosophy that has guided his own life. True to his name he withdraws, victorious and hermit-like, back to his own house, where presumably new chapters in the unfolding story of his complicated relationship with his writing desk continued to unfold.)[134] So we are left with four philosophical characters who each provide us with a philosophy of life, and I will argue that all four of them are very happy nihilists.

That the two characters in Part I—A and Johannes the Seducer—are both nihilists is widely accepted, so I won't spend much time arguing unnecessarily for that conclusion. However, understanding the two characters in Part II as nihilists—B and his friend the Stocky Little Pastor—is a much more unorthodox conclusion that will require a more detailed argument. Once the nihilism of all four characters has been established I'll argue that they are all deeply in love with their nihilism, which is also an unusual claim that will require some argument.

A and Johannes the Seducer are nihilists

A makes no secret of his nihilism. He declares it openly right out of the gate in the very first lines of Part I—the quotation he chooses to set the stage for the "Diapsalmata":

> Greatness, knowledge, renown,
> Friendship, pleasure and possessions,
> All is only wind, only smoke:
> To say it better, all is nothing. (*EOI* 18)

A few pages later in the "Diapsalmata" A writes,

> How empty and meaningless life is.—We bury a man; we accompany him to the grave, throw three spadefuls of earth on him; we ride out in a carriage, ride home in a carriage; we find consolation in the thought that we have a long life ahead of us. But how long is seven times ten years? Why not settle it all at once, why not stay out there and go along down into the grave, and draw lots to see to whom will befall the misfortune of being the last of the living who throws the last three spadefuls of earth on the last of the dead? (*EOI* 29)

And this is just the beginning. One reason *Either/Or* Part I is famous for its comedy is because A proclaims his nihilism so explicitly, thoroughly, and systematically, as if he were announcing to the world a revolutionary discovery that had never occurred to anyone else. He's clearly capable of expressing these ideas very succinctly, as he did in the passages above, but instead he chooses to prepare and deliver three wordy and exhaustive discourses on the themes of tragedy, grief, and unhappiness to his club: the Fellowship of the Dead (*EOI* 137–230); he writes a review of a one-act play that is much longer than the play itself (A231–79); he writes a very long-winded parody of contemporary aesthetic theory that begins with an insignificant introduction and concludes with an insignificant postlude (*EOI* 45–135); he constructs an elaborate "theory of social prudence" called "The Rotation of Crops" that is meant to solve what he considers the greatest problem facing mankind: boredom (*EOI* 281–300).[135] Clearly A is a very verbose and enthusiastic nihilist. He's something like an evangelist for nihilism: he loves to preach this gospel.

Though A proclaims his own nihilism with endless enthusiasm, he still claims to be shocked by the manuscript that he found in the unlocked writing desk of the man he calls Johannes the Seducer.[136] But he also finds it irresistible.[137] He hastily makes his own transcript of this scandalous text, and later he studies and comments on it at length. Like Victor Eremita he makes himself the editor of someone else's writing, but in this case the writing is stolen rather than found and A knows exactly who the author is. Johannes had innocently and casually labeled his manuscript "*Commentarius Perpetuus No. 4*, as if it were nothing more than the latest collection of field notes from an ongoing and perfectly normal research project, but A assigns it a far more spectacular and salacious title: "The Seducer's Diary."

A claims that he was so stunned when he first read this diary that he nearly fainted (*EOI* 304), but he recognizes that the text brings to life the very same ideas that he himself expressed in his own writing. "The Seducer's Diary" is the concrete manifestation of the abstract ideas that A himself advocated, most notably in his essay, "The Rotation of Crops." Johannes simply takes seriously A's own philosophy. He enacts A's own aesthetic theory of existence, which A himself has acknowledged is nihilistic. For this reason A thinks of Johannes as an actor on a stage behind the stage where his own life is performed:

> Behind the world in which we live, far in the background, lies another world, and the two have about the same relation to each other as do the stage proper and the stage one sometimes sees behind it in the theatre. Through a hanging of fine gauze, one sees, as it were, a world of gauze, lighter, more ethereal, with a quality different from that of the actual world. Many people who appear physically in the actual world are not at home in it but are at home in that other world. . . . The latter was the case with this man. . . . He did not belong to the world of actuality, and yet he had very much to do with it. He continually ran lightly over it, but even when he most abandoned himself to it, he was beyond it. (*EOI* 306)

Since A has loudly and repeatedly proclaimed himself to be a nihilist, and A immediately recognizes Johannes as someone who has scrupulously put into practice the principles and methods that he himself advocated—someone who has carefully followed the script that A composed—then Johannes is obviously a nihilist as well.

B and his friend the Stocky Little Pastor are nihilists

A flat out tells us that he's a nihilist, and since we recognize A's rotation method in the "Diary of a Seducer" it's easy to recognize Johannes the Seducer as a nihilist as well. However, it's more of a challenge to understand B and his friend, the Stocky Little Pastor, as nihilists. They claim to be just the opposite, but there is abundant evidence in the text that we should not take this claim seriously.

To see this we first have to remind ourselves of a few important details concerning how Victor Eremita edited the papers of B. Please recall that Victor Eremita told us that even though he found internal and external differences in the papers that he thought justified him in organizing them into two groups (*EOI* 6–7), he also recognized that he couldn't rule out the possibility that both sets of papers were written by the same person and he even found himself quite persuaded by this thought. If this were the case, he notes, the papers would certainly "take on a new aspect" (*EOI* 13). I promised to explore this fascinating possibility later on, and now that time has arrived!

Perhaps Victor Eremita meant to suggest that A and B are literally the same person, meaning they share the same consciousness and the same body. This would certainly make for a spectacular ending, à la *Fight Club*, if *Either/Or* is ever made into a movie; but a far more interesting albeit less spectacular possibility is that A and B are distinct individuals with distinct lives but are still the same conceptual persona. This is the reading that I'll argue for: that the texts of A and B provide us with two different aspects of a single conceptual persona: a nihilist who denies that humans can create meaning and value in existence. A demonstrates how aesthetics can be employed in the service of nihilism, and B shows us how the same thing can be accomplished with ethics. Victor Eremita tells us that he had the single author theory in mind when he chose the title *Either/Or* (*EOI* 13), which suggests that we should understand the title not as an exclusive disjunction with fundamentally different and irreconcilable alternatives, but rather as an inclusive disjunction or even as a conjunction—just as the Queen of Denmark suggested.

Please recall also that Victor Eremita not only gave the book as a whole its title, he's also responsible for many of the titles assigned to particular chapters and essays in the book (including all of the letters of B assembled in Part II) and for the order in which each essay appears. He claims to have found a logical order for the contents of Part II, and he also thinks that the titles he assigned to the letters in Part II make sense, but he freely admits that he may have gotten both of these wrong (*EOI* 10–11). Once we recognize that there's nothing necessary about the order of the texts in Part II many interesting possibilities emerge. If we simply reverse the order that Victor Eremita selected B's character as a nihilist becomes much more apparent, so I propose that we start at the end of Part II and read that volume backward.[138]

If we start with the "Ultimatum" at the end of Part II we get an astoundingly direct, succinct, and unambiguous statement of what *Either/Or* Part II is all about, and also the principles that B stands for. Because B is well aware that his two letters are dense and heavy in every possible sense (if he actually mailed these enormous letters, he says, the postage would be very expensive [*EOII* 5]), he fully expects that by the time the reader has finished reading his two very long letters she will have forgotten most of the contents "just as I have" (*EOII* 337). So he appends a helpful summary of his letters in the form of another short text (just fourteen pages) that he didn't write. B chooses the brief undelivered sermon of his friend, the Stocky Little Pastor, to summarize his own very lengthy and rambling letters (which even he has forgotten), and he heartily endorses this text with these words: "In this sermon he has grasped what I have said and what I would like to have said to you; he has expressed it better than I am able to" (*EOII* 338). Just as Part I ends with A recognizing that another author's writing clarifies the meaning of his own words and theories, Part II ends with B doing the same.[139] Later in this chapter I will argue that if you do make the effort to analyze exactly what B writes in his two extremely long letters you discover inconsistencies and contradictions that make the letters quite comical, but before we get to those details we should first give thanks that B has made it so much easier to understand the overall essence and spirit of his ideas by appending this additional short text by his less-long-winded friend and informing us that this short and straightforward sermon of just fourteen pages summarizes all the most important and essential ideas contained in his own 327 pages of excessive and exorbitant paternal exhortation.[140]

The sermon from B's stocky little friend presents a version of religion which is summarized very precisely and succinctly by its title: "In Relation to God We Are Always in the Wrong." Here are the core principles of this version of religion:

(1) It's impossible for humans to figure out what's good for them, and they should not even try because they will always be wrong. (*EOII* 341) Values are simply beyond us; we can't begin to comprehend them. We will always need someone to tell us what to do because we cannot determine for ourselves what is valuable without tumbling into an unstoppable infinite regress.

> If a person is sometimes in the right, sometimes in the wrong, to some degree in the right, to some degree in the wrong, who, then, is the one who makes that decision except the person himself, but in the decision may he not again be to some degree in the right and to some degree in the wrong? Or is he a different person when he judges his act than when he acts? Is doubt to rule, then, continually to discover new difficulties, and is care to accompany the anguished soul and drum past experiences into it? Or would we prefer continually to be in the right in the way irrational creatures are? Then we have only the choice between being nothing in relation to God or having to begin all over again every moment in eternal torment, yet without being able to begin, for if we are able to decide definitely whether we are in the right at the present moment, then this question must be decided definitely with regard to the previous moment, and so on further and further back. (*EOII* 346)

(2) God treats humans as a single group, not as individuals, so everyone should give up all their striving to be an individual (*EOII* 342). God cares so little for individuals that he doesn't hesitate to punish entire generations when they offend him—and also the children, and the children's children of those generations—and to expect otherwise is "dismal" and "cowardly" (*EOII* 343).

> Do you think, Christ says, that those Galileans whose blood Pilate let be shed were worse sinners than all the other Galileans because they suffered this? Or the eighteen whom the tower in Siloam fell upon and killed, do you think that they were worse offenders than all the others who lived in Jerusalem? Consequently some of those Galileans were not worse sinners than other people, those eighteen were not more guilty than everybody else who lived in Jerusalem—and yet the innocent shared the same fate as the guilty. (*EOII* 343)

(3) The only way to be happy is to resign yourself to the facts summarized above. This thought is upbuilding and calming; it allows you to live

your life as the Stocky Little Pastor lives his: content to "let things take their course" (*EOII* 337). If you resist this counsel and insist in taking responsibility for your own life you will be gripped by a terrible overwhelming anxiety, which he describes with these words:

> [D]id not a terrible anxiety seize you when the thought could momentarily arise in your soul that you could be in the right, that God's governance was not wisdom but your plans were, that God's thoughts were not righteousness but your deeds were, that God's heart was not love but your feelings were? . . . Therefore this thought, that in relation to God we are always in the wrong, is an upbuilding thought; it is upbuilding that we are in the wrong, upbuilding that we are always in the wrong. It manifests its upbuilding power in a twofold way, partly by putting an end to doubt and calming the cares of doubt, partly by animating to action. (*EOII* 351)

According to this theory of religion, trying to figure out how to live is utterly futile. Such an effort will produce nothing but anxiety and unhappiness, and in the end you will always be wrong—so why bother? As the Stocky Little Pastor informed us right in the title of his undelivered sermon: in relation to God we are always in the wrong.

This is a stunningly concise and comprehensive nihilistic theory. It maintains that humans are incapable of creating their own values or even understanding what is good or bad for them. According to this theory, all we can do, and should do, is make ourselves blindly obedient members of a herd, since we are incapable of making our own lives meaningful and since individuality is simply an empty and meaningless illusion. B's friend, the Stocky Little Pastor, presents this nihilistic theory in the form of a sermon and so for him it is a theory of religion, but B says very clearly that his friend's sermon expresses all that he himself said and all that he wanted to say in his own account of ethics, and we should take that seriously as B himself clearly does since he has made this text the last word in Part II and has urged us to accept it as the summation of everything that he expressed much more verbosely in his two long letters. So what can we say about B's ethical principles now? B told us in his letters that he was presenting a theory of ethics and arguing for the superiority of an ethical life. Since B concludes by telling us that the Stocky Little Pastor has expressed "what I have said and what I would like to have said to you; he has expressed it better than I am able to" (*EOII* 338), we are justified in transposing the Stocky Little Pastor's nihilistic religious theory into a nihilistic ethical theory built around the same core principles. The foundational principles of such an ethical theory would be:

(1) It's impossible for humans to figure out what's good for them and they should not even try because they will always be wrong. Values are simply beyond us; we can't begin to create them or even comprehend them. We will always need someone to tell us what to do because we cannot think or create for ourselves.

(2) Individuals do not matter, only collectives or groups are important, so we should all give up our striving to be individuals.

(3) The only way to be happy is to resign yourself to the facts summarized above. This thought is upbuilding and calming and makes for a peaceful life. The alternative is a wasted life of anxiety and utterly futile striving.

Both B and his friend the Stocky Little Pastor have endorsed and embraced an impressively unambiguous and thorough nihilistic theory of human existence. Both of them deny that humans are capable of giving meaning and value to their own lives: the Stocky Little Pastor expresses this point of view from the perspective of religion, and B expresses the same conclusions from the perspective of ethics. There is more evidence within the two very long (and very boring) letters that B wrote (and then forgot about) that his approach to ethics is just another mask for nihilism, and I will explore that evidence later in this chapter, but already at this point in our backward reading of Part II we have enough evidence to conclude that both B and his friend the Stocky Little Pastor are nihilists since B has explicitly connected his own thinking to that of his friend.[141] If we take seriously the authority that B assigns to the "Ultimatum" in Part II we really can't conclude otherwise even before we begin reading B's two long letters in detail; this is one of the great values of reading part II backwards.[142]

All of these characters are deeply in love with their nihilism

On this point there is an interesting reversal: whereas it was A who declared freely and frankly that he is a nihilist, while the three other characters lied about it (or at least—in the case of Johannes the Seducer—didn't talk about it openly), the inverse is the case here. Johannes the Seducer, B, and B's friend the Stocky Little Pastor all tell us they are very happy, and there is no reason to doubt them. A, on the other hand, claims to be miserable, but there are good reasons to be suspicious of this claim. So I'll proceed in reverse order again, saving the discussion of A until the end (though even in A's case it won't take much to show that he does in fact take great pleasure in his nihilistic life, just like the other three characters).

B describes his friend the pastor as "a stocky little fellow, lively, cheerful, and unusually jovial" (*EOII* 337). Though he was somewhat disappointed to be assigned to a rural parish, by now "he has regained his contentment" (*EOII* 338). He loves his life and he loves his job. He's very proud of the sermon he has written, which informs his parishioners that in relation to God they will always be in the wrong (*EOII* 338). In short, though the Stocky Little Pastor lives according to a thoroughly and profoundly nihilistic worldview, he is very happy with his life.

B proclaims his own happiness just as loudly and excessively as A proclaims his nihilism, and in both cases there is no reason not to believe them. Later on I'll argue that there is a comical gulf between the ideals and aspirations that B brings to his marriage and the actual ethical practice that B prescribes for his marriage (and all other marriages), but this doesn't change the fact that he is, as he claims, a very happily married man. He's also obviously quite happy with his job as a judge, and his position in the world, and the opportunities they afford him to write documents so excessively long that no one could be expected to remember what is in them (*EOII* 337). So B, like his friend the Stocky Little Pastor, is quite content with his life; another very happy nihilist

Johannes the Seducer, like B and his friend the Stocky Little Pastor, is also very happy with his profession, which happens to be seducing young girls. In his *Commentarius Perpetuus No. 4* he appears to have perfected A's crop rotation method, and he seems to have accomplished the number one objective of that particular discipline: avoiding boredom. A remarks that Johannes has attained "truly aesthetic, objective mastery or himself and the situation" (*EOI* 304). "His life has been an attempt to accomplish the task of living poetically. With a sharply developed organ for discovering the interesting in life, he has known how to find it and after having found it has continually reproduced his experiences half poetically" (*EOI* 304). In short, he loves his job and he's very good at it. He's living exactly the life he wants to live and finding great pleasure in it.

A, on the other hand, claims to be miserable; however, all his actions belie this claim. A preaches the gospel of nihilism with such energy and enthusiasm that it's impossible to imagine him unhappy. The same man who claims that life can have no purpose still finds plenty to do in proclaiming this doctrine. He writes long speeches and delivers them at his club: The Fellowship of the Dead (which also seems like a pretty happy group). He reviews books, plays, and music[143] and composes elaborate theories concerning how to avoid ever getting bored. Though he claims to be depressed, he also says that he loves his depression (*EOI* 20), just as he loves his sorrow (*EOI* 21, 33). The most famous entry in the "Diapsalmata" is subtitled "An

Ecstatic Discourse," and A is clearly enjoying himself when he proclaims the principles of this impious and irreverent parody of the Hegelian dialectic. This text is so often cited as evidence that A is unhappy, because (apparently) he regrets everything; but if you consider the complete text of this long, uninterrupted paragraph and not just the opening fusillade about how everything is regretful, it's clear that A is actually enjoying himself immensely as he delivers his Ecstatic Discourse:

> Marry, and you will regret it. Do not marry, and you will also regret it. Marry or do not marry, you will regret it either way. Whether you marry or you do not marry, you will regret it either way. Laugh at the stupidities of the world, and you will regret it; weep over them, and you will also regret it. Laugh at the stupidities of the world or weep over them, you will regret it either way. Whether you laugh at the stupidities of the world or you weep over them, you will regret it either way. Trust a girl, and you will regret it. Do not trust her, and you will also regret it. Trust a girl or do not trust her, you will regret it either way. Whether you trust a girl or do not trust her, you will regret it either way. Hang yourself, and you will regret it. Do not hang yourself, and you will also regret it. Hang yourself or do not hang yourself, you will regret it either way. Whether you hang yourself or do not hang yourself, you will regret it either way. This, gentlemen, is the quintessence of all the wisdom of life. It is not merely in isolated moments that I, as Spinoza says, view everything *aeterno modo*, but I am continually *aeterno modo*. Many believe they, too, are this when after doing one thing or another they unite or mediate these opposites. But this is a misunderstanding, for the true eternity does not lie behind either/or but before it. Their eternity will therefore also be a painful temporal sequence, since they will have a double regret on which to live. My wisdom is easy to grasp, for I have only one maxim, and even that is not a point of departure for me. One must differentiate between the subsequent dialectic in either/or and the eternal one suggested here. So when I say that my maxim is not a point of departure for me, this does not have the opposite of being a point of departure but is merely the negative expression of my maxim, that by which it comprehends itself in contrast to being a point of departure or not being a point of departure. My maxim is not a point of departure for me, because if I made it a point of departure, I would regret it, and if I did not make it a point of departure, I would also regret it. If one or another of my esteemed listeners thinks there is anything to what I have said, he merely demonstrates that he has no

> head for philosophy. If he thinks there is any movement in what has been said, this demonstrates the same thing. But for those listeners who are able to follow me, although I do not move, I shall now elucidate the eternal truth by which this philosophy is self-contained and does not concede anything higher. That is, if I made my maxim a point of departure, then I would be unable to stop, for if I did not stop, I would regret it, and if I did stop, I would also regret it, etc. But if I never start, then I can always stop, for my eternal starting is my eternal stopping. Experience shows that it is not at all difficult for philosophy to begin. Far from it. It begins, in fact, with nothing and therefore can always begin. But it is always difficult for philosophy and philosophers to stop. This difficulty, too, I have avoided, for if anyone thinks that I, in stopping now, actually stop, he demonstrates that he does not have speculative comprehension. The point is that I do not stop now, but I stopped when I began. My philosophy, therefore, has the advantageous characteristic of being brief and of being irrefutable, for if anyone disputes me, I daresay I have the right to declare him mad. The philosopher, then, is continually *aeterno modo* and does not have, as did the blessed Sintenis, only specific hours that are lived for eternity. (*EOI* 39–40)

It's also worth noting that though the "Diapsalmata" seems to overflow with expressions of despair, the last word in this section of the book suggests that A finds all of it hilarious, and is enjoying the show that he is putting on immensely:

> Something marvelous has happened to me. I was transported to the seventh heaven. There sat all the gods assembled. As a special dispensation, I was granted the favor of making a wish. "What do you want," asked Mercury. "Do you want youth, or beauty, or power, or a long life, or the most beautiful girl, or any one of the other glorious things we have in the treasure chest? Choose—but only one thing." For a moment I was bewildered; then I addressed the gods, saying: My esteemed contemporaries, I choose one thing—that I may always have the laughter on my side. Not one of the gods said a word; instead, all of them began to laugh. From that I concluded that my wish was granted and decided that the gods knew how to express themselves with good taste, for it would indeed have been inappropriate to reply solemnly: It is granted to you. (*EOI* 42–43)

A is laughing as he proclaims his nihilistic gospel, not crying. He too loves his nihilism deeply; he too is a very happy nihilist.[144]

This completes my argument for the first conjunction that connects Parts I and II of *Either/Or:* that all the characters in the book are nihilists who are deeply in love with their nihilism. Though these characters all represent different forms of life (aesthetic, ethical, and religious), they all find great pleasure in living their lives nihilistically.

The second conjunction: *Either/Or* is a comedy from beginning to end, and therefore great fun to read when that comedy is recognized

I don't think there's any controversy about Part I being comical, and also enormous fun to read.[145] There's a long history of reading A's many nihilistic theories, case studies and rants, and also the "Diary of a Seducer," as works of comedy. Perhaps the only impediment to such a reading is the thought that some readers might have that A and Johannes the Seducer are unhappy (as A especially insists) and therefore Part I should be read as the tragic record of two lost and unhappy souls. But as I just argued, there is abundant evidence that both Johannes and A are in fact very happy nihilists and A's claim to be unhappy is just part of his aesthetic performance and should not be taken seriously. So rather than waste time arguing that Part I is comical (a conclusion that seems quite obvious to almost everyone) I will instead focus on demonstrating that Part II is just as much of a comedy as Part I.

Most honest readers will confess that they find Part II of *Either/Or* to be a very boring book—perhaps even one of the most boring books in the entire history of philosophy (which is certainly saying something).[146] B's two letters, which are respectively 150 and 177 pages long (in the English translation by the Hongs) contain so many ideas, arguments, stories, anecdotes, parables, exhortations, and attempts (though not always successful) at jokes that it is quite difficult to sort through everything that is there, and B himself acknowledges that the letters are so verbose and tedious that even he feels punch drunk by the time he reaches the end of this 327-page epistolary slog and can't remember much of the journey, so dense and admittedly dull it was. It's easy to see the comedy in Part I because it's so easy to laugh at A when he wears his nihilism on his sleeve and complains about how unfair the world is like a petulant child while at the same time displaying many telltale signs that he's actually enjoying his nihilistic life very much. B, on the other hand, is trying very hard to be the responsible adult in the room, and this is proven by the fact that he is extremely boring. But most readers accept that Part II is so boring as a necessary, unavoidable consequence of the fact that the discussion it contains is so serious. Typically the justification goes something like this: To respond to the sarcastic nihilism of A that was so plainly evident in Part I, B really has no choice but to write in a paternal and ponderous way as he defends "The Aesthetic Validity of Marriage" and "The Balance of the Aesthetic and the Ethical in the Development of the Personality." These profoundly serious topics have been belittled and dismissed by A, so it's understandable that the Judge must present something like an exhaustive legal argument to defend the honor of these ethical institutions. Thus, the story goes, it's not surprising that Part II is boring—really we had no right to expect otherwise—but it's our duty to slog through the boring parts and to look beyond the book's soporific style to appreciate the sober and serious truths that it contains.

One consequence of this style of reading Part II is that most readers have regarded B as a sort of stock figure or caricature: a father figure who is ready to offer exhortation and advice anytime and anyplace and can talk everyone else right under the table. We know what such a stock figure will say, and we also are not surprised that what he has to say is extremely long-winded and boring; but we know that he means well so we forgive him for this. We do not, however, feel the need to pay close attention to everything that such a caricature says when he lectures us about ethics given how predictable and dull we rightly expect this lecture to be. The experience of reading B's two long letters feels like being beaten slowly over the head with a broomstick, and so most readers just close their eyes and submit to the firehose of paternal advice B directs at them without paying careful attention to the contents. The enormous quantity of ideas, arguments, stories, anecdotes, parables, exhortations, and attempted jokes in the 327 pages that constitute B's two very long letters is so vast that it truly is quite difficult to sort through everything that is there. These 327 pages provide us with a remarkable example of why the *argumentum ad nauseam* works so well: the reader is simply worn down and exhausted by the seemingly endless stream of words. The fact that we're aware from the outset that B is defending a position that we know we ought to agree with—that an ethical life is superior to a life dedicated to the single-minded pursuit of pleasure—also contributes to the soporific success of these 327 pages, because this understanding causes most readers to drop their guards immediately. There doesn't seem to be any reason to be suspicious of a middle-aged judge who is defending the honor of an ethical life, and the fact that this judge chooses to do so in an extremely long-winded way doesn't even seem particularly surprising. So most readers very quickly stop paying close attention to what B writes in his two long letters and just allow themselves to be carried along in the slow and meandering current of B's many, many words.[147]

One of the great advantages of reading Part II backwards is that we discover immediately that B—just like the other three philosophical characters in this book—is a nihilist since the theory presented as the ultimatum to Part II by the Stocky Little Pastor is blatantly nihilistic and B says that he agrees with this theory completely. "In case you've forgotten everything I wrote in those very long letters, as I myself have" (B tells us) "all you really need to know is this: my friend the Stocky Little Pastor 'has grasped what I have said and what I would like to have said to you; he has expressed it better than I am able to'" (*EOII* 338). Knowing this puts us in a position to read B's two long letters not with an attitude of resignation, hoping only to stay awake and survive until the end, but instead with an attitude of justified suspicion. How is it possible for a nihilist to write 327 pages in defense of ethics? What is really going on in this 327-page ethical manifesto that allows it to conceal B's underlying nihilism from almost everyone, including (apparently) B himself? Now we have a good reason to stay awake and pay attention to all of B's words. If B is in fact a nihilist he has managed to construct a very elaborate mask for himself in these letters by making himself into the spokesperson for ethics, the defender of ethical theory and practice, and this calls for a very attentive, suspicious reading of his letters.

Fortunately a wide awake, attentive, and suspicious reading of B's long letters is rewarded by the discovery of some excellent moments of comedy. B is actually just as funny as A—in fact, I would argue that B is even funnier because while A did not take himself seriously at all, B most certainly does. To appreciate B as a comedian we have to peel away the many layers of pious conventionality and respectability that he wears as a mask. A wears no mask in Part I as he demonstrates, with obvious humor, how nihilism can be derived from aesthetics. But while aesthetics openly embraces comedy and is agnostic regarding nihilism, ethics is supposed to be allergic to both comedy and nihilism, so B's comedy and his nihilism must be hidden under layers of apparent solemnity and seriousness.

Victor Eremita has given B's two letters (which comprise all of Part II except the "Ultimatum" by the Stocky Little Pastor) the titles "The Aesthetic Validity of Marriage" and "The Balance between the Aesthetic and the Ethical in the Development of the Personality." These titles are Victor Eremita's creations and they may not accurately reflect the actual contents of the letters at all, so we should not let them predetermine our interpretation of the letters. Victor Eremita also chose the order of these letters and may have gotten that order completely wrong—as he freely admits—so there's no reason we have to respect the order that he chose. Reading Part II backwards is, once again, enormously helpful in clarifying what's really happening in this strange philosophy book. There are fundamental contradictions in B's letters, and it's easiest to see these contradictions when the letters are read backwards. As Socrates demonstrated, contradictions are hilarious, and they are also potentially the beginning of wisdom since they are the animating force behind *reductio ad absurdum* arguments that clarify mistakes in assumptions so that those mistakes can be corrected. (Socrates made this opportunity available to his many interlocutors, of course, though most of them chose not to avail themselves of the privilege and instead opted to require Socrates to drink hemlock and die so that he would no longer bother them.) The contradictions in B's letters follow this same Socratic pattern: they are funny for sure, but more importantly that comedy gives us an opportunity to learn something important. While Part I of *Either/Or* has been widely recognized as a work of comedy, the purpose of which is to demonstrate that an aesthetic form of life can be nothing more than a thinly disguised form of nihilism, Part II has generally been read as a serious work that was meant to be the antidote to the unfortunate illness that was diagnosed in Part I. But this is a serious and unfortunate mistake. Part II is just as much of a comedy as Part I, and the purpose of this comedy is to show us another form of life which is actually nihilism in disguise.

A backwards reading of Part II reveals the contradictions in B's letters more readily and also clarifies that Part II is structured something like a three-act comedy with an epilogue.

- Act I is B's first letter, in which he summarizes his vision of ethics: what he wants an ethical life to be. Act I is a purely subjective statement of desire and not an argument.
- Act II is the first section of the second letter, which is an argument for an ethical theory that is capable of realizing the vision of ethics that B summarized in his first letter.
- Act III is the second section of the second letter, which presents an argument concerning ethical practice: B's account of what an ethical life looks like as it is actually lived.
- Finally the epilogue is the "Ultimatum" by B's friend the Stocky Little Pastor, a religious argument for the conclusion that "in relation to God we are always in the wrong" with which B says that his own ethical arguments agree completely and therefore he suggests that we use this ultimatum as a summary of his own views on ethics.

In the first two acts B is subjective and creative. He insists upon what he wants from an ethical life even if what he wants is unorthodox and even if empirical evidence suggests that it is improbable, and then he creates an ethical theory that explains how his vision of ethics can be realized. Then in Act III B embraces an account of ethical practice that effectively undermines everything that he declared he wanted and everything that he created in the first two acts, and in the epilogue he explicitly endorses a nihilistic worldview in which humans are incapable of creating any meaning or value for themselves and should stop trying. The contradictions that make Part II comical emerge from the contrast between the first two acts and the third act (plus the epilogue). Part II begins with an attempt to reconceptualize ethics in an innovative, affirmative, and creative way, and then it ends with a collapse into an ethical paradigm that is purely conventional and completely allergic to individuality and innovation. This particular narrative arc—beginning with innovation, idealism, and individuality and ending with a collapse under the weight of convention, conformity, and the challenge of being an individual—is not at all unusual on Planet Earth, but it is nevertheless always comical because of the contradictions inherent in it. The comedy that B performs for us in Part II demonstrates that ethics too can be a mask for nihilism just as easily as aesthetics, and also how easily individual idealism can be overwhelmed by the supposed authority of tradition and convention.

To see this comedy it's best to read Part II backwards, so I'll begin, once again, at the end of Part II with B's second letter.

B's Second Letter

B's second letter is very long (177 pages in the English translation), but it divides neatly into two distinct sections: a theory section (the first 109 pages, which functions as Act II in this three-act comedy), and a practice section (the remaining sixty-eight pages, which is Act III in the comedy). In the theory section many profound and beautiful ideas concerning the nature of ethics are presented and consequently these portions of the second letter have often been cited as the essence of B's ethical theory and the proof that it is vastly superior to A's aesthetic and nihilistic form of life. But this isn't the whole story of the second letter. Such a selective reading overlooks the fact that in the practice section of the letter (the final sixty-eight pages) all of these profound and beautiful ideas concerning ethics are undermined or flat out contradicted, resulting in a strange and comical conflict between theory and practice in B's account of ethics. It's easier to see the conflict, the contradiction, and the comedy if we read the second letter backwards and start with Act III—everything B writes about ethical practice in the final sixty-eight pages, and then go back to the beginning of the letter and read

Act II, which is B's ethical theory—whereupon the clash between theory and practice immediately becomes evident and the befuddled reader is led to exclaim: "This is certainly an awesome ethical theory, but it seems to have nothing in common with the account of ethical practice that I just read. Were these two sections written by the same author? And if so, were they meant to be a joke?"

B begins the practice section of his second letter right at the top of page 266 (in the Hong English translation) with these words:

> Here I shall cease my theorizing; I am well aware that I am not cut out for it, nor is that my ambition, but I shall be perfectly contented if I might be assumed to be a passable practitioner. Then, too, theorizing takes so much time; any act I can do in a moment or embark upon promptly involves a great deal of trouble and difficulty before it can be put into words or into writing. Now, it is not my intention to give you a lecture on a doctrine of duty so to speak according to custom about duties to God, oneself, and one's neighbor. Not that I would spurn this grouping or that what I would have to teach would be too profound to be joined to Balle's catechism or would presuppose much more previous knowledge than this catechism presupposes—not at all for those reasons, but because I believe that with the ethical it is not a matter of multiplicity but of its intensity. (*EOII* 266)

B then proceeds in the remaining sixty-eight pages to present what the intensity of ethical duty looks like not in theory, but in practice. As I've noted several times, and as B himself also acknowledges several times, B writes in a ponderous, plodding, pontificating style that causes readers to forget the contents of his letters as soon as they have finished reading them. So the weary reader who does make it to the finish line of the second letter, feeling like Pheidippides returning to Athens from Marathon, can certainly be forgiven for not noticing, but there is a natural progression in B's presentation of ethical practice with six distinct stages—and all of them are worth noting because they are quite comical when they are contrasted with B's ethical theory (Act II in this backwards reading), so I will summarize each of them briefly. I certainly don't want to be tedious, but I do think that a complete catalogue of B's account of ethical practice is essential for understanding the contradictions in B's letters, so here's a blow-by-blow account of all six of the stages that make up Act III in this three-act comedy:

(1)

In practice ethics is simply doing what you are told, following the rules (pp. 266–71). B begins his account of ethical practice with a fascinating and very revealing story. He explains that he can derive his entire ethical view of life from the experience of completing a homework assignment he was given as a five-year-old child.

> When a person has felt the intensity of duty with all his energy, then he is ethically matured, and then duty will break forth within him. The fundamental point, therefore, is not whether a person can count on his fingers how many duties he has, but that he has once and for all felt the intensity of duty in such a way that the consciousness of it is for him the assurance of the eternal validity of his being. . . . Let me illustrate what I mean by an example. To that end I select an impression I preserved from my earliest childhood. When I was five years old, I was sent to school. That such an event makes an impression on a child is natural, but the question is—what impression? Childish inquisitiveness is fascinated by all the bewildering ideas about what it may really mean. That this was also the case with me was to be expected; however the main impression I received was entirely different. I arrived at school; I was presented to the teacher and was given my assignment for the next day—the first ten lines in Balle's catechism, which I was to learn by heart. Every other impression was now erased from my soul; only my task stood vividly before it. . . . It seemed to me that heaven and earth would tumble down if I did not do my homework, and on the other hand it seemed to me that if heaven and earth did tumble down this upheaval would in no way excuse me from doing what had once been set before me—doing my homework. At that age I knew very little about my duties; I had not yet become acquainted with them in Balle's catechism. I had but one duty, to do my homework, and yet I can derive my whole ethical view of life from this impression. (*EOII* 266–67)

This story sets the stage for the entire account of ethical practice in Act III. The main theme of this account is that in practice ethics is simply figuring out what the rules are and then following them, and therefore ethics is basically the same as completing a homework assignment. Ethical rules are clear and precise and available to all, and any departure from the rules is unacceptable, so in practice the rules of ethics are very much like the rules of grammar.

> In my day, we studied Latin grammar with a rigor that is unknown today. From this instruction I received an impression that in a different way affected my soul similarly. Insofar as I dare attribute to myself any capacity for taking a philosophical view of things, I owe it to this impression from childhood. The unconditioned respect with which I regarded the rule, the veneration I felt for it, the contempt with which I looked down on the miserable life the exception endured, the to my eyes righteous way in which it was pursued in my exercise book and always stigmatized—what else is this but the distinction that is the basis of all philosophic reflection? (*EOII* 269)

As one might expect from a judge, Judge Wilhelm is a defender of the rule of law: a system of rules that apply to all, are always already in place, and require only our obedience. As soon as he begins discussing what living an ethical life means in practice he makes it clear immediately that it is first and foremost a life dedicated to following the rules: doing what you are told, whether you are a five-year-old completing your first homework assignment or a fifty-five-year-old judge following the rules dictated to you by convention and tradition. After clarifying this fact—that in practice an ethical life is just following the rules—there's nothing left for B to do in the remainder of the second letter but to illustrate some of the particular details of what such a life looks like in practice: "What is left now is to show how life looks when it is regarded ethically" (*EOII* 271). The five remaining sections of B's account of ethical practice are devoted to this work of illustration.

(2)

The first point that B wants to make to illustrate ethical practice is that an ethical life absorbs aesthetics and elevates it to a higher level (pp. 271–77). B presents this synthesis of aesthetics and ethics in the quasi-mystical language of Hegelian dialectic. It is not the case, B argues, that "the ethical is entirely different from the esthetic, and when it advances it completely annihilates the latter" (*EOII* 271). Instead there is a "metamorphosis" and "everything comes back again, but transfigured" (*EOII* 271).

> Therefore, it is not until I look at life ethically that I see it according to its beauty; not until I look at my own life ethically do I see it according to its beauty. If you say that this beauty is invisible, I shall reply: in one sense it is, in another, it is not; that is, it is visible in the footprints of the historical, visible in the sense in which one says: *Loquere, ut videam te*. It is certainly true that I

do not see the consummation but the struggle, but yet I also see the consummation at any moment I want to if I have the courage for it, and without courage I see nothing eternal at all, and consequently nothing beautiful either (*EOII* 275).

(3)

After arguing for the mystical synthesis of the aesthetic and the ethical B moves from this sublime and abstract topic to the concrete and utterly prosaic and mundane. To be more specific, B says, the ethical life looks like this: everyone needs to get a job (pp. 277–97). The reason for this is, to be blunt, because "money is and remains the absolute condition for living" (*EOII* 277). In the fifteen pages that follow B makes working for a living not just a mere fact of life or economic necessity but instead an essential demand of ethical practice.

> It is every person's duty to work for a living. Consequently, insofar as a person does not need to work, he is the exception, but to be an exception, as we agreed before, is not something great but inferior. If a person looks at the matter ethically he will look upon having money as a humiliation, for every preferential favor is a humiliation. (*EOII* 281)

> The question whether it is impossible to conceive of a world where it is unnecessary to work for a living is really a futile question since it does not have to do with the given actuality but a fictitious one. At the same time it is still always an attempt to disparage the ethical view. If it really were indeed a perfection in existence that one did not need to work, then the person who did not need this would have the most perfect life. Then one could say that it is a duty to work only in the sense that those words are understood to mean a dismal necessity. Then duty would not express the universally human but the ordinary, and here duty would not be the expression for the perfect. (*EOII* 281–82)

Such a world, B argues, is unacceptable. Getting a job is a duty that applies to everyone; it's one of the rules of the game that everyone must follow. However, the fact that everyone has a duty to work is not as oppressive as it might sound because everyone also has a calling—a vocation. In other words, everyone has a natural aptitude that determines what sort of work they should do and what their place in the social hierarchy should be (pp.

292–97). In this way, B claims, individual talent is brought into harmony with the universal rule that everyone must work for a living.

> What the esthete said about the aristocratic talents is confusing and skeptical talk about that which the ethical man clarifies. The esthete's view of life always involves the difference that some people have talent and others do not, and yet what separates people is a more or less quantitative determinant.... Their life-view, therefore, establishes a division in all existence, which they do not see their way to eliminating; instead, they recklessly and callously try to arm themselves against it.
>
> The ethicist, however, reconciles the person with life, for he says: every human being has a calling. He does not annihilate the differences but declares: In all the differences there still remains the universal, that it is a calling. The most eminent talent is a calling, and the individual who possesses it cannot lose sight of actuality; he does not stand outside the universally human, because his talent is a calling. (*EOII* 292)
>
> So our hero has found what he was looking for, a work from which he can live; he has also found a more significant expression for the relation of this work to his personality: it is his calling—consequently, the carrying out of it is bound up with a satisfaction for his whole personality. He has also found a more significant expression for the relation of his work to other people; inasmuch as his work is his calling, he is thereby placed essentially on the same level as all other human beings. Hence through his work he is doing the same as everyone else—he is carrying out his calling. (*EOII* 293)

The fact that everyone has a vocation in life—a pre-established calling that designates a particular position for each individual within the larger communal whole, the larger social structure—this fact, B argues, makes the ethical requirement that everyone get a job meaningful and fulfilling rather than oppressive and alienating.

(4)

Everyone has an ethical obligation not only to get a job but also to get married, and these two ethical obligations have the added virtue that they eliminate all individuality and extraordinariness (pp. 297–306). Because of this B announces that the time has come to stop calling the ethical person he has been imaginatively constructing (his "client") as a "hero."

> There is just one thing to which I must object—that you call your client a hero. . . . A jobholder and a married man, I have all respect for him, but a hero—even he himself does not claim to be that. . . . Therefore, if I have him marry, I'll quietly manage to get him off my hands and happily hand him over to his wife. Through the recalcitrance displayed earlier, he has qualified himself to be placed under special surveillance. His wife will assume this task, and then everything will go well, for every time he is tempted to want to be an out-of-the-ordinary person, his wife will immediately straighten him out again . . . . (*EOII* 298)

What, then, does marriage do? Does it rob him of anything, does it deprive her of any beauty, does it cancel a single difference? Not at all. But it shows him all these things as accidentals when he is outside marriage, and not until he gives the differences the expression of the universal, and only then, is he in secure possession of them. The ethical teaches him that the relationship is the absolute. The relationship is, namely, the universal. It takes away from him the vain joy of being out-of-the-ordinary in order to give him the true joy of being the ordinary. . . . This he will realize, and he will turn back again to the ethicist's position that it is every human being's duty to marry, and he will perceive that it has not only truth but also beauty on its side. (*EOII* 304)

(5)

Married men can learn many wonderful things from their wives, and their wives definitely don't want to be "emancipated" or to have their position in life altered in any way (pp. 306–23). The main thing that married men can learn from their wives, according to B, is that women have a deep understanding of time; specifically, how to pass the time.

> It sometimes happens to me . . . that I sit and settle into myself. I have taken care of my work; I have no desire for any diversion, and something melancholy in my temperament gains the upper hand over me. I become many years older than I actually am, and I become a stranger to my home life. I can very well see that it is beautiful, but I look at it with different eyes than usual. It seems to me as if I myself were an old man, my wife my happily married younger sister in whose house I am sitting. In such hours, time almost begins to drag for me. Now if my wife were a man, the same thing would perhaps happen to her, and we might both come to a halt, but she is a woman and in harmony

with time. . . . When I am sitting this way, desolate and lost, and then I watch my wife moving lightly and youthfully around the room, always busy—she always has something to take care of—my eyes involuntarily follow her movements. I participate in everything she is doing, and in the end I find myself within time again, time has meaning for me again, and the moment hurries along again. (*EOII* 307)

I come back to my wife—I never grow weary of watching her. What she does I cannot explain, but she does it all with a charm and a graciousness, with an indescribable lightness, does it without preliminaries and ceremony, like a bird singing its aria. Indeed I do believe that her occupation can best be compared to a bird's work, and yet her arts seem to me to be genuine magic. . . . Yes, my wise fellow, it is unbelievable what a natural virtuoso a woman is; she explains in the most interesting and beautiful manner the question that has cost many a philosopher his reason: time. (*EOII* 308)

On the whole, woman has a native talent, an original gift, an absolute virtuosity for explaining the finite. When man was created, he stood there as nature's lord and prince, nature's magnificence and splendor; all the riches of finitude awaited only his nod, but he did not comprehend what he should do with it all. He looked at it, but everything seemed to vanish under this intellectual gaze; it seemed to him that if he moved he would be past it all in one single step. Thus he stood, an imposing figure, lost in thought and yet comic, because one had to smile at this rich man who did not know how to use his riches, but also tragic, because he could not use them. Then woman was created. She was in no quandary, knew at once how one should take hold of the situation; without any fuss, without any preparation, she was ready to start at once. This was the first solace that was given to man. She approached the man, happy as a child, humble as a child, wistful as a child. She wished only to be a solace to him, to alleviate his need—a need she did not understand, but which she did not think she was filling either—she wished only to shorten the intervening time for him. . . . A woman comprehends the finite; she understands it from the ground up. (*EOII* 310–11)

Following consistently and thoroughly the principle that ethical practice is all about following the rules and fulfilling the roles that have been pre-established for everyone, B maintains that there are clearly defined roles and rules in marriage for every woman and man, and that these rules and roles are exactly as they should be.

> Woman explains the finite; man pursues the infinite. This is the way it must be, and everyone has his pain, for woman bear children in pain, but man conceives ideas in pain, and woman is not supposed to know the anxiety of doubt or the agony of despair. She is not supposed to stand outside the idea, but she has it at second hand. . . . That is why I hate all that detestable rhetoric about the emancipation of women. God forbid that it may ever happen. I cannot tell you with what pain the thought can pierce my soul, nor what passionate indignation, what hate, I harbor toward anyone who dares express such ideas. (*EOII* 311)[148]

(6)

B's account of ethical practice ends with a blunt prescription: Stop trying to be extraordinary; instead surrender yourself to the universal ethical rule and embrace being ordinary (pp. 323–33).

> For the sake of order, I shall here and now promptly state my idea of what an extraordinary person is. The genuinely extraordinary person is the genuinely ordinary person. The more of the universally human an individual can actualize in his life, the more extraordinary a human being he is. The less of the universal he can assimilate, the more imperfect he is. It is true that he may then be an extraordinary person, but not in the good sense. (*EOII* 328).

This concludes the six stages of B's account of ethical practice which make up Act III in this comedy, so now the time has come to go back to the beginning of the second letter (Act II) and consider how B's account of ethical theory contradicts his account of ethical practice, and why this makes the second letter as a whole quite funny.

The first thing to notice is how much B sounds like Hegel when he describes what ethics looks like in practice. The final words of the second letter sound remarkably similar to the final paragraph of Hegel's preface to *The Phenomenology of Spirit*:

> For the rest, at a time when the universality of Spirit has gathered such strength, and the singular detail, as is fitting, has become correspondingly less important, when, too, that universal aspect claims and holds on to the whole range of the wealth it

has developed, the share in the total work of Spirit which falls to the individual can only be very small. Because of this, the individual must all the more forget himself, as the nature of science implies and requires. Of course, he must make of himself and achieve what he can; but less must be demanded of him, just as he in turn can expect less of himself, and may demand less for himself.[149]

Throughout his account of ethical practice B emphasizes the necessity of surrendering oneself to the larger whole of the community, taking your predetermined place within a social structure in which no one is supposed to be extraordinary or unusual in any way. Everyone must get a job and get married, and then allow work and marriage to disabuse them of any desire they may have entertained to be extraordinary. Individuality is not the goal of ethical practice as B explains it; the goal is to stop trying to be an individual and instead surrender oneself to the universal.

Beyond these arguments against individuality, which are very much in the spirit of Hegel, there is also an explicit argument for something like a Hegelian synthesis of the aesthetic and the ethical—a quasi-mystical *Aufheben* in which nothing of the aesthetic is lost or left behind and all apparent contradictions between the aesthetic and the ethical are overcome. This is the second main argument that B gives in his account of ethical practice, right after he insists that an ethical life is simply a life of following the rules and therefore not fundamentally different from a homework assignment given to a five-year-old child. This argument is rather jarring since it is so abstract and mystical, while everything else in B's account of ethical practice is utterly specific, concrete, and mundane (get a job; get married; stop trying to be a hero). B endorses a Hegelian synthesis most obviously and explicitly in the second argument he presents in the section on ethical practice, when he argues that the aesthetic and ethical are unified in a higher synthesis—that the aesthetic is absorbed into the ethical such that nothing is lost and nothing is left behind—but really all of the second letter's practice section can be seen as an enthusiastic endorsement of Hegelian synthesis.

At this point my extremely long-suffering reader may very well point out that B is certainly not the first person to advocate a Hegelian approach to ethics, and also that there is nothing particularly funny about him doing so—and I did promise that the point of this entire long analysis of B's second letter was to demonstrate that the letter is actually comical, and B too is comical. To this completely understandable complaint I can finally reply: you're right, it was quite a long walk, but we have almost reached the punch line so hopefully you'll soon conclude that the journey was worth it. The first hilarious contradiction to notice in the second letter is that B is completely in favor of a Hegelian approach to ethics in practice, but completely opposed to such an approach in theory. While the final sixty-eight pages of the second letter are very much in tune with the spirit of Hegel, the initial 109 pages of the letter are completely discordant with Hegel's philosophy, and they also contain many explicit denunciations of the pernicious effects of Hegel's thought on contemporary ethics. The first glaring and comical contradiction in the second letter is the way that in the practice section of the letter (Act III) B enthusiastically embraces the Hegelian project of denying the existence of contradictions and urging individuals to lose themselves in a higher universal and abstract synthesis, while in the theory section of the same letter (Act II) he criticizes these same ideas mercilessly. In other words, the first moment of comedy in the second letter is the way that B contradicts himself when he argues that there are no contradictions.

Consider how emphatically B denounces Hegelian synthesis in his initial arguments about ethical theory. There he argues that current (that is, nineteenth-century) philosophy does nothing at all to clarify the true nature of ethical choices because it is obsessed with the Hegelian project of mediating and canceling all contradictions in a higher unity. Thus it fails to grasp the decisive nature of an ethical choice, and it also mediates itself right out of existence. B faults A for denying that there are any meaningful ethical choices to be made, since according to A's theory every choice one makes leads to the same result ("You will regret it"). This, B argues, "has a strange similarity to modern philosophy's pet theory that the principle of contradiction is canceled" (*EOII* 170), a pet theory that he regards as incompatible with ethics:

> You mediate the contradictions in a higher lunacy, philosophy in a higher unity. You turn toward the future, for action is essentially future tense; you say: I can either do this or do that, but whichever I do is equally absurd—*ergo*, I do nothing at all. Philosophy turns toward the past, toward the totality of experienced world history; it shows how the discursive elements come together in a higher unity; it mediates and mediates. It seems to me, however, that it does not answer the question I am asking, for I am asking about the future. (*EOII* 170)

Consequently, B says, if I look to philosophy for ethical guidance "I receive no answer, for philosophy mediates the past and is in the past—philosophy hastens so fast into the past that, as a poet says of an antiquarian, only his coattails remain in the present" (*EOII* 171). This results in one of the most absurd facts of the present age: that every philosopher can mediate every apparent contradiction, but none of them have the slightest idea how to live (*EOII* 171). When the question of ethics is posed to philosophy, "it is truly an enormous argument against philosophy that it has nothing to answer. Has the movement of life come to a standstill?" (*EOII* 172). By denying that there are any genuine contradictions, and by advocating a life lived in the abstractions of the past instead of the constitution of a personality by creating values in the present, B argues that modern (Hegelian) philosophy stands in the way of authentic ethical choices.[150]

When expounding his ethical theory B explains that modern philosophy's obsession with mediation results from the fact that Hegelian philosophy has relocated philosophy to a new, non-human address: a new world where individual humans who must make ethical choices in their own finite lives are no longer present. This world of speculation and synthesis is a lovely place to visit, but no one can live there, including the philosophers who insist so adamantly on defending the honor of Hegelian speculation.

> But since I have come this far, I want to give a little closer consideration to the philosophical mediation of contradictions.... The time in which the philosopher lives is not absolute time: it is itself a moment.... Therefore, time itself becomes a moment, and the philosopher himself becomes a moment in time. Then in turn our age will appear to a later age as a discursive moment, and in turn a philosopher of a later age will mediate our age, and so on. To that extent, then, philosophy is in the right, and it would be regarded as an incidental error on the part of the philosophy of our age to confuse our time with absolute time. Yet it is easy to perceive that the category of mediation thereby has suffered a considerable blow and that absolute mediation is not possible until history is finished, in other words, that the system is in a continual process of becoming. What philosophy has retained, however, is the acknowledgment that there is an absolute mediation. This is, of course, extremely important for it, because if one abandons mediation then one abandons speculation. On the other hand, it is a dubious matter to admit this, for if one admits mediation, then there is no absolute choice, and if there is no such thing, then there is no absolute Either/Or. This is the difficulty: yet I believe it is due partially to a confusion of the two spheres with each other, the spheres of thought and of freedom. For thought, the contradiction does not exist; it passes over into the other and thereupon together with the other into a higher unity. For freedom, the contradiction does exist, because it excludes it. (*EOII* 173)

B presents very articulate and compelling arguments against the speculative and mediative spirit of Hegelian philosophy when he is discussing ethical theory in Act II, but when he turns to ethical practice in Act III he discards all of those criticisms and thoroughly embraces Hegelian synthesis, as well as Hegel's many arguments against individuality. This is quite funny, and it's the first contradiction—in this case a contradiction concerning the nature of contradictions—that makes the second letter a work of comedy overall.[131]

The rest of B's account of the nature of ethical life in Act III also contradicts his ethical theory in Act II. Once again theory and practice in the second letter are completely at odds with each other, as if they had been written by two different people who don't get along at all. The picture of ethical practice that B presents can be distilled down to two main ideas or themes:

- Ethics is simply following the rules and conventions of society: doing what you're told.
- The rules and conventions that everyone must follow include: every man must get a job and get married, and then learn from his wife (who has also followed the rules and stepped into the role of a married housewife that was predetermined for her) how to make the time pass. Following these rules and assuming the appropriate roles that society has determined for everyone will have the effect of eliminating any individuality or extraordinariness from everyone, which is entirely appropriate. Everyone should stop trying to be extraordinary or individual in any way; instead everyone should lose themselves in the universal and the utterly ordinary.

Both of these aspects of ethical practice are contradicted quite starkly in the ethical theory B presents in the first sixty-eight pages of the second letter. First of all, in his ethical theory B argues that authentic ethical choices don't just confirm or recover values that were always already there; instead they create new values. B emphasizes that the fundamental ethical choice is the choice to will, and to create by willing—to recognize that the will can create new values.

> Rather than designating the choice between good and evil, my Either/Or designates the choice by which one chooses good and evil or rules them out. Here the question is under what qualifications one will view all existence and personally live. That the person who chooses good and evil chooses the good is indeed true, but only later does this become manifest for the esthetic is

not evil but the indifferent. And that is why I said that the ethical constitutes the choice. Therefore it is not so much a matter of choosing between willing good or willing evil as of choosing to will, but that in turn posits good and evil. The person who chooses the ethical chooses the good, but here the good is altogether abstract; its being is thereby merely posited, and this by no means precludes that the one choosing cannot in turn choose evil even though he chose the good. Here you see again how important it is that a choice is made and that it does not depend so much on deliberation as on the baptism of the will, which assimilates this into the ethical. (*EOII* 169)

In addition to creating new values, B's ethical theory argues that authentic ethical choices also create a person in the deepest sense: they constitute and consolidate a personality. Ethical choices first create an *ethos*—a form of life, and then they create the individual within that form of life.[152]

> What is important in choosing is not so much to choose the right thing as the energy, the earnestness, and the pathos with which one chooses. In the choosing the personality declares itself in its inner infinity and in turn the personality is thereby consolidated. (*EOII* 167)

> The choice itself is crucial for the content of the personality: through the choice the personality submerges itself in that which is being chosen, and when it does not choose, it withers away in atrophy. (*EOII* 163)

Without authentic ethical choices there is no deeper self, just a series of masks worn by a person who no longer even knows how to recognize himself.

> I have seen people in life who have deceived others for such a long time that eventually they are unable to show their true nature. . . . Or can you think of anything more appalling than having it all end with the disintegration of your essence into a multiplicity, so that you actually become several, just as that unhappy demoniac became a legion, and thus you would have lost what is most inward and holy in a human being: the binding power of the personality. (*EOII* 160)

> And this is what is sad when one contemplates human life, that so many live out their lives in quiet lostness; they outlive themselves, not in the sense that life's content successively unfolds and is now possessed in this unfolding, but they live, as it were, away from themselves and vanish like shadows. Their immortal

souls are blown away, and they are not disquieted by the question of its immortality, because they are already disintegrated before they die. (*EOII* 168–69)

B's ethical theory presents ethics as a fundamentally creative act—creating new values and creating a person in the process—which completely contradicts B's account of ethical practice—an ethical practice that is fundamentally about following rules and conventions that are already in place, rather than creating anything new. For B, ethical practice is thoroughly allergic to any kind of creation or innovation or individuality whatsoever, and this is apparent also in how much B emphasizes (especially in arguments 3–6) that ethical practice requires stepping into roles and forms of life that are already in place, just waiting for you to step into them like a well-worn but sturdy pair of shoes that has been handed down from one generation to another. For example: everyone must get a job and get married, and the roles for men and women within this required marriage are prescribed for everyone, so that the final result of work and marriage (exactly the right result according to B) is that everyone learns to stop trying to be extraordinary or trying to be an individual in any way. In the first 109 pages of the second letter B presents a clear and profound account of ethical theory that is creative, affirmative, and individualistic; and then in the remaining sixty-eight pages he contradicts and undermines this theory with his account of ethical practice. By first summarizing very succinctly and powerfully an affirmative, non-nihilistic ethical theory that explains how humans can create meaning and value in their lives, and then immediately contradicting that theory with its polar opposite, B makes it clear that he is fully capable of conceptualizing ethics in an affirmative and creative way but chooses instead to embrace a nihilistic ethics that insists humans are helpless, incapable of creating their own values, and (as his friend the Stocky Little Pastor put it), "always in the wrong." All of these contradictions are quite glaring and quite funny, and they make B's second letter an excellent work of comedy.

To conclude this backwards reading of B's letters in Part II, we turn now to B's first letter, which gets this whole comedy started.

B's First Letter

B's first letter is Act I in the overall comedy of Part II. In this first act B explains very clearly what he wants—the ideals that he aspires to. The first letter has the quality of a very personal confession, a statement of B's highest aspirations, an unabashed declaration of his hopes and dreams. In the first letter B declares what he wants, and then in the second letter he initially proposes an ethical theory that explains how what he wants is possible—and then in the final section of the second letter he gives up on all of that and reverts to a prescription of ethical practice that is utterly conventional and nihilistic and that completely contradicts the ethical ideals and the ethical theory that he presented first. The first letter contributes to the overall comic contradiction between B's ethical theory and his ethical practice by setting the stage with an emphatic declaration of desire: pure, unconventional, unorthodox, and unapologetic subjective desire, which is obviously where all works and dreams and experiments and love affairs and philosophical theories must begin.

The first letter begins with a surprising and seemingly unnecessary proclamation: B wants to make it very clear at the outset that this is a letter we are reading, and not an argumentative treatise. The first thing that B wants the reader to understand is that this text should be read as a very personal communication: a description of his desires, and not a prescription for an ethical theory or an ethical form of life. It's true, B says, that he didn't have time to write a treatise—"my time has not permitted the more painstaking elaboration that a treatise requires"—but also he didn't want "to miss the opportunity of addressing you in the more admonishing and urgent tone appropriate to the epistolary form" (*EOII* 5). B wants to make sure that the reader approaches this text in a very particular way, lest it be mistaken for something that it is not.

> The letter that you hereby receive is rather long; if it were weighed on a post office scale, it would be an expensive letter; on the troy-weight scale of keen critical analysis, it would perhaps appear to be very negligible. I ask you, therefore, not to use any of these scales, not the post office scale, for it comes to you not for forwarding but as a deposit, and not the scale of critical analysis, since I would be loath to see you make yourself guilty of such a gross and uncongenial misunderstanding. (*EOII* 5–6)

It would be a "gross and uncongenial misunderstanding" to read the first letter as if it were a theory or an argument because B has no intention of presenting an ethical theory here, or defending a particular form of ethical practice; instead he's going to bare his heart in a congenial way, he's going to present a summary of what he wants, what he desires, and he'll save the arguments for both theory and practice until later. B's first letter must be understood in this way—as a purely subjective and non-argumentative statement of desire—in order to appreciate how it sets the stage for the arguments concerning theory and practice that follow in the second letter.

B is emphatic and explicit in his description of what he wants to realize: an ethical life that also includes all possible aesthetic value, a life in which both the aesthetic and the ethical flourish together, even though most people (including A) assume that aesthetics and ethics are mutually exclusive. Victor Eremita chooses the rather tepid title "The Esthetic Validity of Marriage" to summarize the contents of the first letter, but this title doesn't begin to do justice to B's passionate and persistent declarations of desire in this letter. B declares that he wants nothing less than a form of marriage in which all of the aesthetic attraction, beauty, and excitement that abound when one first falls in love are preserved, with no diminution whatsoever. B uses the phrase "the first love" or "the first infatuation" or "erotic love" as shorthand for this rich collection of aesthetic experiences, and so he can succinctly summarize the entirety of the first letter thus:

> There are two things that I must regard as my particular task: to show the esthetic meaning of marriage and to show how the esthetic in it may be retained despite life's numerous hindrances. (*EOII* 8)

Or, to express the same thing in slightly different words:

> [T]he task I have chiefly set for myself is to show that the first love can continue to exist in marriage ... that it can be taken up into a higher concentricity. (*EOII* 46–47)[153]

This may sound like the language of Hegelian dialectic, but B is very far from presenting any sort of theory—Hegelian or otherwise—in the first letter. He's simply declaring what he wants without venturing yet into any attempt to theorize concerning how what he wants might be possible. B makes no attempt to conceal the fact that this is a purely subjective project, that he is fighting to realize something that matters deeply and personally to him, and that he is driven by a stubborn insistence in spite of all the evidence that suggests that what he wants is not possible.

> So you see the nature of the task I have set for myself: to show that romantic love can be united with and exist in marriage—indeed, that marriage is its true transfiguration.... No matter how many painful confusions life can still manifest, I fight for two things: the enormous task of showing that marriage is the transfiguration of the first love and not its annihilation, is its friend and not its enemy; and for the task—to everyone else so very insignificant but to me all the more important—of showing that my humble marriage has had this meaning, whereby strength

and courage are gained for the continual accomplishment of this task. (*EOII* 31)

For me the phrase "the first love" has no sadness at all, . . . for me it is a password, and although I have been a married man for several years, I have the honor to fight under the victorious banner of the first love. (*EOII* 37)

In the first letter B makes it very clear that his ideal of marriage—which forever includes all of the aesthetic fascination and enjoyment of the first love—is not realized in many marriages, perhaps even most of them. Scattered throughout the first letter are remarkably blunt summaries of B's empirical observations of the abundance of marriages he has witnessed that fall far short of his ideal. Many of these observations take the form of B completely agreeing with A's assessment that most marriages are quite awful; here are a few choice examples:

How often you entertained me—yes, I readily admit it—but how often you also tormented me with your stories of how you had stolen your way into the confidence of one and then another married man in order to see how deeply bogged down he was in the swamp of marital life. You are really very gifted at slipping in with people; that I will not deny, nor that it is very entertaining to hear you relate the consequences of it and to witness your hilarity every time you are able to peddle a really fresh observation. (*EOII* 8).

I assure you that this subject is so much on my mind that I, who ordinarily feel only slightly tempted to write books, actually could be tempted to do that if I dared to hope I could save just one single marriage from the hell into which it has perhaps plunged itself . . . . (*EOII* 9)

All marriages of that kind [B has just devoted several pages to analyzing and criticizing marriages that have no aesthetic dimension, such as people who get married just to have children, or just to have a home] suffer from the mistake of making a particular feature of the marriage the purpose for marriage, and therefore they often feel deceived, especially those mentioned first, when they have to admit that marriage means little more than acquiring a comfortable, cozy, suitable home. . . . It is not given to everyone to operate on a very large scale, and many of those who imagine they are working for something great sooner or later find themselves laboring under a delusion. (*EOII* 78)

> When you see a married couple whose life together, so it seems to you, drags on in the most dreadful boredom, "in the most insipid repetition of the sacred institutions and sacraments of erotic love," then, yes, then a fire rages within you, a fire that wants to consume them. And this is not something arbitrary on your part; you are indeed justified; you are indeed entitled to let the lightning of irony strike them and the thunder of anger terrify them. As a matter of fact, you do destroy them not because you have a liking for it but because they have deserved it. (*EOII* 129)

It's clear that B recognizes how often married life falls short of his own ideals—how many marriages are hellish, torturous, completely lacking in aesthetic joy, and very much like prison. In this regard he is happy to agree with A. But in spite of all the empirical evidence to the contrary, B clings to his stubborn and purely subjective insistence that his marriage can be different.

Overall, the first letter constitutes a very personal manifesto for B, a proclamation of his own vision of ethical life that does not surrender any aesthetic value whatsoever. It is a stubborn, tenacious declaration of his desires, and thus it sets the stage perfectly for the second letter, where B will first present arguments for an innovative and affirmative ethical theory that explains how it is possible to realize the sort of ethical life that he said he wants. But then when the second letter shifts to an argument about ethical practice, and later when B recommends the undelivered sermon of his friend the Stocky Little Pastor as an accurate summary of his own beliefs about ethics, all of the creative and affirmative elements of the first two acts of this comedy are renounced and B slides into a comfortable and conventional form of everyday nihilism, like almost everyone else in the world.

The comedy in Part II has generally been overlooked because so many readers have singled out particular moments in B's letters, removing those moments from the overall comic progression of Part II. In isolation and taken out of context there are certainly pieces of B's letters that are creative, profound, and affirmative, and based on selections such as these B would hardly seem to be a nihilist. In fact, B isn't a nihilist at first: initially he's unafraid to express his own subjective desire for an ethical life that includes every possible aesthetic value, and he's innovative and unconventional enough to create an ethical theory that explains how such subjective ideals can be realized. But then in Act III B's independent thinking collapses under the weight of the supposed authority of tradition and convention, and the genuinely difficult task of thinking and being for oneself. B descends into nihilism in Act III at the end of a very long performance, and thus he becomes a cautionary tale of how easy it is to back into a nihilistic form of ethical practice, or collapse into it, even when one has a vision of a completely different form of ethics, and a creative theory to support that vision. This is still, however, a very funny story, and we should recognize the comedy that B performs for us in the three acts (plus an epilogue) of Part II so that we can absorb this important lesson: ethics can be just as much of a mask for nihilism as aesthetics, and perhaps it's an even more effective and insidious mask.

So yes, Part II of *Either/Or* is just as much of a comedy as Part I, and this is one more way in which the two parts of the book are connected and continuous, conjoined rather than disjoined.

In conclusion: In praise of the inclusive disjunction

When the Queen of Denmark called his book *Either and Or* Kierkegaard did not correct her, and everyone in the room (including the King, who gave Kierkegaard a meaningful look [*KJN* 5:234]) probably assumed that this was simply because one does not correct the Queen. However, it's also possible that Kierkegaard liked the title the Queen gave to his strange book, and recognized that she had correctly understood the conjunctive continuity between Part I and Part II. I prefer to think that the author kept silent out of respect for the Queen's logical insight, and not merely out of respect for royal protocol.

As every student in a formal logic class learns very quickly, disjunctions in natural language are ambiguous. An inclusive disjunction is true whenever any one or both of its disjuncts are true, so it's more like saying "and/or," while an exclusive disjunction excludes the possibility of both disjuncts being true: only one of them is allowed to be true, not both. Here are the respective truth tables for these logical operators, which I am including mainly because I think it likely that this will be the first book on Kierkegaard that contains truth tables, and being the first author to attain that pointless distinction is deeply important to me.

exclusive disjunction		inclusive disjunction	
p q | p cr q		p q | p or q	
t t | f		t t | t	
t f | t		t f | t	
f t | t		f t | t	
f f | f		f f | f	

Either/Or has been read by almost everyone as an exclusive disjunction: you can choose A's aesthetic life or B's ethical life, but you cannot choose both. But the book is much more interesting and educational when it's read as an inclusive disjunction. Such a reading reveals a great deal about the nature of nihilism: that ethics can be just as much a mask for nihilism as aesthetics; that even someone as respectable and pious as Judge Wilhelm can be essentially a nihilist; and that nihilism can be a perfectly enjoyable form of life regardless of the mask that conceals it—be it aesthetic, religious, or ethical. Victor Eremita told us right at the beginning of the book that A and B might be a single person, and now I believe we have the evidence to prove this suspicion correct. If A and B turned out to share the same body that would be spectacular but inconsequential; however, if A and B are the same conceptual persona that is indeed significant and revelatory, because this singular conceptual persona would shed light on the multifaceted phenomena of nihilism. A and B are in fact the same person in every sense that counts toward a deeper understanding of nihilism, and this makes *Either/Or* (or *Either and Or*), a very funny book from which we can learn valuable lessons about the nature of nihilism and the nature of comedy.[154]

CHAPTER 6

How to misunderstand *Repetition* by ignoring the fact that the book's author, Constantin Constantius, loves a good farce

or

Repetition repeats itself in *Repetition*: first as tragedy and then as farce

> He who knows how to keep silent discovers an alphabet that has just as many letters as the ordinary one; thus he can express everything in his jargon, and no sigh is so deep that he does not have the laughter that corresponds to it in his jargon, and no request so obtrusive that he does not have the witticism to fulfill the demand. (R 145)

RIGHT IN THE MIDDLE of the opening Report which marks the beginning of the very strange book called *Repetition*, Constantin Constantius sets aside some sixteen pages—much more than he ever devotes to clarifying the technical, philosophical meaning of the concept "repetition," which is supposedly what the book is all about—to explain to us why he loves to go to the Königstädter Theater to see a good farce. When pressed to account for this strange moment in the text, readers have almost universally agreed on one thing: it is a digression.[155] Constantin Constantius's love of farce and his long discussion of the way it is performed in the Königstädter Theater is essentially an aside that can safely be ignored. *Repetition* is a serious book with a serious message, almost everyone has agreed; and if you want to see that serious message you can't afford to get bogged down in this strange digression about farce.

In this chapter I will argue that the failure to take seriously Constantin Constantius's love of farce is a serious mistake. When pseudonyms such as Constantin Constantius address the subject of comedy their comments often contain important insights for understanding the indirect communications of which they are the authors. By offering what appear to be abstract comments on the general theory of comedy, the pseudonyms often provide crucial concrete clues into their own projects of indirect communication—clues that could not be provided in any other way without betraying those very projects. Given these facts, it seems very likely that Constantin Constantius's great love of farce—which leads him to spend a great deal of time in the middle of the story of his trip to Berlin singing the praises of this particular form of comedy—can hardly be an accidental detail that is irrelevant to the meaning of the work as a whole.

I will argue that Constantin Constantius's enthusiasm for farce is actually extremely relevant to the text of which he is the author, because this text is itself a farce.[156] The farce of *Repetition* has two comic actors, each of which I will consider more closely in this essay. Before the curtain goes up on act I, however, I want first to look more carefully at Constantin Constantius's discourse on farce and the joys of attending the Königstädter Theater, because this will serve as a prologue to the whole performance. (There will also be a brief curtain call at the end by a certain Mr. X, Esquire, if we can find him by the time the comedy is finished.)[157]

Prologue: Constantin Constantius on the theater of existence

> Berlin has three theaters. The opera and ballet performances in the opera house are supposed to be *groszartig*; performances in the theater are supposed to be instructive and refining, not only for entertainment. I do not know. But I do know that Berlin has a theater called the Königstädter Theater .... (R 154)

Constantin Constantius[158] loves the theater because it mirrors the existential process of creating an identity. This process is one of trying on different roles, experimenting with different parts in an imaginative shadow play that (if it is to be successful) has to be protected from the demands of actuality. The theater presents this play of becoming in microcosm. It attracts us precisely because we recognize the activity on stage as a reflection of our own hidden life story—the story of the construction of the self through constant experimentation with different roles. Constantin Constantius views the self as a kind of play, a spontaneous performance where various shadows of an individual's possibility are set in motion under the imagination's direction.

> There is probably no young person with any imagination who has not at some time been enthralled by the magic of the theater and wished to be swept along into that artificial actuality in order like a double to see and hear himself and to split himself up into every possible variation of himself, and nevertheless in such a way that every variation is still himself. . . . In such a self-vision of the imagination, the individual is not an actual shape but a shadow, or, more correctly, the actual shape is invisibly present and therefore is not satisfied to cast one shadow, but the individual has a variety of shadows, all of which resemble him and which momentarily have equal status as being himself. As yet the personality is not discerned, and its energy is betokened only in the passion of possibility, for the same thing happens in the spiritual life as with many plants—the main shoot comes last. (R 154)

The theater mirrors the experimentation and role playing required for the construction of every self, and it solves the problem of how to accomplish this experimentation in a world where even selves that are under construction are still subject to the demands of responsibility.

> [T]he individual's possibility wanders about in its own possibility, discovering now one possibility, now another. But the individual's possibility does not want only to be heard; it is not like the mere passing of the wind. It is also configuring and therefore wants to be visible at the same time. That is why each of its possibilities is an audible shadow. . . . At the very same moment the cock crows and the twilight shapes vanish, the nocturnal voices fall silent. If they keep on, then we are in an altogether different realm where all this takes place under the disquieting supervision of responsibility, then we approach the demonic. Then, in order not to gain an impression of his actual self, the hidden individual needs an environment as superficial and transient as the shapes, as the frothing foam of words that sound without resonance. The stage is that kind of setting, and therefore it is particularly suitable for the shadow play of the hidden individual. (R 155–56)

Constantin Constantius argues that the development of an individual identity always requires acting. Possibilities need to be enacted in the theater of the imagination before they can have any meaning, before they can become serious candidates for acting out on the stage of actuality. But this kind of role playing requires protection from the world—from the "disquieting supervision of responsibility" that always accompanies the self's actual identity (R 156). The individual needs to be free to wander about in her own possibilities, "discovering now one possibility, now another" (R 155), free to perform these possibilities in her own imagination, but free also from the gaze of obligation that observes the performance of her actual identity. Constantin finds in the theater a kind of virtual reality, an alternative universe, that perfectly embodies his view of life as constant experimentation with one's own identity—without, however, sacrificing the demands of responsibility in the process. He loves the theater because it imitates the hidden life of the "cryptic individual" that he wants to defend (R 155).

All forms of theater are attractive to Constantin Constantius because they imitate the process of self-creation that everyone should follow, but he prefers farce above everything else. What makes farce so perfect in his mind is its imperfection—imperfection that mirrors the imperfection of life. For this reason, Constantin Constantius predicts, an adult who rekindles her childhood love of the theater will naturally gravitate to farce. Such an adult "desires the comic effect and wants a relation to the theatrical performance that generates the comic. Since tragedy, comedy, and light comedy fail to please him precisely because of their perfection, he turns to farce" (R 157–58). An adult will immediately appreciate the "imperfections" of farce for their existential implications. Of all forms of theater, Constantius argues, farce comes closest to the theater of human existence in the demands that it makes on both the actors and the spectators.

To be a successful farce actor, Constantius argues, one must be fundamentally unreflective. The greatest actors (such as Beckmann and Grobecker) are not intellectual geniuses, but rather "generative geniuses" (R 161) who create comedy without foresight or planning and without any reference to concepts.

> They must be children of caprice, intoxicated with laughter, dancers of whimsy who, even though they are at other times like other people—yes, the very moment before—the instant they hear the stage manager's bell they are transformed and, like a thoroughbred Arabian horse, they begin to snort and puff, while their distended nostrils betoken the chafing of spirit because they want to be off, want to cavort wildly. They are not so much reflective artists who have studied laughter as they are lyricists who themselves plunged into the abyss of laughter and now let its volcanic power hurl them out on the stage. Thus they have

> not deliberated very much on what they will do but leave everything to the moment and the natural power of laughter. They have the courage to venture what the individual makes bold to do only when alone, what the mentally deranged do in the presence of everybody, what the genius knows how to do with the authority of genius, certain of laughter. (R 161)

Such an actor creates comedy spontaneously and almost effortlessly. His "generative genius" is his ability to create *ex nihilo*.

> He is not great in the commensurables of the artistic but is admirable in the incommensurables of the individual. He does not need the support of interaction, of scenery and staging; precisely because he is in an ebullient mood, he himself carries everything along. At the same time that he is being inordinately funny, he himself is painting his own scenery as well as a set painter. (R 163)

Constantin Constantius emphasizes that this kind of acting can't be blocked out in advance. It will only succeed if it is genuinely spontaneous, and therefore surprising to both the performer and her audience. Actors who are capable of farce "know that their hilarity has no limits, that their comic resources are inexhaustible, and they themselves are amazed at it practically every moment" (R 161). The lack of rational control that characterizes farce brings this form of comedy dangerously close to offensiveness, and even to insanity. The way that an actor in a farce provokes laughter "requires the authority of genius; otherwise it is most repellent" (R 164). "He is an incognito in whom dwells the lunatic demon of comedy, who quickly extricates himself and carries everything away in sheer abandonment" (R 164). Such an actor has "the courage to venture what the individual makes bold to do only when alone, what the mentally deranged do in the presence of everybody, what the genius knows how to do with the authority of genius, certain of laughter" (R 161). The proximity of offense and madness infuses farce with a sense of danger that adds energy to the actor's performance, and makes the audience all the more appreciative of the ease with which the actor navigates the tightrope between these two potential disasters. But this kind of tightrope walking is only possible if the actor remains firmly rooted in the moment, trusting in her spontaneity.

Constantin Constantius's characterization of the farce actor has very clear existential overtones. This actor "is not great in the commensurables of the artistic but is admirable in the incommensurables of the individual" (R 163). Such an actor succeeds by enacting the same qualities of spontaneity and responsiveness to the moment that are required of every existing individual. Both the actor on the stage and the existing individual are incapable of fully understanding what they are actually doing in any given moment, since life can only be understood backwards but it must be lived forwards. Neither of them can base their performance on reflective concepts, but instead they must act as "generative geniuses," creating subjectively in a way that has the potential to surprise everyone, even themselves. So the requirements that farce places on an actor give this form of theater unique existential dimensions, which helps to close the gap between the Königstädter Theater and the theater of existence in which everyone lives.

The existential dimension of farce is apparent also on the other side of the stage: in the demands that the play makes of the audience. In this respect, what Constantius loves most about farce is that it cannot be contained in a general system of categories. Farce resists conceptualization. It demands that the spectator approach it strictly as an individual, without making any appeals to the general public or to accepted rules of aesthetic judgment. In this way, farce requires the audience member—just as it requires the actor—to be a self-active "generative genius" who has forsaken the "commensurables of the artistic" in favor of "the incommensurables of the individual."

> Every general esthetic category runs aground on farce; nor does farce succeed in producing a uniformity of mood in the more cultured audience. Because its impact depends largely on self-activity and the viewer's improvisation, the particular individuality comes to assert himself in a very individual way and in his enjoyment is emancipated from all esthetic obligations to admire, to laugh, to be moved, etc. in the traditional way. For a cultured person, seeing a farce is similar to playing the lottery, except that one does not have the annoyance of winning money. But that kind of uncertainty will not do for the general theater-going public, which therefore ignores farce or snobbishly disdains it, all the worst for itself. (R 159)[159]

The general theater-going public disdains farce because the meaning of farce is resistant to any sort of general agreement. When the general public attends the theater, "it wishes to have had—or at least fancies that it has had—a rare artistic enjoyment; it wishes, as soon as it has read the poster, to be able to know in advance what is going to happen that evening" (R 159–60). But "[s]uch unanimity cannot be found at a farce, for the same farce can produce very different impressions, and, strangely enough, it may so happen that the one time it made the least impression it was performed best" (R 160). Consequently, when farce is performed at the Königstädter Theater the general public stays home. Those who do attend must accept the fact that, even though they are surrounded by people, in their judgment of the play they are essentially on their own. The non-reflective spontaneity and generative genius of the actor circumvent any general conceptual constructions and appeal directly to each audience member's own spontaneity and generative genius. The spectator will discover the humor in the farce only if she lowers her rational defenses and allows this direct appeal to happen; and if she does allow this to happen she is also exposing herself to the risk of upsetting the expectations of her peers, (and perhaps even breaking, my goodness, the social bond).[160] "Seeing a farce can produce the most unpredictable mood, and therefore a person can never be sure whether he has conducted himself in the theater as a worthy member of society who has laughed and cried at the appropriate places" (R 160). "Thus a person cannot rely on his neighbor and the man across the street and statements in the newspaper to determine whether he has enjoyed himself or not. The individual has to decide that matter for himself" (R 160). Since the enjoyment created by farce "consists largely in the viewer's self-relating to the farce, something he himself must risk, whereas he seeks in vain to the left or the right or in the newspapers for a guarantee that he actually has enjoyed himself" (R 160).

The individuality that farce requires of its audience leaves most members of the audience anxious or confused. They're not sure if they liked it, and if they did like it, they're not sure why. What farce requires of an audience member is "sufficient unconstraint to dare to enjoy himself entirely solo, sufficient self-confidence to think for himself without consulting others as to whether he has enjoyed himself or not" (R 160). Such a viewer, Constantin Constantius suggests, will discover in farce a form of comedy whose meaning will remain impenetrable to anyone who doesn't approach the work strictly as an existing individual.

The "imperfections" of farce, which make it existentially demanding for both the actors and the audience, and which make it the preferred form of theater for Constantin Constantius, are readily apparent in *Repetition*. Like every good farce, *Repetition* has a small core of actors who are unreflective, generative geniuses. "A completely successful performance of a farce requires a cast of special composition. It must include two, at most three, very talented actors" (R 161). "Two such geniuses are enough for a farce theater; three are the most that can be used advantageously, for otherwise the effect is diminished, just as a person dies of hypersthenia" (R 161). In the farce called *Repetition* there are two primary actors who support the weight of the farce: the narrator, Constantin Constantius, and the anonymous young man who engages Constantin's services. Both of these actors perform their parts brilliantly, and the consequence is that the general public has no idea what to make of the book. It would like to know that it has enjoyed itself, or been edified in some way, or learned something important, but it can't be sure that it has. Everyone is left to himself in his attempt to understand the comedy, (which apparently is just what the author wanted [R 149–50]). *Repetition* forces every audience member to set aside her reliance on general rules and the general public if she is to appreciate the comedy that it stages for her benefit. That almost all readers of the book have failed to do so is witnessed by the history of its interpretation, wherein there is very little laughter to be heard. On the other hand, for one who has "sufficient unconstraint to dare to enjoy himself solo, sufficient self-confidence to think for himself without consulting others as to whether he has enjoyed himself or not" (R 160), this farce still has the power to create "a very singular meaning" (R 160)—and also to be very funny.[161]

To recover the singular meaning and the farcical dimension of *Repetition*, I will turn now to its two principal comic actors and the two moments of comedy that they create in this farce.

The first comic actor: Constantin Constantius and the trials of the experimental psychologist

> Thus do you hold me captive with an indescribable power, and this same power makes me anxious; thus do I admire you, and yet at times I believe that you are mentally disordered. Is it not, in fact, a kind of mental disorder to have subjugated to such a degree every passion, every emotion, every mood under the cold regimentation of reflection! Is it not mental disorder to be normal in this way—pure idea, not a human being like the rest of us, flexible and yielding, lost and being lost! Is it not mental disorder always to be alert like this, always conscious, never vague and dreamy! (R 189)

Constantin Constantius is a spy. The author of *Repetition* regards his book as a case study in what he calls "experimenting psychology."[162] He has convinced the anonymous young man to consider him his confidant, and to share with him his most secret thoughts and moods (R 134). Constantin Constantius uses the information he receives to construct experimental situations so that he can study his subject better (R 137). And the young man is not his only experimental subject: Constantin Constantius claims to have a similar relationship "with several like him" (R 140), a few of whom are discussed in passing (e.g., R 147, 167, 181). The young man suggests that Constantius has sacrificed his humanity for the sake of this research project

(R 189). "Are you not afraid," he writes, "of running headlong into a dreadful passion called contempt for men?" (R 192) But Constantin Constantius is unmoved by these criticisms. He takes great pride in being someone who has trained himself "every day for years to have only an objective theoretical interest in people" (R 180), and who has mastered the art of disguising himself so that his subjects will drop their own disguises and reveal themselves completely. This requires transforming himself into a scientific instrument in order to obtain the material evidence that he is looking for, which is nothing less than the content of his subjects's consciousness.

> An observer knows how to appear easygoing; otherwise no one opens up. Above all, he guards against being ethically rigorous or portraying himself as the morally upright man. There is a degenerate man, one says, he has taken part, has had some wild experiences, *ergo*, I certainly can confide in him, I who am far superior to him! Well, so be it. I ask nothing of men but the substance of their consciousness. I scale it, and if it is weighty, no price is too high for me. (R 183)

The observer's vocation, according to Constantin Constantius, is purely scientific. His goal in studying his subjects is to uncover the objective truth of the world, the hidden reality behind the masks of human behavior. His desire is to use his relationship with his subjects as an occasion for attaining a more complete relationship with the Idea. Constantin Constantius describes this occupation in a remarkable passage whose unmistakably sexual character suggests that the observer's deepest intimacy is reserved not for his subjects but rather for the ideas which are put into play in their lives:

> So I am by nature: with the first shudder of presentiment, my soul has simultaneously run through all the consequences, which frequently take a long time to appear in actuality. Presentiment's concentration is never forgotten. I believe that an observer should be so constituted, but if he is so constituted, he is also sure to suffer exceedingly. The first moment may overwhelm him almost to the point of swooning, but as he turns pale the idea impregnates him, and from now on he has investigative rapport with actuality. If a person lacks this feminine quality so that the idea cannot establish the proper relation to him, which always means impregnation, then he is not qualified to be an observer, for he who does not discover the totality essentially discovers nothing. (R 146)

On this account, the goal of Constantin Constantius, the observer and experimenting psychologist, is a vaguely Hegelian one: to discover the objective whole, the totality, which is behind the particulars of human behavior and human history. This vocation is both passionate and demanding, but Constantin Constantius regards it as a noble calling because everything is done for the greater good of science. "[I]t is often distressing to be an observer—it has the same melancholy effect as being a police officer. And when an observer fulfills his duties well, he is to be regarded as a secret agent in a higher service, for the observer's art is to expose what is hidden" (*R* 135).

The role of the scientific, experimenting observer, as Constantin Constantius describes it, is no doubt worthy of a certain admiration and praise. The only problem with it is that it is completely out of place when one is attempting to understand repetition. The nature of repetition (as Constantius explains it) and the function of the experimenting observer (as Constantius explains it) are completely at odds, and this is the primary source of the comedy that he generates as one of the comic actors in the farce called *Repetition*. Constantin Constantius turns *Repetition* into a farce and proves himself to be a great comic actor when he attempts to discover by means of objective, experimental, scientific observation whether or not repetition is possible. To see how funny this really is we need to piece together Constantin Constantius's various remarks on repetition in order to create at least a rudimentary picture of what he is looking for when he conducts his experiments. Then the comic incongruity between what he is looking for and how he is looking for it will become apparent.

In his discussion of the nature of repetition Constantin Constantius follows the same pattern that he alludes to in a passing remark on the pseudonym "A" from *Either/Or*: as an author he is "at times somewhat deceitful, not in the sense that he says one thing and means another, but in the sense that he pushes the thought to extremes, so that if it is not grasped with the same energy, it reveals itself the next instant as something else" (*R* 133). While Constantin Constantius seems to believe that he himself knows what repetition is, he doesn't bother to tell us everything that he knows. The "question of repetition" that Constantin Constantius poses for himself in the very first paragraph of the book is limited to "whether or not it is possible, what importance it has, whether something gains or loses in being repeated" (*R* 131). We are left to piece together a theory of the nature of repetition from scattered remarks that Constantius makes in the course of his experimenting, and then to interpret these fragments with the same passion and energy with which Constantius has infused them, in order to arrive at something approaching a complete picture or theory of the meaning of repetition. Once that is in place, we can then consider whether or not

How to misunderstand *Repetition* 179

that theory of repetition is compatible with Constantin Constantius's own attempt to verify whether or not repetition exists.[163]

Constantin Constantius defines repetition by contrasting it with recollection. Recollection and repetition are inverse mirror images of each other. "Repetition and recollection are the same movement, except in opposite directions, for what is recollected has been, is repeated backward, whereas genuine repetition is recollected forward" (R 131). Both recollection and repetition are attempts to take the present moment seriously, either by forming some connection between the present and the past (recollection), or the present and the future (repetition). Constantin Constantius argues that since the "now" of the present is always a singular instant—a blink of the eye that immediately disappears and in itself has no preestablished or lasting meaning—it follows that without either recollection or repetition to give meaning to the present moment "all life dissolves into an empty, meaningless noise" (R 149).

According to Constantin Constantius, recollection was the preeminent category of Greek philosophy.[164] For the Greeks, recollection gave meaning to existence by connecting it with a past that is always already beyond one's reach. In Greek thought there is nothing new under the sun; no genuine discoveries are possible. To know is not to create or uncover but to remember, and this memory provides an anchor of stability and significance to the fleeting moments of one's experience. In this way recollection bestows meaning on the present, but because that meaning is rooted in a past that is always unrecoverable, it is tinged with sadness (R 132). Recollection makes security and sadness inseparable. "Recollection has the great advantage that it begins with the loss; the reason it is safe and secure is that it has nothing to lose" (R 136).

What recollection was to ancient philosophy, Constantin Constantius argues, repetition will be to modern philosophy, even though modern philosophy is not yet aware of this (R 131).[165] At present, Constantius writes, philosophy remains ignorant of repetition because philosophy "makes no movement; as a rule it makes only a commotion, and if it makes any movement at all, it is always within immanence, whereas repetition is and remains a transcendence" (R 186). But Constantin Constantius predicts that this ignorance of repetition will be replaced in the future. "Repetition is the new category that will be discovered" (R 148), and if his prediction is realized it would mark a radical paradigm shift for philosophy, because it would transfer the source of meaning out of the past and into the future.

> The dialectic of repetition is easy, for that which is repeated has been—otherwise it could not be repeated—but the very fact

that it has been makes the repetition into something new. When the Greeks said that all knowing is recollecting, they said that all existence, which is, has been. When one says that life is a repetition, one says: actuality, which has been, now comes into existence. (R 149)[166]

The paradigm shift involved here is not complicated, but its consequences for philosophy are enormous. Shifting the source of meaning into the future creates a fundamentally new relationship to time as well as a fundamentally new relationship to the idea of the new. Repetition is an attempt to bring together both new and old in a movement that—like existence—always faces the future. To explain this, Constantin Constantius uses the analogy of a marriage that constantly renews and reinvigorates itself.

> Hope is a lovely maiden who slips away between one's fingers; recollection is a beautiful old woman with whom one is never satisfied at the moment; repetition is a beloved wife of whom one never wearies, for one becomes weary only of what is new. One never grows weary of the old, and when one has that, one is happy. He alone is truly happy who is not deluded into thinking that the repetition should be something new, for then one grows weary of it. It takes youthfulness to hope, youthfulness to recollect, but it takes courage to will repetition. He who will merely hope is cowardly; he who will merely recollect is voluptuous; he who wills repetition is a man, and the more emphatically he is able to realize it, the more profound a human being he is. But he who does not grasp that life is a repetition and that this is the beauty of life has pronounced his own verdict and deserves nothing better than what will happen to him anyway—he will perish. For hope is a beckoning fruit that does not satisfy; recollection is petty travel money that does not satisfy; but repetition is the daily bread that satisfies with blessing. (R 132)

According to this analogical argument, the only way for a marriage not only to endure through time but also to be a continuing source of happiness and growth for both partners is through repetition. The partners in the marriage are the same people every day of their lives, and they wake up each morning to find themselves married to the same person they were married to yesterday, and the day before that; all of these components of the marriage are the same, but the relationship itself—if it is going to be a happy and fulfilling relationship—must be constantly renewed. In one sense the relationship is always old, in that it is based on a commitment that was made long ago, but in another sense it can be always new, in that it is renewed with each new day, and willed into existence with a courage that insists on discovering greater depth and uncharted territory in what is (apparently at least, on the surface of things) the same as it ever was (except for the fact that everyone involved is getting older). Repetition seeks innovation and novelty within the borders of the same. It seeks to prove that a single personality has infinite depth,[167] which means that a relationship between the same two people can be continually, inexhaustibly new even as it grows old, while at the same time remaining always, in appearance at least, the same. A relationship of repetition brings together change and continuity by moving the source of meaning into the future.

In contrast to a relationship of repetition, typified by a marriage that constantly renews itself, consider a relationship of recollection, typified by the young man's "poetic relationship" to his beloved. The young man who is the subject of Constantin Constantius's observation is "deeply and fervently in love," and yet after just a few days . . .

> He was essentially through with the entire relationship. In beginning it, he took such a tremendous step that he leaped over life. If the girl dies tomorrow, it will make no essential difference; he will throw himself down again, his eyes will fill with tears again, he will repeat the poet's words again. What a curious dialectic! He longs for the girl, he has to do violence to himself to keep from hanging around her all day long, and yet in the very first moment he became an old man in regard to the entire relationship. Underneath it all, there must be a misunderstanding. For a long time nothing has affected me so powerfully as this scene. It was obvious enough that he was going to be unhappy; that the girl would also become unhappy was no less obvious, although it was not immediately possible to predict how it would happen. But so much is certain: if anyone can join in conversation about recollection's love, he can. Recollection has the great advantage that it begins with the loss; the reason it is safe and secure is that it has nothing to lose. (R 136)

> His mistake was incurable, and his mistake was that he stood at the end instead of at the beginning, but such a mistake is and remains a person's downfall. (R 137)

The young man who is the subject of Constantin Constantius's observation has poeticized his relationship to his beloved right out of existence. The girl has been reduced to a memory, and her actual existence is now an obstacle to the recollected relationship. The young man must find a way to get the actual, existing girl out of the picture so that he can pursue his relationship with the idealized, remembered girl without any interference from the demands of actuality. Because it fixes its gaze strictly on what is past, recollection's love cannot really be love, Constantius argues. It can only be nostalgia: a longing for that which is past and gone, forever out of one's reach (R 137). And since the actual girl has been removed from the picture the young man's love is really a kind of self-love. There is no relationship because there is no other party to share in the relationship.

> The young girl was not his beloved: she was the occasion that awakened the poetic in him and made him a poet. That was why he could love only her, never forget her, never want to love another, and yet continually only long for her. She was drawn into his whole being; the memory of her was forever alive. She had meant much to him; she had made him a poet—and precisely thereby had signed her own death sentence. (R 141)

Constantin Constantius observes that in a recollected "relationship" such as this effectively there is really only one person in the room. "In a sense, her existence or non-existence was virtually meaningless to him" (R 138). "It was impossible for him to create a real relationship out of this misunderstanding" (R 141). Having transformed the relationship with the girl into a poetic longing, idealized in a memory, the only one left in existence to be an object of the young man's affection is himself.

Repetition emphasizes this point with an abundance of masturbatory imagery. For example, writing of the young man's intellectual abilities Constantius notes:

> The young man was so constituted and endowed by nature that I would have wagered that he had not been caught in the snare of erotic love. The fact is that there are exceptions in this respect that cannot be declined into the usual case forms. He had unusual mental powers, particularly imagination. As soon as his creativity was awakened, he would have enough for his whole life, especially if he understood himself properly and limited himself to a cozy domestic diversion, together with mental activity and pastimes of the imagination, which are the most perfect substitute for all erotic love, are not at all accompanied by the inconveniences and disasters of erotic love, and have a definite similarity to what is most beautiful in the bliss of erotic love. Anyone with that nature does not need feminine love, something I usually account for by his having been a woman in a previous existence and his having retained a recollection of it now that he has become a man. (R 183–84)

More imagery of auto-eroticism is found in the young man's letters to Constantin Constantius, especially in the final letter. After the young man learns that the girl has married someone else, the language of self-absorption and self-love intensifies dramatically. He writes:

> Let existence reward her as it has, let it give her what she loved more; it also gave me what I loved more—myself. (*R* 220)

> I am myself again; the machinery has been set in motion. The inveiglements in which I was entrapped have been rent asunder; the magic formula that hexed me so that I could not come back to myself has been broken. There is no longer anyone who raises his hand against me. My emancipation is assured; I am born to myself, for as long as Ilithyia folds her hands, the one who is in labor cannot give birth. It is over, my skiff is afloat. In a minute I shall be there where my soul longs to be, there where ideas spume with elemental fury, where thoughts rise uproariously like nations in migration. (*R* 221)

Finally, in the final paragraph of the final letter from the young man, the auto-erotic self-absorption that has been apparent throughout the book finally climaxes in a paragraph which seems very much like the textual equivalent of an orgasm:

> The beaker of inebriation is again offered to me, and already I am inhaling its fragrance, already I am aware of its bubbling music—but first a libation to her who saved a soul who sat in the solitude of despair: Praised be feminine generosity! Three cheers for the flight of thought, three cheers for the perils of life in service to the idea, three cheers for the hardships of battle, three cheers for the festive jubilation of victory, three cheers for the dance in the vortex of the infinite, three cheers for the cresting waves that hide me in the abyss, three cheers for the cresting waves that fling me above the stars! (*R* 221–22)

The bottom line in this comparison between a relationship of repetition (such as an ideal marriage) and a relationship of recollection (such as the young man's poeticized relationship with the girl, which in the end is really just a relationship with himself) is that repetition is capable of discovering meaning in a future that has not happened yet—and that therefore leaves room for change and becoming, while recollection can only find meaning in an unchangeable past—a relationship in which one is inevitably removed from the present moment of existence. Both recollection and repetition bring meaning to existence, and if neither of them is present, 'all life dissolves into an empty, meaningless noise" (*R* 149). But recollection can give meaning to existence only at the cost of transforming the existing individual into "a memorial volume of the past" (*R* 133). Repetition, on the other hand, gives meaning to existence without contradicting the relationship to time that the existing individual finds herself in. Repetition allows the individual to continue to live her life forward, but without thereby becoming "a tablet on which time writes something new every instant" (*R* 133).

The theory of repetition that Constantin Constantius articulates is clear and existentially coherent. What is incoherent, and therefore very funny, is the attempt that Constantin Constantius makes to study repetition through scientific observation. Constantius becomes a comic actor, and *Repetition* becomes a farce, when he tries to combine a theory of repetition that is subjective and a method of observation that is objective.

To see the comedy of such a combination, consider Constantin Constantius's trip to Berlin. The trip is conceived as a scientific experiment that will prove once and for all whether or not repetition is possible. Such a plan assumes that repetition is something that is publicly observable, subject to objective measurement and analysis. Not surprisingly, with this goal in mind Constantius is disappointed at every turn. All the external details of his previous visit to Berlin, which he longed to find repeated again, have changed. His landlord is now married; the city lacks the beauty he remembers from his last visit; and in the Königstädter Theater, the performance of *Der Talisman* is not as enjoyable as before (and he can't even get the same seat that he had last time). He had hoped to verify the possibility of repetition by repeating the same satisfactions of his previous visit, but the experiment fails miserably. Nothing is the same, except for the features of the trip that he wanted to change; everything else that repeats, repeats differently; and consequently Constantin Constantius can't get no satisfaction.

Constantin Constantin's assumptions about satisfaction play an important role in the Berlin experiment, and they serve to clarify further the comedy of his approach to repetition.[168] The only repetition he finds is not the kind that brings happiness, but rather the kind that brings frustration and annoyance, such as the repetition he discovers in the restaurant he used to frequent:

> —It was just the same, the same witticisms, the same civilities, the same patronage; the place was absolutely the same—in short, the same sameness. Solomon says that a woman's nagging is like rain dripping from the roof; I wonder what he would say about

this still life. What an appalling thought—here a repetition was possible! (*R* 170)

Constantin Constantius assumes that repetition should bring a certain kind of happiness, but his conception of that happiness as undisturbed tranquility and satisfaction show that he is still under the spell of recollection. Consider the bitter conclusions about the possibility of happiness that Constantin Constantius tosses out at the end of the Berlin experiment:

> The older a person grows, the more he understands life and the more he relishes the amenities and is able to appreciate them—in short, the more competent one becomes, the less satisfied one is. Satisfied, completely, absolutely satisfied in every way, this one never is, and to be more or less satisfied is not worth the trouble, so it is better to be completely dissatisfied. Anyone who has painstakingly pondered the matter will certainly agree with me that it has never been granted to a human being in his whole life, not even for as much as a half hour, to be absolutely satisfied in every conceivable way. (*R* 172–73)

It follows, he says, that no one can be satisfied, and no one can find happiness. Everyone is certain to be disappointed.

> And is it not the case that the older a person grows, the more and more of a swindle life proves to be, that the smarter he becomes and the more ways he learns to shift for himself, the bigger the mess he makes of life and the more he suffers! (*R* 172)

Constantin Constantius then proceeds to tell the story of the one day in his life when he got closest to perfect satisfaction, and actually began to think that it was possible—but of course his hopes were dashed and he was disappointed in the end.

> At one time I was very close to complete satisfaction. I got up feeling unusually well one morning. My sense of well-being increased incomparably until noon; at precisely one o'clock, I was at the peak and had a presentiment of the dizzy maximum found on no gauge of well-being, not even on a poetic thermometer. My body had lost its terrestrial gravity; it was as if I had no body simply because every function enjoyed total satisfaction, every nerve delighted in itself and in the whole, while every heartbeat, the restlessness of the living being, only memorialized and declared the pleasure of the moment. . . . All existence seemed to have fallen in love with me, and everything quivered in fateful rapport with my being. . . . As stated, it was one o'clock on the

dot when I was at the peak and had presentiments of the highest of all; when suddenly something began to irritate one of my eyes, whether it was an eyelash, a speck of something, a bit of dust, I do not know, but this I do know—that in the same instant I was plunged down almost into the abyss of despair, something everyone will readily understand who has been as high up as I was and while at that point has also pondered the theoretical question of whether absolute satisfaction is attainable at all. Since that time, I have abandoned every hope of ever feeling satisfied absolutely and in every way, abandoned the hope I had once nourished, perhaps not to be absolutely satisfied at all times but nevertheless at certain moments, even though all those instances of the moment were no more, as Shakespeare says, than "an alehouse keeper's arithmetic would be adequate to add up." (*R* 173–74)

It's clear from this story, and from all of Constantin Constantius's complaints about the impossibility of satisfaction, that he is in the grip of a rather extreme utilitarian fantasy wherein happiness consists of the complete elimination of all pain and the institution of pure unadulterated pleasure. This is a conception of happiness as *stasis*, as the maintenance of a previous—now past—state of happiness, all of which boils down to a theory of happiness as recollection. Constantin Constantius is not prepared to accept the true happiness of repetition, which he himself explained prior to his second trip to Berlin (*R* 131–33), and consequently he believes that his experiment has demonstrated the impossibility of happiness. He finds repetition only in the miserable and painful details of the trip, such as the stagecoach ride, where, unfortunately, everything repeated itself (*R* 151). (This is not terribly surprising, given that Constantin Constantius is a person who dislikes all change, even housekeeping [*R* 171]). After enduring such undesirable repetition for several days in Berlin, Constantin Constantius writes: "I became so furious, so weary of the repetition, that I decided to return home. My discovery was not significant, and yet it was curious, for I had discovered that there simply is no repetition and had verified it by having it repeated in every possible way" (*R* 171). This comical conclusion to Constantin Constantius's Berlin experiment is the direct result of the comical assumptions that the experiment was based upon.

But the comic performance that Constantin Constantius gives in act I of *Repetition* plays a valuable part in the book's indirect communication of the meaning of repetition. It brings into relief one aspect of repetition that is essential, and yet very easy to overlook or even to contradict in a text that aims to tell the truth about this concept. The meaning that repetition finds in the future can only be a personal meaning.[169] Repetition creates meaning by discovering newness in what is apparently (and as far as any observer can detect, since an observer is only capable of observing exterior surfaces) old.[170] Therefore, what Constantin Constantius says of the young man actually applies with perfect accuracy to his own project of observation:

> It is characteristic of the young man, however, precisely as a poet, that he can never really grasp what he has done, simply because he both wants to see it and does not want to see it in the external and visible, or wants to see it in the external and visible, and therefore both wants to see it and does not want to see it. (R 230)

True repetition gives significance to the present moment by discovering depth beneath the surfaces that are objectively apparent. A form of repetition that is observable would lead to what Constantin Constantius explicitly says true repetition is intended to avoid: "Who could want to be a tablet on which time writes something new every instant or to be a memorial volume of the past? Who could want to be susceptible to every fleeting thing, the novel, which always enervatingly diverts the soul anew?" (R 133). The task of the book of which Constantin Constantius is the author is an impossible task: explaining the meaning of a concept whose meaning is never general, but rather always particular and individual, and therefore always hidden from objective observation. Given this impossible task, the only way for Constantin Constantius to succeed is to fail. By assuming the role of a comic actor, Constantin Constantius fails in the task that he sets for himself—to verify the possibility of repetition by objective, scientific means—but succeeds, indirectly, in communicating something important about the essentially subjective nature of repetition.

The second comic actor: The anonymous young man and the trials of Job

> I do not converse with people, but in order not to break off all communication with them, as well as not to give them blather for their money, I have collected quite a few poems, pithy sayings, proverbs, and brief maxims from the immortal Greek and Roman writers who have been admired in every age. I have added to this anthology several superb quotations from Balle's catechism published under the license of the orphans's home. If anyone asks me anything, I have a ready answer. I quote the classics as well as Per Degn, and as a bonus I quote Balle's catechism.

> "Even if we have attained all desirable honor, we ought not to let ourselves be carried away by pride and haughtiness." Then I deceive no one. . . . What could be gained if I did say something? There is no one who understands me. My pain and my suffering are nameless, even as I myself am nameless . . . . (R 203)

The second comic actor in the farce called *Repetition* is the anonymous young man who is the subject of Constantin Constantius's scientific observation.[171] The young man is in love with the story of Job. He is, in every way, a Job-intoxicated man.

> Although I have read the book again and again, each word remains new to me. Every time I come to it, it is born anew as something original or becomes new and original in my soul. Like an inebriate, I imbibe all the intoxication of passion little by little, until by this prolonged sipping I become almost unconscious in drunkenness. (R 205)

Having fled from his beloved, and from the scientific gaze of Constantin Constantius, the young man isolates himself from the world, with only Job as his companion. In Job he finds a voice for his suffering, and also a model to follow in leveling a complaint against the universe.

> [Y]ou did not disappoint men when everything went to pieces—then you became the voice of the suffering, the cry of the grief-stricken, the shriek of the terrified, and a relief to all who bore their torment in silence, a faithful witness to all the affliction and laceration there can be in a heart, an unfailing spokesman who dared to lament. (R 197)

"I need you, a man who knows how to complain so loudly that he is heard in heaven" (R 198). ("[B]ut woe also to him," the young man adds, "who would cunningly cheat the sorrowing of sorrow's temporary comfort in airing its sorrow and 'quarreling with God'" [R 197]). Cutting himself off from the rest of the world, the young man reads and re-reads the Book of Job, finding endless shades of meaning for himself within its pages (R 204). He devotes two of his eight letters to expressing his general passion and enthusiasm for the Book of Job, and two more letters to giving his interpretation of the text. That interpretation focuses on freedom. "Job's greatness is that freedom's passion in him is not smothered or quieted down by a wrong expression," the young man writes. "In similar circumstances, this passion is often smothered in a person when faintheartedness and petty anxiety have allowed him to think he is suffering because of his sins, when that was not at all the case" (R 207). Job demonstrates that—in spite of all human frailties—"in freedom [humanity] still has something of greatness" (R 208).

The Book of Job is, no doubt, a very mysterious and powerful story, and no one can read it without being moved by its depiction of humankind's ultimate vulnerability. But when the young man adopts Job as his role model, and tries to imitate his complaint to heaven, everything is transformed into farce. The second main source of the comedy in the farce called *Repetition* is the incongruity between the trials of the young man and the trials of Job. While the young man sees a perfect fit between Job's loss and his own, their stories actually diverge at two important points.

First of all, it's impossible to keep a straight face when comparing the suffering of Job and the suffering of the young man. In one day, Job loses five hundred yoke of oxen, five hundred she-asses, seven thousand sheep, three thousand camels, seven sons, three daughters, and an unspecified number of household servants. Finally, he himself is smitten with boils from head to toe, which he has to scrape off with a potsherd (Job 1–2).[172] To add insult to injury, these disasters are not just the result of bad luck; they are deliberately (albeit indirectly) inflicted upon him by God, whom Job has feared and worshipped all his life in a perfectly upright manner. On the other hand, what exactly is the young man suffering from? He's involved in an unhappy love affair that he wants to end even though the girl still loves him, and he can't quite bring himself to break up with her. That's it. Constantin Constantius notes that the first time he met the young man he immediately knew he was a poet because "a situation that would have been taken easily in stride by a lesser mortal expanded into a world event for him" (R 230). The young man's suffering is so trivial in comparison to the trials of Job that even mentioning the two of them in the same breath is hilarious.[173] All of the young man's protestations, his complaints about the injustice of the universe, his terrible cries, which frighten even the birds at the fishery when he meets Constantin Constantius there at dawn (R 140)—the triviality of the young man's complaints make his story seem like nothing more than a self-indulgent parody of Job's experience of profound and genuine suffering.

Consider, for example, perhaps the most famous text in all the young man's letters: his tirade against the meaninglessness of existence in letter number three.

> I am at the end of my rope. I am nauseated by life; it is insipid—without salt and meaning. If I were hungrier than Pierrot I would not choose to eat the explanation people offer. One sticks a finger into the ground to smell what country one is in; I stick my finger into the world—it has no smell. Where am I? What does it

> mean to say: the world? What is the meaning of that word? Who tricked me into this whole thing and leaves me standing here? Who am I? How did I get into the world? Why was I not asked about it, why was I not informed of the rules and regulations but just thrust into the ranks as if I had been bought by a peddling shanghaier of human beings? How did I get involved in this big enterprise called actuality? Why should I be involved? Isn't it a matter of choice? And if I am compelled to be involved, where is the manager—I have something to say about this. Is there no manager? To whom shall I make my complaint? (R 200)

This text has been invoked repeatedly as the paradigm of one of the fundamental ideas of existentialism: that humans are thrown into a world that, in itself, is meaningless.[174] That's a very serious principle, but in this context the young man's appeal to that principle is impossible to take seriously because it is so clearly a parody of Job's speech about the injustices inflicted on him, which begins with the words, "Let the day perish wherein I was born, and the night in which it was said, There is a man child conceived" (2:3). It is comical that the young man is so lost in his poetic existence that—unable to see the tremendous gulf that separates the unhappiness of his imperfect love affair from the pain and suffering of losing seven sons and three daughters (not to mention quite a bit of cattle)—he calls upon Job, of all people, as the only person who can possibly comprehend his misery, and then tries to imitate the Book of Job with his own juvenile rant against a universe that has not granted all his wishes.

Letter number three also brings to the foreground the second, and most important, disconnection between Job and the young man. As the young man affirms, Job becomes great through the use of his own freedom (R 207–8). In spite of all the tragedies that have befallen him, in spite of the terrible circumstances to which he has been reduced, Job still asserts himself as a person who is free and responsible. The young man, on the other hand, consistently refuses to exercise his own freedom. His overriding obsession is the fact that he might be considered guilty for the way he behaved with the young girl, and he finds this extremely annoying. To avoid being called guilty, he casts about for every possible excuse. Someone or something else, he argues, must have been to blame:

> My mind is numb—or is it more correct to say I am losing it? One moment I am weak and weary, yes, practically dead with apathy; the next moment I am in a rage and in desperation rush from one end of the world to the other to find someone on whom I can vent my anger. My whole being screams in self-contradiction. How did it happen that I became guilty? Or am I

> not guilty? Why, then, am I called that in every language? What kind of miserable invention is this human language, which says one thing and means another? Has something happened to me, is not all this something that has befallen me? (*R* 200–201)

> Who is to blame but her and the third factor, from whence no one knows, which moved me with its stimulus and transformed me? After all, What I have done is praised in others. —Or is becoming a poet my compensation? I reject all compensation, I demand my rights—that is, my honor. I did not ask to become one, and I will not buy it at this price. —Or, if I am guilty, then I certainly should be able to repent of my guilt and make it good again. Tell me how. On top of that, must I perhaps repent that the world plays with me as a child plays with a beetle? . . . Shall I allow myself to be shoved out in this manner? Why, then, was I shoved in? I never requested it. Someone imprisoned on bread and water is better off than I am. (*R* 202–3)

The young man insists upon his innocence in the strongest possible terms. Like Job, he argues strenuously with anyone who would say that he is at fault (although, unlike Job, it's not at all apparent to whom he is speaking). "Even if the whole world rose up against me, even if all the scholastics argued with me, even if it were a matter of life and death—I am still in the right. No one shall take that away from me" (*R* 201). On this point, as on all others, the young man aligns himself with Job, who "despite everything, is in the right" (*R* 207). But on this point, once again, the identification is absurd. While Job is innocent, the young man clearly is not. He has walked out on a relationship without any explanation, leaving the girl alone and confused; and even before that he was guilty of concealing his true feelings from her, which ultimately did neither of them any good. Clearly, these are not capital crimes, but their triviality only underscores the depth of the young man's stubbornness in refusing to accept responsibility for his own actions. But when this effort to evade his own freedom and responsibility leads him to adopt Job, of all people, as his guide and role model, the incongruity becomes hilarious.

Perhaps the height of this comedy, which results from the young man's refusal to acknowledge his own freedom, is the moment in his seventh letter when he announces that he is waiting for a thunderstorm (*R* 214–15). For an entire month he sits and waits, "*suspenso gradu*," for the thunderstorm that will remake his entire personality (*R* 214).

> I am waiting for a thunderstorm—and for repetition. And yet I would be happy and indescribably blessed if the thunderstorm

would only come, even in my sentence were that no repetition is possible. What will be the effect of this thunderstorm? It will make me fit to be a husband. It will shatter my whole personality—I am prepared. It will render me almost unrecognizable to myself—I am unwavering even though I am standing on one foot. My honor will be saved, my pride will be redeemed, and no matter how it transforms me, I nevertheless hope that the recollection of it will remain with me as an unfailing consolation, will remain when I have experienced what I in a certain sense dread more than suicide, because it will play havoc with me on quite another scale. (R 214)

The young man models his expectation of such a thunderstorm on the climactic ending of the Job story, where Job gets back everything that the Lord took from him—but here again the inapplicability of Job's repetition to the young man's situation is really quite hilarious.[175] Job asserts his freedom and demonstrates his integrity by holding fast to his claim that all of the disasters in his life cannot be divine punishments because he has done nothing to deserve such punishment. In the end God commends him for this, and gives him back twice as much as he had before (42:7–10). "So the LORD blessed the latter end of Job more than his beginning" (42:12). This is Job's story of repetition, and it turns on the fact that he clings to his freedom even when everything else is taken from him. He uses his freedom in the only way that remains to him in his strange and particular situation: to ask sincerely why all of this has happened to him, since the God that he believes in does not punish the just. The young man's misappropriation of Job's story of repetition underscores the fact that every story of repetition is a personal story whose meaning cannot be separated from the particular, subjective context in which it occurs.

The only thing that can be generalized from Job's story of repetition is the centrality of freedom and responsibility to any story of repetition. The young man's relationship problems are not going to be resolved by the Lord speaking to the unhappy couple from the whirlwind. The repetition that the young man claims to want, a life of ever-deepening love in a marriage that constantly renews itself, can only be achieved when he uses his own freedom to transform his personality in order to make such a repetition possible—something he claims he is helpless to do (R 214–15). Waiting for some objective event, like a thunderstorm, to transform him subjectively, creates a strange comic picture: somewhat akin to the picture that Constantius paints of the person who can find happiness only by "standing on one leg in a picturesque pose" (R 158). While the young man waits passively in this strange pose for repetition to happen to him, the girl marries someone else, and the possibility of repetition passes him by forever. The young man celebrates this fact and ecstatically claims that this is the thunderstorm for which he was waiting, and the repetition that it has accomplished is to give him back what he loved most of all: himself (R 220-22). But the comedy of this climax is obvious. The young man is left, like Narcissus, admiring his own gaze in a relationship of recollection that has given up on finding any meaning in the future.

Like Constantin Constantius, the young man's comic performance plays an important part in *Repetition*'s indirect communication of the meaning of repetition. While Constantius clarified the subjective nature of repetition by attempting to comprehend it objectively, the young man demonstrates the centrality of freedom and responsibility in repetition by attempting to evade them both.[176] In each case, one essential dimension of repetition is made available to the reader by means of a farcical presentation of its absence. This indirect method ensures that whatever the reader understands about repetition is understood strictly through her own effort, so that the understanding gained is a purely personal understanding that is independent of the book, and its author, and likewise of everyone else on the planet. So in the end *Repetition* doesn't tell us very much about the idea to which its title refers. The farce that Constantin Constantius and the young man act out for us provides only a preliminary sketch of repetition, leaving the details to be filled in by each individual as she acts out the story of repetition in her own life.[177] By the end of the book all we really know about repetition is that it is a method of bringing meaning to the present moment by means of referring the present moment to the future rather than the past, and that both subjectivity and freedom are essential to it. Other than that, the meaning of this strange quasi-concept remains to be discovered, or created, by each individual. The full significance of repetition, like the full significance of the life of the individual who seeks to accomplish repetition in his own existence, waits to be realized in the future.

This strange and satisfying conclusion is very effectively communicated by this strange and wonderful book, but most readers have failed to understand this communication because they have failed to see that the book is a farce, written by an author who has a great love for this particular form of comedy and who has crafted his text in this way to ensure that 'the heretics are unable to understand it" (R 225). *Repetition* has been understood as a tragedy by most readers, and it is certainly presented that way—with unrestrained wailing and melodrama by its two principal characters; but once these characters are understood as comic actors *Repetition* gets a chance to repeat itself as a truly hilarious farce, worthy of a long run in the Königstädter Theater.

Curtain call: Paging Mr. X, Esq.

> Let everyone form his own judgment with respect to what is said here about repetition; let him also form his own judgment about my saying it here and in this manner, since I, following Hamann's example, express myself in various tongues and speak the language of sophists, of puns, of Cretans and Arabians, of whites and Moors and Creoles, and babble a confusion of criticism, mythology, rebus, and axioms, and argue now in a human way and now in an extraordinary way. Assuming that what I say is not a mere lie, I perhaps did right in submitting my aphorism to a systematic appraiser. Perhaps something may come of it, a footnote in the system—great idea! Then I would not have lived in vain! (R 149–50)

Who, then, is the real reader of *Repetition*? "Who in our day thinks of wasting any time on the curious idea that it is an art to be a good reader, not to mention spending time to become that?" (R 225). The general public has no time for such things. Almost everyone, Constantin Constantius claims, approaches a book "for one or another superficial reason unrelated to the book" (R 225).[178] He goes on to enumerate several specific types of readers who will find his book a great disappointment. These include: the inquisitive female, the concerned family man, the temporary genius, the convivial family friend, the vigorous champion of reality, the experienced matchmaking woman, His Reverence, and the ordinary reviewer (R 225–26). The last of these will have the dubious privilege of explaining to the world everything that the book is not, namely: "it is not a comedy [or so he thinks, and almost all reviewers to date would agree with him], tragedy, novel, short story, epic or epigram"—and to make matters even worse, it is not susceptible to the Hegelian dialectic (R 226). This unfortunate reviewer "will also find it difficult to understand the movement in the book, for it is inverse; nor will the aim of the book appeal to him, either, for as a rule reviewers explain existence in such a way that both the universal and the particular are annihilated" (R 226).

The movement of *Repetition* is inverse in the sense that instead of leading the reader out into the world—to Berlin, for example—to discover the meaning of repetition, it inverts that movement and leads the reader back into herself. Repetition, if there is such a thing, can only be found in the unique, subjective experience of an individual who freely and subjectively enacts that role on the stage of her own existence. And the text is exceptional in that it does not try to reduce the existence of such an individual in order to bring it within the bounds of general categories, but instead aims to defend the subjective and extraordinary character of repetition in the face of an omnivorous demand for universality which is the spirit of the times. "Eventually one grows weary of the incessant chatter about the universal and the universal repeated to the point of the most boring insipidity," Constantin Constantius writes. "There are exceptions. If they cannot be explained, then the universal cannot be explained, either" (R 227).[179]

The real reader of *Repetition* must be someone who does not read book reviews, but instead reads and understands the book for herself, and is capable of seeing the farce that is staged on its pages by Constantin Constantius and the anonymous young man. Such a reader is, of necessity, "fictional" (R 225) in that Constantin Constantius must conjure her up in his imagination, like a work of fiction, since it is impossible for him to have a direct relationship with her. The meaning of repetition, if it is not going to be contradicted by the method of its presentation, must be communicated indirectly.[180]

All of this is very serious business. The repetition that *Repetition* is pointing to amounts to nothing less than the possibility of happiness and progress in existence. But this fact can only be appreciated when one learns to appreciate *Repetition* not as a tragedy, but as a highly educational farce performed by two excellent comic actors.

Chapter 7

How to misunderstand Johannes Climacus by missing the methodological manifesto that it contains
or
Lessons on how to end (and also begin) a philosophy book, from a philosophy book that did not end

RENÉ DESCARTES IS THE author of several excellent jokes, for which he rarely receives credit. For example:

> Good sense is the best distributed thing in the world: for everyone thinks himself so well endowed with it that even those who are the hardest to please in everything else do not usually desire more of it than they possess.[181]

> [N]ot content with knowing everything which is intelligibly explained in their author's writings, they wish in addition to find there the solution to many problems about which he says nothing and about which perhaps he never thought.... In this they seem to resemble a blind man who, in order to fight without disadvantage against someone who can see, lures him into the depths of a very dark cellar.[182]

> The high degree of perfection displayed in some of their actions makes us suspect that animals do not have free will.[183]

> I have almost never encountered a critic of my views who did not seem to be either less rigorous or less impartial than myself.[184]

> [P]hilosophy gives us the means of speaking plausibly about any subject and of winning the admiration of the less learned.[185]

While Descartes almost never gets the attention he deserves as a writer of comedy, there has been no shortage of recognition for him as a master of methodology. Descartes is the author not only of the *Discourse on Method*—the quintessential statement of modern philosophy's obsession with method—but also of two more unpublished works that attempt to lay down the law on the practice of philosophy: *Rules for the Direction of the Mind* and *The Search for Truth by Means of the Natural Light*. Some may doubt that Descartes had a sense of humor, but no one doubts that he was thoroughly committed to giving philosophy a solid methodological foundation.

Søren Kierkegaard is also the author of many excellent jokes. In fact, some have suggested that his entire authorship can be understood as one long and rather complicated joke. Even if one doesn't go to that extreme, it's clear that an author who wrote under at least twenty-eight different pseudonyms, who composed an entire book consisting of nothing but prefaces, who wrote no less than five different conclusions to his work as a pseudonymous author, whose master's thesis was titled *The Concept of Irony*, and who also penned the immortal lines—

> Were there no hell, one would have to come into being in order to punish the assistant professors, whose crime is indeed precisely of the sort that cannot very well be punished in this world. (*KJN* 10:99)

—is someone who cares about comedy. While not everyone has appreciated Kierkegaard's sense of humor, nearly all of his readers have at least acknowledged that he had one.

On the other hand, almost no one has thought of Kierkegaard as someone who had any particular interest in philosophical method.[186] In this chapter I will try to rectify that fact. I will argue that *Johannes Climacus, or, De Omnibus Dubitandum Est* can be read as Kierkegaard's own statement concerning philosophical method, his own version of the *Discourse on Method*. *Johannes Climacus* is a strange text that has been interpreted in many ways, but it has not yet been fully appreciated as something of a methodological manifesto.[187] In what follows I will argue for such a reading by focusing on three key issues of methodology that are explored in *Johannes Climacus*: (a) time and its relation to the philosophical investigator; (b) the nature of doubt and its role in philosophy; and (c) the possibility of connecting ideas without disconnecting from the world.

All of these matters of methodology are occasioned for Johannes Climacus by Descartes's attempt to give philosophy a legitimate beginning, so I'll begin with that beginning.[188]

(1) Philosophy's dubious beginning(s)

> The Dialectic of Beginning.
>
> Scene in the Underworld.
>
> Characters: Socrates
>   Hegel
>
> Socrates is sitting by running water, listening to it in the cool air. Hegel sits at a desk and is reading Trendelenburg's *Logische Untersuchungen:* Part 2 p. 198 and walks over to Socrates to complain.
>
> Socrates: Should we begin by disagreeing entirely or by agreeing about something that we will call a presupposition?
>
> Hegel: [says nothing—apparently stunned speechless by the stupidity of Socrates's question]
>
> Socrates: what presupposition are you starting from?
>
> Hegel: from none whatever.
> Socrates: now you're talking; so perhaps you do not begin at all.
>
> Hegel: I? Not begin—I, who have written 21 volumes?
>
> Socrates: Ye gods, you have sacrificed a hecatomb.
>
> Hegel: But I start with nothing.
>
> Socrates: isn't that with something?
>
> Hegel: No—the inverse movement. It becomes clear only at the conclusion of the whole, where I have treated all knowledge, world history, etc.
>
> Socrates: How can I overcome this difficulty. . . . You know that I did not even allow Polus to speak for more than 5 minutes at a time, and you want to speak XXI volumes. (*KJN* 11.2:30)

It is well known that Descartes was obsessed with beginnings. The *Discourse on Method* records and preserves this obsession for all of Descartes's philosophical posterity. In Part One of the *Discourse* Descartes tells the story of the intellectual awakening that led him to conclude that philosophy, even though it's the oldest of the disciplines, had nevertheless begun badly, and hence had never really begun. As with most intellectual awakenings, this one took place after he had finished school:

> From my childhood I have been nourished upon letters, and because I was persuaded that by their means one could acquire a clear and certain knowledge of all that is useful in life, I was

> extremely eager to learn them. But as soon as I had completed
> the course of study at the end of which one is normally admitted
> to the ranks of the learned, I completely changed my opinion.
> For I found myself beset by so many doubts and errors that I
> came to think I had gained nothing from my attempts to become
> educated but increasing recognition of my ignorance. And yet I
> was at one of the most famous schools in Europe . . . .[189]

Descartes's post-graduate skepticism is directed particularly at philosophy because it has had far longer than any other intellectual endeavor to produce some meaningful results, and yet in spite of this it has never managed to finish anything. He remarks on this fact with a terse dismissal that makes no attempt to conceal his disdain for so much wasted time.

> Regarding philosophy, I shall say only this: seeing that it has
> been cultivated for many centuries by the most excellent minds
> and yet there is still no point in it which is not disputed and
> hence doubtful . . . [a]nd, considering how many diverse opin-
> ions learned men may maintain on a single question—even
> though it is impossible for more than one to be true—I held as
> well-nigh false everything that was merely probable. As for the
> other sciences, in so far as they borrow their principles from
> philosophy I decided that nothing solid could have been built
> upon such shaky foundations.[190]

Philosophy's long history of false starts leads Descartes to a drastic conclusion: "when I cast a philosophical eye upon the various activities and undertakings of mankind there are almost none which I do not consider vain and useless."[191]

From this point on the *Discourse* takes on the tone of an engineering textbook, as Descartes sounds the alarm about the dangers of shaky foundations.[192] The intellectual world needs to be completely rebuilt, he argues, starting with philosophy, which needs to be given (finally!) a solid foundation to support its lofty aspirations. After a bizarre series of dreams on November 10, 1619,[193] Descartes is inspired to use doubt as the method to secure such an unshakable foundation.

Like the *Discourse on Method*, *Johannes Climacus* is a story about a young man who has just come to realize that everything may not be precisely as he was taught in school. The peculiar intellectual history of Johannes Climacus follows a strange trajectory that leads him into a confrontation with Descartes's theory of beginnings.

Johannes Climacus says that he was in love with thinking long before he even knew there was such a thing as philosophy. Kierkegaard emphasizes that what Johannes loves about thinking is not the beginning or the ending, but rather a certain movement. This movement is generated by making connections between ideas. Johannes has no particular ideological convictions, nor does he regard himself as a philosopher (or even a "philosophizer"). "[T]o want to devote himself exclusively to speculation, had not occurred to him; he was not profound enough for that" (JC 123). Thinking for him is a far more superficial activity. It is the movement from one thought to another that glides along the surface of ideas, disinterested in putting down roots or throwing out anchors by committing to any given principles. "The least significant and the most significant things tempted him alike as points of departure for his pursuits; for him the result was not important—only the processes interested him" (JC 123).

For Johannes Climacus, the movement of thinking is like climbing a ladder, but this ladder is not one that gets pushed away after the climb is complete. The pleasure of thinking comes from both ascending and descending—from linking ideas into a chain and then moving along the chain in both directions. This movement twists Climacus's ladder into a circular ladder, something more like a spiral staircase or a Moebius strip. The pleasure of thinking is not complete until Johannes has made a complete circle and returned to the precise point from which he departed.

> It was his delight to begin with a single thought and then, by way of coherent thinking, to climb step by step to a higher one, because to him coherent thinking was a *scala paradisi*, and his blessedness seemed to him even more glorious than the angels's. Therefore, when he arrived at the higher thought, it was an indescribable joy, a passionate pleasure, for him to plunge headfirst down into the same coherent thoughts until he reached the point from which he had proceeded. Yet this did not always turn out according to his desire. If he did not get just as many pushes as there were links in the coherent thinking, he became despondent, for then the movement was imperfect. Then he would begin all over again. If he was successful, he would be thrilled, could not sleep for joy, and for hours would continue making the same movement, for this up-and-down and down-and-up of thought was an unparalleled joy. In those happy times, his step was light, almost floating.... (JC 118–19)

In the movement of Climacus's thought there is no climax, and there is no predetermined starting point. There is no beginning, nor is there an ending; everything in Johannes Climacus's passionate description suggests that those categories simply don't apply. Thinking (which is not the same thing as philosophy for Johannes—it never occurred to him that his love of thinking made him a philosopher) is all about movement, and the beginning or the end of movement is no longer movement in the strict sense of the word. For everyone but the Unmoved Mover all movement has a beginning and eventually it has an end, but that isn't what interests Johannes Climacus. His interest lies in the *inter-esse,* the zone in-between beginnings and endings where thought is in motion. His passion is to keep the movement of thought moving—forever if possible—by advancing and then receding, up and down, backwards and forwards, along the chain of interconnected ideas. Ideally this movement would never stop: the web of ideas would be expanded until every possible thought was interconnected, and then Johannes Climacus could spend eternity moving from one connected thought to another and then back again. It's not the first or the last link in a chain of ideas that Johannes Climacus is in love with, but rather the movement that is possible between those two points. "At times, he did become aware of how he would arrive at one and the same result from quite different points, but this did not attract his attention in a deeper sense. His desire at all times was only to press his way through. Wherever he suspected a labyrinth, he had to find the way. Once he began, nothing could influence him to stop" (JC 123–24). Thinking, for Johannes Climacus, is all about continuity, not about beginnings and endings.

Johannes Climacus discovers philosophy for the first time as a university student when he attempts to read some recent philosophical books. Unfortunately his first brush with modern philosophy is a great disappointment:

> At times, a title would tempt him, and he would go to the book gladly and expectantly, but, lo and behold, it would discuss many other things, least of all that which one would have expected. If at length he worked his way little by little through to what the title had justified his searching for, the thought process would frequently be interrupted and the matter left undecided. He was often annoyed to find so much attention paid to what appeared to him to be incidentals. The investigation would be interrupted in order to correct one or another singular opinion advanced by some author totally unknown to him. For him to understand this digression properly would require a prior reading of that man's book. That in turn perhaps would presuppose others etc. He also thought he observed that the reason for incorporating a particular opinion of a particular author would be a very peculiar one: because he lived in the same city as the writer, because he wrote in the same journal, etc. He did not

always find rigorous, dialectical movement; he sadly missed the wonderful sport of dialectic, its puzzling surprises. (*JC* 129–30)

What Johannes finds lacking in modern philosophy is the connection and continuity that he loves so much in his own thinking. The philosophy books that he reads are filled with interruptions. Some of these interruptions are due to the fact that the authors are more concerned with dropping the right names and with standing guard over their own tiny plots of ideological real estate than with creating the kind of dialectical movement that, for Climacus, constitutes the great pleasure of thinking. But an even more significant obstacle comes from the fact that modern philosophy is distracted by a preoccupation with beginnings, and by an insistence upon a certain kind of methodologically respectable and uncontaminated beginning. The one thesis that is "always praised, always venerated" and always repeated by modern philosophy is the claim that philosophy begins in doubt: *De omnibus dubitandum est* (*JC* 131). Johannes Climacus is enthused by this thesis because he senses that it may be the key that will allow him finally to comprehend modern philosophy, which has so far eluded him. To this end he seeks "to clarify for himself the connection between that thesis and philosophy" (*JC* 132). The thesis *de omnibus dubitandum est* "became a task for his thinking. Whether it would take a long or a short time to think it through, he did not know. But this he did know: until that time came, he would not let go of it, even though it were to cost him his life" (*JC* 131).

Unfortunately this project quickly turns problematic, because when he attempts to think the thesis *de omnibus dubitandum est* it immediately fractures into multiple theses, all of which resist his attempts to get a chain of coherent thinking started. *De omnibus dubitandum est,* which seemed to provide such a clean and concise beginning to philosophy, disintegrates before Johannes Climacus's eyes into three different propositions, leaving him once again unsure about where to begin. These three different propositions are: (a) philosophy begins with doubt; (b) in order to philosophize, one must have doubted; (c) modern philosophy begins with doubt (*JC* 132). "What struck him at once in these three theses was that they did not seem to be at all of the same kind" (*JC* 133). Each one of these three different starting points for philosophy turns out to be, in its own way, exceedingly dubious. Not knowing where to begin, he begins at the end: with the proposition that comes last in the sequence and also seems to be situated last in time.

(2) Three possible meanings of *de omnibus dubitandum est*

(a) Modern philosophy begins with doubt

The first possible meaning of Descartes's insistence that philosophy must begin with doubt is that modern philosophy begins with doubt. According to this thesis, philosophy does not, and should not, have a single history. Modern philosophy has its own unique genealogy, with its own unique beginning. But Climacus notes two problems with the claim "modern philosophy begins with doubt," one having to do with the use of the term "modern," and one having to do with the use of the term "philosophy."

First of all, Climacus points out that it makes no sense to use the word "philosophy" to refer to both modern and pre-modern philosophy if they have different histories. In the Cartesian view, modern and premodern philosophy are fundamentally different due to the fact that pre-modern philosophy has no *fundamentum* while modern philosophy has the only possible *fundamentum*, which is doubt. According to this view, pre-modern philosophy is baseless and therefore not really philosophy. "In that case, modern philosophy is essentially philosophy, and to call that older version philosophy is merely an accommodation" (JC 134). And to give only modern philosophy—the philosophy that begins with doubt—the deed of ownership to all of philosophy is also inconsistent, Climacus points out, because the idea that philosophy must begin with doubt—an idea which must be in place before modern philosophy can begin—is itself a philosophy (JC 137). Hence, even when modern philosophy takes the extreme measure of cutting itself off from the rest of the history of thought that preceded it, it still seems unable to avoid the infinite regress that it wants to be rid of. The absolute, unmediated beginning that Descartes promised is nowhere in sight.

Secondly, Climacus argues that it is incoherent to call any philosophy "modern" if it has a static, singular beginning in time—such as that particular moment in 1637 when Descartes first said: "Philosophy must begin with doubt." Modern philosophy can only remain "modern" if it is allowed to transform itself in time. If it defines itself wholly in terms of one static moment—in 1637, or whenever—then it has immediately lost the developmental, evolutionary dimension that is essential to its modernity. "Modern philosophy must be assumed to be even yet in the process of becoming," Climacus writes; "otherwise there already would be something more modern, in relation to which it would be older" (JC 135). So in both of these respects, "modern" and "philosophy" are rendered meaningless when one postulates the thesis "modern philosophy begins with doubt."

(b) Philosophy begins with doubt

Unable to make any sense of the first version of *de omnibus dubitandum est,* Climacus turns to another version of the thesis that seems to avoid the confusion surrounding both "modern" and "philosophy." "Philosophy begins with doubt" seems to be the straightforward embodiment of what Descartes promised: a foundation that will get philosophy started. But Climacus is quick to note that this principle is not as simple and straightforward as it seems, because "Philosophy begins with doubt" immediately posits an antecedent to philosophy that is itself outside of philosophy. Thus, the beginning is again deferred, and philosophy is once more left standing at the altar, still waiting to get underway.

This consequence is the result of the peculiar properties of doubt. Doubt is a negative principle that always isolates itself, asserting a discontinuity with both past and future. Doubt can't be a beginning for the whole of philosophy that is also continuous with philosophy itself, because it instantly ruptures any continuity that exists within philosophy.

> When a later philosopher said: Philosophy begins with wonder—he was straightway in continuity with the Greeks. They had wondered, and he also wondered; they perhaps had wondered about one thing, and he wondered about something else. But every time a later philosopher repeats or says these words: Philosophy begins with doubt—the continuity is broken, for doubt is precisely a polemic against what went before. (JC 145)

Doubt is not a beginning that pulls philosophy together on a unitary foundation from which it can begin. The negative force of doubt individuates thinking, and refers it back to another starting point that (once again) is prior to philosophy—a theory that precedes the formal and official commencement of theorizing. Doubt fractures the community that Cartesian foundationalism seemed to promise, and instead leaves every man for himself. Hence the great irony of the admonition that Climacus hears repeated all around him, that "one must begin to philosophize by doubting."

> He was well able to comprehend that an individual could take it into his head to doubt, but he could not understand how it could occur to him to say this to another person, least of all as advice (it would be another matter if it were said to deter), for if the

other person was not too slow, he might very well say, "Thank you, but please forgive me for also doubting the correctness of that statement." (JC 146)[194]

The negativity of doubt makes it incapable of beginning philosophy, or anything else. Doubt can at best be an antecedent or prerequisite to philosophy—not the unifying foundation that Descartes imagined, but an individualizing moment before the beginning of philosophy that makes such a beginning possible. If doubt is conceptualized as the beginning of philosophy, philosophy is once again unable to move forward, but instead is thrown into an infinite regress in search of its foundation, its starting point. The principle, "philosophy begins with doubt," when pursued philosophically, leads only to an abyss of questions that one must ignore if philosophy is ever going to get underway. Mindful of this, Johannes Climacus assures us that,

> he did not ask questions like these: Is doubt as the beginning of philosophy a part of philosophy or is it the whole of philosophy? If it is a part, what, then, is the other part? Could it be certainty? Are these parts forever separated? How can we speak of a whole if its parts exclude one another? What Epicurus had sophistically maintained about the fear of death seemed to him to apply here—namely, that one should not concern oneself about it, because when I am, death is not, and when death is, I am not. Was there something that united these two parts into a whole? He did not ask questions such as these . . . . (JC 147)

. . . but he did allude to them, and that is enough to establish the self-contradictory status of the principle "philosophy begins with doubt." "The more Johannes Climacus thought about this matter, the more obvious it became to him that this was not the way into philosophy, because that thesis destroyed the very connection" (JC 154–55). "[T]his beginning was a beginning that kept one outside philosophy" (JC 156). All that is left, if Cartesian foundationalism is going to be saved, and if philosophy is ever going to get started, is to allow for the antecedent status of doubt—to allow that the beginning of philosophy is something wholly other than philosophy itself. Understood in this way, the founding principle of philosophy now means—

(c) In order to philosophize, one must have doubted

The retreat to this formulation of *de omnibus dubitandum est* amounts to giving up on the quest to find philosophy's beginning. At this point the beginning of philosophy has been bracketed as a mystery. Doubt is now conceptualized not as what starts philosophy, but as a prerequisite to getting started in philosophy (perhaps just one of many such prerequisites). Doubt is a kind of personal discipline, an ordeal, an initiation that one goes through in order to make oneself worthy of philosophy, just as one must be initiated and purified in order to join a holy order (JC 157–58).

To this final formulation of Cartesian foundationalism Johannes Climacus has two, very personal, objections. First of all, he argues that the principle enjoins an attitude toward thinking that is too arrogant. As an initiation it is not humble enough. The initiate who doubts does not kneel in submission before her teacher, but rather stands over her in a posture of superiority (JC 158). Philosophy, Climacus argues—whatever it is, and however it manages to get started—deserves more respect than that. Secondly, Climacus criticizes the idea of making universal doubt into one of philosophy's prerequisites because it doesn't own up to the difficulty of the task. Modern philosophy gives lip service to the project of universal doubt without acknowledging how difficult and even debilitating it really is.

> The thesis remained unexplained, but an explanation was precisely what he needed, and his own private thinking had made him more receptive to instruction by others. But the explanation was not forthcoming; on the contrary, at times the thesis was repeated so swiftly by those speaking that he almost became dizzy because of the uniformity. Then he would always return home troubled, because what seemed so easy for others, so that they only needed to outline it vaguely, was so hard for him to think. He thought through the thesis again and again, tried to forget what he had thought in order to begin again, but, lo and behold, he always arrived at the same point. Yet he could not abandon the thesis; it seemed as if a mysterious power held him to it, as if something were whispering to him: Something is hiding behind this misunderstanding. (JC 139)

This flippancy concerning universal doubt leads Johannes Climacus to suspect that no one who advocates such a prerequisite to philosophy has actually done it.

> [I]n the philosophizers's discussions there was scarcely a word about all the fates and adventures in which one must be tried when going forth to doubt everything. And yet one would have expected to hear this; one would think that this would be their favorite topic, just as seafarers love to talk about their close calls, especially if they meet men who have navigated the same ocean. If some of them had wanted to lie about such an experience

> without actually having had it, he would have understood, but he also hoped to be able to distinguish the experienced man from the parrot by the fervency of what was said. But it was inexplicable that everyone remained silent. Could it be that what they had seen was so terrible that they dreaded to speak of it? Yet they were indeed associated with men who must have seen the same thing. (JC 164)

The silence of the philosophers (or philosophizers) leads Johannes Climacus to wonder if maybe all this heated discussion about universal doubt is just "a pious fraud" (JC 158).

> When, for example, he once heard a lecture on the importance of having doubted as a preliminary to philosophy the following statement was made in his presence: "One must not waste time on doubting but should just start out at once in philosophy." The listeners seized this information with the same joy with which Catholics seize the announcement of an indulgence. Johannes, however, was so ashamed on behalf of the speaker that he wished himself far away so that no one could see it on his face. (JC 164)

No one who has actually tried to doubt everything that can be doubted could so easily dismiss the task as if it were a thing of naught—easily undertaken and quickly completed so that one can move on, once and for all, to bigger and better things. Once again, Johannes Climacus feels that he's been lied to. He has discovered that *De omnibus dubitandum est* is not a singular and simple proposition, nor can it be the beginning of either modern philosophy or of philosophy in general, nor can it be lightly and easily used as a prerequisite that situates itself before the beginning of philosophy. This series of deceptions leads Johannes Climacus to lose all faith in the philosophers of his generation who so flippantly speak in the name of doubt.

> Johannes then bade the philosophizers farewell forever. Even if he now and then heard a particular observation by them, he decided to pay no more attention to them, inasmuch as he had had so many sad experiences of how deceitful their words were. He now followed the method he was in the habit of following—namely, to make everything as simple as possible. (JC 165)[195]

(3) What really matters for philosophical method according to Johannes Climacus

(a) Time and temporality

When Johannes Climacus gives up on the modern philosophy of doubt and begins to follow his own "method of simplicity" a more general theory of philosophical method begins to take shape. The exploration of Cartesian foundationalism and beginnings in philosophy that comes at the beginning of the book leads Johannes Climacus first of all to formulate a more general theory of subjective time—time as it relates to the individual thinker who attempts to think philosophically.

Johannes Climacus argues that all attempts to give philosophy a beginning, or to pin down the precise moment when philosophy did in fact begin, require the individual thinker to falsify her own experience of time. Descartes's foundationalism, which was intended to provide a simple and straightforward starting place for philosophy, so that individual philosophers could get underway (finally!)—so that philosophy could start to make some progress (at last!)—actually ends up making philosophical thought something so fantastically difficult that the single individual finds it almost unbearable. Thinking philosophically, after Descartes has discovered the correct foundation for philosophy, now requires such a prodigious head that the individual philosopher nearly collapses under its weight.

> [T]o be a philosopher these days must be something indescribably difficult.... [T]he individual philosopher *must become conscious of himself and in this consciousness of himself also become conscious of his significance as a moment in modern philosophy; in turn modern philosophy must become conscious of itself as an element in a prior philosophy, which in turn must become conscious of itself as an element in the historical unfolding of the eternal philosophy.* Thus the philosopher's consciousness must encompass the most dizzying contrasts: his own personality, his little amendment—the philosophy of the whole world as the unfolding of the eternal philosophy. It was a long time before Johannes managed to think this enormous thought correctly and definitely. (JC 140, all emphasis is in the original)

It's no wonder, then, that when Johannes Climacus finally does manage to think this enormous thought "it overwhelmed him and *he fainted!* When he recovered consciousness, he hardly dared to turn his attention to that thought. It dawned on him that it could drive a person to madness" (*JC* 141, all emphasis is in the original). This charming bit of melodrama illustrates how the temporality of foundationalist Cartesian philosophy becomes an unendurable intellectual burden, stopping the thinker in her tracks instead of allowing her to get started. Johannes Climacus faints because the thought that he describes really is unthinkable (*JC* 143).

Johannes Climacus's own theory of time emerges in response to the unthinkable burden of Cartesian temporality. Climacus puts this theory as succinctly as possible when he writes:

> [T]he individual's knowledge was always merely knowledge about himself as a moment and about his significance as a moment. On the presupposition that this was actually possible—something he still could not really grasp, since it was not clear to him how a moment could become conscious of itself merely as a moment, inasmuch as this consciousness was an impossibility without a consciousness that was more than a consciousness of oneself at a moment, because otherwise my consciousness would have to reside in another—this knowledge would then become a very relative knowledge and would by no means be an absolute knowledge. (*JC* 141)

Any other understanding of time is an abstraction, a disconnection from reality, and—when applied to the individual's own lived experience of temporality—merely "a prank" (*JC* 141). The theory of time implied by Cartesian foundationalism suggests that somehow, magically, "a person would become so transfigured to himself that he, although himself present to himself, became past to himself" (*JC* 142). "But how would it be possible for every single moment to become aware also of its eternal validity as a moment in the whole? That, after all, would require that the individual be omniscient and that the world be finished" (*JC* 141). The individual's own experience of time and the world would be completely sacrificed in favor of artificial theoretical constructs.

> It would already be a precarious matter, so it seemed to him, for someone to undertake to prophesy. And yet, just as one could have an intimation of a necessity in the past, was it not also conceivable that one could have an intimation of a necessity in the future. Philosophy, however, wanted to do something even more difficult: it wanted to permeate everything with the thought of eternity and necessity, wanted to do this in the present moment, which would mean slaying the present with the thought of eternity and yet preserving its fresh life. It would mean wanting to

see what is happening as that which has happened and simultaneously as that which is happening; it would mean wanting to know the future as a present and yet simultaneously as a future. (*JC* 142–43)

In contrast to this distortion of individual experience and time, Johannes Climacus's theory of temporality attempts to preserve the individual thinker's place in time. That place is always the present, always her present, always a moment which is both singular and particular. The moment of thought is always the present moment, and the present "did not obtain permission to become a present out of eagerness to become a past, the sooner the better" (*JC* 142). This means that every beginning in philosophy is always a subjective beginning. It can have no objective, universal, mathematical necessity, even if it is the thesis "philosophy begins with doubt" (*JC* 153). There is no beginning to "philosophy as a whole" because "philosophy as a whole" is an empty abstraction. There are only particular philosophers, and philosophy has always already begun at that particular moment when each one of them begins to wonder about the present moment. No further analysis or explanation of this moment is necessary: "if no one had ever explained what it is to wonder, every human being would still have done it" (*JC* 151).[196]

(b) Doubt and consciousness

Subjectivity is central to the second methodological issue that Johannes Climacus takes up in response to Descartes's argument that philosophy needs a foundational beginning. In the final section of the book Johannes Climacus explores the true nature of doubt. This section of the book, which is titled "What must the nature of existence be in order for doubt to be possible?" is extraordinarily dense and rich in concepts with methodological implications.[197]

To answer the question posed by this title Johannes Climacus analyzes the structure of consciousness. The consciousness of an infant is, apparently, immediate. It knows the world directly, but does not distinguish itself from the world. There is no mediation between the self and the world, no obstacle to the infant's direct, unreflected experience of reality. But this direct relationship with the world is transformed by the introduction of language. As the child acquires language her consciousness is transformed. As soon as a child is no longer an *infans* she no longer experiences the world directly, because language brings a dimension of ideality into consciousness. The consciousness of an *infans* is a mystery to us, and its unmediated character is a purely speculative presupposition. The form of consciousness that we ourselves recognize is situated between the raw reality of the world (which is like the Kantian *Ding an sich*), and the ideality of the word.

Mediated consciousness can also be understood as interested consciousness. Consciousness is inter-ested because it finds itself always already between the ideality of language and the actuality of existence. Consciousness as we experience it doesn't exist until it is bracketed by both actuality and ideality. "Reality is not consciousness, ideality no more so. Yet consciousness does not exist without both, and this contradiction is the coming into existence of consciousness and is its nature" (*JC* 168). Consciousness is inter-ested because it exists in the tension between ideality and actuality. The subject of consciousness feels the pull of both the real and the ideal and she cannot be indifferent to this tension because she lives in it. The difference between the actual and the ideal structures all the contours of her experience.

Johannes Climacus explains the interested and mediated nature of consciousness by contrasting it with reflection. Reflection is the gap between ideality and actuality regarded in the abstract, without the presence of the subject who is situated within that gap. Reflection is the condition of the possibility of consciousness; but it is not yet consciousness since it remains a simple dichotomy, whereas consciousness is always a trichotomy because an existing subject is added to the simple oppositions of reflection.

> Reflection is the *possibility of the relation;* consciousness is *the relation, the first form of which is contradiction.* As a result, he also noted, reflection's categories are always *dichotomous*. For example, ideality and reality, soul and body, to know the true, to will the good, to love the beautiful, God and the world, etc. are categories of reflection. In reflection they touch each other in such a way that a relation becomes possible. The categories of consciousness, however, are *trichotomous*, as language also demonstrates, for when I say, *I am conscious of this sensory impression,* I am expressing a triad. Consciousness is mind, and it is remarkable that when one is divided in the world of mind, there are three, never two. Consciousness, therefore, presupposes reflection.... [A]s soon as I as mind become two, I am *eo ipso* three. (*JC* 169)

Reflection is only the abstract "possibility" of a relation between the ideal and the actual, whereas consciousness is that trichotomous relationship between the world, language that attempts to express the truth about the world, and the existing subject who finds herself thrown into the tension between this opposition (*JC* 170).

Doubt is only possible because consciousness is mediated, trichotomous, and interested. The infant is not capable of doubt because her consciousness is not mediated. Doubt only becomes possible when language is added to consciousness, bringing with it the interested space that the conscious subject occupies between the actual and the ideal. "The possibility of doubt, then, lies in consciousness, whose nature is a contradiction that is produced by a duplexity and that itself produces a duplexity" (*JC* 168). "If there were nothing but dichotomies, doubt would not exist, for the possibility of doubt resides precisely in the third, which places the two in relation to each other" (*JC* 169). Doubt is always situated in the space of the interested, existing subject. That same separation of the actual and the ideal that makes doubt a possibility continues to structure the experience of consciousness for the interested subject.

It follows from this analysis of consciousness that doubt has nothing to do with objectivity. Objective thought is on the same level as reflection. It regards the separation of the ideal and the actual in the abstract. The dichotomies that it considers never include an interested subject who lives in the tension between reality and language. Interested consciousness assumes the simple oppositions of reflection as conditions of its own possibility, but it goes beyond those dichotomies to a more complicated level of trichotomy. In Johannes Climacus's methodology subjective interest is a higher form of thought than objective reflection. Therefore it makes no sense to try and find the "solution" to doubt in objective thought, because doubt is not even possible until one rises to the level of subjective thought.

> [A]ll disinterested knowledge (mathematics, esthetics, metaphysics) is only the presupposition of doubt. As soon as the interest is canceled, doubt is not conquered but is neutralized, and all such knowledge is simply a retrogression. Thus it would be a misunderstanding for someone to think that doubt can be overcome by so-called objective thinking, for it presupposes the latter but has something more, a third, which is interest or consciousness. (*JC* 170)

Modern philosophy, which begins in the same space that was cleared by Descartes when he applied universal doubt to human experience, misunderstands the true nature of doubt when it responds to doubt with an objective "system."

> [I]t was an inconsistency, seemingly based on ignorance of what doubt is, that motivated modern philosophy to want to conquer

> doubt systematically. Even if the system were absolutely perfect, even if the actuality exceeded the advance reports, doubt would still not be overcome—it only begins—for doubt is based on interest, and all systematic knowledge is disinterested. (JC 170)

Johannes Climacus wants to reposition doubt as the beginning—not of philosophy—but rather of an engaged, interested form of subjective thinking that is a step beyond the objectivity of reflection. Doubt is "the beginning of the highest form of existence, because it can have everything else as its presupposition" Climacus argues (JC 170).

There are several implications of this analysis of doubt for a philosophical methodology. Perhaps the most important is the way that it valorizes subjective thought, rescuing it from the ill repute that followed Descartes's attempt to give philosophy the same legitimacy as the sciences. Johannes Climacus points out that using doubt to tear down the rotten edifice of philosophy should have led to an entirely different paradigm shift than the one that Descartes effected, since the very possibility of doubt points the way to the superiority of subjective thought. But Descartes, and his followers, took the wrong turn at this crossroads because they failed to appreciate the interested nature of consciousness. Philosophy can begin with doubt—not in the sense of an objective, absolute, foundational beginning, which is what Descartes proposed, but rather as a subjective moment of recognition when the individual realizes doubt's conditions of possibility in the structure of consciousness, and the fact that they illuminate an interested, subjective form of thought where philosophy has always already begun.[198]

(c) Connecting ideas without disconnecting from the world

The *Discourse on Method* is, in part, a very personal autobiography that narrates the story of one René Descartes. Descartes explicitly acknowledges this dimension of the text. Though he believes his method is a universal method that has great potential to reinvent all of philosophy as a science, he recounts the story of the method's discovery in the form of a purely personal history, filled with the accidents and idiosyncrasies of his own existence, and he recognizes that the peculiarities of his own life may have introduced into his method some elements that are not worthy of imitation.

> But I say without hesitation that I consider myself very fortunate to have happened upon certain paths in my youth which led me to considerations and maxims from which I formed a method whereby, it seems to me, I can increase my knowledge gradually and raise it little by little to the highest point allowed by the

> mediocrity of my mind and the short duration of my life. . . . I shall be glad . . . to reveal in this discourse what paths I have followed, and to represent my life in it as if in a picture, so that everyone may judge it for himself. . . . I am presenting this work only as a history or, if you prefer, a fable in which among certain examples worthy of imitation, you will perhaps also find many others that it would be right not to follow.[199]

Johannes Climacus follows the same pattern as the *Discourse on Method*. All of Johannes Climacus's thoughts on method are presented in the context of a very personal narrative that tells the story of his own intellectual development, and we should not hesitate to apply Descartes's admonition to the philosophical methods that develop out of both of these personal histories: "among certain examples worthy of imitation, you will perhaps also find many others that it would be right not to follow."[200] Both the *Discourse on Method* and *Johannes Climacus* give us an opportunity to consider how a philosophical method of connecting ideas need not lead to a disconnection from the world. Exploring the personal narratives in this text may seem like pointless psychologizing at best and a voyeuristic invasion of privacy at worst, but I think that it's an important part of what *Johannes Climacus* has to say about method. From the very beginning Johannes Climacus emphasizes that the narrative structure of his text is one of its essential elements (JC 117). I will argue that the narrative of *Johannes Climacus* is, among other things, a very explicit commentary on how philosophy can lead to a disconnection from the world, but this is an avoidable accident: there is no necessary connection between philosophical method and disconnection from the world.[201]

The Cartesian tradition is famous for emphasizing detachment from the world as an essential prerequisite for philosophical thought. This theme is especially pronounced in the *Discourse on Method* when Descartes tells the story of his day alone in the stove-heated room (probably in 1619). This day of meditation was only possible, Descartes reports, because there was "no conversation to divert me and fortunately . . . no cares or passions to trouble me."[202] This day of isolation resulted, of course, with Descartes arriving at the conclusion that he could be more certain of himself, of his own mind, than of anyone or anything else in the world.[203] In the *Discourse* Descartes elaborates on how this detached, isolationist approach to philosophy carried over into his life as a whole. Describing his itinerant lifestyle, Descartes writes, "I did nothing but roam about in the world, trying to be a spectator rather than an actor in all the comedies that played out there."[204]

In his detachment from the world and his efforts to be a spectator rather than a participant, Johannes Climacus mirrors Descartes. Johannes is absorbed in a world of his own creation: the world of carefully arranged ladders of coherent thoughts, which he struggles to balance as he makes his way through the world.

> When we see someone carrying a number of fragile and brittle things stacked one upon the other, we are not surprised that he walks unsteadily and continually tries to maintain balance. If we do not see the stack we smile, just as many smiled at Johannes Climacus, not suspecting that his soul was carrying a stack far taller than is usually enough to cause astonishment, that his soul was anxious lest one single coherent thought slip out, for then the whole thing would collapse. He did not notice that people smiled at him, no more than at other times he would notice an individual turn around in delight and look at him when he hurried down the street as lightly as in a dance. He did not pay any attention to people and did not imagine that they could pay any attention to him; he was and remained a stranger in the world. (JC 119)

The level of self-absorption involved in Johannes Climacus's thinking is indicated by the erotic, masturbatory imagery invoked by the text. His long-standing relationship with thinking clearly has an erotic dimension. For him, thinking is the greatest possible pleasure; it is an eroticism that transcends sex, and this erotic pleasure comes from making connections:

> No young lover can be more intensely moved by the incomprehensible transition that comes when erotic love awakens in his breast, by the stroke of lightning with which reciprocated love bursts forth in the beloved's breast, than he was moved by the comprehensible transition in which one thought connects with another, a transition that for him was the happy moment when, in the stillness of his soul, his presentiments and expectations were fulfilled. (JC 118)

The pleasure of that moment, when one idea connects with another, is the pleasure that Johannes Climacus lives for. In pursuit of that singular and solitary pleasure he lives like "a stranger in the world" (JC 119), "occupied with himself and with his own thoughts" (JC 120). "[H]e did not express his views, never betrayed what was going on inside him—the erotic in him was too deep for that" (JC 123).

"Coherent thinking" as Johannes Climacus understands it is the ability to start anywhere in a chain of interconnected ideas and then work your way through the connections between the ideas for as long as possible. The pleasure that Johannes Climacus finds in thinking comes from being able to plunge into a labyrinth of ideas, and then find his way back out again (*JC* 124). "In this way his life was always adventurous. He did not require forests and travels for his adventures, but merely what he had: a little room with one window" (*JC* 124). The eroticism of his thought is something like tantric sex: "If he was successful, he would be thrilled, could not sleep for joy, and for hours would continue making the same movement, for this up-and-down and down-and-up of thought was an unparalleled joy" (*JC* 119). And the same consistency (and endurance) that typify his joy in thinking also characterize his life as a whole. "[N]ow in his twenty-first year he was to a certain extent the same as he had always been" (*JC* 119). "[S]ince he practically never went out, he very early became accustomed to being occupied with himself and with his own thoughts" (*JC* 120).

> What other children have in the enchantment of poetry and the surprise of fairy tales, Johannes Climacus had in the repose of intuition and the interchange of dialectic. These delighted the child, became the boy's play, the young man's desire. In this way his life had a rare continuity, not marked by the various transitions that generally denote the separate periods. As Johannes grew older, he had no toys to lay aside, for he had learned to play with what would be his life's earnest occupation, and yet it did not thereby lose its appeal. A little girl plays so long with her doll that at last it is transformed into her beloved, for woman's whole life is love. His life had a similar continuity, for his whole life was thinking. (*JC* 122–23)

It's clear that Johannes Climacus, like Descartes, lives on the margins of his world, "trying to be a spectator rather than an actor in all the comedies that played out there."[205] He exchanges thinking for love, but infuses thinking with an eroticism that transcends the infatuation of love.

> Those who knew him somewhat intimately tried to explain his enclosed nature, which shunned all close contacts with people, by supposing that he was either melancholy or in love. In a certain sense, those who supposed the latter were not incorrect, although they erred if they assumed that a girl was the object of his dreams. Such sentiments were totally foreign to his heart, and just as his external appearance was delicate and ethereal, almost transparent, his soul was likewise far too intellectual and spiritual to be captivated by a woman's beauty. In love he was, ardently in love—with thought, or, more accurately, with thinking. (*JC* 118)

The intensity of this eroticism reinforces his separation from the world. He maintains the carefully balanced connections between all his thoughts only by disconnecting himself from other people and the world.

Disconnection from the world is not a necessary consequence of a philosophical method that emphasizes connecting ideas. *Johannes Climacus* clarifies that this idiosyncratic result has an idiosyncratic cause in the personal history of Johannes Climacus himself. The source of Johannes Climacus's fascination with the methodology of coherent thinking was his father, who is described as moody, depressed, full of self-loathing, but also a dialectical genius.

> Once in a while, when an older, trusted friend visited the family and engaged in a more confidential conversation with his father, Johannes frequently heard him say, "I am good for nothing; I cannot do a thing; my one and only wish would be to find a place in a charitable institution." This was no jest. There was not a trace of irony in his father's words; on the contrary, there was a gloomy earnestness about them that troubled Johannes. Nor was it a casual comment, for his father could demonstrate that a person of the least importance was a genius compared with him. No counter-demonstration achieved anything, for his irresistible dialectic could make one forget what was most obvious, could compel one to stare fixedly at the observation he made as if there were nothing else in the world. Johannes, whose whole view of life was, so to speak, hidden in his father, since he himself did not get to see very much, became entangled in a contradiction, because it was a long time before it dawned on him that his father contradicted himself—if by nothing else, then by the skill with which he could vanquish any opponent and reduce him to silence. (*JC* 124–25)

Since Johannes Climacus's "whole view of life was hidden in his father," the descriptions of his father's personal and emotional idiosyncrasies also serve to illustrate Johannes's own state of mind, and the text goes to great lengths to inform us that his father was not a happy person. Johannes Climacus's "formative influence," we are told, "was not a man who knew how to propound his knowledge as valuable but was instead one who knew how to render it as unimportant and valueless as possible" (*JC* 125).

Johannes's father teaches him to surround himself with artificial worlds. Instead of taking Johannes out on a walk through the city, they simply walk through the house while his father erects an artificial city with words, describing everything in such perfect detail that "after a half-hour's walk with his father he was so overwhelmed and weary as if he had been out a whole day. . . . For Johannes, it was as if the world came into existence during the conversation" (*JC* 120). This kind of almost fantastical idealism has a profound impact on Johannes Climacus.

> Although he was led into ideality at an early age, this by no means weakened his belief and trust in actuality. The ideality by which he was nourished was so close to him, everything took place so naturally, that this ideality became his actuality, and in turn he was bound to expect to find ideality in the actuality all around him. His father's depression contributed to this. (*JC* 124)

The last sentence in this paragraph is by far the most interesting in terms of the connection between methodology and personality that I'm considering here. Johannes Climacus decision to use philosophy to disconnect from the world reflects his own unhappiness, which apparently he learned from his father. Johannes Climacus has no confidence that the world is a place where beauty and happiness are possible, and his use of philosophy as a means to disconnect from the world reflects this desperation and despair. There is a strong suggestion in this narrative that this particular aspect of his philosophical method is, as Nietzsche might say, merely a symptom. In *Twilight of the Idols* Nietzsche presents the irreverent thought that even Socrates can be seen as a sick man.

> These wisest men of all ages, let us start by looking at *them* more closely! Perhaps they had become a bit unsteady on their feet? Perhaps they were late? Doddering? Decadent? Perhaps wisdom appears on earth as a raven, inspired by a little scent of carrion. . . . . The *consensus sapientium*—I see this with increasing lucidity—proves least of all that the wisest men were right about what they agreed on: instead it proves that they were in *physiological* agreement about something, and consequently adopted—*had* to adopt—the same negative attitude towards life. Judgments, value judgments on life, for or against, can ultimately never be true: they have value only as symptoms, they can be taken seriously only as symptoms,—in themselves, judgments like these are stupidities.[206]

The narrative of *Johannes Climacus* presents strong evidence that Johannes Climacus's use of philosophy to disconnect from the world is symptomatic of a depressed perspective on the world, a negative judgment concerning the value of life that Johannes may have inherited from his father. This is a surprising message to find in a text concerned with method, but the way that the book foregrounds the story of Johannes Climacus suggests that this warning that a philosophical method can emphasize connecting ideas without requiring disconnection from the world—that there is no necessary connection between those two ideas, and that if one chooses to disconnect from the world as Johannes Climacus did, that's really just a symptom of one's own judgment concerning the value of life—all of this is an essential part of the exploration of philosophical methodology that *Johannes Climacus* presents.[207]

(4) In conclusion: Back to the beginning

Johannes Climacus is known primarily as Kierkegaard's book that never ends. Kierkegaard didn't publish the work in his lifetime, and to everyone who examined the manuscript when it was found among Kierkegaard's papers after his death in 1855, poor *Johannes Climacus* looked like an orphaned child, a book that had been abandoned by its author. While it is not entirely certain when Kierkegaard began writing the work,[208] it does seem clear that he never finished it.[209]

The closest thing that this unending book has to a formal beginning is a "Please Note" that comes before the first of three introductions in the book, like a preliminary appendix—or perhaps a warning that what follows is a text that has not quite made up its mind about how to get started. This initial *nota bene* takes the form of two sentences, the second of which seems like it's never going to end:

> Someone who supposes that philosophy has never in all the world been so close as it is now to fulfilling its task of explaining all mysteries may certainly think it strange, affected, and scandalous that I choose the narrative form and do not in my small way hand up a stone to culminate the system. But someone who has become convinced that philosophy has never been so eccentric as now, never so confused despite all its definitions (much like the weather last winter when we heard simultaneously things never heard before at the same time—shouts of "mussels," "shrimp," and "watercress"—so that someone who was attentive to a particular shout at one moment would think it was winter, then spring, and then midsummer, while anyone who heard them all would think that nature had become confused and that the world would not last until Easter)—that person will surely find it in order that I, too, by means of the form seek to counteract the detestable untruth that characterizes recent philosophy, which differs from older philosophy by having discovered that it is ludicrous to do what a person himself said he would do or had done—he will find it in order and will merely lament, as I

do, that the one who here begins this task has no more authority than I have. (*JC* 117)

In the debate about the role of method in philosophy most people have not recognized that *Johannes Climacus* had anything whatsoever to say. That's how slight its authority has been. It seems appropriate that the important points about methodology that one finds in *Johannes Climacus* are inscribed in a book that has no clear ending and an ambiguous beginning, since the unbracketed nature of the text mirrors human existence itself, which—as Kierkegaard repeatedly emphasized throughout all of his writings—cannot be reduced to a system.

Conclusion

(actually more like a personal apology)

And now this crumby book is finally over

or

Concluding ecstatic discourse in praise of scrappy philosophy

> Nor, therefore, can the humorist ever really become a systematizer, for he regards every system as a renewed attempt in the familiar Blicherian manner to blow up the world with a single syllogism, whereas he himself has come alive to the incommensurable which the philosopher can never figure out and therefore must despise. He lives in the fullness of things and is therefore sensitive to how much is always left over, even if he has expressed himself with all felicity (hence this disinclination to write). The systematizer believes that he can say everything, and that whatever cannot be said is erroneous and secondary.
> (A note scribbled in the margins of Kierkegaard's DD Journal, probably sometime in 1837 when he was twenty-four years old. *KJN* 1:226.)

THERE IS ALWAYS so much left over, so much more that could be said, even if one has expressed himself with all felicity (which I certainly have not). But if you want to write a philosophy book that doesn't attempt to blow up the world, at some point you just have to stop writing and say "farewell" and "good luck" to your scrappy little book and send it out into the world to begin having adventures on its own. For a crumby book such as this there can be no illusion of any necessary finish line or last word; you just stop writing—hopefully before you have completely exhausted the endurance and the patience of the last extremely-long-suffering reader who hasn't yet thrown the book away.

To make this non-concluding conclusion perhaps just a little less arbitrary I would like to conclude with an expression of gratitude. I first discovered Kierkegaard as an eighteen-year-old college student, and that proved to be one of the most important discoveries of my life. Kierkegaard's philosophy has enriched my life in so many ways, and Kierkegaard's writing has constantly reminded me that philosophy is supposed to be joyous. I hope this book has successfully conveyed my gratitude for those gifts.

Endnotes

1   Regarding the excessive and disjunctive chapter titles that I have adopted throughout this book, I plead guilty to being unable to resist the seductive appeal of a title that is nearly as long as the book itself, and as a rather pathetic defense of my weakness of will I note that Kierkegaard seemed to suffer from the same disorder, which is evident from the many clever titles he auditioned in his journals—titles for books that were never written. Here are a few examples:

> Metaphysical Lectures by the tax collector Zacchaeus in a sycamore tree. For diversion and consolation of anguished consciences in dark and sorrowful hours, tediously compiled by his grateful colleague, the former assistant tax collector, with immortal commentary by a young philologist. In order to promote sales of the book, a short summary of conversation topics *beliebich* arranged *zum Gebrauch für Jedermann* is included.
> The Drone House, printed this year.
> Enclosed please find a list of abusive words one can use without being taken to court (*KJN* 2:77).

> *Memoirs of My Life*
> By
> *Nebuchadnezzar*
> Formerly an Emperor. Subsequently an Ox.
> Published
> By
> *Nicolaus Notabene* (*KJN* 2:168)

> Godly Phrasebook
> or
> Handbook for Priests
> Containing 500 Platitudes
> Ordered Alphabetically
> by

> A Sexton Who Has Been Employed at All Churches, and Who
> Therefore Has Detailed Knowledge of Platitudes
> Dedicated to Councillor of Justice Hiorthøoy,
> the exceptional Connoisseur, the
> Painstaking Collector of Platitudes (*KJN* 4:236)
>
> 3 Moral Tales
> For children, adults, but especially for childlike souls
> Most respectfully
> Sent into the world
> By
> Hilarius Bookbinder
> By order (*KJN* 11.2:31).

2   Of course it is possible to embrace certain contradictions in a serious and completely non-hilarious way as Graham Priest has argued thoroughly and convincingly for years (e.g., Priest, *Contradiction*, 3–124 and Priest, *Doubt*, 1–74). But I think it's safe to say that even the most enthusiastic proponent of dialetheism would regard the particular contradictions embraced in this particular philosophical Hail Mary as proof that while some contradictions may be profound and worthy of deeper study other contradictions do not merit anything more than a good hearty laugh because they are simply funny incongruities that do not harbor any deeper truths—and thank God (whichever one you want) for that because if it were no longer possible to laugh at contradictions at least some of the time life would be almost unbearably somber and grim.

3   Louis Mackey ("Scratch," 1–22) argues that even though there was no explicit comedy in this dissertation, there was, nevertheless, an undercurrent of irony in the project since Kierkegaard managed to write the whole dissertation using the (required) language of Hegel's philosophy, while still undercutting and undermining Hegel's philosophy. I agree that the only way to find any humor in *The Concept of Irony* is to see the whole book as an exercise or performance of irony. When the book is understood in this way texts such as the following become quite hilarious:

> Hegel clearly provides a turning point in the view of Socrates. Therefore, I shall begin with Hegel and end with Hegel, without giving attention to his predecessors, since they, insofar as they have any significance, have been corroborated by his view, or to his successors, since they have only relative value in comparison with Hegel. (*CI* 220–21).

> For a new mode of irony to be able to appear now, it must result from the assertion of subjectivity in a still higher form. It must be subjectivity raised to the second power, a subjectivity's subjectivity, which

corresponds to reflection's reflection. With this we are once again world-historically oriented—that is, we are referred to the development that modern philosophy attained in Kant and that is completed in Fichte, and more specifically again to the positions that after Fichte sought to affirm subjectivity in its second potency.... Finally, here irony also met its master in Hegel. (*CI* 242)

4   Amir, *Humor*, 101–208 presents a strong defense of the centrality of comedy to all of Kierkegaard's philosophical writing, with no exceptions, and Williams, *Legitimacy*, 1–118 also argues that comedy can be a legitimate aspect of both ethics and religion, in case anyone needed to be persuaded to accept this conclusion.

5   Here I agree wholeheartedly with Joakim Garff when he writes:

> And if one could wish for a future reading of Kierkegaard, I would wish for a less reverent, more flippant reading than in earlier generations. A reading that delivers a type of restrained affection or a "sympathetic antipathy"—to say it along with Vigilius Haufniensis. A reading that makes use of the rhetorical discipline and irony that the authorship itself prefers, but at the same time turns irony upon itself in order to counteract itself. ("Esthetic," 69–70)

6   Nietzsche, *Ecce Homo*, 36.

7   Deleuze and Guattari, *What Is Philosophy*, 28–29.

8   Deleuze and Guattari, *What Is Philosophy*, 83. Deleuze, of course, thought that it was possible to write about the history of philosophy in a different way that did create new concepts. "What is the best way to follow the great philosophers? Is it to repeat what they said or *to do what they did*, that is, create concepts for problems that necessarily change" (Deleuze and Guattari, *What Is Philosophy*, 28). He wrote several books that followed this pattern, books on Nietzsche, Hume, Bergson, Spinoza, Leibniz, Kant, and others that used those classic texts as springboards or catalysts to create new concepts of his own. He described his approach to the history of philosophy using very memorable imagery:

> I belong to a generation, one of the last generations, that was more or less bludgeoned to death with the history of philosophy. The history of philosophy plays a patently repressive role in philosophy, it's philosophy's own version of the Oedipus complex: 'You can't seriously consider saying what you yourself think until you've read this and that, and that on this, and this on that." Many members of my generation never broke free of this; others did, by inventing their own particular methods and new rules, a new approach. I myself "did" history of philosophy for a long time, read books on this or that author. But I compensated in various ways.... I suppose the main way I

coped with it at the time was to see the history of philosophy as a sort of buggery or (it comes to the same thing) immaculate conception. I saw myself taking an author from behind and giving him a child that would be his own offspring, yet monstrous. It was really important for it to be his own child, because the author had to actually say all I had him saying. But the child was bound to be monstrous too, because it resulted from all sorts of shifting, slipping, dislocations, and hidden emissions that I really enjoyed. (Deleuze, *Letter*, 5–6)

9   Deleuze and Guattari, *What Is Philosophy*, 5–6. Understanding philosophy as fundamentally the activity of creating new concepts provides a perspective on the history of philosophy that doesn't panic every time the death of philosophy is announced, or any time some new fashion becomes all the rage.

> To say that the greatness of philosophy lies precisely in its not having any use is a frivolous answer that not even young people find amusing any more. In any case, the death of metaphysics or the overcoming of philosophy has never been a problem for us: it is just tiresome, idle chatter. Today it is said that systems are bankrupt, but it is only the concept of system that has changed. So long as there is a time and a place for creating concepts, the operation that undertakes this will always be called philosophy, or will be indistinguishable from philosophy even if it is called something else. (Deleuze and Guattari, *What Is Philosophy*, 9)

10 Other connections between Deleuze and Kierkegaard are explored in Jampol-Petzinger, "Deleuze," 177–88.

11 I'll give a much more complete argument for the claim that Xnty is a collection of new philosophical concepts in chapter 1.

12 The complexity of Kierkegaard's relationship with his father is certainly enormous, and I am delighted that I can ignore it completely. For anyone with more ambition than I who cares to sally forth and try to make sense of this utterly confusing relationship, I will simply suggest this journal entry, which is tossed out in a parenthesis, as a good starting point: "(Merciful God, what a dreadful wrong my father did me in his melancholia—an old man who shifts the entire burden of his melancholia onto a poor child, to say nothing of what was more dreadful, and yet for all that the best of fathers.)" (*KJN* 4:168).

Ok, maybe one more journal entry, and then I'll stop: "But my father's death was a circumstance that also shook me fearfully; in what way, I have never talked about with one single person. The entire foreground of my life is altogether shrouded in the darkest melancholia and in the deepest mists of brooding wretchedness to such a degree that it is no wonder that I was as I was. But all of that remains my secret" (*KJN* 4:401).

Just one more: "And to my father I owe everything, humanly speaking. In every way he made me as unhappy as possible, made my childhood an unparalleled torture, and made me, in my heart of hearts, not far from being offended by Xnty, or I was indeed offended, even if out of respect for it resolved never to say a word about it to any person and, out of love to my father, to portray Xnty as truly as possible in contrast to the drivel that is called Xnty in Xndom" (*KJN* 4:401–2).

This is the last one, I promise. "[I]t's a sad satire on the human race that Governance has so richly endowed nearly every child because it knew in advance what it means to be brought up by 'parents,' i.e., to be messed up as much as humanly possible" (*KJN* 6:95).

13 In Nietzsche's telling, these are the words of the satyr Silenus when King Midas captured him and demanded that he answer the question, "What is the best and most excellent thing for human beings?" Selenus answered: "Wretched, ephemeral race, children of chance and tribulation, why do you force me to tell you the very thing it would be most profitable for you *not* to hear? The very best thing is utterly beyond your reach not to have been born, not to *be*, to be *nothing*. However, the second best thing for you is: to die soon" (Nietzsche, *Birth*, 23). Nietzsche absorbed this nihilistic philosophy from Schopenhauer early in his life, then later he decided that he didn't want to be a nihilist after all so he rejected Schopenhauer's nihilistic worldview and from that point on focused his own philosophy on unmasking and overcoming nihilism everywhere in all the many insidious forms that it could possibly take. Kierkegaard independently created his own, more extreme version of Schopenhauer's argument for anti-natalism, and added to it a glorification of martyrdom that would have been foreign even to Schopenhauer. When Kierkegaard discovered Schopenhauer toward the end of his life his only criticism of Schopenhauer's nihilism was that it didn't go far enough. (I'll have more to say about Kierkegaard's nihilism later in this introduction/confession.)

14 As in almost everything, Socrates is Kierkegaard's ideal in this respect. Socrates demonstrated the sort of existential performance art that Kierkegaard believed should take the place of lecturing.

> The more a person strives in daily existence himself, the less he is inclined to give speeches. Take Socrates. Someone like him understands only all too well that these splendid speeches and masterpieces of eloquence do not lead people into, but away from, the existential. ... Therefore a person of that sort will say, Oh good Lord, what does an hour's oratory once a week or once a year amount to[?] No, therefore a person of that sort becomes an ironist, a tease. And what does that mean? It means that he constantly connects the insignificant things of life to what is highest, the difficulty is precisely the fact that

> it also involves the most everyday sorts of things—in short, he does not place the tasks at a distance aesthetically.
> On the other hand, the less a person himself exists, the greater the need for effusions of eloquence. (*KJN* 8:205)

Failing to follow the example of Socrates and instead falling back on lecturing can be understood as the assistant professor's primary contribution to the problem that Kierkegaard diagnoses in "The Present Age": that today everyone exhausts all their energy in talking, deliberation, and reflection and never actually does anything (e.g., *PA* 70–71). This is one example of an argument for "ethical silence" in Kierkegaard's writing, an argument that is analyzed in Shakespeare, *Language*, 110–38 and Hay, *Silence*, 61–76.

15 Mooney, "Personality," 39–47 extends this idea by arguing that Kierkegaard understood creating a personality to be an essential part of ethics.

16 *Philosophical Crumbs* is a wonderful translation of *Philosophiske Smuler*, which M. G. Piety adopts for her translation of the book, and I won't hesitate to use the delightful word "crumbs" whenever the mood strikes me; but out of respect for the Hong translation that I'm using I will generally refer to the book as *Philosophical Fragments*, and I'll cite the book as *PF*.

17 Fiskvik, "Dance," 149–76, devotes an entire essay to Kierkegaard's frequent use of dance imagery throughout his writing.

18 Louis Mackey ("Earnest," 150–51) points out what a scandal it was even to call the book *Philosophical Fragments* in Kierkegaard's speculative nineteenth century: "In the wake of the Hegelian revelation, calling a book *Philosophical Fragments or a Fragment of Philosophy* was a bit like calling a treatise in geometry *Reflections on Round Squares*, so egregious was the self-contradiction." Mackey also points out that *Philosophical Fragments* is "multidimensionally fragmented: each chapter begins from scratch with what looks like a new topic; the discussion is interrupted by irrelevant digressions and by imaginary conversations with an impertinent interlocutor; the book has a motto and a moral and a problem, but no conclusion; the author confesses no opinion of the matters he discusses."

19 Here again I agree with Joakim Garff concerning the value of the marginal and the scrappy in Kierkegaard's writing:

> [T]he seemingly most useless parts of the Kierkegaardian corpus—everything in the margins and all the fragmentary material—is in reality the most indispensable, since it opposes every attempt to instrumentalize the texts and thereby be done with them. And if one

asks why such a sense is important, the answer is simple: the indispensability of the useless corresponds to—in fact, is repeated in—the most fundamental existential phenomena that the authorship captures and illuminates both negatively and positively: phenomena like anxiety, despair, trust, devotion, faith, and forgiveness—which also are just as useless and indispensable ("Esthetic," 70).

20 Other aspects of Kierkegaard's thinking, and his biography, applied to death are explored in Stokes, "Death," 365–84 and in the collection of essays *Kierkegaard and Death*.

21 Caputo, *How*, 111–21 is a rare and noteworthy exception to this general tendency. Caputo devotes the entire concluding chapter of his excellent guide through Kierkegaard's life and ideas to the "world-weariness" that overcame Kierkegaard in the final years of his life.

22 On the place of Kierkegaard as one of the founding voices of existentialism, please see Cooper, "Philosophical," 27–49; McBride, "Cultural," 50–72; Hannay "Individual," 73–95; Dreyfus, "Monster," 96–110; and Ricoeur, "After," 9–25.

23 I would include in this group even those who make the argument that Kierkegaard's philosophy is a kind of anti-philosophy—a *reductio ad absurdum* argument that shows the impossibility of philosophical argument—such as Henry Allison ("Nonsense," 432–60) and M. Holmes Hartshorne (*Godly Deceiver*, 1–84).

24 Roger Poole ("Unknown," 48–75) provides a very thorough and useful general summary of how Kierkegaard's philosophy has been read and appropriated, particularly in the twentieth century, and also notes the important role that the journals and notebooks have played in that reception.

25 The idea that philosophy can be a kind of theatre is inspired by the book *What Is Philosophy?* by Gilles Deleuze and Felix Guattari. I'll have more to say about this book when we get to Act 3 where their arguments that "philosophy is the discipline that involves *creating* concepts*" (*What Is Philosophy*, 5) will be especially relevant, but I want to acknowledge my debt to this book right at the outset. Other authors have also argued very effectively that philosophy can be understood as a kind of theatre. For example, please see Foucault's essay on Deleuze called *Theatrum Philosophicum*, the collection of essays on Deleuze (edited by Boundas) titled *Gilles Deleuze and the Theatre of Philosophy*, Also, Stephen Crites suggested long ago that Kierkegaard's philosophy in particular is best understood as a kind of theatre ("Pseudonymous Authorship," 183–229), and Pickett, "Beyond," 99–114 argues that the *Concluding Unscientific Postscript* is both theatrical and anti-theatrical at the same time.

26 This awkward moment in the story of Kierkegaard's journals and papers is described in a delightful chapter of Joakim Garff's biography of Regine (*Muse*, 51–55).

27 Jensen, "Diaries," 74–97 provides a very interesting summary of the contents of Peter's own diaries, which have not yet been published though it seems inevitable that eventually they will, and when that happens it will be fascinating to compare the journals of the two brothers.

28 Cappelørn, *Images*, 40.

29 Cappelørn, *Images*, 55.

30 To appreciate fully the long, strange trip that Kierkegaard's journals, notebooks, and assorted papers have traveled in order to arrive finally in the completely unabridged form in which they are now available, I strongly recommend the book, *Written Images: Søren Kierkegaard's Journals, Notebooks, Booklets, Sheets, Scraps, and Slips of Paper*, by Niels Jørgen Cappelørn, Joakim Garff, and Johnny Kondrup. This fascinating book narrates "the story of packets and sacks of paper covered with writing, which after a vagabond existence, first in a couple of apartments in Copenhagen, then in the bishop's residence in northern Jutland, finally landed in the Royal Danish Library, where they are today guarded with the greatest of care" (Cappelørn *Images*, 7). Henning Fenger dedicates a fine chapter of his book (*Myths*, 32–61) to the history of Kierkegaard's journals and papers, especially to the earliest years right after Kierkegaard's death, and there's also a good summary of the history and the contents of Kierkegaard's journals and other posthumous papers in Tullberg, "Textual Inheritance," 11–27.

31 New biographies of Kierkegaard continue to appear with a methodical regularity, though it is difficult to imagine how anyone could surpass Joakim Garff's thorough and massive (867 pages) *Søren Kierkegaard: A Biography*. The latest Kierkegaard biography in English is *Philosopher of the Heart: The Restless Life of Søren Kierkegaard* by Clare Carlisle. Reviewing the book for the *New York Times* Parul Sehgal writes: "The book ambles along the well-trodden conclusions," but "the attractions of Kierkegaard—his severity and wit, the force of his rhetoric, his defense of the individual and the example of his solitary spiritual striving—survive even a middling biography" (Sehgal, "Short Life"). Of course, Kierkegaard's other books, aside from his journals, can also be consumed as grist for the mill of biography, and many authors have done so. Even a writer such as George Steiner, who says that "as a rule" he finds "current modes of 'psycho-biography' fatuous" (Steiner, "Wound," 105), is unable to resist a biographical reading of *Fear and Trembling* and *The Book on Adler*.

32 One example of this approach—using Kierkegaard's journals as something like the answer key or instruction manual for Kierkegaard's other texts—is the fact that all the Princeton University Press editions of Kierkegaard's books include a supplement, that is often nearly as long as the text itself, titled: "selected entries from Kierkegaard's journals pertaining to (insert the name of the book you are holding here)." The editors (Howard and Edna Hong) include in this supplement every entry from Kierkegaard's journals that they consider relevant to understanding this particular book. This format clearly suggests that Kierkegaard's journals were meant to be used as supplements to clarify the meaning of his other writing, so if you're trying to make sense of some strange book that Kierkegaard wrote you should immediately turn to the journals, where Kierkegaard himself decoded and explained the book for you. Other instructive examples of this approach include Frederick Sontag's *A Kierkegaard Handbook*, which aims to provide a guide to all of Kierkegaard's thought, and relies primarily on the journals to do that, and Gregor Malantschuk's *Kierkegaard's Thought* which uses the journals to establish the intentions behind all of Kierkegaard's writing, since the author's intentions are presumed to determine the only possible meaning of those texts.

33 As Louis Mackey notes ("Aesthete," 1), Kierkegaard's "entire life was a retelling—to his journals, to himself, to God, and to posterity—of a grief inexpressibly out of proportion to the events that occasioned it."

34 Bruce Kirmmse has thoroughly explored this history in many fine works, including his books *Kierkegaard in Golden Age Denmark* and *Encounters with Kierkegaard*, and the articles "'Out with it!'" 15-47; and "End," 28-43. Pattison, "Copenhagen," 44-61 also explores this territory.

35 Gabriel Josipovici ("Kierkegaard and the Novel," 114-28) explores the literary qualities of all of Kierkegaard's writing and how it complicates any distinction between philosophy and literature, and the anthology edited by Schleifer and Markley (*Kierkegaard and Literature*) includes several more essays that analyze the connections and disconnections between Kierkegaard's philosophy and literature. Sylviane Agacinski devotes most of her book (*Aparté*, 127-258) to a reading of Kierkegaard's journals that takes them seriously both as works of literature and as works of philosophy. Malpas, "Literature," 291-321 discusses Kierkegaard's writing within the overall context of existentialism as literature. Lorentzen, *Cannibals*, 17-303 offers many compelling comparisons between the writing of Melville and Kierkegaard, as does Mooney, *Living*, 43-66. Jamie Lorentzen, *Becoming*, 39-73 extends his analysis of the connections between Kierkegaard and Melville, and also adds Kierkegaardian readings of additional literary works such as *Huckleberry Finn* (8-38),

Peer Gynt (74–92), and *Brothers Karamazov* (93–124). Lisi, "European," 550–69 considers Kierkegaard's legacy within European literature, and Pyper, "English," 570–89 does the same within the Anglo-American literary tradition. David Lodge discusses his own appropriation of Kierkegaard's philosophy and his life story for his marvelous novel *Therapy* in "Special Purposes, 34–47.

36 Cappelørn, *Images*, 38–42.

37 Peter did later allow more of his brother's journals and papers to be published, after much effort and argument from H. P. Barford, whom Peter had hired to catalogue the contents of the collection. But his first thought—that *The Point of View* said everything that needed to be said, and therefore nothing else needed to be published—is still very instructive. To this day *The Point of View* continues to be used just as Peter wanted to use it: as the last word and simplifying reduction that explains Kierkegaard's whole authorship. Hough, *Dancing*, 22–25 is a good recent example of this. A fine corrective to this persistent tradition are the essays by Joakim Garff ("Eyes of Argus," 75–102), and Christopher Norris ("Fictions," 87–107), which argue that *The Point of View* cannot be used as so many have tried to use it—to reduce the range of possible meanings that can be assigned to Kierkegaard's pseudonymous texts—because the meaning of *The Point of View* itself remains in question and is ultimately undecidable. Furchert, "Spiritual," 359–76 strangely and inexplicably characterizes the readings of Garff and Norris as "reductive," even though they are manifestly the polar opposite of that, and then proceeds to argue once again that *The Point of View* simplifies and systematizes all of Kierkegaard's authorship under a religious umbrella, thereby demonstrating the durability of the tradition that Peter Christian Kierkegaard started when he insisted that *The Point of View* was all that needed to be published from Søren's unpublished papers since it worked so perfectly to clean up the mess that his little brother bequeathed to the world.

38 Nietzsche, *Zarathustra*, 105–8.

39 Nietzsche, *Zarathustra*, 99–102.

40 Nietzsche, *Zarathustra*, 55–59. I explored these arguments in *Zarathustra* concerning teaching and learning in "Statue," 79–90.

41 I will have much more to say about the many non-concluding conclusions that Kierkegaard wrote in chapter 2 where I will argue that these manifold conclusions undermine the very possibility of any conclusion or simplifying last word on Kierkegaard's philosophy.

42 Michael Strawser provides an insightful analysis of the indirectness of

The Point of View and the other supposedly direct communications from Kierkegaard concerning the meaning of his writing in the concluding section of his book (*Both/And*, 173–97).

43 This claim—that "Søren Kierkegaard" should be understood as a pseudonym in Kierkegaard's Journals and Notebooks may seem to contradict the argument that I made in the first act of this chapter: that the journals have philosophical value because they "demonstrate what a true work of existential philosophy looks like ... they present a true picture of human existence, including all of its confusion and disorder. All the features of human existence that Kierkegaard explored and analyzed in his philosophy come to life in his journals." Understanding "Søren Kierkegaard," the author of *Kierkegaard's Journals and Notebooks,* to be a pseudonym doesn't contradict that argument from Act One because the argument is just as strong if the "picture of human existence, including all of its confusion and disorder" is about a fictional character and not about the actual historical person named Søren Kierkegaard. If the journals are understood as works of fiction that doesn't undermine their value as works of existential philosophy. Similarly it remains true that Søren Kierkegaard is an unreliable narrator in these journals even if Søren Kierkegaard is a pseudonym or a fictional character.

44 Geoffrey Hale points out that if "Søren Kierkegaard" is given authority over all the pseudonyms this would effectively undermine any possible authority that any of the authors and voices in Kierkegaard's authorship, including "Søren Kierkegaard," could possibly have (Hale, *Language*, 1–36). Louis Mackey ("Points of View," 160–92) makes the same point about the necessity of understanding "Søren Kierkegaard" as a pseudonym, and the impossibility of identifying a single authoritative point of view for Kierkegaard's complicated authorship. Joakim Garff argues for adopting a "subversive strategy" in reading Kierkegaard that renders impossible any single authoritative point of view ("Argus," 77), and Henning Fenger (*Myths*, 1–31) is also appropriately skeptical of any unitary or authoritative reduction of Kierkegaard's writing using "The Point of View." Other commentators who take this conclusion seriously—that there is no single authoritative point of view for Kierkegaard's complicated authorship—include Pat Bigelow (*Problem*, 176–209), Peter Fenves (*Chatter*, 113–44), and Joseph Westfall (*Author*, 4–17). It should also be noted that the impossibility of a single authoritative point of view for Kierkegaard's authorship entails the impossibility of any hope of systematizing these unruly texts, including even more nuanced and self-aware recent attempts such as that proposed by Michael Strawser (*Both/And*, 89–226). For an example of the polar opposite position with regard to pseudonyms, pseudonymity, and the author-ity of the author, see M. Holmes Hartshorne's argument (*Godly Deceiver*, 1–84) for an absolute

separation of Kierkegaard's own thinking and the (deceptive and dangerous, according to Hartshorne) ideas expressed by his pseudonyms.

45 Plato, *Collected Works*, 1659–61.

46 Howland, "Shimmering," 23–35 is right to note that "Kierkegaard's existential debt to Socrates is inseparable from his literary debt to Plato and Aristophanes" (24). Connell, "Matters," 66–81 makes a similar point, arguing that Kierkegaard's lasting importance is due to the fact that he is both Socratic and Platonic.

47 Mark Wrathall writes: "One must always proceed with caution in attributing to Kierkegaard the positions espoused by his pseudonymous authors. In this paper, however, I am going to largely ignore the distinction between Kierkegaard, Climacus, and his other pseudonyms because (as will become apparent), the pseudonymous authors' claims about subjectivity and immortality are repeated, developed, or assumed by Kierkegaard in his journals and in several of the 'Discourses' published under his own name." ("Trivial," 419–20). There are two problems with this argument: (1) It ignores the possibility that the author of Kierkegaard's journals is also a pseudonym, just like Climacus et al. (2) It really is not at all evident that Kierkegaard (whoever that is) and also the various pseudonyms, such as Johannes Climacus, agree on anything. One can arrive at that conclusion only through a highly selective reading of these texts (and it is evident that Wrathall's reading of the journals is highly selective since he relies on the "greatest hits" version of the text edited by the Hongs).

48 As K. Brian Söderquist's notes, "irony shows up in Søren Kierkegaard's authorship from one end to the other" ("Irony," 344), it's not limited to just a few books that are famous for being funny, and Andrew Cross ("Neither Either," 125–53) argues further that "existential irony"—irony as form of life—is just as important for Kierkegaard as verbal irony. Likewise, I would argue that indirect communication is present in Kierkegaard's authorship from one end to the other; it's not limited just to the books that were written by pseudonyms who inform the reader that they don't know what they are doing. Pat Bigelow is the rare writer who takes this fact seriously, and attempts to consider all the implications that follow from it, in his two books (*Writing*, 3–8, and *Conning*, xi–xxiii) and in his truly delightful article "Brokenness," 310–38.

49 Edward F. Mooney ("Examplars, 129–49" and "Pseudonyms," 191–210) provides a great overview of Kierkegaard's theory and practice of indirect communication, and also the reasons why indirect communication is a necessity. Another good summary of Kierkegaard's theory of indirect communication, this time with a focus on how indirect communication

aims to correct an existential inadequacy within language itself, is given by David Wood (*Limit*, 105–17). Indirect communication, of course, creates more possibilities to be badly misunderstood, a phenomenon explored in Piety, "Dangers," 163–74.

50 The many forms and uses of irony in Kierkegaard's writing is thoroughly explored by John Vignaux Smyth (*Eros*). Andrew Cross ("Neither Either," 125–53) argues that "existential irony"—irony as form of life—is just as important for Kierkegaard as verbal irony.

51 Many discussions of indirect communication in Kierkegaard's writing seek to delineate networks and hierarchies among the many different voices found in Kierkegaard's texts. For example, Nerina Jansen ("Deception," 125) proposes that there is a "first" and a "second" authorship in Kierkegaard's writing. The "second" authorship would consist of everything Kierkegaard published under his own name. W. Glenn Kirkconnell (*Sin and Salvation*) shares a similar concern for Kierkegaard's "direct" writings, which he believes have been wrongly overshadowed by the pseudonymous texts. Mark C. Taylor (*Pseudonymous*, 19) argues for just the opposite conclusion: that "the pseudonymous authorship forms the most important part" of Kierkegaard's corpus. Michael Strawser ("Indirectness," 73–90) allows that Kierkegaard's signed writings may also contain indirect communication, but he still maintains that there is a division, and therefore an implicit hierarchy, between the pseudonymous and what he proposes to call the "veronymous" texts. Other authors, such as C. Stephen Evans (*Fragments*, 6–9, *Making Sense*, 5–12), try to steer clear of hierarchies among the many voices in Kierkegaard's authorship, but still advocate very complicated networks that require the reader to be aware at all times who is speaking. It is clear from all of these contortions that many of us have yet to embrace the argument by "A.F. . . ." that it really doesn't matter who is speaking.

52 Deleuze and Guattari use many terms in a unique fashion that can be confusing, so I'll now provide a brief lexicon for some of their key terms, roughly in the order in which those terms occur in this chapter.

- "Concepts" for Deleuze and Guattari are philosophical creations. Art creates "sensations" and science creates "functions," but only philosophy creates concepts. These three creations are all honest and authentic ways of creating order out of chaos because they do not falsify or deny chaos and they seek to preserve the energy and intensity of chaos, as opposed to—

- "Opinions," which merely deny chaos or seek to impose a veneer that conceals it. Opinions are dogmas that refuse to wrestle with chaos in order to wring meaning and energy from it. Concepts are authentic and hard-won creations that generate meaning and value;

opinions are lazy and thoughtless and therefore dangerous because they falsify the truth of our chaotic world.

- "Intensity" and similar terms are often used by Deleuze and Guattari to refer back to that part of chaos that we want to preserve—the original energy of chaos that needs to be structured and made meaningful but not silenced.

- "Plane of immanence" refers to the insistence that philosophy remain on the stage of immediate experience and refuse the temptation of transcendence. Insisting on creating concepts that remain always on an immanent plane is one of the features that distinguishes philosophy from religion, they argue. The plane of immanence can be understood as the stage on which philosophy performs all of its concepts, never asking the audience to imagine that there is some other stage that they cannot experience where some or perhaps all of the show takes place. The "plane of immanence" for Deleuze and Guattari can be understood as essentially the same as an immanentist perspective or point of view, which Steven Shakespeare has defined as "a view of being that is neither hierarchical nor analogical. It is a refusal of the two-world ontology of Platonism. Negatively, it rejects any dependence of the world upon an otherworldly transcendence that is unified, simple, and noncontingent. More positively, immanence is an affirmation of the world in its worldliness, its gratuitous whylessness" (Shakespeare *Refusal*, 11).

- "Immanent idealism" should be understood as a version of idealism that insists on remaining on the plane of immanence. Sartre used the phrase "transcendence within Immanence" to express essentially the same idea (*Being and Nothingness*), and contemporary authors such as Patrice Haynes opt for the phrase "immanent transcendence" (Haynes, *Immanent*). The basic idea remains the same in all of these formulations.

- "Events" that are generated by philosophical concepts can be understood as essentially a pragmatic standard for evaluating the value of any philosophical concept that is created: it's only valuable if it makes things happen and allows you to do things.

53 It seems very possible to me that Deleuze and Guattari were not entirely sure themselves about what they were doing at first, but it does seem clear that by the time they finished *A Thousand Plateaus* they had arrived at the paradigm of philosophy that they outline in *What Is Philosophy?* This comes through in Deleuze's interview with Christian Descamps shortly after the release of *A Thousand Plateaus* ("On *A Thousand Plateaus*"), in the conversation with Raymond Bellour and François Ewald ("On Philosophy"), and in Deleuze's essay (sort of an interview with himself)

"What Is the Creative Act?

54 Deleuze and Guattari, *What Is Philosophy*, 5.

55 Deleuze and Guattari, *What Is Philosophy*, 6.

56 Deleuze and Guattari, *What Is Philosophy*, 29.

57 Deleuze and Guattari, *What Is Philosophy*, 28.

58 Deleuze and Guattari, *What Is Philosophy*, 206.

59 Deleuze and Guattari, *What Is Philosophy*, 201–2.

60 Deleuze and Guattari are keen to differentiate philosophy from art and science, but they never suggest that philosophy is superior to art or science. They are three "daughters of chaos"—three siblings all engaged in the same work but using different tools and producing different results. Collectively, philosophy, art, and science constitute "thought," as opposed to mere opinion or belief, which is thoughtless.

> In short, chaos has three daughters, depending on the plane that cuts through it: these are the *Chaoids*—art, science, and philosophy—as forms of thought or creation. We call *Chaoids* the realities produced on the planes that cut through the chaos in different ways. (Deleuze and Guattari, *What Is Philosophy*, 208)

> What defines thought in its three great forms—art, science, and philosophy—is always confronting chaos, laying out a plane, throwing a plane over chaos. But philosophy wants to save the infinite by giving it consistency: it lays out a plane of immanence that, through the action of conceptual personae, takes events or consistent concepts to infinity. Science, on the other hand, relinquishes the infinite in order to gain reference: it lays out a plane of simply undefined coordinates that each time, through the action of partial observers, defines states of affairs, functions, or referential propositions. Art wants to create the finite that restores the infinite: it lays out a plane of composition that, in turn, through the action of aesthetic figures, bears monuments or composite sensations. . . . Thinking is thought through concepts, or functions, or sensations and no one of these thoughts is better than the other, or more fully, completely, or synthetically "thought." (Deleuze and Guattari, *What Is Philosophy*, 197–98)

61 Deleuze and Guattari, *What Is Philosophy*, 203.

62 Deleuze and Guattari, *What Is Philosophy*, 43. There can be any number of planes of immanence, Deleuze and Guattari argue, and a single philosopher may create many different planes (Deleuze and Guattari, *What Is Philosophy*, 50). Using the language of geometry they describe each plane of immanence as "a secant plane that crosses" chaos (Deleuze and

Guattari, *What Is Philosophy*, 203). The plane of immanence is explained and demonstrated in Deleuze's book, *Pure Immanence: Essays on a Life*.

63 Deleuze and Guattari, *What Is Philosophy*, 44.

64 Deleuze and Guattari, *What Is Philosophy*, 45.

65 Deleuze and Guattari, *What Is Philosophy*, 49.

66 Because concepts can only be evaluated pragmatically in terms of the concrete results that they produce—the specific new events and new concepts that they generate on the plane of immanence—in the abstract it's easiest to say what concepts are not. This results in some very rarefied but certainly elegant descriptions of concepts from Deleuze and Guattari that sound almost like negative theology, such as the following:

> There is a long series of misunderstandings about the concept. It is true that the concept is fuzzy or vague not because it lacks an outline but because it is vagabond, nondiscursive, moving about on a plane of immanence. It is intensional or modular not because it has conditions of reference but because it is made up of inseperable variations that pass through zones of indiscernibility and change its outline. It has no reference at all, either to the lived or to states of affairs, but a consistency defined by its internal components. The concept is neither denotation of states of affairs nor signification of the lived; it is the event as pure sense that immediately runs through the components. It has no number, either whole or fractional, for counting things that display its properties, but a combination that condenses and accumulates the components it traverses and surveys. The concept is a form or a force; in no possible sense is it ever a function. (Deleuze and Guattari, *What Is Philosophy*, 143–44)

67 Deleuze and Guattari, *What Is Philosophy*, 21.

68 Deleuze and Guattari, *What Is Philosophy*, 34.

69 Another implicit normative prescription in *What Is Philosophy?* is that the activity of creating new concepts on a plane of immanence should be playful, affirmative, and joyous. This is clear from the style of this book, as well as all the other books that Deleuze and Guattari wrote together. For example, in *What Is Philosophy?* Deleuze and Guattari endorse the portraits of various philosophers created by the artist Jean Tingueley (which are actually large and very clunky Rube Goldberg machines), and they don't hesitate to include their own bizarre drawings which represent their own take on the philosophical machines created by several famous philosophical concepts, such as Descartes's *cogito* (Deleuze and Guattari, *What Is Philosophy*, 25) and the Kantian "I think" "as an ox head wired for sound" (Deleuze and Guattari, *What Is Philosophy*, 56).

Clearly laughter too is an essential part of philosophy.
Jean Tinguely's work can be seen here:
https://www.tinguely.ch/en.html
and here:
https://www.youtube.com/watch?v=GmrDEX4P5l8

70 Deleuze and Guattari, *What Is Philosophy*, 7–8.

71 Here are two examples of creatively naming a new concept in *What Is Philosophy?* (a) In a sense the whole book is required to explain what they mean by the new concept they have created which they name "concept." This is an old word with many accumulated meanings and associations, none of which exactly match the meaning of the new philosophical concept that Deleuze and Guattari name with this word. (b) In the book's conclusion, "From Chaos to the Brain," "brain" names a newly created concept, but obviously this is a very old word. This whole chapter can be seen as an explanation of the meaning of this new concept. Deleuze and Guattari explain, for example, that they are talking about a "nonobjectifiable brain" (Deleuze and Guattari, *What Is Philosophy*, 209) which is "*the* junction—not the unity—of the three planes" (the planes of science, art, and philosophy) (Deleuze and Guattari, *What Is Philosophy*, 208). This is something new, so why did they choose to call it "the brain"? Apparently they had their reasons, and it remains the responsibility of the reader to discern the "philosophical athleticism" and the "strange necessity for these words and for their choice" (Deleuze and Guattari, *What Is Philosophy*, 8). All philosophical language must be allowed to exceed the limits of traditional meaning and create something new. The names of new concepts are just one example of this more general phenomenon. "If philosophy is paradoxical by nature, this is not because it sides with the least plausible opinion or because it maintains contradictory opinions but rather because it uses sentences of a standard language to express something that does not belong to the order of opinion or even of the proposition" (Deleuze and Guattari, *What Is Philosophy*, 80).

72 The argument that I'm presenting here about Xnty as a new philosophical concept only works if we resist the impulse and the tradition of immediately branding Kierkegaard as nothing more than a religious thinker, so this is a good time to repeat Michael Strawser's point (*Both/And*, xxvii) that "there is no obvious connection between Kierkegaard's real or feigned religiosity and his interpretation of his authorship. Whether Kierkegaard was a true Christian is certainly undecidable. . . . Consequently, it is misleading to speak of Kierkegaard the person as either a Christian or a non-Christian. This should not even be a question." Also, as Michael O'Neil Burns has noted (*Matter*, 97–98), "For a thinker so strongly associated with the Christian tradition, it is important to note

that Kierkegaard has shockingly little to say about the actual theological content of this tradition. . . . Kierkegaard's Christianity is basically content-less. . . . This lack of a discussion of the theological content of Kierkegaard's Christianity has made it all too easy for religious thinkers with a host of theological commitments to adopt Kierkegaard for their own personal usage and impose a variety of theological contents into Kierkegaard's purely formal account of religion."

73 Holm, "Church," 112–28 provides a good summary of Kierkegaard's complicated and often tempestuous relationship with the religion of his birth.

74 All of these characteristics of Xnty are best understood as events that this concept produces. I will have more to say about these events shortly. I am certainly not the first person to suggest that Kierkegaard's thoughts and arguments which on the surface seem to be about religion can also be understood in a purely secular way. David Wood's essay "Thinking God in the Wake of Kierkegaard" provides a summary of some of the most creative attempts to do this, and Jacques Derrida demonstrates one such creative interpretation in chapter 3 of his book *The Gift of Death*, as does Jean-Paul Sartre's essay "The Singular Universal." Sartre's appropriation of Kierkegaard's philosophy is further analyzed by William McBride ("Sartre's Debt," 18–42), and Derrida's debt to Kierkegaard is explored by John Caputo ("Instants," 216–38).

75 Two excellent recent books, Steven Shakespeare's *Kierkegaard and the Refusal of Transcendence* and Michael O'Neil Burns *Kierkegaard and the Matter of Philosophy*, both present compelling readings of Kierkegaard as a philosopher intent upon creating a purely immanent philosophy. My argument here for understanding Xnty as a new philosophical concept determined to remain on a plane of immanence is very much in the spirit of these fine books.

76 Deleuze and Guattari, *What Is Philosophy*, 206.

77 Deleuze and Guattari, *What Is Philosophy*, 34.

78 The confusion about the ontological status of groups is what makes the *ad populum* fallacy work. There is a fascinating extended analysis of the *ad populum* fallacy—how "the numerical exercises a sensory power over us human beings"—in *KJN* 8:123–24.

79 Martin J. Matuštík ("Radical," 239–64) argues that individuality in Kierkegaard's philosophy is truly radical, truly something fundamentally new that exceeds individuality as it is conceived in liberalism, communitarianism, and postmodernism.

80 In a sense Kierkegaard's goal was to "increase the price" of Xnty until it was almost impossible to afford. Xnty had become so discounted so cheap that everyone took it for granted. Kierkegaard wanted to restore Xnty to its true difficulty, its true cost.

> Through many, many generations there has been a continual knocking off of the price of Xnty, making it milder and milder, more and more subdued, until finally it is not Xnty. (*KJN* 8:77)

> The ideality of it has been completely lost. The result is that being Xn is regarded as something that can surely be done by everyone. Then, by contrast, it becomes a mark of distinction to go further, to become a philosopher, a poet, or God knows what. (*KJN* 8:342)

> When a person first comes to reflect on Xnty, it must at first—before he has immersed himself in it—undoubtedly have been his downfall, a cause of offense. Indeed, he must have wished that it had never come into the world, or at least that the question regarding it had never arisen in his consciousness. It is therefore revolting to hear all this talk by officious and chattering middlemen about how Xt is the greatest hero, etc., etc.—therefore the humorous view is far preferable. (*KJN* 2:76)

> For Xnty is heterogeneity with this world—at the very instant that it begins to be official Xnty, even in the least way, at that very instant Xnty begins to become homogeneity with this world.
> Official Xnty is the precise, diametrical opposite of true Xnty; in every way, every way, even in the least things, it reverses things . . . . (*KJN* 9:312)

81 Kierkegaard suggests Socrates as an example of the immanent idealism inherent in Xnty:

> I maintain that this is Xnty, and I maintain that old man Socrates was infinitely ahead of the geographical Christendom of today. Yet obviously Socrates, who was called practical in contrast to the theoretical philosophers, was just as impractical, almost as impractical, as Xnty. How impractical not to take money for his teaching, how impractical not to defend himself in a way that he knew would effect his acquittal, how impractical not to escape from prison, how impractical to die for the truth. That a sailor dies out on the ocean, where he had ventured in hope of profit, that a soldier falls in battle, where he had ventured in hope of becoming a general: this can be understood, this is practical—but to die for the truth[?] (*KJN* 4:301)

Of course it's hardly surprising to see Kierkegaard point to Socrates as the exemplar of everything excellent. Jon Stewart (*Subjectivity*, 6–21) argues that Kierkegaard's relationship to Socrates is the key to understanding all of Kierkegaard's philosophy, or at least the best way to get started down that road.

82 The transformation of time effected by this event deserves to be added to the catalogue of the various uses and theories of time in Kierkegaard's philosophy summarized in Grøn, "Time," 273–91.

83 The implications of subjective truth in the ethical sphere are explored and analyzed at length in Mackey, "Loss," 141–59.

84 I should note here at the beginning that throughout this chapter I will freely jump between these two conclusions—sometimes using the language of authorial intent, and sometimes using the language of textual effect. The conclusion about textual effect is independent of the conclusion concerning authorial intent, and it is also what I am mainly concerned to demonstrate in this chapter, so I could have just left out any discussion of what Kierkegaard might have had in mind when he wrote what he wrote; but I chose not to for the following reasons. First of all, in Kierkegaard's case the text that is generally thought to present the closest thing to his authorial intent—the journals and notebooks in which he wrote obsessively throughout his life—is so monumental that it's hard to ignore. Obviously these journals can't be regarded simply as the unifying, master key to Kierkegaard's work, as I argued in chapter 1. But Kierkegaard-the-Journal-Writer is certainly one of the most interesting readers of Kierkegaard-the-Author-of-Philosophical-Books, so I have felt free to draw upon the journals for purposes of textual interpretation in order to support my conclusion about textual effect. But I will also, along the way, make some attempt to form a case from the journals—for whatever it's worth (which may be very little or even nothing)—in support of the idea that Kierkegaard intended for his prefaces and conclusions to have the effect that they do have. This second argument about authorial intent should be regarded as subordinate to the argument about textual effect, and as ultimately undecidable (though certainly interesting).

My second reason is simply a desire not to be tedious. Imposing technical language in this chapter to differentiate constantly between arguments for the conclusion about textual effect (which is an argument that concerns a body of writings that we collectively label "Kierkegaard"), and arguments for the conclusion about authorial intent (which is an argument that concerns a person who lived in Copenhagen between 1813 and 1855), would have made the chapter far less readable. The distinction between the two conclusions should be obvious from the context, without constantly calling attention to it.

85 Cf. Derrida, "Outwork," 3.

86 Hegel, *Phenomenology*, 1.

87 Hegel, *Phenomenology*, 1.

88 Derrida, "Outwork," 15. Three valuable studies of further connections between Kierkegaard and Derrida are: Dooley, "Margins," 85–105, Caputo, "Instants," 216–38, and Caputo, "Undecidability," 14–41.

89 *The Phenomenology of Spirit* can also be seen as a preface to Hegel's *Encyclopedia*, which would make the preface to the *Phenomenology* a preface to a preface. William McDonald ("Circular," 227–46) takes this as the starting point of his analysis of the connections and disconnections between Hegel's preface to the *Phenomenology* and Kierkegaard's *Postscript*.

90 See, for example, *CUP* 106–25.

91 See *CUP* 111–17. Climacus's arguments against basing any kind of knowledge on "immediacy" are summarized by W. S. K. Cameron ("Writing," 58).

92 Joakim Garff ("Produce," 75–93) describes how Kierkegaard's unpublished manuscripts and other papers were found to be in a state of readiness and careful preparation immediately after his death.

93 Whitmire, "Witnessing," 325–58 argues that "My Activity as a Writer" succeeds as a direct communication of the unified religious meaning of Kierkegaard's authorship because it is a straightforward act of "witnessing" with none of the aesthetic indirection that afflicts *The Point of View*. As I will argue in the remainder of this chapter, I think this argument overlooks the bigger picture within which "My Activity as a Writer" must be situated. The fact that "My Activity as a Writer" is a definitely shorter and apparently less poetic and more direct text than *The Point of View* does not make it immune to the effects of Kierkegaard's larger project of indirect communication, and it does not erase the fact that it is just one of many systematic and reductive conclusions that Kierkegaard offered for his complicated authorship.

94 Garff, "Argus," 75–102.

95 Louis Mackey ("Points of View," 160–92) analyzes the many cracks in the argument for a systematization of Kierkegaard's authorship that *The Point of View* creates. All of those same fissures are present in "My Activity as a Writer." *The Point of View* only amplifies the incongruities by amplifying the basic argument for religious unity that is briefly sketched in "My Activity as a Writer."

96 Cf. Jean-François Lyotard's reflections in the preface to *Differend* (xv) on

the way books will be consumed in the future:

> So in the next century there will be no more books. It takes too long to read, when success comes from gaining time. What will be called a book will be a printed object whose "message" (its information content) and name and title will first have been broadcast by the media, a film, a newspaper interview, a television program, and a cassette recording. It will be an object from whose sales the publisher (who will also have produced the film, the interview, the program, etc.) will obtain a certain profit margin, because people will think that they must "have" it (and therefore buy it) so as not to be taken for idiots or to break (my goodness) the social bond! The book will be distributed at a premium, yielding a financial profit for the publisher and a symbolic one for the reader.

A. B. C. D. E. F. Godthaab, the author of *Writing Sampler*, is clearly thinking along the same lines when he (?) (she?) (they?) writes a preface to the preface, asking people to read the preface, and then explains:

> It might seem to be an excess to write a preface to a preface, but it is not that at all; on the contrary, it is only a characteristic expression for the increasing haste with which our age exerts itself, with the result that it takes a great deal to halt it for only a moment and in order to come under consideration for only a moment. Prefaces are no longer read. A person must hit upon something new if he wants to be noticed, like this, now, to write a preface to the preface. (*WS* 73–74)

97 For a good summary of Kierkegaard's mostly negative reflections on how the reading public reads, see Pattison, "Why Read," 291–309. For summaries of Kierkegaard's thoughts on journalism and its role in preventing the reading public from reading, see, Jansen, "Individual," 1–22; and also Best and Kellner, "Modernity," 23–62.

98 As Strawser argues in *Both/And*, xv–xxxiv the religious dimension of Kierkegaard's texts cannot be ignored, but neither can it be elevated above the aesthetic dimension. The priority of the religious and the aesthetic—the edifying and the ironic—remains undecidable in Kierkegaard's work.

99 The ultimate example of this misunderstanding is Henning Fenger's *Kierkegaard: The Myths and Their Origins*.

100 This phrase is a constant throughout Kierkegaard's authorship in both the pseudonymous works and the texts published under his own signature. Stephen Dunning ("Task," 18–32) provides an overview of Kierkegaard's views on authority, with regard to religion and his own authorship.

101 As Michael Strawser points out, "what would be the point of the dialectical structure of an authorship which in the end is annulled by a direct report to history that shows the entire authorship was religious from the start? Is this a result that Kierkegaard was willing to accept or impinge on readers? It seems, rather, that to say S.K. was a religious writer or S.K. was a Christian implies a result that Kierkegaard could never in good faith claim to have attained" ("Socrates," 259–60). Hughes, "Earnestness," 205–37 also argues that *The Point of View* is written in a way that renders undecidable any claim to the ultimate unification of Kierkegaard's writing around a singular religious purpose. Tietjen, *Authorship as Edification*, 75–88, and "Trust," 78–103 argues for the opposing view, maintaining that the whole authorship was a religious project and *The Point of View* organizes everything perfectly with a backwards perspective in a way that should not surprise us, since it was Kierkegaard himself who said that life can only be understood backwards. (However, this interpretation overlooks the fact that Kierkegaard was himself still alive when he wrote *The Point of View*, and therefore was in no position to provide a systematic summary of his still unfinished life.) In a similar vein, Helms, "Serious," 238–67 argues that *The Point of View* should be taken seriously and at face value as a direct communication, and that failing to do so would be to err on the side of being overly suspicious. Law, "Cacophony, 12–47 argues that *The Point of View* is best understood as a project of self-understanding in which Kierkegaard was trying to make sense of his own writing but encountering therein both internal and external aporias which undermine any totalizing or systematic organization of his ideas. Caputo, "Undecidability," 32 argues against any such attempt to treat *The Point of View* "as if it were outside the authorship . . . as if this were not still one more text for his readers to interpret. The very structure of writing insures an ironic distance between the text and the author, on both sides of the aesthetic/religious divide, so that his readers are always and as a structural matter on their own." Joakim Garff points out the awkwardness of reading *The Point of View* as a conclusion to Kierkegaard's authorship since,

> [I]t has fundamental difficulties in coming to the end. Its "Epilogue" is not even its last word, but serves as a prologue to a subsequent "Conclusion," which turns out not to be a conclusion because it is succeeded by "Two Notes," which are themselves preceded by a new "Preface," after which follows more writing, followed by an additional "Postscript," the true postscript of which is yet another "Postscript," that urgently pleads for "just one word more." Thus it was both symptomatic and parodic when somewhere about halfway through *The Point of View* Kierkegaard permitted himself to write, "The whole thing can be stated in a single word." The whole thing never can. (*Biography*, 552)

Finally, Matuštík, "Drama," 411 suggests reading *The Point of View* "as stage directions for the dramatization of Kierkegaard's works. On this reading the authorship becomes accessible through a play or film called *Kierkegaard*. And I am reading *The Point of View* as an exemplar of indirect communication of Kierkegaard's living drama." This is a very creative idea that demonstrates yet another way that *The Point of View* can be read productively in an expansive and non-reductive manner.

102 Merold Westphal ("Anxiety," 5–22) focuses on the last of these—the need to preserve the reader's independence—in his account of Kierkegaard's theory of indirect communication. Westphal also contrasts Kierkegaard's thoughts on the "anxiety of authorship" with contemporary theories of the "death of the author" which originate in Gadamer, Barthes, Foucault, Derrida, and others. Stephen Dunning ("Paradoxes," 125–41) focuses exclusively on the connections between Kierkegaard and Gadamer.

103 Steven Emmanuel ("Reading," 240–55) suggests that we shift our focus from the actual author to an "implied author" as the organizing principle of Kierkegaard's texts. Yet the pseudonymous works would seem to argue that the author in any form (actual or "implied") is "irrelevant" to understanding the texts. An "implied" author remains a method of systematization that the texts themselves resist.

104 Per Lønning ("Stumbling-Block," 94–106) argues that an authentic "follower" of Kierkegaard is someone who does not agree with Kierkegaard, especially with regard to the meaning of Kierkegaard's own books. The ironic interpretation of "My Activity as a Writer" and *The Point of View* that I'm defending here fits nicely with the theory of self-referential irony defended by Andrew Cross ("Neither Either," 125–53). Cross compares the accounts of irony in *The Concept of Irony* and *Concluding Unscientific Postscript* and concludes that the latter is an improvement over the former because it allows irony to be applied to the subject's own existence. In my view that is precisely what Kierkegaard is doing at the end of his career as a writer, by means of two texts which appear to be the most un-ironical items in his authorship.

105 Mooney, "Disruptions," 55–70, argues that Kierkegaard attempted to disrupt and undermine completeness and systematicity in every aspect of his writing, and in his own personal identity as a nineteenth-century Socrates in Copenhagen. Barnett, *Technology*, 97–112 argues that Kierkegaard's fears concerning the dangers of systems and systematic thinking have new relevance today in the age of information technology that offers new ways of systematizing human experience.

106 Roger Poole defends a similar view of the resistance of Kierkegaard's texts to systematic interpretation in his book *Indirect*, 1–27, and his

argument is also summarized in his article "Wish," 156–76. In Pocle's reading, however, Kierkegaard's concluding summaries of his own work, such as "The Point of View," are to be taken at face value; he does not include these texts in Kierkegaard's "indirect communication" (see for example *Indirect*, 21). My argument is that Kierkegaard's multiple points of view, along with his prefaces, are essential components in his indirect communication.

107 That's Roman numeral X, meaning 10. The incredible cleverness of this chapter title will soon become apparent.

108 For a succinct and excellent summary of some of the most important results that follow from taking Kierkegaard's arguments about religion and faith in a non-metaphorical sense, please see Westphal, "Religion," 322–41 and Barrett, "Theologian," 528–49. Kirkconnell, "Unity," 377–90 presents a good example of this perfectly legitimate approach to Kierkegaard's writing when he argues that it is possible to read all of Kierkegaard's work in this way—as fundamentally religious—but acknowledges that this is not the only possible reading. I would never argue that there is anything wrong with understanding religion in a non-metaphorical sense; I'm only arguing that it's wrong to insist that this is the *only possible* meaning religion can have in Kierkegaard's writing.

109 Jacobellis v. Ohio.

110 Aumann, "Art," 166–176 reminds us that indirect communication as Kierkegaard practiced it belongs in the larger genus called "art," including performance art.

111 Deleuze and Guattari, *What Is Philosophy*, 7–8.

112 Deleuze and Guattari, *What Is Philosophy*, 7–8.

113 Holm, "Church," 112–128 analyzes Kierkegaard's very complex relationship with, and critique of, institutional Christianity; Law, "Theology," 166–190 does the same for Kierkegaard and the history of theology.

114 Nietzsche, *Zarathustra*, 5.

115 The Ass Festival at the end of *Zarathustra* (255–258) seems to be a celebration of Zarathustra's recognition that it's up to other people to figure out what his philosophy means, and how to use it.

116 There are numerous interesting readings of *Philosophical Fragments* that focus on the second theory of education, the one that considers what happens when God assumes the role of teacher. For example: Pyper, "Eternity," 129–145, and McCombs, *Paradoxical*, 133–159 (who argues that in *Philosophical Fragments* Socrates "longs for and prepares himself

for the mystery of Christ" (133–134). There are also quite a few readings of *Philosophical Fragments* that don't recognize the first theory of (merely human) education at all, and instead see the entire book as an investigation of how it's possible to learn from God. Nielsen, *Passion*, is an example of this approach, which can only result from begging the question from the outset, and assuming that Climacus could not possibly have anything to say about merely human education. The polar opposite of this approach is represented well by Manheimer, *Educator*, 1–58, whose analysis of "Kierkegaard as Educator" recognizes that Kierkegaard has something to say about merely human education, as well as divine education. There are also treatments of the relevance of Kierkegaard to education studies generally that say nothing at all about *Philosophical Fragments*. Hall, "Education," 490–501 is a wonderful example of this, and in this article several other authors are also cited who think that Kierkegaard may be relevant to education but that *Philosophical Fragments* is not.

117 So many readers see *Philosophical Fragments* as having the simplest possible structure: three questions are asked on the title page, and then everything that follows is an answer to those questions. A question followed by an answer: simple as that. The crumby approach refuses to see the structure of the book in such simplistic terms. Andrew J Burgess analysis of the *Postscript* ("Bilateral Symmetry," 329–345) did a marvelous job of clarifying the complex structure of the *Postscript*; I hope he will someday do something similar for *Philosophical Fragments*.

118 As Jaron Lanier notes, education is the only thing that gives humans an advantage over other animals—for example, cephalopods (such as octopi and cuttlefish). "The raw brainpower of cephalopods seems to have more potential than the mammalian brain. Cephalopods can do all sorts of things, like think in 3-D and morph, which would be fabulous innate skills in a high-tech future.... From the point of view of body and brain, cephalopods are primed to evolve into the high-tech-tool-building overlords. By all rights, cephalopods should be running the show and we should be their pets. What we have that they don't have is neoteny. Our secret weapon is childhood.... While individual cephalopods can learn a great deal within a lifetime, they pass on nothing to future generations. Each generation begins afresh, a blank slate, taking in the strange world without guidance other than instincts bred into their genes" (*Gadget*, 188–189).

119 Among current English translations of *Philosophical Fragments* the Hong translation renders the first sentence of the "Thought Project" as "Can the truth be learned?" while the Piety translation opts for "To what extent can the truth be taught?" I see no reason to settle for either of

these translations. While "Can the truth be learned and/or taught?" is certainly more awkward, and almost painful to the ear, it is truer to the original text and doesn't settle for arbitrarily choosing only one dimension of the word *laere*.

120 Ronald M. Green claims (*Kantian*, 171). that "[t]he problem explored in this opening chapter" of *Philosophical Fragments* is "the question of whether religious and moral truth is resident within us or must be learned from without" But Kierkegaard doesn't just ask "Can religious and moral truths be learned and/or taught," he asks if anything can be learned and/or taught. Green's interpretation is an example of how the theory of merely human education, which is such an interesting and useful crumb in *Philosophical Fragments*, gets overlooked completely when readers rush to impose an exclusively religious interpretation on the book.

121 E.g. Plato, *Apology* 20b; *Theaetetus* 145d–146a; *Laches* 186a–c; *Protagoras* 311d–314c; *Gorgias* 447d–448a; *Greater Hippias* 282b–283c.

122 Failing to recognize how Climacus's theory of merely human education in *Philosophical Fragments* is not identical with Plato's theory of learning as recollection leads to the mistake that Merold Westphal makes when he argues: "In *Philosophical Fragments*, Johannes Climacus seeks to show the difference between recollection as the key to knowledge and revelation as the key to faith" ("Johannes," 13–14). Climacus is not simply repeating or defending Plato's theory of recollection; he's borrowing a few elements from Plato but leaving out all of Plato's metaphysics and adding several of his own pedagogical insights and innovations.

123 These *reductio ad absurdum* proofs deserve to be added to the catalogue of the many uses of comedy in Kierkegaard's writing that Hugh S. Pyper assembles ("Beyond," 149–167). Many readings of *Philosophical Fragments* don't recognize that the book presents a theory of merely human education along with a theory of divine education, and therefore they also don't recognize that the merely human theory of education is given an absurd defense, using *reductio ad absurdum* proofs. The *reductio ad absurdum* proofs that I will outline are instead read in a completely humorless fashion, as if they were proofs that humans require a divine teacher, instead of demonstrating (as I will argue) that it is patently ridiculous when merely human education proceeds according to a paradigm that requires teachers to be gods, and that requires education to be understood in a transcendent, religious paradigm. In this respect my argument in this paper is quite a departure from the interpretative orthodoxy, so this seems like a good time to remind readers of Per Lønning's excellent arguments against orthodoxy in Kierkegaard studies ("Stumbling-Block," 94–106).

124 Nietzsche, *Zarathustra*, 255–258.

125 The orthodox interpretation of *Philosophical Fragments* doesn't recognize a theory of merely human education in this book at all, and therefore doesn't recognize the *reductio ad* absurdum defense of that theory. C. Stephen Evans is one author who seems to miss the comedy in the defense of Socratic teaching/learning completely, and thus he concludes that Climacus has presented an account of God "as the indispensable teacher of humans sunk in error" ("Apologetic," 65). This conclusion is only possible if you miss the joke: turning merely human education into a religion is funny. Another good example of missing this joke is provided by George Connell and Heather Servaty, who argue that the picture of humans in such a wretched and fallen condition that they need to be rescued by god-like teachers entails an incoherent theory of personal identity ("Paradox," 86). They then rush in to patch up this incoherent theory of identity without ever considering that the incoherence could have been meant precisely as an illustration of the absurd consequences that follow when merely human teaching and/or learning is assumed to be possible in a non-Socratic way. David E. Mercer (*Living-Room*, 77) is in the same camp when he argues that the only point of outlining Socratic education in *Philosophical Fragments* is to enable Climacus "to declare the disadvantage of the Socratic position and the value and necessity of the divine teacher." M. G. Piety ("Subversion," 47–62) misses the comedy in Kierkegaard's defense of Socratic teaching and/or learning, which leads her to regard a non-Socratic form of merely human education as a genuine possibility, rather than something that leads to absurd consequences. Another author who doesn't get the joke is Robert C. Roberts (*Faith*, 17), who argues that the only purpose of the discussion of Socratic teaching is to set the stage for the arguments about divine learning. Therefore he recognizes no *reductio ad absurdum* proofs and no comedy generally to defend the theory of Socratic teaching in *Philosophical Fragments*. Though it would be difficult to find anyone who disagrees with K. Brian Söderquist's claim that "Irony shows up in Søren Kierkegaard's authorship from one end to the other" ("Irony," 344), it is striking that the long list of authors above seem to make an exception to this rule for the *Philosophical Fragments*. As I noted at the beginning of this chapter, my reason for mentioning these examples of the authoritative approach to *Philosophical Fragments* is not to argue that they are simply wrong, but rather to remind us of what these readings are overlooking in order to make some space for a crumby approach to the book, and to remind us that *Philosophical Fragments* resists being reduced to a single, simple interpretative point of view.

126 Sheridan Hough can be added to the list of people who miss the joke here, since she claims that in this text Climacus is describing a moment

"of transformation in which the world becomes perfect" (*Dancing*, 105).

127 Aristotle, *Works*, 689. Aristotle gave no argument for this claim; apparently he considered it to be completely obvious—the antithesis of a paradox.

128 Concerning this dimension in *Philosophical Fragments* I highly recommend Walsh, "Echoes," 34–46, and also Barrett, "Paradox," 261–284.

129 Given that the book is called *Philosophical Fragments*, and not *Theological Fragments*, it is amazing how often the book is read exclusively as a theology book and is understood to address only theological questions. For example, Jon Stewart (*Subjectivity*, 133) writes that *Philosophical Fragments* is simply about "the doctrine of the incarnation and revelation of Jesus Christ," and Daphne Hampson (*Exposition*, 60) claims that "*Philosophical Fragments* is the most important text published in theology since the Enlightenment." As Steven Shakespeare points out ("Stirring," 421), given that Kierkegaard says that he found theology to be incredibly boring, it's amazing that any of his books are read as theology books. I have great admiration for George J. Stack's attempt (*Philosophical Fragments*) to resist the tide by reading Kierkegaard as a philosopher and not only as a theologian. I am also a great admirer of Louis Mackey's ability to see that religion, theology and Christianity should not always be taken simply at face value in Kierkegaard's writing. As Mackey argues ("Ram," 102) with regard to *Philosophical Fragments*: "Although the ostensible subject of the book is Christianity, it is Christianity as *wholly other* that structures its discourse. Since the other than language cannot be uttered, the text of the *Fragments* turns back upon itself and becomes an exploration of the limits of language. . . . And it is only in this absolutely indirect way that the book is, importantly, 'about' Christianity." This is a marvelous demonstration of how a willingness to read Kierkegaard as something more than a theologian, and his writing as something more than a defense of Christian theology, opens up so many fascinating new dimensions in these texts. David Wood ("Thinking God," 54) also makes an excellent case for understanding God and Christianity more expansively as "a recognition of the *passion* of thought."

130 Edward F. Mooney ("Exemplars," and "Pseudonyms") provides a wonderful overview of Kierkegaard's theory and practice of indirect communication, and also the reasons why indirect communication is a necessity. Another excellent summary of Kierkegaard's theory of indirect communication, this time with a focus on how indirect communication aims to correct an existential inadequacy within language itself, is given by David Wood (*Limit*, 105–117). Vanessa Rumble ("No-One," 307–321) focuses specifically on the arguments for indirect communication given by the pseudonym Johannes Climacus.

131 Arguments for rejecting the author-ity of the author are often presumed to be based on a different authority: the authority of a postmodern fad—the latest academic hipster disease. That is not at all the case for the argument I've given here, which is derived entirely from taking seriously the theory of education in *Philosophical Fragments* and owes no debt to any fads, postmodern or otherwise. If this theory of education is applied to Kierkegaard's authorship there can no longer be any question of appealing to the intentions of the author. W. Glenn Kirkconnell (*Ethics and Religion*) is an interesting example of someone who wants to read Kierkegaard in a way that does justice to the fact that Kierkegaard "invested much of his thought and effort in settling not only what he wished to say, but how it must be said" (*Ethics and Religion*, 1). This is admirable; however the only solution Kirkconnell can find for this interpretive problem is to fall back on "authorial intent" (*Ethics and Religion*, 2), which he understands to require that the pseudonymous philosophical books be read together with the religious discourses that Kierkegaard authored under his own name and intended to accompany them (*Ethics and Religion*, 1–2). For a cautionary example of what can happen when the author's biography is allowed to assume ultimate authority over his writing, see Strathern, *90 Minutes*, which insists on reading everything Kierkegaard wrote as the direct consequence of events in his life, and engages in the most bizarre speculation in order to follow this imperative.

132 Roger Poole ("First Time," 47) criticizes the simplicity of this very orthodox and very blunt reading of *Either/Or*.

133 Garff, "Formation," 255–259 takes this suggestion and runs with it to offer a fascinating reading of *Either/Or* as an exploration of how individual selves are formed. Hubert Dreyfus ("Self," 11–23) offers a sweeping analysis of Kierkegaard's thinking about the nature of the self, and how selves are formed, and Hannay, "Identity," 48–58 extends the analysis that Dreyfus started, and Aumann, *Selfhood*, 15–100, proposes several different models of selfhood inspired by various Kierkegaardian texts. Louis Mackey notes ("Aesthete," 32) that if Victor Eremita's hypothesis about A and B being the same person is true, "then *Either/Or* becomes a novel and not—as it purports to be—an interchange between two men."

134 Elsebet Jegstrup ("Rose," 71–87) argues that *Either/Or* is a book that has no real author, only a collection of different voices and characters.

135 McDonald, "Boredom," 61–84, explores this argument and many others that are found throughout Kierkegaard's works concerning the theme of boredom.

136 Rumble, "Difference," 167 argues that A is likely the author of "The

Seducer's Diary," given the "suspiciously high degree of anxiety" he expresses concerning its contents.

137 Louis Mackey explores at length the fascinating dialectical relationship between A and Johannes the Seducer in "Aesthete," 24-32.

138 Joakim Garff "Esthetic," 61 points out that another value of reading all of *Either/Or* backwards, not just Part II, is that it would make it even more clear that A and B are completely unaffected by each other's arguments. If we understand everything A writes in Part I as having been written after B sent him the very long letters that comprise Part II, then it would be abundantly evident that B's attempts to persuade A to turn from an aesthetic to an ethical form of life have had no effect whatsoever. Along similar lines, Carlsson, *Eros*, 1-106 and "ethical," 135-144 argues that there is very little evidence that B has read or is responding to anything that A wrote, and that rather than reading Part II of *Either/Or* as a response to Part I, it makes more sense to read Part I as a response to *The Concept of Irony*, since there is a genuine dialogue between those two texts.

139 As Louis Mackey writes ("All in All," 87): "The suspicion that there is a dishonesty lurking in the upright heart of Judge Wilhelm is borne out by the 'Ultimatum' that concludes *Either/Or*. As the Diary of the Seducer draws the ultimate consequences of aestheticism, so this ultimatum exposes the presuppositions of the ethical life."

140 I completely agree with Law, "Place," 233-258 when he points out that the "Ultimatum" has received very little attention for the role that it plays in *Either/Or*, although I don't agree with the rest of his analysis of how the "Ultimatum" functions in the text, since he argues that the concluding sermon transposes all of *Either/Or* into a religious key.

141 Plekon, "Knight," 125-138 argues that what we should really conclude from the sermon that B selects for the last word of Part II is that B is himself presenting a message that is essentially religious—that B is a sort of Proto-Knight-of-Faith. Perkins, "Parson," 207-232 argues for a similar conclusion—that the concluding sermon announces that Part II is really, ultimately about religion and not ethics. Watkin, "Christian," 113-124 thoroughly disagrees with these arguments, as do I.

142 Here are just a few readings of *Either/Or* which ignore this textual evidence and therefore regard B as anything but a nihilist: Baskin, *Ordinary Unhappiness*, 121-122 argues that in *Either/Or* Part II B presents a straightforward argument for "moral perfectionism" in the tradition of Emerson, Wittgenstein, and Cavell. Quinn, "Christian Ethics," 349-375 argues that *Either/Or* Part II contains nothing but a standard approach to secular ethics. Westphal, "Society," 311-314 maintains that B "is a

representative of the ethical stage" who stages a straightforward debate with an aesthete named A. Hannay, *Philosophy*, 90 argues that "if, as Kierkegaard himself says, *Either/Or* gets 'no further' than the ethical, it does at least get that far." Elrod, *Being*, who uses B throughout his chapter on ethics (114–142) as the spokesperson for the ethical. Dunning, *Dialectic*, 74–104, argues that Judge Wilhelm is simply Kierkegaard's pseudonym who represents the ethical stage, and can be relied upon to instruct us in its contents. Louis Mackey argues that B is the one and only ethical man in Kierkegaard's writing ("World Enough," 84), but also allows that B is not "an overly acute thinker" ("World Enough," 39). Karsten Harries (*Nihilism*, 111–148), argues that Part II of *Either/Or* is less exciting than Part I precisely because B is exactly what he claims to be: a representative of ethical life. Mehl, *Pluralistic*, 13–40 argues that B simply represents the viewpoint of "strong evaluative identity and moral content." Fremstedal, "Normative Ethics," 113–125, assigns B to his traditional place—as a spokesperson for ethics who must respond to the aesthetic challenges presented by A—and detects no trace of nihilism in B's performance of these duties. MacIntyre, *After Virtue*, 39–41 famously argues that B is the spokesperson for a "modern" approach to ethics, which he thoroughly criticizes, but in that criticism there is no suggestion that B is actually using ethics as a mask to conceal a deeper nihilism. (MacIntyre's critique of the ethical theory in *Either/Or* has itself been critiqued many times; just one example is Lillegard, "MacIntyre," 83–112. Compaijen, *Internal*, 11–37 provides a thorough summary of MacIntyre's criticisms and responses to them.) Green, "Transcendental," 139–154 argues that B is undertaking a critique of empiricism in his letters via a Kantian transcendental deduction, which is certainly a novel interpretation, but again it makes B into anything but a nihilist.

143 These works of aesthetic theory and criticism by A have generally been very well received as serious works of scholarship, which is more evidence that A takes this work seriously and enjoys it enough to do an excellent job. Three examples of contemporary appreciation for A's aesthetic theories are Yaffe, "Unsung," 73–90; Holler, "Tragedy," 125–142; Norris, "Ibsen's," 143–158. Pattison, "Art," 76–100 explores the broader meaning of aesthetics in Kierkegaard's writing and in his philosophy, which is a very useful context within which to consider A in *Either/Or* Part I as an aesthetic theorist.

144 The view of A as someone who is obviously unhappy originates with B. B insists on this, and uses it as evidence for the superiority of his own ethical theory, but a careful reading of A's own words in Part I doesn't support this conclusion. McCarthy, "Narcissism," 51–72 starts with the standard assumption—inherited from B—that A is obviously unhappy, and then proceeds to diagnose his despair with tools and concepts from

Freudian psychology. Hannay, "Despair," 329–348 considers B's claims that A must be in despair, and situates these arguments within the broader context of Kierkegaard's many explorations of despair. Kierkegaard certainly did explore the phenomenon of despair in many other works, as Marino, "Depression, 121–128 catalogues, but A in Part I of *Either/Or* is not part of that research project. All the evidence we have in the text of *Either/Or* itself suggests that A was actually quite far from despair.

145 Actually there's at least one exception: Pattison, "Bonfire," 47 argues that *Either/Or* as a whole, including all of Part I, is one of Kierkegaard's least funny books.

146 Karsten Harries, in a demonstration of absolutely hyperbolic understatement, writes that "[t]he second volume of *Either/Or* is a bit duller than the first" (*Nihilism*, 111). And of course even after 327 pages B was not done sharing his opinions concerning marriage, since he shows up again in *Stages on Life's Way* to deliver another speech on the subject, this one a mere ninety-six pages long (*SLW* 87–184). Louis Mackey ("World Enough," 81) suggests perhaps the most charitable interpretation possible for B's long-windedness: "So Judge Wilhelm concludes—or rather does not conclude, for he is as garrulous as time itself. The length of his letters suggests that his wife's expert management of his finitude leaves him infinite leisure for distributing extra-professional counsel."

147 The abridged version of *Either/Or* published in a single volume by Penguin (1992) and edited and translated by Alastair Hannay is primarily an attempt to make Part II less boring and more readable (most of the material that is missing in this abridged version was removed from B's letters in Part II). In the introduction to this edition Hannay writes that the cuts in Part II "are designated primarily to bring the line of Wilhelm's argument into greater relief and thus to help it make a more immediate impact upon the reader" (4). This project of providing the reader with cleaned-up and more coherent version of B is obviously well-intended but it does make it impossible for the reader to discover, as I will argue in this chapter, that B is actually a nihilist and also that the arguments he presents in his long letters are comical because they are contradictory. These discoveries can be made only by slogging through the unabridged version of B, which is certainly, a less pleasant experience in the short term, though ultimately it is much more rewarding.

148 Louis Mackey directs appropriate skepticism toward the idea that all women will be perfectly satisfied with the role that B assigns them in his picture of ethical life. ("All in All," 85–87). As he notes: "One need not be a cynic (though perhaps one needs to be married) to remark that such an idyllic relationship could only be imagined by a bachelor like

Kierkegaard" ("All in All," 85). Joakim Garff "Esthetic," 66 notes that "[t]he woman to whom Wilhelm is married essentially appears to be a principle rather than a person; she does not even have a name..." Since B neglects to name his wife, Garff decides to call her C, and he devotes several interesting pages (66-68) to exploring her forgotten perspective in *Either/Or*. Amy Laura Hall clarifies how much the submission and exploitation of B's wife is necessary for his ethical system to work. Her marvelous chapter on *Either/Or* is titled: "The Married Man as Master Thief in *Either/Or*" (*Treachery,* 108-138). Berry, "Judging," 33-58 covers all of these topics deftly and argues that B demonstrates classic essentialism, rather than the existentialism with which he is so often associated, in his thinking about women. Her analysis of the blindspots in A's "heterosexual imagination" (Berry, "Imagination," 201-228) is also quite delightful. Walsh, "Divide," 191-205 considers these particular moments of *Either/Or* within the larger field of challenges that confront anyone reading Kierkegaard critically on the topic of gender.

149 Hegel, *Phenomenology,* 45.

150 Compaijen and Vos, "Reflection," 67-77 explore the general theme of ethical reflection as evasion of responsibility and action in Kierkegaard's thought, with a particular focus on Kierkegaard's unpublished and undelivered 1847 lectures titled "The Dialectic of Ethical and Ethical-Religious Communication." Nelson, "Lectures," 391-410 also analyzes this fascinating little project, this time in the context of the many explanations for his authorship that Kierkegaard entertained in the years between 1847 and 1851.

151 Carlisle, *Becoming,* 49-66 argues that the main purpose of *Either/Or* is to establish the reality of contradiction in the face of the Hegelian insistence upon mediation, and therefore presents B as the opponent of all contradiction. I would argue that B does assume this role initially in Part II, but then later abdicates that job and embraces his own contradictions in a rather hilarious fashion. Westphal, "Kierkegaard and Hegel," 101-124 explores the broader context of Kierkegaard's relation to Hegel—a relation that Westphal characterizes as an *Aufhebung* in its own way. Hühn and Schwab, "German Idealism," 62-93 also explores Kierkegaard's response to Hegel and German idealism generally, as does Stewart, *Idealism,* 79-119 and "View," 50-65. Binetti, "Relations, 98-111 aims to clarify and demystify once and for all the whole question of how Kierkegaard is related to Hegel specifically and German Idealism generally.

152 This rightly famous aspect of B's ethical theory—so famous that it is often allowed to overshadow and drown out everything else that B says in his letters to A—is thoroughly explored in Mooney, "Self-Choice," 5-32.

153 Ferreira, "Love," 329–331 emphasizes this aspect of B's first letter—the claim that nothing aesthetic need be lost in marriage, that all the aesthetic values of the first love can be preserved in an enduring relationship. Wood, "First Kiss," 88–111 also explores this idea thoroughly.

154 As Louis Mackey writes:

> *Either/Or* is incomplete and necessarily so. It is unfinished and open-ended in the same way that man is infinite and always exposed to further possibilities. It has not one protagonist, but two, three, who-knows-how-many *personae*, none of whom is any sort of hero. Each *persona* stands for an existential option which he has taken up, and no author with superior insight evaluates his choice *vis-à-vis* those of the others. There is no narrative resolution of the stretto among A, Judge Wilhelm, the priest from Jutland, and all the rest of putative others. Each is stuck fast in his own categories, by his own choice; none of them develops; their actions merely reiterate their choices. The novel in which they live is a *Bildungsroman*, but without *Bildung* ("Poet," 274).

In the *Concluding Unscientific Postscript* Johannes Climacus offers a similar take on *Either/Or* as part of "A Glance at a Contemporary Effort in Danish Literature":

> That there is no conclusion and no final decision is an indirect expression for truth as inwardness and in this way perhaps a polemic against truth as knowledge. The preface itself says something about it, but not didactically, for in that case I could know something with certainty, but in the jovial form of jest and hypothesis. The absence of an author is a means of distancing (*CUP* 252).

155 For example, Roger Poole makes the following argument: "Set into the middle of the Berlin section is a long disquisition about the theater. The design of this section is to frustrate the reader (who is presumably interested in repetition) as much as possible. The disquisition about the nature of farce deliberately holds up the advance of the argument in a series of deferrals. The description of the great actor Beckmann and his gait upon the stage seems to wish to bog the reader down with details in what is already a parenthesis ... All this brilliant display of *belles lettres* is there for a single purpose: to divert the attention of the reader from the concept of repetition" (*Indirect*, 69–70). See also: Louis Mackey, "Once More," 69, 78–81. In most cases, commentators have simply had nothing to say about Constantin's discourse on farce, thereby establishing indirectly their conviction that these pages are irrelevant to the text as a whole. For example, Eriksen, *Repetition*, 3–170 doesn't mention it once in his entire "reconstruction" of Kierkegaard's category of repetition. Two notable exceptions to this rule are Sylviane Agacinski, who argues

that, "[i]t is not by accident that the theater can be found at the very heart of *Repetition*" (*Aparté*, 159), and George Pattison, who argues that "Constantin's discourse on dramatic art and farce . . . [is] a clue to the labyrinth not only of this small but complex book but of wider aspects of Kierkegaard's authorship" ("Magic," 360).

156 Boven, "Theatre," 123–127 does not regard *Repetition* as a farce in particular, but does argue that the text should be understood as a work of philosophical theatre. Stack, "Theatrical," 367–380 also argues that the theatrical dimension of *Repetition* is important to recognize, though again without a particular focus on farce.

157 One thing that I will not do in this chapter is offer any opinion on the possible connections between the text of *Repetition* and Søren Kierkegaard's relationship with Regine Olsen. The following quotations summarize my thinking concerning such an approach:

> After my death no one will find in my papers (this is my consolation) the least information about what has *really* filled my life, find *that* script in my innermost being that explains everything, and which often, for me, makes what the world would call trifles into events of immense importance, and which I too consider of no significance once I take away the secret note that explains it. (*KJN* 2:157)

> [I]n the pseudonymous books there is not a single word by me. I have no opinion about them except as a third party, no knowledge of their meaning except as a reader, not the remotest private relation to them . . . My facsimile, my picture, etc., like the question whether I wear a hat or a cap, could become an object of attention only for those to whom the indifferent has become important—perhaps in compensation because the important has become a matter of indifference to them. (*CUP* 626)

158 The repetition contained in Constantin Constantius's name is just one of the many repetitions in the book called *Repetition* that Vincent McCarthy argues can serve as "a point of entry and possible clue to the meaning(s) of the book" ("Repetition's *Repetitions*," 264). Mooney, *Polemics*, 160 makes a similar point.

159 Adorno insists that this text proves that the theory of farce in *Repetition* is "a theory in which not only Kierkegaard's doctrine of art, but his entire systematics of the concept of existence disintegrates" (*Construction*, 129). This might be a very interesting argument, if Kierkegaard had anything like a "doctrine of art" or a "systematics of the concept of existence."

160 Cf. Lyotard, *Differend*, xv.

161 With regard to the farcical dimension of *Repetition*, the comments of Vigilius Haufniensis, author of *The Concept of Anxiety*, on his reading of *Repetition* are very interesting:

> This is no doubt a witty book, as the author also intended it to be. To my knowledge, he is indeed the first to have a lively understanding of 'repetition'... But what he has discovered he has concealed again by arraying the concept in the jest of an analogous conception. What has motivated him to do this is difficult to say, or more correctly, difficult to understand... Since he wanted to occupy himself with repetition only esthetically and psychologically, everything had to be arranged humorously so as to bring about the impression that the word in one instant means everything and in the next instant the most insignificant of things, and the transition, or rather the constant falling down from the clouds, is motivated by its farcical opposite. (*CA* 17–18n)

162 McDonald, "Experimenting," 39–51 explores the many versions of "experimenting psychology" in Kierkegaard's writing including *Repetition*.

163 Mark Lloyd Taylor ("Ordeal," 36–37) does an admirable job of pulling together Constantin's three main discussions of the meaning of repetition.

164 Crites. "Blissful," 225–246 contrasts the categories of recollection and repetition, and also eternal recurrence. Furtak, "Greek," 129–149 explores the broader context of Kierkegaard's thinking about and appropriation of Greek philosophy generally.

165 One notable exception to contemporary philosophy's ignorance of repetition is Heidegger, who ontologized repetition and recast it as "authenticity" in *Being and Time*, though he was not very forthcoming about the inspiration for his ideas. A good summary of how Heidegger was influenced by the concept of repetition he found in Kierkegaard is offered by Huntington, "Heidegger's Reading," 44–47. For a more complete account of Kierkegaard's influence on Heidegger, above and beyond *Repetition*, see Caputo, *Demythologizing*, and also Carlisle, "Heidegger," 421–439.

166 A musical metaphor found in the Journals and Notebooks of one Søren Kierkegaard sheds some light on what Constantin Constantius is saying here about repetition: "The presupposition or, as it were, musical key of consciousness steadily rises, but within that key the same thing repeats itself." (*KJN* 2:211).

167 Gregor Malantshuk emphasizes the theme of depth in his interpretation of repetition. He writes: "Kierkegaard wishes to say that development in the individual life consists of a steadily deeper and more concrete knowledge of oneself. One is not to look at himself abstractly but 'ought to use a special map' and thereby clearly recognize the numerous factors and motivations in his life. Kierkegaard believes that by taking this

path a person can obtain, on the human level, an insight into his own inadequacy" (*Thought*, 136).

168 T. F. Morris (Acceptable," 309–334) discusses the aesthetic assumptions behind the failure of Constantin's Berlin experiment.

169 Pat Bigelow makes this point: "[R]epetition is the name for what irresistibly tries to become an object of a science but necessarily can never become an object for any science . . . repetition can neither be said nor shown but can only be performed" (*Writing*, 163). Because repetition can never be demonstrated objectively, Bigelow argues, "it is essentially undecidable whether or not we can understand repetition" (*Writing*, 167).

170 David J. Gouwens ("Understanding," 283–308) examines the role played by observers in both *Repetition* and *Fear and Trembling*, focusing in particular on the incongruity of assigning to those observers the task of understanding somebody else's subjective experience.

171 While some commentators have been willing to view part 1 as a comic interlude, most have continued to insist that when the young man takes over in part 2 the book turns serious. One example of this way of breaking down the text is the first chapter of John Caputo's *Radical Hermeneutics*. Caputo argues that part 1 of *Repetition*—the story of Constantin Constantius's trip to Berlin—is indeed a parody, but part 2—the story of the young man's love affair, as explained in his letters to Constantin Constantius—is not a parody, but rather a serious "drama of the ethico religious fate of the nameless young man" (23). Caputo makes the same claims in "Foundering," 201–224.

172 All citations of the Book of Job are taken from the King James translation of the Bible.

173 The young man anticipates and protests my criticism thus: "But one who owned very little may indeed also have lost everything; one who lost the beloved has in a sense lost sons and daughters, and one who lost honor and pride and along with it the vitality and meaning of life—he, too, has in a sense been stricken with malignant sores" (*R* 198–199). This comment only serves to accentuate the comedy inherent in the young man's attempt to make himself Job's equal in suffering. There remains a tremendous gap between the irritations that the young man suffers in his romantic life and losing all your children and being stricken with malignant sores. This comedy is lost completely on Andrew J. Burgess ("Suffering," 24–262). Kramer, "Present Past," 57–73 argues that *Repetition* is a study of traumatic memory that can contribute to the current analysis of the unbinding of memory. I would argue that the fact that much of *Repetition* deals with a supposed trauma which is not really

as traumatic as the Young Man claims only adds an additional layer of ironic depth to this dimension of the text.

174 Of course, this is just the beginning of an existentialist theory of meaning. As Sartre has argued, ultimately an existentialist has to accept responsibility even for her own birth. See for example, Sartre, *Nothingness*, 406–408.

175 Niels Thulstrup (*Hegel* 349) doesn't appreciate the humor of the young man's insistence on a thunderstorm. He declares that the only genuine repetition that occurs in *Repetition* occurs in the form of a thunderstorm. Constantius, on the other hand, apparently does see the comedy in the young man's account of waiting to be struck by lightning. "It is impossible to get involved with him," he writes, "because to correspond with a man who holds a trump card such as a thunderstorm in his hand would be ludicrous" (*R* 216).

176 For a terrific application of some Kierkegaardian arguments about the centrality of freedom and responsibility to contemporary culture, see Dreyfus and Rubin, "Addiction," 3–19.

177 Louis Mackey articulates this thought concisely when he writes: "Repetition cannot be written. *Repetition* is a way of writing this" ("Once More," 100). Stephen Crites concurs: "There are occasional hints about the meaning of repetition, but we are never permitted to see the movement itself except in the distorting mirror of the esthetic." ("Pseudonymous," 217.) David Cain ("Coach Horn," 345–350) argues that *Repetition* needs to be understood in the context of "revocation"—an idea that the pseudonyms return to time and again.

178 This shift in emphasis from the writer to the reader occurs in many Kierkegaardian texts. For more on this theme see: Pattison, "Reading," 291–309.

179 Boven, "Theatre," 119–123 argues that repetition is presented as an "existential category" rather than a logical category, and that the presentation of this existential category guarantees that its meaning will always be in dispute. Mooney, "Getting," 282–307 argues that repetition is not at all a straightforward concept, and defends this conclusion with a careful reading that emphasizes the complexities of the text.

180 The inability to see the comedy in *Repetition*, or in the other Kierkegaardian texts, has created some moments of comedy that are rather remarkable in their own right. For example, consider the comments that Emmanuel Levinas made after reading a paper at a Kierkegaard conference in 1964. Levinas suggests, in a very ominous tone, that Kierkegaard's "reckless" style may even be partly to blame for the appearance of

national Socialism:

> [W]hat shocks me about Kierkegaard is his violence. An impulsive and violent style, reckless of scandal and destruction, was added to the philosophical repertory by Kierkegaard, even before Nietzsche. Philosophers could now philosophize with a hammer. The new style aspired to permanent provocation, and the total rejection of everything, and I think we can see it as anticipating certain other verbal violences that once passed themselves off as pure and considered. I refer not only to National Socialism itself, but also to the various ideas that it promoted" (Levinas, "Ethics," 34).

For more on the differences, and the similarities, between the philosophy of Levinas and Kierkegaard, see: Kemp, "Another Language," 5–28; Dooley, "Totality," 199–213; and also, Westphal, "Shadow," 265–281. Gibbs, "Dash," 143 argues that Kierkegaard's "Christian ethics," which he says is presented primarily in *Works of Love*, has much in common with Levinas.

181 Descartes, *Discourse*, 111.

182 Descartes, *Discourse*, 147.

183 Descartes, "Early," 5.

184 Descartes, *Discourse*, 146.

185 Descartes, *Discourse*, 113.

186 Two notable exceptions to this rule are Michael Strawser, who devotes one very interesting chapter of his book *Both/And* (62–86) to taking *Johannes Climacus* seriously as a critique of modern philosophy, especially its focus on hyperbolic doubt, and David Kangas, who also devotes an excellent chapter of his excellent book (*Instant*, 65–90) to a reading of *Johannes Climacus* as an exploration of the problem of getting philosophy started. Kangas argues that "[t]he critical meaning of *Johannes Climacus* is thus to point to a beginning that cannot be grasped as a principle, a beginning whose origin does not lie in the self-positing movement of self-consciousness" (66).

187 Actually, it would be more accurate to say that *Johannes Climacus* has by and large been ignored. For example, in the *International Kierkegaard Commentary* on *Philosophical Fragments* and *Johannes Climacus*, the editor's introduction does not mention *Johannes Climacus* once, and only one essay out of thirteen deals with the text in any way. It's a little odd, and misleading, that they even chose to include *Johannes Climacus* in the title. Barrett, "Method," 17–27 makes an admirable attempt to aggregate and organize the various threads of Kierkegaard's thought that

could be regarded as methodological in nature, but does not mention *Johannes Climacus* in this summary. Turnbull, "Methodology," 52–64 does something similar: presenting a summary of Kierkegaard's methodology with no mention of *Johannes Climacus*. Davidshofer, "Method," 28–38 presents a dialectical method that the author finds in the writings of Johannes Climacus, but again does not mention the book that bears that author's name. One exception to the general tendency to ignore what *Johannes Climacus* has to say about methodology is Malantschuk, *Thought*, 160–178 (but Malantschuk's reading of the methodological message in *Johannes Climacus* is significantly different from mine).

188 Strictly speaking, *Johannes Climacus* does not have a pseudonym. (In fact, no author is designated on the manuscript's title page.) Because of this I have felt free to alternate between "Johannes Climacus" and "Søren Kierkegaard" in my references to the author of this text, according to what seemed appropriate in each case, (and also according to my own foolish whims). Rather than being disturbed by this lack of authorial consistency, I urge the reader to adopt the attitude of "A. F...." in her/his article, "Who is the Author of *Either/Or*": "Most people, including the author of this article, think it is not worth the trouble to be concerned about who the author is. They are happy not to know his identity, for then they have only the book to deal with, without being bothered or distracted by his personality" (*CA* 16). See also, Lønning, "Stumbling-Block," 94–106.

189 Descartes, *Discourse*, 112–113.

190 Descartes, *Discourse*, 114–115.

191 Descartes, *Discourse*, 112.

192 cf. Descartes, *Discourse*, 117, 112.

193 The most complete account of these three dreams that I know if is in Cole, *Olympian Dreams*, 59–88.

194 This brings to mind the bumper sticker, often seen in university parking lots, which commands the reader to "Question Authority." I was recently delighted to discover one of these bumper stickers (attached to the bumper of a Volvo, which is probably not relevant), on which a clever rogue had penned the response: "OK, if you say so...."

195 Stephen N. Dunning ("Illusory Grandeur," 203–222) summarizes Climacus's three different responses to the three different versions of *de omnibus dubitandum est*. Dunning then goes on to contrast the account of doubt in *Johannes Climacus* with the account of doubt given by Judge Wilhelm in *Either/Or* and the account by Anti-Climacus in *The Sickness*

unto Death. When Johannes Climacus rejects modern philosophy as a kind of madness he is not alone; there are many other instances in Kierkegaard's that repeat this claim, as Llewelyn, "Borderline, 88–111 demonstrates.

196 This means that the "beginning" of philosophy can only be understood as an individual leap. M. Jamie Ferreira ("Leap," 207–234) discusses the various leaps in Kierkegaard's writings, including, but not limited to, the leap of faith.

197 Michael Strawser (*Both/And*, 74–81) argues that this section of the book provides one of the earliest, and most complete, sources for the arguments about the gap between language and the world that Kierkegaard worked out more extensively in the pseudonymous works that followed.

198 Rudd, "Sceptics," 71–88 discusses this theme of doubt as a threshold to authentic subjectivity as it plays out in the later works of Johannes Climacus, the *Postscript* and the *Fragments*. Another good general discussion of Kierkegaard's work vis á vis the sceptical tradition is Popkin "Scepticism," 342–372.

199 Descartes, *Discourse*, 112.

200 Descartes, *Discourse*, 112.

201 Julie E. Maybee ("Madness" 387–406) takes a similar approach, but with an even broader focus. She argues that Kierkegaard equates all objective, systematic rationality with a kind of madness that "will make you sick" (387). This is a very interesting way of turning the tables on one traditional criticism of Kierkegaardian subjective thinking and subjective truth: the claim that they are not fundamentally different from insanity.

202 Descartes, *Discourse*, 116.

203 Descartes, *Meditations*, 17–62.

204 Descartes, *Discourse*, 125.

205 Descartes, *Discourse*, 125.

206 Nietzsche, *Twilight*, 162.

207 Robert C. Roberts ("Passion," 87–106) discusses many of Kierkegaard's arguments in favor of passionate engagement with the world, and opposed to detached spectatorship. Roberts ("Virtue," 177–206) also discusses issues of health and "character" in Kierkegaardian texts. Julia Watkin ("Boom!" 95–114) looks at contemporary efforts in physics to produce a theory of everything as some of the most current examples of the futility of attempting to create an existential system.

208 Most likely it was between November 1842 and April 1843, after he had written *Either/Or* and before he wrote the three books which appeared in 1843 (*Repetition, Fear and Trembling,* and *Three Upbuilding Discourses.* Michael Strawser (*Both/And,* 64–69) discusses the uncertainty surrounding the dates.

209 Louis Mackey speculates that the book was never finished "because Kierkegaard came to see that it was not an excess of doubt—the philosophers after all never really doubted—but an excess of assurance that was the real peril. Not skeptical modesty but the grandiloquent self-confidence of speculative thought prevented men from apprehending the contradictions of existence and the necessity of faith" ("Earnest," 150). Michael Strawser argues (*Both/And,* 80) that "the incomplete form achieves Kierkegaard's purpose, in that the life-doubt of Johannes Climacus cannot be concluded; it cannot be stopped through thinking or knowledge." As an unfinished and unpublished text, *Johannes Climacus* bears a strong resemblance to Descartes's *Rules for the Direction of the Mind,* which was also unpublished and left unfinished by its author (although Descartes did manage to set forth twenty-one rules for thinking—apparently this wasn't nearly enough). Perhaps by leaving *Johannes Climacus* unfinished Kierkegaard intended a deliberate commentary on the impossibility of creating a complete list of rules, or any other kind of totalizing methodology, that would control thinking.

Bibliography

Adorno, Theodor. *Kierkegaard. Construction of the Aesthetic*. Edited and Translated by Robert Hullot-Kentor. Minneapolis: University of Minnesota Press, 1989.
Agacinski, Sylviane. *Aparté: Conceptions and Deaths of Søren Kierkegaard*. Translated by Kevin Newmark. Tallahassee, FL: Florida State University Press, 1988.
Allison, Henry E. "Christianity and Nonsense." *The Review of Metaphysics* 20.3 (1967) 432–60.
Amir, Lydia B. *Humor and the Good Life in Modern Philosophy: Shaftesbury, Hamann, Kierkegaard*. Albany, NY: SUNY Press. 2014.
Aristotle. *The Basic Works of Aristotle*. Edited by Richard McKeon. Translated by W. D. Ross. New York: Random House, 1941.
Aumann, Antony. *Art and Selfhood: A Kierkegaardian Account*. New York: Lexington, 2019.
———. "Kierkegaard and the Value of Art: An Indirect Method of Communication." In *The Kierkegaardian Mind*, edited by Adam Buben, Eleanor Helms, and Patrick Stokes, 166–76. London: Routledge, 2019.
Baskin, Jon. *Ordinary Unhappiness: The Therapeutic Fiction of David Foster Wallace*. Stanford: Stanford University Press, 2019.
Barnett, Christopher B. *Kierkegaard and the Question Concerning Technology*. London: Bloomsbury, 2019.
Barrett, Lee D. "Kierkegaard as Theologian: A History of Countervailing Interpretations." In *The Oxford Handbook of Kierkegaard*, edited by John Lippitt and George Pattison, 528–49. Oxford: Oxford University Press, 2013.
———. "The Paradox of Faith in *Philosophical Fragments*: Gift or Task." In *International Kierkegaard Commentary: Philosophical Fragments and Johannes Climacus*, edited by Robert L. Perkins, 261–84. Macon, GA: Mercer University Press, 1994.
———. "The Passion of Kierkegaard's Existential Method." In *The Kierkegaardian Mind*, edited by Adam Buben, Eleanor Helms, and Patrick Stokes, 17–27. London: Routledge, 2019.
Berry, Wanda Warren. "The Heterosexual Imagination and Aesthetic Existence in Kierkegaard's *Either/Or, Part One*." In *International Kierkegaard Commentary: Either/Or Part I*, edited by Robert L. Perkins, 201–29. Macon, GA: Mercer University Press, 1995.
———. "Judge William Judging Woman: Existentialism and Essentialism in *Either/Or Part II*." In *International Kierkegaard Commentary: Either/Or Part II*, edited by Robert L. Perkins, 33–58. Macon, GA: Mercer University Press, 1995.

Best, Steven, and Kellner, Douglas. "Modernity, Mass Society, and the Media: Reflections on the Corsair Affair." In *International Kierkegaard Commentary: The Corsair Affair*, edited by Robert L. Perkins, 23–62. Macon, GA: Mercer University Press, 1990.

Bigelow, Pat. "The Brokenness of Philosophic Desire: Edifying Discourses and the Embarrassment of the Philosopher." In *Kierkegaard Revisited*, edited by Niels Cappelørn and Jon Stewart 310–338. Berlin: de Gruyter, 1997.

———. *The Conning, The Cunning of Being: Being a Kierkegaardian Demonstration of the Postmodern Implosion of Metaphysical Sense in Aristotle and the Early Heidegger*. Tallahassee, FL: Florida State University Press, 1990.

———. *Kierkegaard and the Problem of Writing*. Tallahassee, FL: Florida State University Press, 1987.

Binetti, Maria J. "Kierkegaard's Relations to Idealism Demystified." In *Kierkegaard in Context: A Festschrift for Jon Stewart*, edited by Lee C. Barrett and Peter Šajda, 98–111. Macon, GA: Mercer University Press, 2019.

Boundas, Constantin, and Olkowski, Dorothea, eds. *Gilles Deleuze and the Theatre of Philosophy*. London: Routledge, 1994.

Boven, Martijn. "A Theatre of Ideas: Performance and Performativity in Kierkegaard's *Repetition*." In *Kierkegaard, Literature and the Arts*, edited by Eric Ziolkowski, 115–30. Evanston, IL: Northwestern University Press, 2018.

Burgess, Andrew J. "The Bilateral Symmetry of Kierkegaard's *Postscript*." In *International Kierkegaard Commentary: Concluding Unscientific Postscript to "Philosophical Fragments,"* edited by Robert L. Perkins, 329–45. Macon, GA: Mercer University Press, 1997.

———. "*Repetition*—A Story of Suffering." In *International Kierkegaard Commentary: Fear and Trembling and Repetition*, edited by Robert L. Perkins, 247–62. Macon, GA: Mercer University Press, 1993.

Burns, Michael O'Neill. *Kierkegaard and the Matter of Philosophy: A Fractured Dialectic*. London: Rowman and Littlefield, 2015.

Cain, David. "Notes on a Coach Horn: 'Going Further,' 'Revocation,' and 'Repetition.'" In *International Kierkegaard Commentary: Fear and Trembling and Repetition*, edited by Robert L. Perkins, 345–50. Macon, GA: Mercer University Press, 1993.

Cameron, W. S. K. "[Writing] about Writing about Kierkegaard." *Philosophy Today* 39.1 (1995) 58.

Cappelørn, Niels Jørgen, et al. *Written Images: Søren Kierkegaard's Journals, Notebooks, Booklets, Sheets, Scraps, and Slips of Paper*. Translated by Bruce H. Kirmmse. Princeton: Princeton University Press, 2003.

Caputo, John D. *Demythologizing Heidegger*. Bloomington, IN: Indiana University Press, 1993.

———. "Either-Or, Undecidability, and Two Concepts of Irony." In *The New Kierkegaard*, edited by Elsebet Jegstrup, 14–41. Bloomington, IN: Indiana University Press, 2004.

———. *How to Read Kierkegaard*. New York: Norton, 2007.

———. "Instants, Secrets, and Singularities: Dealing Death in Kierkegaard and Derrida." In *Kierkegaard in Post/Modernity*, edited by Martin J. Matuštík and Merold Westphal, 216–38. Bloomington, IN: Indiana University Press, 1995.

———. "Kierkegaard, Heidegger, and the Foundering of Metaphysics." In *International Kierkegaard Commentary: Fear and Trembling and Repetition*, edited by Robert L. Perkins, 201–24. Macon, GA: Mercer University Press, 1993.
———. *Radical Hermeneutics.* Bloomington, IN: Indiana University Press, 1987.
Carlisle, Clare. "Kierkegaard and Heidegger." In *The Oxford Handbook of Kierkegaard*, edited by John Lippitt and George Pattison, 421–39. Oxford: Oxford University Press, 2013.
———. *Kierkegaard's Philosophy of Becoming: Movements and Positions.* Albany, NY: State University of New York Press, 2005.
———. *Philosopher of the Heart: The Restless Life of Søren Kierkegaard.* New York: Farrar, Straus and Giroux, 2020.
Carlsson, Ulrika. "The Ethical Life of Aesthetes." In *The Kierkegaardian Mind*, edited by Adam Buben, Eleanor Helms, and Patrick Stokes, 135–44. London: Routledge, 2019.
———. *Kierkegaard and Philosophical Eros: Between Ironic Reflection and Aesthetic Meaning.* London: Bloomsbury, 2021.
Cole, John R. *The Olympian Dreams and Youthful Rebellion of René Descartes.* Urbana, IL: University of Illinois Press, 1992.
Compaijen, Rob. *Kierkegaard, MacIntyre, Williams, and the Internal Point of View.* New York: Palgrave Macmillan, 2018.
Compaijen, Rob, and Pieter Vos. "Ethical Reflection as Evasion." In *The Kierkegaardian Mind*, edited by Adam Buben, Eleanor Helms, and Patrick Stokes, 67–77. London: Routledge, 2019.
Connell, George. "Why Kierkegaard Still Matters." In *Why Kierkegaard Matters: A Festschrift in Honor of Robert L. Perkins*, edited by Marc A Jolley and Edmon L. Rowell, 66–81. Macon, GA: Mercer University Press, 2010.
Connell, George, and Heather Servaty. "A Paradox of Personal Identity in Kierkegaard's *Philosophical Fragments*." In *International Kierkegaard Commentary: Philosophical Fragments and Johannes Climacus*, edited by Robert L. Perkins, 85–107. Macon, GA: Mercer University Press, 1994.
Cooper, David E. "Existentialism as a Philosophical Movement." In *The Cambridge Companion to Existentialism*, edited by Steven Crowell, 27–49. Cambridge: Cambridge University Press, 2012.
Crites, Stephen. "'The Blissful Security of the Moment': Recollection, Repetition, and Eternal Recurrence." In *International Kierkegaard Commentary: Fear and Trembling and Repetition*, edited by Robert L. Perkins, 225–46. Macon, GA: Mercer University Press, 1993.
———. "Pseudonymous Authorship as Art and as Act." In *Kierkegaard: A Collection of Critical Essays*, edited by Josiah Thompson, 183–229. New York: Doubleday, 1972.
Cross, Andrew. "Neither Either Nor Or: The Perils of Reflexive Irony." In *The Cambridge Companion to Kierkegaard*, edited by Alastair Hannay and Gordon D. Marino, 125–53. Cambridge: Cambridge University Press, 1998.
Dalton, Stuart. "Existence and Comedy: An Interpretation of the *Concluding Unscientific Postscript*." *Kinesis* 18.2 (1992) 1–26.
———. "How to Avoid Getting Killed by a Statue: Some Lessons on Teaching and Lying from Nietzsche's *Thus Spoke Zarathustra*." *Think: A Journal of the Royal Institute of Philosophy* 21.60 (2022) 79–90.

———. "How to Avoid Writing: Prefaces and Points of View in Kierkegaard." *Philosophy Today* 44.2 (2000) 123–36.

———. "How to Be a Terrible Teacher: Kierkegaard's *Philosophical Fragments* on What Education Is Not." *Philosophy and Social Criticism* 45.3 (2019) 241–64.

———. "*Johannes Climacus* as Kierkegaard's Discourse on Method." *Philosophy Today* 47.4 (2003) 360–77.

———. "Kierkegaard's *Repetition* as a Comedy in Two Acts." *Janus Head* 4.2 (2001) 287–326.

———. Review of *Kierkegaard's Journals and Notebooks Volumes 6 and 7: Journals NB11–NB14 and NB15–NB20*. Edited by Niels Jørgen Cappelørn, Alastair Hannay, David Kangas, Bruce H. Kirmmse, George Pattison, Joel D. S. Rasmussen, Vanessa Rumble, and K. Brian Söderquist. *Philosophy in Review* 36.2 (2016) 63–66.

———. Review of *Kierkegaard's Journals and Notebooks Volume 8: Journals NB21–NB25*. Edited by Niels Jørgen Cappelørn, Alastair Hannay, David Kangas, Bruce H. Kirmmse, George Pattison, Joel D. S. Rasmussen, Vanessa Rumble, and K. Brian Söderquist. *Philosophy in Review* 36.5 (2016) 204–9.

———. Review of *Kierkegaard's Journals and Notebooks Volume 9: Journals NB26–NB30*. Edited by Niels Jørgen Cappelørn, Alastair Hannay, David Kangas, Bruce H. Kirmmse, George Pattison, Joel D. S. Rasmussen, Vanessa Rumble, and K. Brian Söderquist. *Philosophy in Review* 39.1 (2019) 8–11.

———. Review of *Kierkegaard's Journals and Notebooks Volume 10: Journals NB31–NB36*. Edited by Niels Jørgen Cappelørn, Alastair Hannay, David D. Possen, Bruce H. Kirmmse, Joel D. S. Rasmussen, and Vanessa Rumble. *Philosophy in Review* 40.2 (2020) 59–63.

———. Review of *Kierkegaard's Journals and Notebooks Volume 11: Part 1, Loose Papers, 1830–1843*. Edited by Niels Jørgen Cappelørn, Alastair Hannay, David D. Possen, Bruce H. Kirmmse. *Philosophy in Review* 40.3 (2020) 94–98.

———. Review of *Kierkegaard's Journals and Notebooks Volume 11: Part 2, Loose Papers, 1843–1855*. Princeton and Oxford: Princeton University Press 2020. *Philosophy in Review* 42.1 (2022) 7–12.

———. Review of *Written Images: Søren Kierkegaard's Journals, Notebooks, Booklets, Sheets, Scraps, and Slips of Paper* by Niels Jørgen Cappelørn, Joakim Garff and Johnny Kondrupp. *Philosophy in Review / Comptes rendus philosophiques* 24.1 (2004) 15–17.

———. "Three Forms of Philosophical Theatre in Kierkegaard's Journals and Notebooks." *Philosophy and Social Criticism* 48.1 (2022) 86–127.

Davidshofer, Claudine. "Johannes Climacus and the Dialectical Method: from Dialectics Back to Existence." In *The Kierkegaardian Mind*, edited by Adam Buben, Eleanor Helms, and Patrick Stokes, 28–38. London: Routledge, 2019.

Deleuze, Gilles. "Letter to a Harsh Critic." In *Negotiations*, translated by Martin Joughin, 3–12. New York: Columbia University Press, 1995.

———. "On *A Thousand Plateaus*." In *Negotiations*, translated by Martin Joughin, 25–34. New York: Columbia University Press, 1995.

———. "On Philosophy." In *Negotiations*, translated by Martin Joughin, 135–55. New York: Columbia University Press, 1995.

———. *Pure Immanence: Essays on a Life*. Translated by Anne Boyman. New York: Zone, 2005.

---. "What Is the Creative Act?" In *Two Regimes of Madness: Texts and Interviews 1975–1995*, edited by David Lapoujade, translated by Ames Hodges and Mike Taormina, 317–29. New York: Semiotext(e), 2007.

Deleuze, Gilles, and Felix Guattari. *What Is Philosophy?* Translated by Hugh Tomlinson and Graham Burchell. New York: Columbia University Press, 1994.

Derrida, Jacques. *The Gift of Death*. Translated by David Wills. Chicago: University of Chicago Press, 1995.

---. "Outwork, prefacing." In *Dissemination*, translated by Barbara Johnson, 1–59. Chicago: University of Chicago Press, 1981.

Descartes, René. *Discourse on the Method*. Translated by John Cottingham, Robert Stoothoff and Dugald Murdoch. In *The Philosophical Writings of Descartes*, volume 1, 111–76. Cambridge: Cambridge University Press, 1985.

---. "Early Writings." Translated by John Cottingham, Robert Stoothoff and Dugald Murdoch. In *The Philosophical Writings of Descartes*, volume 1, 2–5. Cambridge: Cambridge University Press, 1985.

---. *Meditations on First Philosophy*. Translated by John Cottingham, Robert Stoothoff and Dugald Murdoch. In *The Philosophical Writings of Descartes*, volume 2, 3–62. Cambridge: Cambridge University Press, 1985.

Dooley, Mark. "Kierkegaard and Derrida: Between Totality and Infinity." In *The New Kierkegaard*, edited by Elsebet Jegstrup, 199–213. Bloomington, IN: Indiana University Press, 2004.

---. "Kierkegaard on the Margins of Philosophy." *Philosophy and Social Criticism* 21.2 (1995) 85–105.

Dreyfus, Hubert. "Kierkegaard on the Self." In *Ethics, Love, and Faith in Kierkegaard: Philosophical Engagements*, edited by Edward F. Mooney, 11–23. Bloomington, IN: Indiana University Press, 2008.

---. "'What a monster then is man': Pascal and Kierkegaard on being a contradictory self and what to do about it." In *The Cambridge Companion to Existentialism*, edited by Steven Crowell, 96–110. Cambridge: Cambridge University Press, 2012.

Dreyfus, Hubert, and Jane Rubin. "Kierkegaard and the Nihilism of the Present Age: The Case of Commitment as Addiction." *Synthese* 98 (1994) 3–19.

Dunning, Stephen N. "The Illusory Grandeur of Doubt: The Dialectic of Subjectivity in *Johannes Climacus*." In *International Kierkegaard Commentary 7: Philosophical Fragments and Johannes Climacus*, edited by Robert L. Perkins, 203–22. Macon, GA: Mercer University Press, 1994.

---. *Kierkegaard's Dialectic of Inwardness: A Structural Analysis of the Theory of Stages*. Princeton: Princeton University Press, 1985.

---. "Paradoxes in Interpretation: Kierkegaard and Gadamer." In *Kierkegaard in Post/Modernity*, edited by Martin J. Matuštík and Merold Westphal, 125–41. Bloomington, IN: Indiana University Press, 1995.

---. "Who Sets the Task? Kierkegaard on Authority." In *Foundations of Kierkegaard's Vision of Community: Religion, Ethics, and Politics in Kierkegaard*, edited by George B. Connell and C. Stephen Evans, 18–32. Atlantic Highlands, NJ: Humanities, 1992.

Elrod, John W. *Being and Existence in Kierkegaard's Pseudonymous Works*. Princeton: Princeton University Press, 1975.

Emmanuel, Steven. "Reading Kierkegaard." *Philosophy Today* 36.3 (1992) 240–55.

Eriksen, Niels Nymann. *Kierkegaard's Category of Repetition: A Reconstruction.* Berlin: de Gruyter, 2000.

Evans, C. Stephen. "Apologetic Arguments in *Philosophical Fragments*." In *International Kierkegaard Commentary: Philosophical Fragments and Johannes Climacus*, edited by Robert L. Perkins, 63–83. Macon, GA: Mercer University Press, 1994.

———. *Passionate Reason: Making Sense of Kierkegaard's Philosophical Fragments.* Bloomington, IN: Indiana University Press, 1992.

———. *Kierkegaard's "Fragments" and "Postscript": The Religious Philosophy of Johannes Climacus.* New York: Humanities, 1983.

Fenger, Henning. *Kierkegaard: The Myths and Their Origins.* Translated by George C. Schoolfield. New Haven, CT: Yale University Press, 1980.

Fenves, Peter. *Chatter: Language and History in Kierkegaard.* Stanford: Stanford University Press, 1993.

Ferreira, M. Jamie. "Faith and the Kierkegaardian Leap." In *The Cambridge Companion to Kierkegaard*, edited by Alastair Hannay and Gordon Marino, 207–34. Cambridge: Cambridge University Press, 1998.

———. "Love." In *The Oxford Handbook of Kierkegaard*, edited by John Lippitt and George Pattison, 328–43. Oxford: Oxford University Press, 2013.

Fiskvik, Anne Margrete. "'Let No One Invite Me, for I Do Not Dance': Kierkegaard's Attitudes toward Dance." In *Kierkegaard, Literature and the Arts*, edited by Eric Ziolkowski, 149–76. Evanston, IL: Northwestern University Press, 2018.

Foucault, Michel. "Theatrum Philosophicum." In *Language, Counter Memory, Practice*, edited and translated by Donald F. Bauchard, 165–95. Ithaca, NY: Cornell University Press, 1980.

Fremstedal, Roe. "Kierkegaard's Views on Normative Ethics, Moral Agency, and Metaethics." In *A Companion to Kierkegaard*, edited by Jon Stewart, 113–25. Oxford: Blackwell, 2015.

Furchert, Almut. "From the God of the Father to God the Father: Kierkegaard's Spiritual Narrative as His Point of View." In *International Kierkegaard Commentary: The Point of View*, edited by Robert L. Perkins, 359–76. Macon, GA: Mercer University Press, 2010.

Furtak, Rick Anthony. "Kierkegaard and Greek Philosophy." In *The Oxford Handbook of Kierkegaard*, edited by John Lippitt and George Pattison, 129–49. Oxford: Oxford University Press, 2013.

Garff, Joakim. "'The Esthetic Is Above All My Element.'" In *The New Kierkegaard*, edited by Elsebet Jegstrup, 59–87. Bloomington, IN: Indiana University Press, 2004.

———. "The Eyes of Argus: The Point of View and Points of View on Kierkegaard's Work as an Author." Translated by Jane Chamberlain and Belinda Ioni. In *Kierkegaard: A Critical Reader*, edited by Jonathan Rée and Jane Chamberlain, 75–102. Oxford: Blackwell, 1998.

———. "Formation and the Critique of Culture." In *The Oxford Handbook of Kierkegaard*, edited by John Lippitt and George Pattison, 252–72. Oxford: Oxford University Press, 2013.

———. *Kierkegaard's Muse: The Mystery of Regine Olsen.* Translated by Alastair Hannay. Princeton: Princeton University Press, 2017.

———. *Søren Kierkegaard: A Biography.* Translated by Bruce H. Kirmmse. Princeton: Princeton University Press, 2005.

———. "'To Produce Was My Life': Problems and Perspectives within the Kierkegaardian Biography." In *Kierkegaard Revisited*, edited by Niels Cappelørn and Jon Stewart, 75–93. Berlin: de Gruyter, 1997.

Gibbs, Robert. "I or You: The Dash of Ethics." In *The New Kierkegaard*, edited by Elsebet Jegstrup, 141–60. Bloomington, IN: Indiana University Press, 2004.

Glenn, John D. Jr. "Kierkegaard and Anselm." In *International Kierkegaard Commentary: Philosophical Fragments and Johannes Climacus*, edited by Robert L. Perkins, 223–43. Macon, GA: Mercer University Press, 1994.

Gouwens, David J. "Understanding, Imagination, and Irony in Kierkegaard's *Repetition*." In *International Kierkegaard Commentary: Fear and Trembling and Repetition*, edited by Robert L. Perkins, 283–308. Macon, GA: Mercer University Press, 1993.

Green, Ronald M. "Kierkegaard's Great Critique: *Either/Or* as a Kantian Transcendental Deduction" In *International Kierkegaard Commentary: Either/Or Part II*, edited by Robert L. Perkins, 139–54. Macon, GA: Mercer University Press, 1995.

———. "Kierkegaard's *Philosophical Fragments*: A Kantian Commentary." In *International Kierkegaard Commentary: Philosophical Fragments and Johannes Climacus*, edited by Robert L. Perkins, 169–202. Macon, GA: Mercer University Press, 1994.

Grøn, Arne. "Time and History." In *The Oxford Handbook of Kierkegaard*, edited by John Lippitt and George Pattison, 273–91. Oxford: Oxford University Press, 2013.

Hale, Geoffrey A. *Kierkegaard and the Ends of Language*. Minneapolis: University of Minnesota Press, 2002.

Hall, Amy Laura. *Kierkegaard and the Treachery of Love*. Cambridge: Cambridge University Press, 2002.

Hall, Timothy. "Making Kierkegaard Relevant to Education Today." In *A Companion to Kierkegaard*, edited by Jon Stewart, 490–501. London: Blackwell, 2015.

Hampson, Daphne. *Kierkegaard: Exposition and Critique*. Oxford: Oxford University Press, 2013.

Hannay, Alastair. "Introduction." In *Either/Or*, abridged version edited and translated by Alastair Hannay, 1–26. New York: Penguin, 1992.

———. *Kierkegaard and Philosophy: Selected Essays*. London: Routledge, 2003.

———. "Kierkegaard and the Variety of Despair." In *The Cambridge Companion to Kierkegaard*, edited by Alastair Hannay and Gordon D. Marino, 329–48. Cambridge: Cambridge University Press, 1998.

———. "Kierkegaard on Commitment, Personality and Identity." In *Ethics, Love, and Faith in Kierkegaard: Philosophical Engagements*, edited by Edward F. Mooney, 48–58. Bloomington, IN: Indiana University Press, 2008.

———. "Kierkegaard's Single Individual and the Point of Indirect Communication." In *The Cambridge Companion to Existentialism*, edited by Steven Crowell, 73–95. Cambridge: Cambridge University Press, 2012.

Harries, Karsten. *Between Nihilism and Faith: A Commentary on Either/Or*. Berlin: de Gruyter, 2010.

Hartshorne, M. Holmes. *Kierkegaard: Godly Deceiver*. New York: Columbia University Press, 1990.

Hay, Sergia. *Ethical Silence: Kierkegaard on Communication, Education, and Humility*. New York: Lexington, 2020.

Haynes, Patrice. *Immanent Transcendence: Reconfiguring Materialism in Continental Philosophy*. London: Bloomsbury, 2012.

Hegel, G. W. F. *The Phenomenology of Spirit*. Translated by A. V. Miller. Oxford: Oxford University Press, 1977.
Helms, Eleanor D. "Can Kierkegaard Be Serious? A Phenomenological Point of View for Kierkegaard's Authorship." In *International Kierkegaard Commentary: The Point of View*, edited by Robert L. Perkins, 238–67. Macon, GA: Mercer University Press, 2010.
Holler, Clyde. "Tragedy in the Context of Kierkegaard's *Either/Or*." In *International Kierkegaard Commentary: Either/Or Part I*, edited by Robert L. Perkins, 125–42. Macon, GA: Mercer University Press, 1995.
Holm, Anders. "Kierkegaard and the Church." In *The Oxford Handbook of Kierkegaard*, edited by John Lippitt and George Pattison, 112–28. Oxford: Oxford University Press, 2013.
Hough, Sheridan. *Kierkegaard's Dancing Tax Collector: Faith, Finitude, and Silence*. Oxford: Oxford University Press, 2015.
Howland, Jacob. "A Shimmering Socrates: Philosophy and Poetry in Kierkegaard's Platonic Authorship." In *A Companion to Kierkegaard*, edited by Jon Stewart, 23–35. London: Blackwell, 2015.
Hughes, Carl S. "Communicating Earnestness: Kierkegaard and Derrida Respond to Their (Poorest) Readers." In *International Kierkegaard Commentary: The Point of View*, edited by Robert L. Perkins, 205–37. Macon, GA: Mercer University Press, 2010.
Hühn, Lore, and Phillip Schwab. "Kierkegaard and German Idealism." In *The Oxford Handbook of Kierkegaard*, edited by John Lippitt and George Pattison, 62–93. Oxford: Oxford University Press, 2013.
Huntington, Patricia. "Heidegger's Reading of Kierkegaard Revisited: From Ontological Abstraction to Ethical Concretion." In *Kierkegaard in Post/Modernity*, edited by Martin J. Matuštík and Merold Westphal, 43–65. Bloomington, IN: Indiana University Press, 1995.
Jacobellis v. Ohio, 378 U.S. 184 (1964).
Jampol-Petzinger, Andrew. "Deleuze on Kierkegaard." In *The Kierkegaardian Mind*, edited by Adam Buben, Eleanor Helms, and Patrick Stokes, 177–88. London: Routledge, 2019.
Jansen, Nerina. "Deception in the Service of Truth: Magister Kierkegaard and the Problem of Communication." In *International Kierkegaard Commentary: Concluding Unscientific Postscript to "Philosophical Fragments,"* edited by Robert L. Perkins, 115–28. Macon, GA: Mercer University Press, 1997.
———. "The Individual Versus the Public: A Key to Kierkegaard's Views of the Daily Press." In *International Kierkegaard Commentary: The Corsair Affair*, edited by Robert L. Perkins, 1–22. Macon, GA: Mercer University Press, 1990.
Jegstrup, Elsebet. "A Rose by Any Other Name . . . ." In *The New Kierkegaard*, edited by Elsebet Jegstrup, 71–87. Bloomington, IN: Indiana University Press, 2004.
Jensen, Finn Gredal. "The Diaries of P. C. Kierkegaard: An Overview." In *Kierkegaard in Context: A Festschrift for Jon Stewart*, edited by Lee C. Barrett and Peter Šajda, 74–97. Macon, GA: Mercer University Press, 2019.
Josipovici, Gabriel. "Kierkegaard and the Novel." In *Kierkegaard: A Critical Reader*, edited by Jonathan Rée and Jane Chamberlain, 114–28. Oxford: Blackwell, 1998.
Kangas, David J. *Kierkegaard's Instant: On Beginnings*. Bloomington, IN: Indiana University Press, 2007.

Kemp, Peter. "Another Language for the Other: From Kierkegaard to Levinas." *Philosophy and Social Criticism* 23.6 (1997) 5–28.

Kierkegaard, Søren. *Concluding Unscientific Postscript to Philosophical Fragments*. Translated by Howard Hong and Edna Hong. Princeton: Princeton University Press, 1992. (All citations are from volume 1.)

———. *The Corsair Affair and Articles Related to the Writings*. Edited and Translated by Howard Hong and Edna Hong. Princeton: Princeton University Press, 1982.

———. *Either/Or Part I*. Edited and Translated by Howard Hong and Edna Hong. Princeton: Princeton University Press, 1987.

———. *Either/Or Part II*. Edited and Translated by Howard Hong and Edna Hong. Princeton: Princeton University Press, 1987.

———. *Johannes Climacus, or De Omnibus Dubitandum Est*. In *Philosophical Fragments and Johannes Climacus*, translated by Howard Hong and Edna Hong, 113–73. Princeton: Princeton University Press, 1985.

———. *Kierkegaard's Journals and Notebooks, Volume 1: Journals AA–DD*. Edited and Translated by Niels Jørgen Cappelørn, Alastair Hannay, David Kangas, Bruce H. Kirmmse, George Pattison, Vanessa Rumble, and K. Brian Söderquist. Princeton: Princeton University Press, 2007.

———. *Kierkegaard's Journals and Notebooks, Volume 2: Journals EE–KK*. Edited and Translated by Niels Jørgen Cappelørn, Alastair Hannay, David Kangas, Bruce H. Kirmmse, George Pattison, Vanessa Rumble, and K. Brian Söderquist. Princeton: Princeton University Press, 2008.

———. *Kierkegaard's Journals and Notebooks, Volume 3: Notebooks 1–15*. Edited and Translated by Niels Jørgen Cappelørn, Alastair Hannay, David Kangas, Bruce H. Kirmmse, George Pattison, Vanessa Rumble, and K. Brian Söderquist. Princeton: Princeton University Press, 2010.

———. *Kierkegaard's Journals and Notebooks, Volume 4: Journals NB1–5*. Edited and Translated by Niels Jørgen Cappelørn, Alastair Hannay, David Kangas, Bruce H. Kirmmse, George Pattison, Joel D. S. Rasmussen, Vanessa Rumble, and K. Brian Söderquist. Princeton: Princeton University Press, 2011.

———. *Kierkegaard's Journals and Notebooks, Volume 5: Journals NB6–10*. Edited and Translated by Niels Jørgen Cappelørn, Alastair Hannay, David Kangas, Bruce H. Kirmmse, George Pattison, Joel D. S. Rasmussen, Vanessa Rumble, and K. Brian Söderquist. Princeton: Princeton University Press, 2011.

———. *Kierkegaard's Journals and Notebooks, Volume 6: Journals NB11–14*. Edited and Translated by Niels Jørgen Cappelørn, Alastair Hannay, Bruce H. Kirmmse, George Pattison, Joel D. S. Rasmussen, Vanessa Rumble, and K. Brian Söderquist. Princeton: Princeton University Press, 2012.

———. *Kierkegaard's Journals and Notebooks, Volume 7: Journals NB15–20*. Edited and Translated by Niels Jørgen Cappelørn, Alastair Hannay, Bruce H. Kirmmse, David D. Possen, Joel D. S. Rasmussen, Vanessa Rumble, and K. Brian Söderquist. Princeton: Princeton University Press, 2014.

———. *Kierkegaard's Journals and Notebooks, Volume 8: Journals NB21–25*. Edited and Translated by Niels Jørgen Cappelørn, Alastair Hannay, Bruce H. Kirmmse, David D. Possen, Joel D. S. Rasmussen, and Vanessa Rumble. Princeton: Princeton University Press, 2015.

———. *Kierkegaard's Journals and Notebooks, Volume 9: Journals NB26–30*. Edited and Translated by Niels Jørgen Cappelørn, Alastair Hannay, Bruce H. Kirmmse,

David D. Possen, Joel D. S. Rasmussen, and Vanessa Rumble. Princeton: Princeton University Press, 2017.

———. *Kierkegaard's Journals and Notebooks, Volume 10: Journals NB31–36.* Edited and Translated by Niels Jørgen Cappelørn, Alastair Hannay, Bruce H. Kirmmse, David D. Possen, Joel D. S. Rasmussen, and Vanessa Rumble. Princeton: Princeton University Press, 2018.

———. *Kierkegaard's Journals and Notebooks, Volume 11, Part 1: Loose Papers, 1830–1843.* Edited and Translated by Niels Jørgen Cappelørn, Alastair Hannay, Bruce H. Kirmmse, David D. Possen, Joel D. S. Rasmussen, and Vanessa Rumble. Princeton: Princeton University Press, 2019.

———. *Kierkegaard's Journals and Notebooks, Volume 11, Part 2: Loose Papers, 1843–1855.* Edited and Translated by Niels Jørgen Cappelørn, Alastair Hannay, Bruce H. Kirmmse, David D. Possen, Joel D. S. Rasmussen, and Vanessa Rumble. Princeton: Princeton University Press, 2020.

———. "My Activity as a Writer" (including the appendix, "My Position as a Religious Author in Christendom' and my Strategy"). In *The Point of View For My Work as an Author and Related Writings*, Translated by Walter Lowrie, 141–58. New York: Harper, 1962.

———. *Philosophical Fragments.* In *Philosophical Fragments and Johannes Climacus*, translated by Howard Hong and Edna Hong, 1–111. Princeton: Princeton University Press, 1985.

———. "The Point of View for My Work as an Author" (including the supplement, "The Single Individual"). In *The Point of View for My Work as an Author and Related Writings*, translated by Walter Lowrie, 5–138. New York: Harper, 1962

———. *The Point of View: Kierkegaard's Writings XXII.* Translated by Howard Hong and Edna Hong. Princeton: Princeton University Press, 1998.

———. *Prefaces: Light Reading for Certain Classes as the Occasion May Require.* Translated by William McDonald. Tallahassee, FL: Florida State University Press, 1989.

———. *Prefaces.* In *Prefaces, Writing Sampler: Kierkegaard's Writings IX*, translated by Todd W. Nichol, 1–68. Princeton: Princeton University Press, 1997.

———. *Repetition.* Translated by Howard Hong and Edna Hong. Princeton: Princeton University Press, 1983.

———. *Repetition* and *Philosophical Crumbs.* Translated by M. G. Piety. Oxford: Oxford University Press, 2009.

———. *Writing Sampler.* In *Prefaces, Writing Sampler: Kierkegaard's Writings IX*, Translated by Todd W. Nichol, 69–90. Princeton: Princeton University Press, 1997.

Kirkconnell, Glenn W. "The Elegant Unity of Kierkegaard's Authorship." In *International Kierkegaard Commentary: The Point of View*, edited by Robert L. Perkins, 377–90. Macon, GA: Mercer University Press, 2010.

———. *Kierkegaard on Ethics and Religion: From Either/Or to Philosophical Fragments.* New York: Continuum, 2008.

———. *Kierkegaard on Sin and Salvation: From Philosophical Fragments through the Two Ages.* New York: Continuum, 2010.

Kirmmse, Bruce, ed. *Encounters with Kierkegaard: A Life as Seen by his Contemporaries.* Translated by Bruce H. Kirmmse and Virginia R. Laursen. Princeton: Princeton University Press, 1996.

———. *Kierkegaard in Golden Age Denmark*. Bloomington, IN: Indiana University Press, 1990.

———. "Kierkegaard and the End of the Danish Golden Age." In *The Oxford Handbook of Kierkegaard*, edited by John Lippitt and George Pattison, 28–43. Oxford: Oxford University Press, 2013.

———. "'Out with it!' The Modern Breakthrough, Kierkegaard and Denmark." In *The Cambridge Companion to Kierkegaard*, edited by Alastair Hannay and Gordon D. Marino, 15–47. Cambridge: Cambridge University Press, 1998.

Kramer, Nate. "Present Past: Traumatic Memory in Kierkegaard's *Repetition*." In *Kierkegaard in Context: A Festschrift for Jon Stewart*, edited by Lee C. Barrett and Peter Šajda, 57–73. Macon, GA: Mercer University Press, 2019.

Lanier, Jaron. *You Are Not a Gadget: A Manifesto*. New York: Vintage, 2011

Law, David R. "A Cacophony of Voices: The Multiple Authors and Readers of Kierkegaard's *The Point of View for My Work as an Author*." In *International Kierkegaard Commentary: The Point of View*, edited by Robert L. Perkins, 12–47. Macon, GA: Mercer University Press, 2010.

———. "Kierkegaard and the History of Theology." In *The Oxford Handbook of Kierkegaard*, edited by John Lippitt and George Pattison, 166–90. Oxford: Oxford University Press, 2013.

———. "The Place, Role, and Function of the 'Ultimatum' of *Either/Or, Part Two*." In *International Kierkegaard Commentary: Either/Or Part II*, edited by Robert L. Perkins, 233–58. Macon, GA: Mercer University Press, 1995.

Llewelyn, John. "On the Borderline of Madness." In *The New Kierkegaard*, edited by Elsebet Jegstrup, 88–111. Bloomington, IN: Indiana University Press, 2004.

Levinas, Emmanuel. "Existence and Ethics." Translated by Jonathan Rée. In *Kierkegaard: A Critical Reader*, edited by Jonathan Rée and Jane Chamberlain, 26–38. Oxford: Blackwell, 1998.

Lillegard, Norman. "Judge William in the Dock: MacIntyre on Kierkegaard's Ethics." In *International Kierkegaard Commentary: Either/Or Part II*, edited by Robert L. Perkins, 83–112. Macon, GA: Mercer University Press, 1995.

Lisi, Leonardo F. "Kierkegaard and Modern European Literature." In *The Oxford Handbook of Kierkegaard*, edited by John Lippitt and George Pattison, 550–69. Oxford: Oxford University Press, 2013.

Lodge, David. "Kierkegaard for Special Purposes." In *Kierkegaard Revisited*, edited by Niels Cappelørn and Jon Stewart 34–47. Berlin: de Gruyter, 1997.

Lønning, Per. "Kierkegaard: A Stumbling-Block to 'Kierkegaardians': What Theological Orientation Would He Favour Today?" In *Kierkegaard Revisited*, edited by Niels Jørgen Cappelørn and Jon Stewart 94–106. Berlin: de Gruyter, 1997.

Lorentzen, Jamie. *Becoming Human: Kierkegaardian Reflections on Ethical Models in Literature*. Macon, GA: Mercer University Press, 2015.

———. *Sober Cannibals, Drunken Christians: Melville, Kierkegaard, and Tragic Optimism in Polarized Worlds*. Macon, GA: Mercer University Press, 2010.

Lyotard, Jean-François. *The Differend: Phrases in Dispute*. Translated by Georges Van Den Abbeele. Minneapolis: University of Minnesota Press, 1988.

McBride, William L. "Existentialism as a Cultural Movement." In *The Cambridge Companion to Existentialism*, edited by Steven Crowell, 50–72. Cambridge: Cambridge University Press, 2012.

———. "Sartre's Debt to Kierkegaard: A Partial Reckoning." In *Kierkegaard in Post/Modernity*, edited by Martin J. Matuštík and Merold Westphal, 18–42. Bloomington, IN: Indiana University Press, 1995.

McCarthy, Vincent. "Narcissism and Desire in Kierkegaard's *Either/Or, Part One*." In *International Kierkegaard Commentary: Either/Or Part I*, edited by Robert L. Perkins, 51–72. Macon, GA: Mercer University Press, 1995.

———. "Repetition's *Repetitions*." In *International Kierkegaard Commentary: Fear and Trembling and Repetition*, edited by Robert L. Perkins, 263–82. Macon, GA: Mercer University Press, 1993.

McCombs, Richard. *The Paradoxical Rationality of Søren Kierkegaard*. Bloomington, IN: Indiana University Press, 2013.

McDonald, William. "Kierkegaard's Demonic Boredom." In *Essays on Boredom and Modernity*, edited by Barbara Dalle Pezze and Carlo Salzani, 61–84. Amsterdam: Brill, 2009.

———. "Kierkegaard's Experimenting Psychology." In *The Kierkegaardian Mind*, edited by Adam Buben, Eleanor Helms, and Patrick Stokes, 39–51. London: Routledge, 2019.

———. "Retracing the Circular Ruins of Hegel's *Encyclopedia*." In *International Kierkegaard Commentary: Concluding Unscientific Postscript to "Philosophical Fragments"*, edited by Robert L. Perkins, 227–46. Macon, GA: Mercer University Press, 1997.

MacIntyre, Alasdair. *After Virtue*. South Bend, IN: Notre Dame University Press, 1981.

Mackey, Louis. "Almost in Earnest: The Philosophy of Johannes Climacus." In *Kierkegaard: A Kind of Poet*, 133–94. Philadelphia: University of Pennsylvania Press, 1971.

———. "The Loss of the World in Kierkegaard's Ethics." In *Points of View: Readings of Kierkegaard*, 141–59. Tallahassee, FL: Florida State University Press, 1986.

———. "Once More with Feeling: Kierkegaard's *Repetition*." In *Points of View: Readings of Kierkegaard*. 68–101. Tallahassee, FL: Florida State University Press, 1986.

———. "Points of View for His Work as an Author: A Report From History." In *Points of View: Readings of Kierkegaard*, 160–92. Tallahassee, FL: Florida State University Press, 1986.

———. "A Ram in the Afternoon: Kierkegaard's Discourse of the Other." In *Points of View: Readings of Kierkegaard*, 102–40. Tallahassee, FL: Florida State University Press, 1986.

———. "Some Versions of the Aesthete: *Either/Or* and Others." In *Kierkegaard: A Kind of Poet*, 1–38. Philadelphia: University of Pennsylvania Press, 1971.

———. "Starting from Scratch: Kierkegaard Unfair to Hegel." In *Points of View: Readings of Kierkegaard*, 1–22. Tallahassee, FL: Florida State University Press, 1986.

———. "A Kind of Poet . . . ." In *Kierkegaard: A Kind of Poet*, 241–96. Philadelphia: University of Pennsylvania Press, 1971.

———. "That God May Be All in All: The World of the Edifying Discourses." In *Kierkegaard: A Kind of Poet*, 85–132. Philadelphia: University of Pennsylvania Press, 1971.

———. "World Enough and Time: The Letters of Judge Wilhelm." In *Kierkegaard: A Kind of Poet*, 39–84. Philadelphia: University of Pennsylvania Press, 1971.

Malantschuk, Gregor. *Kierkegaard's Thought*. Edited and Translated by Howard Hong and Edna Hong. Princeton: Princeton University Press, 1974.

Malpas, Jeff. "Existentialism as Literature." In *The Cambridge Companion to Existentialism*, edited by Steven Crowell, 291–321. Cambridge: Cambridge University Press, 2012.

Manheimer, Ronald J. *Kierkegaard as Educator*. Berkeley: University of California Press, 1977.

Marino, Gordon. "Despair and Depression." In *Ethics, Love, and Faith in Kierkegaard: Philosophical Engagements*, edited by Edward F. Mooney, 121–28. Bloomington, IL: Indiana University Press, 2008.

Matuštík, Martin J. "Kierkegaard's Radical Existential Praxis, or Why the Individual Defies Liberal, Communitarian, and Postmodern Categories." In *Kierkegaard in Post/Modernity*, edited by Martin J. Matuštík and Merold Westphal, 239–64. Bloomington, IL: Indiana University Press, 1995.

———. "Reading Kierkegaard as a Drama." In *International Kierkegaard Commentary: The Point of View*, edited by Robert L. Perkins, 411–30. Macon, GA: Mercer University Press, 2010.

Maybee, Julie E. "Kierkegaard and the Madness of Reason." *Man and World* 29:4 (1996) 387–406.

Mehl, Peter J. *Thinking through Kierkegaard: Existential Identity in a Pluralistic World*. Urbana, IL: University of Illinois Press, 2005.

Mercer, E. David. *Kierkegaard's Living-Room: The Relation between Faith and History in Philosophical Fragments*. Montreal: McGill-Queen's University Press, 2001.

Mooney, Edward F. "Exemplars, Inwardness, and Belief: Kierkegaard on Indirect Communication." In *International Kierkegaard Commentary: Concluding Unscientific Postscript to 'Philosophical Fragments,'* edited by Robert L. Perkins, 129–48. Macon, GA: Mercer University Press, 1997.

———. "Kierkegaard's Disruptions of Literature and Philosophy: Freedom, Anxiety, and Existential Contributions." In *Kierkegaard, Literature and the Arts*, edited by Eric Ziolkowski, 55–70. Evanston, IL: Northwestern University Press, 2018.

———. "Kierkegaard on Self-Choice and Self-Reception: Judge William's Admonition." In *International Kierkegaard Commentary: Either/Or Part II*, edited by Robert L. Perkins, 5–32. Macon, GA: Mercer University Press, 1995.

———. *Living Philosophy in Kierkegaard, Melville, and Others*. London: Bloomsbury, 2020.

———. *On Søren Kierkegaard: Dialogue, Polemics, Lost Intimacy, and Time*. Aldershot, UK: Routledge, 2017

———. "*Postscript* Ethics: Putting Personality on Stage." In *Ethics, Love, and Faith in Kierkegaard: Philosophical Engagements*, edited by Edward F. Mooney, 39–47. Bloomington, IL: Indiana University Press, 2008.

———. "Pseudonyms and 'Style'." In *The Oxford Handbook of Kierkegaard*, edited by John Lippitt and George Pattison, 191–210. Oxford: Oxford University Press, 2013.

———. "Repetition: Getting the World Back." In *The Cambridge Companion to Kierkegaard*, edited by Alastair Hannay and Gordon D. Marino, 282–307. Cambridge: Cambridge University Press, 1998.

Morris, T. F. "Constantin Constantius' Search for an Acceptable Way of Life." In *International Kierkegaard Commentary: Fear and Trembling and Repetition*, edited by Robert L. Perkins, 309–34. Macon, GA: Mercer University Press, 1993.

Nelson, Christopher A. P. "Kierkegaard's Undelivered Lectures and His Author-Activity Writings: 'The Dialectic of Ethical and Ethical-Religious Communication' Revisited." In *International Kierkegaard Commentary: The Point of View*, edited by Robert L. Perkins, 391–410. Macon, GA: Mercer University Press, 2010.

Nielsen, H. A. *Where the Passion Is: A Reading of Kierkegaard's Philosophical Fragments*. Tallahassee, FL: Florida State University Press, 1983.

Nietzsche, Friedrich. *The Birth of Tragedy*. Translated by Ronald Speirs. Cambridge: Cambridge University Press, 1999.

———. *Ecce Homo*. In *The Anti-Christ, Ecce Homo, Twilight of the Idols*, translated by Judith Norman, 69–152. Cambridge: Cambridge University Press, 2005.

———. *Thus Spoke Zarathustra: A Book for All and None*. Translated by Adrian Del Caro. Cambridge: Cambridge University Press, 2006.

———. *Twilight of the Idols*. In *The Anti-Christ, Ecce Homo, Twilight of the Idols*, translated by Judith Norman, 152–230. Cambridge: Cambridge University Press, 2005.

Norris, Christopher. "Fictions of Authority: Narrative and Viewpoint in Kierkegaard's Writing." *Criticism* 25 (1983) 87–107.

Norris, John A. "The Validity of A's View of Tragedy with Particular Reference to Ibsen's *Brand*." In *International Kierkegaard Commentary: Either/Or Part I*, edited by Robert L. Perkins, 143–58. Macon, GA: Mercer University Press, 1995.

Pattison, George. "Art in the Age of Reflection." In *The Cambridge Companion to Kierkegaard*, edited by Alastair Hannay and Gordon D. Marino, 76–100. Cambridge: Cambridge University Press, 1998.

———. "The Bonfire of the Genres: Kierkegaard's Literary Kaleidoscope." In *Kierkegaard, Literature and the Arts*, edited by Eric Ziolkowski, 39–54. Evanston, IL: Northwestern University Press, 2018.

———. "Kierkegaard and Copenhagen." In *The Oxford Handbook of Kierkegaard*, edited by John Lippitt and George Pattison, 44–61. Oxford: Oxford University Press, 2013.

———. "If Kierkegaard is Right about Reading, Why Read Kierkegaard?" In *Kierkegaard Revisited*, edited by Niels Cappelørn and Jon Stewart, 291–309. Berlin: de Gruyter, 1997.

———. "The Magic of Theatre: Drama and Existence in Kierkegaard's *Repetition* and Hesse's *Steppenwolf*." In *International Kierkegaard Commentary: Fear and Trembling and Repetition*, edited by Robert L. Perkins, 359–77. Macon, GA: Mercer University Press, 1993.

Perkins, Robert L. "*Either/Or/Or*: Giving the Parson his Due." In *International Kierkegaard Commentary: Either/Or Part II*, edited by Robert L. Perkins, 207–32. Macon, GA: Mercer University Press, 1995.

———. "Introduction." In *International Kierkegaard Commentary: Philosophical Fragments and Johannes Climacus*, edited by Robert L. Perkins, 1–12. Macon, GA: Mercer University Press, 1994.

Pickett, Howard. "Beyond the Mask: Kierkegaard's Postscript as Antitheatrical, Anti-Hegelian Drama." In *Kierkegaard, Literature and the Arts*, edited by Eric Ziolkowski, 99–114. Evanston, IL: Northwestern University Press, 2018.

Piety, M. G. "The Dangers of Indirection: Plato, Kierkegaard and Leo Strauss." In *Ethics, Love, and Faith in Kierkegaard: Philosophical Engagements*, edited by Edward F. Mooney, 163–74. Bloomington, IN: Indiana University Press, 2008.

———. "A Little Light Music: The Subversion of Objectivity in Kierkegaard's *Philosophical Fragments*." In *International Kierkegaard Commentary: Philosophical Fragments and Johannes Climacus*, edited by Robert L. Perkins, 47–62. Macon, GA: Mercer University Press, 1994.

Plato. *Complete Works*. Edited by John M. Cooper. Indianapolis: Hackett, 1997.

Plekon, Michael. "Judge William: Bourgeois Moralist, Knight of Faith, Teacher." In *International Kierkegaard Commentary: Either/Or Part II*, edited by Robert L. Perkins, 125–38. Macon, GA: Mercer University Press, 1995.

Poole, Roger. *Kierkegaard: The Indirect Communication*. Charlottesville, VA: University Press of Virginia, 1993.

———. "'My Wish, My Prayer': Keeping the Pseudonyms Apart: Preliminary Considerations." In *Kierkegaard Revisited*, edited by Niels Cappelørn and Jon Stewart, 156–76. Berlin: de Gruyter, 1997.

———. "Reading *Either-Or* for the Very First Time." In *The New Kierkegaard*, edited by Elsebet Jegstrup, 42–58. Bloomington, IN: Indiana University Press, 2004.

———. "The Unknown Kierkegaard: Twentieth-century Receptions." In *The Cambridge Companion to Kierkegaard*, edited by Alastair Hannay and Gordon D. Marino, 48–75. Cambridge: Cambridge University Press, 1998.

Popkin, Richard. "Kierkegaard and Scepticism." In *Kierkegaard: A Collection of Critical Essays*, edited by Josiah Thompson, 342–72. New York: Anchor, 1972.

Priest, Graham. *In Contradiction: A Study of the Transconsistent*. Oxford: Oxford University Press, 2006.

———. *Doubt Truth to Be a Liar*. Oxford: Oxford University Press, 2008.

Pyper, Hugh S. "Beyond a Joke: Kierkegaard's *Concluding Unscientific Postscript* as a Comic Book." In *International Kierkegaard Commentary Concluding Unscientific Postscript to "Philosophical Fragments,"* edited by Robert L. Perkins, 149–67. Macon, GA: Mercer University Press, 1997.

———. "The Lesson of Eternity: Christ as Teacher in Kierkegaard and Hegel." In *International Kierkegaard Commentary: Philosophical Fragments and Johannes Climacus*, edited by Robert L. Perkins, 129–45. Macon, GA: Mercer University Press, 1994.

———. "Kierkegaard and English Language Literature." In *The Oxford Handbook of Kierkegaard*, edited by John Lippitt and George Pattison, 570–89. Oxford: Oxford University Press, 2013.

Quinn, Philip. "Kierkegaard's Christian Ethics." In *The Cambridge Companion to Kierkegaard*, edited by Alastair Hannay and Gordon D. Marino, 349–75. Cambridge: Cambridge University Press, 1998.

Ricoeur, Paul. "Philosophy after Kierkegaard." In *Kierkegaard: A Critical Reader*, edited by Jonathan Rée and Jane Chamberlain, 9–25. Oxford: Blackwell, 1998.

Roberts, Robert C. "Dialectical Emotions and the Virtue of Faith." In *International Kierkegaard Commentary: Concluding Unscientific Postscript to "Philosophical Fragments,"* edited by Robert L. Perkins, 73–93. Macon GA: Mercer University Press, 1997.

———. "Existence, Emotion, and Virtue: Classical Themes in Kierkegaard." In *The Cambridge Companion to Kierkegaard*, edited by Alastair Hannay and Gordon D. Marino, 177–206. Cambridge: Cambridge University Press, 1998.

———. *Faith, Reason, and History: Rethinking Kierkegaard's Philosophical Fragments*. Macon, GA: Mercer University Press, 1986.

———. "Passion and Reflection." In *International Kierkegaard Commentary 14: Two Ages*, edited by Robert L. Perkins, 87–106. Macon, GA: Mercer University Press, 1984.

Rudd, A. J. "Kierkegaard and the Sceptics." *British Journal of the History of Philosophy* 6:1 (1998) 71–88.

Rumble, Vanessa. "Love and Difference: The Christian Ideal in Kierkegaard's *Works of Love*." In *The New Kierkegaard*, edited by Elsebet Jegstrup, 161–78. Bloomington, IN: Indiana University Press, 2004.

———. "To Be as No-One: Kierkegaard and Climacus on the Art of Indirect Communication." *International Journal of Philosophical Studies* 3 (1995) 307–21.

Sartre, Jean-Paul. *Being and Nothingness*. Translated by Hazel E. Barnes. New York: Washington Square, 1993.

———. "The Singular Universal." Translated by Peter Goldberger. In *Kierkegaard: A Collection of Critical Essays*, edited by Josiah Thompson, 230–65. New York: Doubleday, 1972.

Schleifer, Ronald, and Markley, Robert, eds. *Kierkegaard and Literature*. Norman, OK: University of Oklahoma Press, 1984.

Sehgal, Parul. "A Short Life Packed with Existential Questions." *New York Times Book Review*, April 29, 2020.

Shakespeare, Steven. *Kierkegaard and the Refusal of Transcendence*. London: Palgrave Macmillan, 2015.

———. *Kierkegaard, Language and the Reality of God*. Aldershot, UK: Ashgate, 2001.

———. "Stirring the Waters of Language: Kierkegaard on the Dangers of Doing Theology." *The Heythrop Journal* 37 (1996) 421–36.

Smith, Daniel W. "Introduction." In *Gilles Deleuze: Essays Critical and Clinical*, translated by Daniel W. Smith and Michael A. Greco, xi–liii. Minneapolis: University of Minnesota Press, 1997.

Smyth, John Vignaux. *A Question of Eros: Irony in Sterne, Kierkegaard, and Barthes*. Tallahassee, FL: Florida State University Press, 1986.

Söderquist, K. Brian. "Irony." In *The Oxford Handbook of Kierkegaard*, edited by John Lippitt and George Pattison, 344–64. Oxford: Oxford University Press, 2013.

Sontag, Frederick. *A Kierkegaard Handbook*. Atlanta: John Knox, 1979.

Stack, J. George. *On Kierkegaard: Philosophical Fragments*. Atlantic Highlands: Humanities, 1976.

Stack, Timothy. "Kierkegaard's Theatrical Aesthetic from Repetition to Imitation." In *A Companion to Kierkegaard*, edited by Jon Stewart, 367–80. London: Blackwell, 2015.

Steiner, George. "The Wound of Negativity: Two Kierkegaard Texts." In *Kierkegaard: A Critical Reader*, edited by Jonathan Rée and Jane Chamberlain, 103–13. Oxford: Blackwell, 1998.

Stewart, Jon. *Idealism and Existentialism: Hegel and Nineteenth- and Twentieth-Century European Philosophy*. London: Continuum, 2010.

———. *Søren Kierkegaard: Subjectivity, Irony, and the Crisis of Modernity*. Oxford: Oxford University Press, 2015.

———. "Kierkegaard's View of Hegel, His Followers and Critics." In *A Companion to Kierkegaard*, edited by Jon Stewart, 50–65. London: Blackwell, 2015.

Stokes, Patrick. "Death." In *The Oxford Handbook of Kierkegaard*, edited by John Lippitt and George Pattison, 365–84. Oxford: Oxford University Press, 2013.

Stokes, Patrick, and Adam Buben. *Kierkegaard and Death*. Bloomington, IN: Indiana University Press, 2011.

Strathern, Paul. *Kierkegaard in 90 Minutes*. Chicago: Ivan R. Dee, 1997.

Strawser, Michael. *Both/And: Reading Kierkegaard from Irony to Edification*. New York: Fordham University Press, 1997.

———. "How Did Socrates Become a Christian? Irony and a Postmodern Christian (Non)-Ethic." *Philosophy Today* 36.3 (1992) 259–60.

———. "The Indirectness of Kierkegaard's Signed Writings." *International Journal of Philosophical Studies* 3 (1995) 73–90.

Taylor, Mark C. *Kierkegaard's Pseudonymous Authorship: A Study of Time and the Self*. Princeton: Princeton University Press, 1975.

Taylor, Mark Lloyd. "Ordeal and Repetition in Kierkegaard's Treatment of Abraham and Job." *Foundations of Kierkegaard's Vision of Community: Religion, Ethics, and Politics in Kierkegaard*, edited by George B. Connell and C. Stephen Evans, 33–54. Atlantic Highlands, NJ: Humanities, 1992.

Thomas, J. Heywood. "Revelation, Knowledge, and Proof." In *International Kierkegaard Commentary: Philosophical Fragments and Johannes Climacus*, edited by Robert L. Perkins, 147–68. Macon, GA: Mercer University Press, 1994.

Thulstrup, Niels. *Kierkegaard's Relation to Hegel*. Translated by George L. Stengren. Princeton: Princeton University Press, 1980.

Tietjen, Mark A. *Kierkegaard, Communication, and Virtue: Authorship as Edification*. Bloomington, IN: Indiana University Press. 2013.

———. "To Believe or Not to Believe: Toward a Hermeneutic of Trust." In *International Kierkegaard Commentary: The Point of View*, edited by Robert L. Perkins, 78–103. Macon, GA: Mercer University Press, 2010.

Tullberg, Steen. "The Textual Inheritance." In *The Oxford Handbook of Kierkegaard*, edited by John Lippitt and George Pattison, 11–27. Oxford: Oxford University Press, 2013.

Turnbull, Jamie. "Methodology and the Kierkegaardian Mind." In *The Kierkegaardian Mind*, edited by Adam Buben, Eleanor Helms, and Patrick Stokes, 52–64. London: Routledge, 2019.

Walsh, Sylvia. "Echoes of Absurdity: The Offended Consciousness and the Absolute Paradox in Kierkegaard's *Philosophical Fragments*." In *International Kierkegaard Commentary: Philosophical Fragments and Johannes Climacus*, edited by Robert L. Perkins, 33–46. Macon, GA: Mercer University Press, 1994.

———. "Issues that Divide: Interpreting Kierkegaard on Woman." In *Kierkegaard Revisited*, edited by Niels Cappelørn and Jon Stewart 191–205. Berlin: de Gruyter, 1997.

Watkin, Julia. "Boom! The Earth is Round!—On the Impossibility of an Existential System." In *International Kierkegaard Commentary, Concluding Unscientific Postscript to "Philosophical Fragments,"* edited by Robert L. Perkins, 95–114. Macon, GA: Mercer University Press, 1997.

———. "Judge William, A Christian?." In *International Kierkegaard Commentary: Either/Or Part II*, edited by Robert L. Perkins, 113–24. Macon, GA: Mercer University Press, 1995.

Westfall, Joseph. *The Kierkegaardian Author: Authorship and Performance in Kierkegaard's Literary and Dramatic Criticism*. Berlin: de Gruyter, 2007.

Westphal, Merold. "Existentialism and Religion." In *The Cambridge Companion to Existentialism*, edited by Steven Crowell, 322–41. Cambridge: Cambridge University Press, 2012.

———. "Johannes and Johannes: Kierkegaard and Difference." In *International Kierkegaard Commentary: Philosophical Fragments and Johannes Climacus*, edited by Robert L. Perkins, 13–32. Macon, GA: Mercer University Press, 1994.

———. "Kierkegaard and the Anxiety of Authorship." *International Philosophical Quarterly* 34.1 (1994) 5–22.

———. "Kierkegaard and Hegel." In *The Cambridge Companion to Kierkegaard*, edited by Alastair Hannay and Gordon D. Marino, 101–24. Cambridge: Cambridge University Press, 1998.

———. "Society, Politics, and Modernity." In *The Oxford Handbook of Kierkegaard*, edited by John Lippitt and George Pattison, 309–27. Oxford: Oxford University Press, 2013.

———. "The Transparent Shadow: Kierkegaard and Levinas in Dialogue." In *Kierkegaard in Post/Modernity*, edited by Martin J. Matuštík and Merold Westphal, 265–81. Bloomington, IN: Indiana University Press, 1995.

Whitmire, John F. Jr. "Reconstructing the Religious: Deconstructing, Transfiguration, and Witnessing in *The Point of View*." In *International Kierkegaard Commentary: The Point of View*, edited by Robert L. Perkins, 325–58. Macon, GA: Mercer University Press, 2010.

Williams, Will. *Kierkegaard and the Legitimacy of the Comic: Understanding the Relevance of Irony, Humor, and the Comic for Ethics and Religion*. New York: Lexington, 2018.

Wood, David. "The First Kiss: Tales of Innocence and Experience." In *The New Kierkegaard*, edited by Elsebet Jegstrup, 128–40. Bloomington, IN: Indiana University Press, 2004.

———. *Philosophy at the Limit*. London: Unwin Hyman, 1990.

———. "Thinking God in the Wake of Kierkegaard." In *Kierkegaard: A Critical Reader*, edited by Jonathan Rée and Jane Chamberlain, 53–74. Oxford: Blackwell, 1998.

Wrathall, Mark. "Trivial Tasks That Consume a Lifetime: Kierkegaard on Immortality and Becoming Subjective." *Journal of Ethics* 19 (2015) 419–41.

Yaffe, Martin D. "An Unsung Appreciation of the 'Musical-Erotic' in Mozart's *Don Giovanni*: Hermann Cohen's Nod toward Kierkegaard's *Either/Or*." In *International Kierkegaard Commentary: Either/Or Part I*, edited by Robert L. Perkins, 73–90. Macon, GA: Mercer University Press, 1995.

www.ingramcontent.com/pod-product-compliance
Lightning Source LLC
Chambersburg PA
CBHW032054220426
43664CB00008B/992